"This is the story about how James Madison, a man small of physical stature, became a giant of American Liberty, even the Father of the United States Constitution. Herein Professor Smith chronicles how Madison—through a lifetime of experience, observation, work, study, debate, service, tenacity, and persistence—enshrined the first natural right of mankind into America's founding creed. The freedom of conscience and religious liberty, as we know and enjoy them today, are chief among the blessings bequeathed to every American by Madison's life of service to this Nation. Every American should know this story."

—GORDON H. SMITH, president of the National Association
of Broadcasters and former United States Senator

JAMES MADISON

The *Father* of *Religious Liberty*

RODNEY K. SMITH

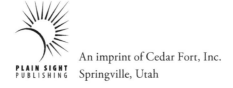

An imprint of Cedar Fort, Inc.
Springville, Utah

To four lawyer-servants,
Arlin Adams, Rex E. Lee, Dallin H. Oaks, and Willis J. Smith,
who have had a profound influence on my life and
without whom this book would never have been written.

ISBN 13: 978-1-4621-2363-6

Published by Plain Sight Publishing, an imprint of Cedar Fort, Inc.
2373 W. 700 S., Springville, UT 84663
Distributed by Cedar Fort, Inc., www.cedarfort.com

LIBRARY OF CONGRESS CATALOGING-IN-PUBLICATION DATA

Names: Smith, Rodney K., author.
Title: James Madison : the father of religious liberty / Rodney Smith.
Description: Springville, Utah : Plain Sight Publishing, An imprint of Cedar
    Fort, Inc., [2019] | Includes bibliographical references and index.
Identifiers: LCCN 2018044256 (print) | LCCN 2018047148 (ebook) | ISBN
    9781462130085 (epub, pdf, mobi) | ISBN 9781462123636 (perfect bound : alk.
    paper)
Subjects: LCSH: Madison, James, 1751-1836. | Presidents--United
    States--Biography.
Classification: LCC E342 (ebook) | LCC E342 .S57 2019 (print) | DDC
    973.5/10912 [B] --dc23
LC record available at https://lccn.loc.gov/2018044256

Cover design by Wes Wheeler
Cover design © 2019 Cedar Fort, Inc.
Edited by Kathryn Watkins and Melissa Caldwell
Typeset by Kaitlin Barwick

Printed in the United States of America

10 9 8 7 6 5 4 3 2 1

Printed on acid-free paper

Contents

Introduction

James Madison: The Religious Roots of the American Constitution

"Every age has its own outlook. It is specially good at seeing certain truths and specially liable to make certain mistakes. We all, therefore, need the books that will correct the characteristic mistakes of our own period."[1]

C. S. Lewis

"Conscience is the most sacred of all property; other property depending in part on positive law, the exercise of that being a natural and unalienable right."[2]

James Madison

A confession is due at the outset—this is primarily a book about a man of faith, James Madison, written by a person of faith, largely for people of faith. That being said, those who consider themselves to be spiritually inclined but disinclined to join any sect will also find the book to be meaningful, because Madison was in many ways just such a person. Those who are agnostic as to matters of faith, but are people of conscience, will find much within the

---

1. C. S. Lewis, Introduction to St. Athanasius's *On the Incarnation*.
2. James Madison, "Property," *The Founder's Constitution*, Chapter 16, Document 23, 29 March 1792, Papers 14: 266–68.

pages of this book to be worthwhile, perhaps even inspiring. It is also a chronicle of the founding period of the United States of America and should be inspiring for those whose faith lies not in God but in the primary achievement of the Revolutionary Era, liberty secured through the rule of law. This book is a tribute to conscience in its many forms, but particularly to religious conscience. It is also a biography of a man who did as much as, if not more than, any other founder to capture the spirit of the Declaration of Independence to form a government of laws conceived in and dedicated to liberty.

Madison had a deep, albeit somewhat untraditional, faith in God. He complemented that faith in God with an abiding faith in the country he did so much to help found and a deep faith in and commitment to family and friendship. In today's world, such values have lost some of their luster in some sectors of the population, particularly in academic circles. In all respects, however, Madison remains an example of the kind of leader and public servant who was seemingly called to fulfill a central role in securing liberty.

Madison believed rights were natural or gifts of God, and he was thoroughly committed to the goal of the founding generation to establish a nation conceived in liberty, the liberty to pursue happiness freed from a naturally overreaching national government. The Declaration of Independence, in many ways, served as the spirit of the American Revolution, a revolution fought to secure liberty, freedom from tyranny of a king or a tyrannical majority. Thomas Jefferson put it well when he noted that he had "sworn upon the altar of god eternal hostility against every form of tyranny over the mind of man."[3] Madison surely shared his dear friend's opposition to tyranny in all forms.

Many who visited with Madison throughout his lifetime were struck by his reverence for the work that he was blessed to be a part of. Those visitors observed a religious quality to Madison's devotion to the American founding and its governing documents. Nevertheless, some writers believe Madison was, at most, a person of limited religious faith. It is often claimed that Madison was a deist, one who believed in a God who can be known through reason but not revelation. Deists

---

3. Jefferson to Benjamin Rush, September 23, 1800, in *PTJ*, 32:168. Transcription available at Founders Online.

also generally believe in the existence of God, a supreme being, but they do not believe that God intervenes in the affairs of human beings. As such, deists do not believe in the concept of a God of miracles, a God who is directly involved in the lives of His children. As Madison's own words and deeds amply demonstrate, however, he firmly believed in a God of miracles. His faith was deeply personal; but he never affiliated with any particular sect. He was generally reluctant to discuss his faith openly, except with very close friends, and he abhorred the idea of using his faith as a tool to secure political support. Nevertheless, minority religionists and sects, particularly the Baptists, provided the votes necessary to place Madison in critical public positions during a determinative time in the history of the United States of America (United States).

Madison was a man of quiet faith, a very spiritual man, who was also intellectually inspired in miraculous ways. He saw the finger of the Divine Providence in his efforts to draft and secure adoption and ratification of the Constitution and Bill of Rights. As Madison's life and writing amply evidenced, the right of conscience was intended to be secured as "the most sacred of all property," the preeminent natural right, the right placed furthest from the touch of any just government. It is also true that Madison feared control of the government by any religious sect. As previously noted, he feared tyranny in any form. This is the Madison whom I have come to revere through years of study. It is the Madison I want to share with readers. In doing so, it is my sincere hope, even prayer, that learning more of the depth and breadth of the faith of the "father" of the Constitution and Bill of Rights will deepen the reader's faith in the miracle of the Constitution and will be a forceful reminder of the grave importance of protecting liberty, including the sacred right of religious conscience during a time of declining faith, a time of increasing assaults on the right of conscience from segments of the progressive left and the conservative right. Some scholars and laypeople claim that religious liberty is little more than a pernicious myth, a fraudulent means of obtaining an exemption from the majority's conception of the public good and a pretext to discriminate against others. This book takes the life of the greatest American proponent of the right of religious conscience as a response to those who believe religious liberty is a lesser or antiquated right or no right at all. More significantly, it is anticipated that this book, and the life of James Madison, will help rally those who believe in the cause of conscience and liberty. Without such an understanding of the importance of the right of conscience and its preeminent place in the panoply of rights, the siege against the right of conscience will persist until the right is no longer anything more than an antiquated parchment barrier.

A few years ago, when I was serving as president of a small, faith-based liberal arts college, I attended a luncheon with many other presidents. The luncheon speaker was David Gergen, who codirects the Center for Public Leadership the Kennedy School at Harvard and who served as an advisor to four presidents: Richard Nixon, Gerald Ford, Ronald Reagan, and Bill Clinton. In his address, Gergen shared his belief that the two primary ingredients of a great leader are authenticity and transparency. He acknowledged that the presidents he served did not fully embody those characteristics. An authentic and transparent leader engenders trust, and such trusted leadership is critical to good government. Madison was just such a president. Such authenticity and transparency, which are a form of honesty, were reflective of Madison's own finely tuned conscience. Even when they attacked Madison for his policy choices, the citizenry respected him as a leader, who was motivated by his conscience and a love of the nation he helped found. It is also not surprising that Madison believed that a firm moral and religious conscience is a critical ingredient in effective leadership. Without it, a government was destined to fail. He started his public career by trying to ensure the right of conscience in Virginia, as a young delegate to Virginia's constitutional convention, and he ended his service as president by vetoing a bill, the substance of which he liked, because it was unconstitutional. In reading of Madison's life, you will sense an ever-active conscience at work, the actions of a true leader, the kind of leadership that is desperately needed in today's world in which political expediency and populism seem to rule at the expense of the kind of transparency and authenticity that are founded in an active commitment to conscience.

When I started writing about James Madison, it was going be another scholarly book, with lengthy citations. I completed over two hundred pages in a form designed to impress and perhaps even persuade scholars, jurists, and lawyers. Early one morning, however, a strong impression came upon me—this biography of Madison and his critical role as the great lawmaker in the founding era needed to be written for a general audience. What follows is a biography of a man, a time, and a country, and it is also a tribute to a man who was a lifelong learner. He acknowledged that only when intellect or reason is founded in faith and humility, including a respect for the views of others, could one hope to approximate truth.

The group of Americans that today join Madison in embracing faith in God, country, and family may be slowly shrinking. Certainly, constitutional literacy is on the decline, and that decline threatens the present and future generations. A recent Annenberg Public Policy Center survey shockingly revealed that more than one-third of Americans cannot name any right guaranteed by the First Amendment of the Constitution. Even more startling was the fact that only 15 percent of Americans knew that the First Amendment protects religious liberty, the right of conscience. The freedom of the press fared worse, with only 14 percent of Americans being able to situate the right in the First Amendment. Hopefully, education and faith are the answer, and this book is intended to provide the reader with a better understanding of the founding of America and the importance of caring for the Constitution and the rights it was intended to secure. In this regard, James Madison wisely counseled that, "A well-instructed people alone can be permanently a free people."[4] Madison was certainly no moral relativist. He wisely emphasized the "great republican principle that the people will have virtue and intelligence to select [leaders] of virtue and wisdom. . . . [If] there is not virtue among us . . . we are in a wretched situation."[5]

There is hope. As I began writing, it became clear to me that this book should speak first to "believers," people who should take the right of religious conscience seriously, as well as others who consider the Constitution and the rule of law to be critical ingredients in the work

---

4. James Madison, Second Annual Message to Congress, Dec. 5, 1810, Founders Online, (National Archives), accessed October 14, 2018, https://founders.archives.gov/documents /Madison/03-03-02-0059.
5. Ibid.

of our founding. A recent Gallup poll noted that over 80 percent of Americans identify themselves as religious. Those who take their religious beliefs seriously ought to be ardent supporters of the right of religious conscience and of liberty, a great gift from a loving God, but they often are apathetic or swept up in the wave of other values that seem to predominate in modern culture. Few persons of faith are even aware that the right of conscience is protected by the First Amendment. Even fewer appreciate why that right is so important, even sacred, to them individually and to America and the world collectively. James Madison knew of the importance of this right. He had lived through times when the right of religious conscience was ignored and sometimes disparaged, and it vexed him more than any other matter. That vexation caused him to spend his lifetime seeking to secure the foremost of a free people to obey the Lord their God and pursue happiness. His life, as such, stands as a testament to the importance of conscience and the Constitution.

A second admission is in order. Together with James Madison and so many others in the founding generation, I believe that human rights are gifts of God, natural rights. Susan B. Anthony, a leading suffragist and women's rights advocate, put it well: "The Declaration of Independence, the United States Constitution, the constitutions of the several states, and the organic laws of the territories all alike propose to protect the people in the exercise of their God-given rights. Not one of them pretends to bestow rights."[6] There has been a revival of sorts of natural rights theory—the belief that rights are gifts of a loving God. Robert P. George, the distinguished holder of the McCormick Professor of Jurisprudence at Princeton, and the director of the James Madison Program in American Ideals and Institutions, is a leader in this effort to revive natural law. Professor George elegantly captures the force of natural law with these words:

> [E]ach human being possesses a profound, inherent, and equal dignity simply by virtue of his nature as a rational creature—a creature possessing, albeit in limited measure (and in the case of

---

6. Susan B. Anthony, "Is It a Crime to Vote?" April 3, 1873, cited in https://susanb anthonyhouse.org/blog/wp-content/uploads/2017/07/Susan-B-Anthony-1872-1873.pdf. See also *Elizabeth Cady, Stanton, Susan B. Anthony: Correspondence, Writings, Speeches*, edited by Ellen C. Dubois (New York: Shocken Books, 1981), 152–53.

some human beings in root or rudimentary form), reason and freedom, powers that make possible such human and humanizing phenomena as intellectual inquiry, aesthetic appreciation, respect for self and others, friendship, and love. This great truth of natural law, which is at the heart of our civilizational and civic order, has its theological expression in the biblical teaching that man, unlike the brute animals, is made in the very image and likeness of the divine creator and ruler of the universe.[7]

Like Madison before him, Professor George recognizes that, "The natural-law argument for religious liberty is founded on the obligation of each person to pursue the truth about religious matters and to live in conformity with his conscientious judgments. . . . The right to religious liberty follows from the dignity of man as a conscientious truth seeker."[8] An increasing number of contemporary scholars, however, sadly consider such a theory to be silly, a manner of thinking as archaic as the Constitution and some of the rights it secures. One need not believe in natural rights to appreciate the importance of remaining vigilant in protecting human rights. Nevertheless, a robust natural rights theory certainly does provide a strong justification for those rights. Madison understood this. It is my hope that readers of this book will join in better understanding Madison and his commitment to natural rights, particularly the right of conscience, even if they disagree with the theory that Madison believed legitimized the importance of the liberty of conscience and underpinned those rights.

One challenge I faced in writing the book for a public audience—including my own grandchildren—involved my determination to regularly rely on actual quotes from Madison and other leaders in the founding generation. That can make for difficult reading, at times; but it also helps ensure accuracy. Madison often warned against placing a contemporary gloss on the words of the founding generation and the words of the Constitution.

This book has been a labor of love. Day after day, as I wandered back into the records of Madison's life, I was inspired. Sometimes it was as if my breath was being taken away, as I sensed the sacrifice and

---

7. Robert P. George, *Conscience and its Enemies* (Wilmington, DE: ISI Books, 2013), 93.
8. Ibid., 85.

commitment of a little, frail man who gave America and the world so much.

My third and final admission involves my belief in miracles, a belief shared with Madison. What some see as grand coincidences, we see as evidence of the hand of God (Providence) in the founding of a new nation conceived in liberty. It is said that faith precedes a miracle. It was just such faith that drove Madison in fulfilling his critical role in the penning of the Constitution and the Bill of Rights and in helping to secure the liberty found in those great documents during his generation of public service. In reading this book, I urge the reader to come to appreciate how one little coincidence built on another little coincidence leads to a grand coincidence, a miracle that evidences the fingerprints of God in the lives of his children. I sometimes joke that I am a member of the Church of Great Coincidences. In all seriousness, the story of Madison's life stands as evidence of a God of miracles who cares deeply for His children. Indeed, each coincidence, like each piece in a beautiful mosaic, is itself a miracle or tender mercy. Senator Dan Coats of Indiana could have been speaking directly about Madison when he reflected, "The only preparation for that one profound decision which can change a life, or even a nation, is those hundreds and thousands of half-conscious, self-defining, seemingly insignificant decision made in private."[9] It is my greatest hope that you will sense each small coincidence, as well as each difficult conscience-driven act, and rejoice in them as I have been blessed to do. If you do, you will sense how Madison's life and work changed this nation. In the process, you may also be inspired to find ways of keeping that legacy alive in your family and community, remembering that every large miracle is the product of a series of small acts of obedience to one's conscience.

---

9. Dan Coats, "America's Youth: A Crisis of Character," *Imprimis*, vol. 20, no. 9 (Sept. 1991), 4.

Chapter One

The Madison Family Comes to America

"You don't choose your family. They are God's gift to you, as you are to them."[1]

Desmond Tutu

"Let the most absent-minded of men be plunged in his deepest reveries—stand that man on his legs, set his feet a-going, and he will infallibly lead you to water, if water there be in all that region."[2]

Herman Melville

The story of any life begins with a time, a place, a mother, a child, and a birth. Reaching back centuries, as we must, some questions remain regarding James Madison's ancestry, but the following depiction seems to be the most accurate. The Madison family story begins in 1588 in London, England, with the birth of James Madison's great-great-great grandfather, the first of the Madison line beckoned to cross the Atlantic Ocean to settle in the Americas.

---

1. Address at his enthronement as Anglican archbishop of Cape Town (7 September 1986), Wikiquote, accessed October 14, 2018, https://en.wikiquote.org/wiki/Desmond_Tutu.
2. *Moby-Dick; or, The Whale* (NewYork: Harper & Brothers, 1851), 2.

The Birth of Isaac Madison

In keeping with the practice common to that period, herbs were sprinkled over the floor, which resulted in the wafting of a sweet smell throughout the room, where Rebecca Madison was preparing to give birth. Together with the rubbing of ointment on her stomach by a midwife, Rebecca felt a measure of relief, as she faced the grave and all too common possibility of death during childbirth, her death or the death of her child. Rebecca found great comfort in loved ones being nearby. She was a woman of strong religious faith, named by her parents after a remarkable woman in the Bible, Rebekah or Rivkah. The prayers of faithful family members also comforted her. She was raised in a home in which the Bible and prayer were centerpieces. Her father, Reverend Richard Horsmanden, was an Anglican clergyman. Nothing, however, could remove the pain of childbirth or Rebecca's abiding fear for her child and family, a fear she shared with other mothers in an era during which so many mothers and children died in childbirth.

After what no doubt seemed like an eternity to Rebecca, a ruddy baby boy was born, a second son. The agony and fear that attended childbirth dissipated as Rebecca nestled her son close, feeling his warmth and the beating of a heartbeat near her own. The birthing process reminded Rebecca that joy comes often through toil and testing, each with their refining power. Birth was, in so many ways, a metaphor for a faithful life.

Isaac Madison's Family

In accordance with their Anglican faith, Isaac's parents arranged for the christening of their newborn son. Isaac, the name given the latest addition to the Madison family, was well chosen. Like his biblical namesake, the son of Abraham and Sarah, Isaac was a child of promise, whose descendant was destined to change the world. Isaac grew to become a dreamer and an adventurer, driven to make something of himself; those dreams were fortuitously timed and blended well with the call to settle the Americas. He toiled daily to provide for his family, as he struggled with the challenges and dangers that consumed each day in the life of a settler in a wild land. He could hardly imagine that his decision to settle a new land would have a powerful influence on his posterity.

Isaac Madison was blessed to be born into a literate family of faith during the Renaissance, a century after the coming of Columbus to the Americas, half a century after the death of Martin Luther, and at the very time that the thinking of Galileo was beginning a scientific revolution. As Isaac grew into manhood, he was exposed to a rapidly changing world. It was a new world for settlers from Europe and a time filled with inspired learning and opportunity. New light was ending the Dark Ages that had consumed Europe for over a thousand years. It was an auspicious but challenging time in which to live, a time of increasing opportunity and danger for an adventurous young man.

Isaac was blessed with the faith of his maternal grandfather, the determination of his mother, and the industriousness of his father. He was a visionary, driven by a dream of a new life in a new world. Isaac was destined to use those traits to find his way to the Americas. Isaac was beckoned by the sea, having been regaled with stories of a new world and a settlement in Jamestown. Those marketing efforts were successful, and Isaac arrived in 1608, not long after the first settlers. It is not surprising that he became known as Isaac the Immigrant.

The Virginia Company of London

In 1606, the Virginia Company of London was formed, as a private enterprise to be owned by stockholders, investors drawn to the promise of a colony in a world they believed to be rich with resources. In time, Isaac became one of those stockholders. This new colony was created primarily for economic reasons. King James also understood that English colonization could counter growing Spanish involvement in the Americas, thereby maintaining a balance of power between the two powerful European nations.

King James wisely determined that the best way to develop a colony was through free enterprise, ownership in a stock company formed under his authority but funded privately. He and the investors saw it as a venture that could create new markets. They could not have fully understood the challenges that attended colonization in Virginia.

Jamestown, Virginia, and King James I

In May 1607, 115 years after Columbus's landing in San Salvador, the first permanent English settlement was formed in the Virginia Colony. With 105 initial settlers, the new community began to grow. As the number of colonists grew, they moved westward to find new lands to plant crops, particularly tobacco. The movement proved to be inexorable. The investors were determined to turn a profit and build the British Empire. They named that first permanent settlement, Jamestown, and the river on which it was located, James, after James I, the King of England who had facilitated formation of the London Company of Virginia, providing the Company with a claim to land stretching from what is today the northern part of South Carolina to Nova Scotia. This is the same King James who commissioned a translation of the Bible for use by the Church of England. The translation of the King James Version of the Bible began in 1604 and was completed in 1611, not long after the settlement of Jamestown.

Laying claim to much of North America was not enough. King James I knew that he had to encourage permanent settlements and the cultivation of new lands to make the venture profitable. New settlements required land. The desire for profits and property to cultivate soon drove settlers to eject the native tribes, who had lived in the Americas for thousands of years, from their lands. That very same desire for productive land in time gave birth to slavery in the Americas, enslaving over twelve million slaves from Africa, as a means of providing inexpensive labor to render the claimed lands productive. Virginia, in time, became home to over 600,000 slaves, men and women who were bought and sold as property; and, in turn, tamed and cultivated the lands and made the formation of a new nation possible. Colonization efforts ultimately brought forth this new nation conceived in liberty, but not liberty for all. Those two great travesties that shaped the United States also shaped the lives of the Madison family, ultimately presenting the one major challenge to his conscience that James Madison faced but proved unable to resolve successfully—emancipation of the awful abomination of slavery.

The King divided his vast land claim into two parts. The northern part was called the London and Plymouth Companies. The southern portion was given the name of South Virginia and included Jamestown. The governing council was made up of seven persons, who elected a president. The names of the governing council were only made known after the ships landed in the Americas. Isaac, embodying the Madison commitment to public service, soon became a member of the local council. The initial intention of the expedition was to settle in Roanoke, but a providential storm drove them northward to a land of many rivers and the settlement that would become Jamestown.

Problems within the Colony

Storms of another sort plagued the colonists. Survival of the colony and each colonist was a perpetual struggle, a daily battle. The leadership of the colony was divided. From the inception of the Colony, there was dissension regarding virtually every topic, with individual leaders seeking to increase their power and authority, as is sadly often the case when a person obtains a little power. Leaders and colonists were jealous of one another but were also zealous in their efforts to draw success, in the form of profits, from their venture. The lack of harmony was attributable in significant measure to the not insignificant challenges of living in a wild and often hostile land. With dissension in the ranks, the colonists were nearly destroyed on multiple occasions as they faced severe hunger, even famine, illness, and hostility from the natives who were unwilling to yield their land without a fight. It is a miracle that Jamestown survived the brutal challenges that rendered every prior effort at colonization a failure. It was, from the beginning, a high-risk venture, which would never pay the dividends anticipated by the investors. In time, however, it would become the home to many of the founding leaders for a new country.

Ships filled with colonists were seeking land and opportunity in what was, for them, a new and hostile world of promise. The increasing numbers of settlers soon created tensions with the native tribes who had inhabited the lands for centuries. The native tribes called the country *Tsenacommacah*, land covering hundreds of square miles, including much of the Tidewater region of Virginia. It was also the name of the tribe. Each tribe also assumed the name of a distinguished chief. In this case, the Tsenacommacah became known as the Powhatan. The native people lived near the rivers that nourished them, through fishing, hunting, and the cultivation of crops. The Tsenacommacah washed in the rivers daily, prizing cleanliness, something largely foreign to many of the European colonists. The Tsenacommacah were a dignified and comely people. Not surprisingly, many of the early colonists developed friendships with them, but those friendships were not to last. Tensions rose as more and more colonists flowed into the country and ousted the Tsenacommacah, rather than share the land with its native inhabitants.

The *Mamanatowick* (emperor or primary chief) of the native tribes at the time of the founding of Jamestown was Chief Powhatan, known as Wahunsenacah or Wahunsenacawh among his people. As chief, Powhatan was a firm and, to the European eye, sometimes cruel leader, who received tribute from each tribe in his empire. He, nevertheless, coveted peace and sought harmony with the colonists. He was a leader of enormous skill, who during his lifetime increased the number of tribes in his empire or confederacy five-fold, from six to over thirty. He unified the tribes through marriage, using coercive power, while drawing on his leadership skills. Powhatan died in 1618, the same year that Isaac's wife, Mary Councilor, arrived in Virginia.

Matoaka (Pocahontas)

Powhatan is, perhaps, best known today as the father of Matoaka, who was initially known among the settlers as Pocahontas, which meant naughty or spoiled one. As a young woman Matoaka regularly visited the Jamestown settlement, often bringing food for the settlers. During one such visit, she was taken captive by Samuel Argall, who intended to use her as ransom, in exchange for prisoners held by Powhatan. During this time, it is reported that John Rolfe, who was about twelve years older than Matoaka, took a "special interest" in Matoaka and may have required that she marry him as a condition to her being freed. It was not surprising that John was smitten by Matoaka—she was young, beautiful, even a bit exotic in appearance, and full of life. Likewise, it is

Matoaka

understandable that Matoaka fell in love with John, a handsome and deeply religious man. Matoaka was impressed with John's faith commitment and Christian beliefs. After her baptism, Matoaka was given a Christian name, Rebecca, which means "captivating" or "knotted cord" in Hebrew. Rebecca was clearly attractive, even captivating, and sought to knit her people together with the colonists.

In order to marry Matoaka, John Rolfe had to write a letter to Thomas Gale, who was then serving as governor of the colony, to obtain his permission. In a letter that subtly evidences the allure of Matoaka, Rolfe wrote:

> Shall the base fears of displeasing the world, overpower and withhold me from revealing unto man these spiritual works of the Lord . . . [I]f the vulgar sort, who square all men's actions by the base rule of their own filthiness, shall tax or taunt me in this my godly labour [in falling in love and sharing his faith with Matoaka]: let them know, it is not any hungry appetite, to gorge myself with incontinency; sure I might satisfy such [a sensual] desire, though note without a seared conscience, yet with Christians more pleasing to the eye, and less fearful in the offense unlawfully committed.

To justify his marriage, Rolfe had to respond to those who opposed such a union by noting that he was marrying to bring the Christian faith to a heathen, although it is certainly clear that he was marrying for love, as well. This unlikely marriage proved to be a means of promoting peace between the Powhatan and the settlers. Some scholars go so far as to refer to that period of peace between the colonists and the Powhatan as the Peace of Pocahontas.

Two years after their marriage, Matoaka (Rebecca) traveled to England in an effort to garner more support for the Virginia colony. During that visit, she met many influential members of the English aristocracy and served as an able emissary for her people. She boarded a ship in 1617 to return home but became deathly ill and died at the tender age of twenty-one. As she lingered at death's door, Matoaka's last words were reported to be, "All must die, but 'tis enough that her child liveth."[3] She had left a son, Thomas Rolfe, whose posterity became distinguished in Virginia, and is reported to have included Dolley Payne Madison. With Pocahontas's death just one year prior to her father's death in 1618, the fragile peace began to deteriorate. Matoaka had called on settlers and tribal members to learn from each other and to find peace for the sake of their children. She understood the benefits of each culture, and the nobility and weaknesses of settlers and tribal members alike, and desperately wanted those she loved to live in peace. It is sad that the colonists and tribal members failed to heed Pocahontas's wise counsel and use the crosscurrents of each culture as a means of bettering all sides, a lesson we seem so disinclined to learn.

Hostility in the ranks of the colonists soon led to mistrust and hostility with the native people, the Powhatan. Initially, relationships with the Powhatan were positive, with each party trading with the other and extending hands of friendship. Led by Chief Powhatan, the natives were anxious to trade with the colonists. Trade was something both the colonists and the native tribes understood, given that it was common among native tribes long before the arrival of Europeans. The Powhatan were particularly interested in acquiring new tools to aid in cultivating their lands. That trade was successful until hunger and a declining store of items used for bartering purposes on the part of the settlers made it difficult for the colonists to trade for food.

By 1609, shortly after Isaac Madison's arrival in Jamestown, the colonists, under the leadership of John Smith were suffering the

---

3. "Pocahontas," History.com, accessed October 8, 2018, https://www.history.com/topics/native-american-history/pocahontas.

ravages of hunger and near death. Raiding parties formed, often burning small native villages and stealing food, driving the Powhatan from their homes and the lands that provided for their temporal and spiritual needs. Despite these raiding parties and efforts to acquire new land on the part of the colonists, many of the settlers continued to die from starvation and sickness. Chief Powhatan, in turn, began to believe, with some reason, that all European settlers wanted to obtain food through force not trading. It was a matter of sadness and perhaps trepidation for the elderly chief who continued his efforts to maintain some semblance of peace. The colonists were undeterred in their continuing move westward, laying claim to native lands and disposing the tribes who had long survived on them. The stage was set for a bitter and brutal conflict that would cost countless lives and sow seeds of distrust and anger.

Early Governance in the Colony

The challenge of bloody skirmishes between the tribal population and settlers was compounded by governance and related problems within the colony. By 1609, the London Company grew increasingly concerned by the lack of return on their investment. They were not realizing the projected profit from their new colony in America. They went to King James to obtain a new charter granting them more power. That charter declared that Thomas West, who was prominently known as Lord De la Warre (hereafter De la War), was to be named as governor over the colony for the entirety of his lifetime. The King granted the Company and its appointed governor near absolute political power over the colony and was given the name, "The Treasurer and Company of Adventurers and Planters for the First Colony in Virginia." Emboldened by these newly granted powers, De la War, who remained in England, quickly began to assert command over the colony and its settlers. He dispatched a fleet of nine ships with five hundred men, commanded by his hand-selected lieutenant, Sir Thomas Gates, and George Somers, who served as admiral of the fleet. Eight ships arrived safely in Jamestown in August 1609. Gates, who was replacing George Percy, was shocked by what he found—a colony of approximately 600 had dwindled to little more than 60. Many of the early colonists had died of starvation during what was known as the "Starving Time."

De la War commanded Gates to bring the Christian faith to the Powhatan and absorb the natives into the colony. Gates was instructed, "If you finde it not best to make [Chief Powhatan] your prisoner yet you must make him your tributary, and all the other his weroances [subordinate chiefs] about him first to acknowledge no other Lord but King James."[4] Gates, in turn, was more interested in assessing the merits of the colony as a business venture and less enamored with the idea of subjecting a powerful chief and his people. War was inevitable, because the Powhatan were a proud people, unwilling to become mere tributaries to a growing influx of colonists. After assessing conditions in the colony, Gates concluded that the venture was doomed to failure and determined to evacuate the colony and return to England.

At the very time Gates had decided to evacuate the colony, Lord de la War sailed into the harbor and assumed command as governor. His first order was to reoccupy the fort. Lord de la War was far more militaristic and unbending in his efforts to subjugate the Powhatan than Captain Smith or his predecessors had been. From the time of his arrival, he sought to develop a strategy to conquer the Powhatan in furtherance of the ambitious mission of the London Company.

When Lord de la War arrived, the Jamestown colony was in disarray. Raids and suffering on all sides continued. For many, the cause seemed hopeless. A wounded Captain Smith had returned to England, leaving the colonists without a strong leader. The colonists were without direction and desperate. At this delicate time, the Powhatan were also suffering and refused to provide the colonists with supplies of provisions. The Powhatan demanded something meaningful in trade for those provisions. The result was famine, intensified conflict, and warfare. The colonists were so ravaged by hunger that they devoured the skins of horses and the bodies of colonists and natives who had died of starvation or sickness or had been killed. Indeed, by the time of de la War's arrival, only 10 percent or 60 of the original 600 colonists

---

4. Alden T. Vaughan, "'Expulsion of the Savages': English Policy and the Virginia Massacre of 1622," *The William and Mary Quarterly* 35, no. 1 (Jan. 1978), 57–84.

were still living in the colony. That is why Gates decided that the wisest course would be to evacuate.

Gates and the remaining colonists had loaded what they owned on ships and embarked, on their way to Britain. As they reached the mouth of the James River, Lord De la War and his ships met them. De la War appeared just in time with supplies of provisions and more men, rejuvenating the colonists. Exerting the power granted by the king and offering the enticement of much need provisions, De la War kept the colony alive.

In 1611, suffering from ill health, De la War returned to England, leaving Thomas Dale in charge of the colony. De la War refused to relinquish his role as governor of the colony and, in 1618, set sail to reclaim his office, only to die while in transit. For his part, in response to the general unwillingness of the colonists to work, Dale gave each colonist three acres of land to cultivate on his own and provided them with released time from the London Company to work that land. Productivity increased. This success led to expansion, as each colonist was assigned another fifty acres, giving birth to a system that the London Company would use in the future—providing land in exchange for work and colonization.

Internal governance issues soon began to exacerbate already frayed relations with the native tribes. With the increase in numbers and power among the colonists and given the governor's decision to provide more native land to the colonists, hostility intensified. In 1618, Chief Powhatan, who sought peace when possible, died and was succeeded by his brother, Opechancanough, who was convinced that peaceful relations could not be maintained with the colonists. He became committed to reclaiming lost lands from the colonists. He was intent on driving out the enemy, those who were colonizing lands that the tribe claimed as their own.

The Massacre of 1622 and Its Aftermath

Despite the harshness and danger that attended the colonization of Virginia, the number of immigrants to the new world had increased significantly in the decade following the founding of Jamestown.

Included in that group was Mary Councilor, a widow who arrived in Jamestown in 1618. It appears that she and Isaac met and fell in love sometime before that, perhaps on one of his trips back to England. Ship records listed Mary as Mary Maddyson. While their marriage date and details regarding their courtship remain unknown, once arriving in the colony, they no doubt followed the path of many new colonists, working their way westward up the James or York Rivers, where fertile land beckoned. Having mapped some of those lands as an employee of the London Company, Isaac was aware of this fact. Years later, James Madison referred to his progenitors as planters and respectable, but not wealthy people.

Just two years after Mary's arrival, the number of colonists increased dramatically, with the arrival of eleven ships, which included 1,260 new colonists, 150 of whom were respectable women sent to become wives of the planter-colonists, for a price of 100–150 pounds of tobacco. Driven like their husbands-to-be, these women embraced a dream, the promise of family and the rewards of hard labor in the new world. The influx of fresh, able-bodied men and women, untouched yet by the hardships of colonial life brought a measure of stability to the colony.

Opechancanough became increasingly troubled, particularly as settlers moved up the various tributaries, including the James River, acquiring, cultivating, and seeking to settle on what was, in the eyes of the colonists, new and available land. Having learned from past battles during the First Anglo-Powhatan War, Chief Opechancanough concluded that it was necessary to begin planning a major, decimating attack on the colonists in their settlements and plantations along the James River. Motivated by the death of his chief counselor at the hands of a colonist in spring of 1622, Opechancanough launched an early morning campaign of deadly surprise attacks on numerous English settlements or plantations.

Early on the morning of March 22, 1622, as the colonists were rising to another full day of work, clearing and cultivating their newly settled lands, native forces led by Opechancanough descended upon the colonists, killing men, women, and children. They even attacked a school, which included the children of natives and colonists. By the time Opechancanough withdrew, his forces had massacred nearly 350 out of approximately 1,200 colonists.

The early morning massacre was brutal, but it could have been much worse. A young Powhatan boy who had been living with colonists along the James River blunted the death toll. He warned some of the colonists of the impending attacks. Isaac and Mary Madison may have been among that group. The colonists, in turn, quickly warned others, so many were prepared for the surprise attacks. Other settlers were not so fortunate. Cries of death from numerous settlers filled the early morning air. Without mercy, women and men were often tortured and then killed. Twenty women became captives. The Powhatan intended to use the women to bargain with the colonists for return of their lands. One-third of all settlers died that fateful day at the hands of Chief Opechancanough and the Powhatan. Fear and anger filled the colonists with a desire for revenge. The massacre justified the settlers' future vicious treatment of the native tribes to satisfy their insatiable desire to obtain additional land.

Opechancanough sincerely believed that his plan had succeeded. He was convinced that the colonists would soon depart. That had historically been the practice among tribes in the region. After suffering major losses, tribes would return to their lands, bringing peace. The colonists, however, were slowly beginning to reap the bounty of their efforts and were disinclined to cross the Atlantic and return to a Britain that had proved inadequate in fulfilling their dreams. The colonists banded together and planned to strike back in a series of equally brutal attacks. Even though many of the remaining colonists were women and children, the colonists began to attack the Powhatan, with superior arms and the use of surprise attacks, which were strategically developed and executed. The colonists burned the Powhatan's corn, destroyed the natives' canoes and homes, and even broke their fishing weirs or barriers built across the rivers to facilitate fishing. As the Powhatan fled from musket fire, the colonists pursued them on horses, led by bloodhounds, reminiscent of a fear-inspiring tactic that would later be used to pursue escaping slaves. This further displacement of the Powhatan opened them up to attack from new enemies, as rival tribes protected their lands from the fleeing Powhatan.

Isaac Madison was among the leaders of those subsequent attacks. For his efforts, he earned the title of captain and the accolades of Captain John Smith, who had returned to the colony. Isaac was protecting his family's safety and lands he believed he owned. In doing so, he earned the respect of fellow colonists for his courage and military leadership and skills.

By the spring of 1623, Opechancanough clearly understood that his people must yield to a superior force and sue for peace with the ever-intruding colonists. He offered to return the twenty women who had been taken captive as leverage for the return of Powhatan lands. Feigning agreement, the colonial leaders set up a meeting to work out the details of peace. One of the colonial women taken captive attended the gathering. Dressed as a native queen, in rich apparel that included beads and furs, she stood as evidence that the women held captive were treated with decency, a token of respect on the part of the tribal leaders for their captives. The colonists, however, used the meeting as an opportunity to kill the tribal leaders by poison. Most of the natives died, but Opechancanough and a few other Powhatan leaders escaped. The fate of the captive women is lost to history, although it is likely that they became members of the tribe and wives of warriors. Peace proved elusive and war between the colonists and the Powhatan and other native tribes persisted, with neither side trusting the other.

That distrust and the cruel treatment of the natives and their chief, Opechancanough, when he sued for peace, may have contributed to a questionable subsequent act on the part of Isaac Madison. As a captain, he was responsible for going among the friendlier native tribes to the north, along the Potomac, to obtain corn for the settlers who continued to suffer from the ravages of hunger and sickness. Evidently, Isaac feared a conspiracy on the part of the native tribes. Even though under orders to trade and build an alliance with the tribes, he doubted their sincerity. Perhaps fearing for his life and his men's lives, rather than working to build trust and an alliance and trading for corn, Isaac and his army killed many of the native men and took their leaders, including the chief, captive as a ransom to receive much-needed corn. He released the leaders when he received the corn and then returned to the settlements. His acts were unacceptable to many of the other settlers.

He returned to England to avoid any legal action. Upon his subsequent return to the colony, the matter seemed to have been forgotten, at least among the colonists.

Other such violent skirmishes with the native tribal populations continued. Finally, in 1644, recognizing defeat, the Powhatan entered into an agreement that mirrored those that other native tribes would be forced to accept in the future. The Powhatan, like tribes after them, were forced to cede most of their land to the colonists, reserving only a limited area for their settlement. The notion of lands reserved for tribal usage (reservations) became common terminology in the American legacy of ill treatment of native tribes.

Isaac and Mary Madison

Internal challenges continued to hamper the colonists as well. In 1624, the London Company was dissolved, and their charter was revoked by King James I. King James took it upon himself to appoint a new governor who, together with twelve councilors, was to provide governance in the new colony. During the time that the London Company poured economic support into the new colony, over 9,000 colonists, including the Madisons, heeded the call of the new land of promise. Life in that new land was so severe, however, that only 2,000 colonists remained when King James dissolved the London Company in 1624. Isaac and Mary were among those who remained.

The new government proved to be even more arbitrary than the London Company had been. In 1636, the colonists seized and sent their governor, Sir John Harvey, as a prisoner back to England. King Charles I, who had succeeded James I, appointed a new governor, Sir William Berkley, instructing him to go to the Virginia colony and permit the colonists to elect representatives.

This endearing act by King Charles I earned the loyalty of the colonists. Their loyalty continued even after Oliver Cromwell had taken control of the British government. In 1652, Parliament responded by sending a fleet to beat the colonists into submission and require Governor Berkley to resign. Before the fleet arrived, Charles II had ascended to the throne and Berkley retained his office. Sadly, Governor Berkley ruled the settlers in a manner that eventually incurred their wrath, resulting in their sending agents to England to express their grievances directly to King Charles II. King Charles II was unresponsive and some of the colonists resorted to rebellion, led by Nathaniel Bacon, a young and somewhat impetuous relative of Francis Bacon and a member of the governing council. Bacon desired to lead a force against the tribes to free lands for settlement, but Berkley denied the request, further fanning the flames of the rebellion. The so-called "Virginia Revolution" transpired during this time of continuing warfare between the colonists and the native tribes to the west of Jamestown. For a short period of time, Bacon wrested control of the government from Berkley, driving Berkley across the Chesapeake Bay to the Eastern Shore, where he began to gather new forces. Bacon and his supporters used this time to destroy Jamestown by fire.

Governor Berkley gathered his small force, led by Robert Beverly, and re-crossed the bay to give battle to Bacon and his forces, leading to a civil war. An English naval squadron was dispatched to deal with the rebels, but before they could arrive, Bacon died of fever, a common form of death in the colony. Joseph Ingram assumed the leadership of the rebels, but the rebellion was soon quelled.

During this period of unrest, Bacon's followers were, in time, reconciled to the government, which hanged twenty-three of the rebels, without a trial, but pardoned two of Bacon's generals in an effort to secure peace. Thereafter, Berkley resumed his role as governor, resulting in the restoration of a semblance of peace among the colonists. During the civil war and Berkley's governance, the people continued to feel oppressed. They often suffered from those three themes that came to characterize the Virginia colonization experience: hunger, internal and external hostility, and sickness. For his part, Sir William Berkley, after having served with minimal distinction for forty years as governor of Virginia, returned to England.

These experiences from the founding of Jamestown to the departure of Berkley were fresh memories on the part of Virginia colonists in the mid-seventeenth century. The Madison family lived through these experiences. Like everyone, the experiences shaped their view of the world. We know little of the details, but it appears that the Madison family shared the early colonists' aversion to oppressive and arbitrary rule and their commitment to independent self-governance. With each new generation, the Madison family also continued their movement westward. That spirit of independence and the acquisition of property through industry and displacement of native tribal populations characterized the colonists who stayed to build Virginia.

The way native tribes and slaves were treated blemished the laudable libertarian commitment of colonists. Isaac's treatment of the native tribes, like the subsequent Madison family legacy regarding slavery and the treatment of native tribes, constitutes what historians may rightfully see as a significant taint on the Madison name. It was certainly a failure of conscience. That assessment is appropriate. It can, however, be understood through the lens of the Madison family. Isaac and the colonists lived through major massacres, watching hundreds of their friends die, sometimes mercilessly, at the hands of the native tribal members. The natives, in turn, believed they were only reclaiming territory that was rightfully theirs and had been under their control for thousands of years. Times are almost always complex, made more so by human frailties that beset us all. Those frailties do not justify such actions, but they do help explain them. If we remember these truths, we will be a little less inclined to become captives to our own cultural and historical moments and more open to understanding matters in a new and more empathetic light.

It is clear other colonists respected Isaac. He served as a captain of military forces and on the local council. The reaction of peers, and not perceived outsiders, is the kind of respect most individuals seek. Such respect is important and is often earned in challenging times and may sometimes be based on questionable actions. Most colonists either did not survive the rigors of settling a new land or simply returned to Britain, refusing to remain to face the perpetual challenges of colonial life. This was not true of Isaac and Mary Madison. They were survivors who planted roots deep in Virginia, raising crops and establishing a strong and respected family. They were courageous and visionary. On occasion, their vision and determination, however, lacked sensitivity to the plight of others.

Some genealogical records indicate that Isaac and Mary both died in 1623 or 1624. Such a conclusion is highly suspect, given that, according to the same genealogical records, two of their three sons were born after that date, with John reportedly being born in 1625 and Thomas in 1630. John Madison carried the name of his mother Mary's father, John Councilor. We have few specifics regarding the formative years for Isaac and Mary's three sons. What is known is drawn from general observations regarding the times and circumstances faced by settlers and planters, like the Madison family, in early Virginia.

Though most settlers continued their westward migration, it is likely that Isaac and Mary Madison remained near Jamestown, where Isaac served for much of his lifetime. The Madison children grew up with justifiable fear—fear of the difficulties attendant with frontier life, including hunger, failed crops, and attacks from the native tribes. Life was difficult in the growing colony, and such challenges provided a crucible in which to build a family generally known for its strength, courage, and civic commitment.

John and Marie (Ambrose) Madison: The Second Generation in America

Given his ties to the Virginia Company of London and his service as a member of the local governing council, Isaac may have helped his son John obtain employment as a ship's carpenter, a coveted job during that era of repeated transatlantic crossings. Such crossings were the basis of trade and growth for the colony, through increased immigration. John's job was to repair loose planks, while shaping and placing wood plugs in leaks. The work of a ship's carpenter was routine, but it was critical to the safety of the cargo and crew and was recognized as a craft requiring a high level of precision and skill. It was a respectable and reasonably well compensated profession for those times. John, nevertheless, was ambitious and viewed his job as a mere stepping-stone to provide a better life for himself and his family. With each clang of his mallet, John dreamed of owning land and beginning life as a planter, taking advantage of the subsidized tobacco market and providing crops to sustain a family.

John was a Madison, with a strong work ethic ingrained into his being. He understood that dreams of becoming a landowner could only come true when accompanied by hard work and self-discipline, frugality, and a capacity to take advantage of opportunities when they presented themselves. He began saving his money with caution, preparing for the day when he would have a sufficient stake to purchase land and lay down roots in the Virginia Colony. The Virginia Company of London, which struggled to become profitable, eventually provided the means to make John's dream a reality.

As the settlers drove the Powhatan and other tribes from their lands, the Virginia Company and their successors in interest became the primary owner of undeveloped land in Virginia. The company's investors and leaders formed the company to make money by trading products, particularly tobacco, produced in the colony. The leaders of the Company understood the need for an increase in human capital in the colony to produce the tobacco necessary to make the Company a success. They lobbied for a subsidy to support tobacco production. More people working within the colony meant more products to sell. It was anticipated that such markets would result in increased profits for the Company. While the Virginia Company never became profitable, it facilitated growth. The colonial population increased sixty-fold from about 400 in 1620 to over 25,000 in 1660. The Virginia Company's plan to use its surplus of undeveloped land was successful in bringing new colonists to Virginia, even though it never was a source of significant profit for the company's investors.

In its efforts to increase population and markets, the Company created a plan by which they could increase the number of landowners and workers in the colony. The Company established the "headright" system, which provided a means for people like John Madison to obtain a patent or grant of land. Under that system, a person who paid the costs of transportation to the colony of a new immigrant, generally an indentured servant or a laborer and sometimes a family member, received a land grant of fifty acres. The London Company believed the headright system would increase productivity and profitability, particularly in the tobacco market.

By 1653, with hard work and postponed gratification, John saved enough to be able to pay the transportation costs of twelve individuals making the crossing to Virginia. Some of those individuals were likely to have been indentured servants who assisted John in developing the grant of six hundred acres of undeveloped land in the Colony that he had received from the Virginia Company. That act, like Isaac and Mary's heroic choice to make a new life in the colony, changed the future for succeeding generations of the Madison family.

In time, John made a wise choice by marrying Marie Ambrose. Marie had been born in Birchington Kent England in 1632. The date and place of John and Marie's marriage is unknown. In 1663, at the age of 31, Marie gave birth to a son, named John after his father and his maternal grandfather. John II, as he is described in these pages, was born in St. Stephen's Parish in New Kent County, which in 1791, became King and Queen County, Virginia. King and Queen County is in the Middle Peninsula of Virginia, just to the east of Richmond. John II subsequently named his third son Ambrose, reflecting the love and admiration he had for his mother.

By the time of his death in 1683, John had acquired an additional 1,300 acres. His land holdings were sufficient to constitute a plantation. John had moved from work as a ship's carpenter to becoming a landowner, finally achieving the rank of a plantation owner and becoming part of a new class, the landed gentry. He had also followed in his father's shoes, achieving the rank of Lieutenant Colonel in the militia. John's dream to become a significant landowner, a planter, came true.

John and Marie instilled in their son, John II, the same frugality, work ethic and entrepreneurial spirit they embodied. Young John worked alongside his father, as they developed the family's extensive land holdings. Owning and developing land, in turn, helped enable young John to earn the respect of other nearby landowners, who had the right to vote. John II's neighbors respected John and elected him to serve in two significant public offices: sheriff and justice of the peace. Like his father and grandfather before him, John II also served as an officer in the militia. By this time, the Madison family commitment to service was a family expectation.

John and Isabella Madison:
The Third Generation in America

At the age of twenty-nine, John II married Isabella Minor Todd, a widow. Some believe that John II had previously been married, as well, which was common in a colony where sickness and disease often led to early death and the need to remarry. Isabella Todd was born in Virginia around 1670. Her father, Captain James Todd came to Virginia in 1653 and died at sea just six years after Isabella's birth. Having suffered the loss of a father and later a husband at a young age, Isabella was well acquainted with hardship, the kind of difficulties that generally either destroy or strengthen a person. Isabella took the latter course—hardship became a source of personal strength. She developed a resilience that surely impressed her second husband, John II, and endeared her sons to her. John II and Isabella had three sons, including their youngest, Ambrose.

Ambrose and Frances (Taylor) Madison:
The Fourth Generation in America

As the youngest son and fourth generation of the Madison family in Virginia, Ambrose understood that land would secure his future. Land to the west in the Piedmont and even further west in the mountainous frontier was alluring for an enterprising young man. That land to the west was in the shadows of the mountains known today as the Blue Ridge. The Blue Ridge Mountains often appear dark blue in the distance. Just as the mountains with a blue hue, typifying faith, those conquering them also had to embrace them as symbols of promise derived from faith. It was a rugged yet beautiful place to raise a family. As a land of adventure and promise, it drew young men like Ambrose ever westward.

In all respects, Ambrose married well. Perhaps he followed his father's wise counsel to marry a strong woman, someone well above himself. Frances also knew she was marrying a man driven to provide for his family. Marrying Frances Taylor, in 1721, facilitated Ambrose's dream of acquiring a vast grant of land to the west. Perhaps even more significantly, the Taylor family also provided Ambrose's family with a much-needed support system. That Taylor strength and stability became necessary for a young family when their father suffered a premature death. Frances was the eldest daughter of James Taylor II, a prominent Virginian who would become the great-grandfather of two presidents, James Madison and Zachary Taylor. Blending the Madison and Taylor families helped ensure that the rising generation within the Madison family would be committed to public service.

While serving as Surveyor-General of Virginia in 1716, James Taylor II joined Governor Spotswood and approximately thirty other individuals on an expedition to explore the wilderness of western Virginia. They contributed significantly to the opening of new lands and providing new opportunities for the increasing flood of colonists and their children, including the Madison family. After the expedition, members received a golden stickpin shaped like a horseshoe with an inscription written in Latin that stated, "Thus, it is pleasant to cross the mountains." Known thereafter as Knights of the Golden Triangle, an honorific title, Taylor and other expedition members earned a well-deserved place in Virginia history.

James Taylor earned more than fame and a gold stickpin. As a surveyor, he used the trip to secure abundant western land, which would provide for the future of his growing family. He took out patents to thousands of acres in western counties of Virginia. The land in Orange County was located on the Rapidan River, a small river that ran through the area, contributing to the beauty and the fertility of the land nearby. The soil was full of promise, brimming with opportunity for a family willing to clear it and make it serviceable as a plantation. Thinking of his children and grandchildren, James Taylor II transferred 4,675 acres of that patented land to each of his sons-in-law, Ambrose Madison and Thomas Chew, making them neighbors and major landowners in one of the most promising and beautiful areas in colonial Virginia.

The land acquired by Ambrose included Mount Pleasant, the land upon which Montpelier, the Madison home, would one day stand. To secure title on the patent given him by his father-in-law, however, Ambrose had to put the land to productive use. Such hard work required a labor force to clear the land and begin the process of planting and cultivating crops.

By this time, using indentured servants to do the backbreaking work of building plantations was considered inefficient, and as such, indentured servants were no longer common in Virginia. Slaves had supplanted the indentured work force as a more efficient and less costly form of clearing and cultivating lands. Although the first slaves came to Virginia in 1619, the use of slaves was uncommon for many decades. By the time Ambrose moved westward, however, the use of African slaves and their children was broadly accepted in the colony.

Making barren land productive by clearing trees and brush, removing rocks, preparing the soil and planting crops was exhausting and demanding work. Ambrose was anxious to secure his patent and prepare the land for his family. Driven by a desire to relocate his family to the land and provide for their needs, Ambrose pushed his overseer to complete the work, which put pressure on the slaves working on the plantation. Overseers were hired to act as middle management between plantation owners and their slaves. Ambrose was driven and may have appeared unduly stern. He clearly demanded much from his overseer and the slaves, ever anxious to secure his patent by working the land and provide a home for his family. Nevertheless, it took years to prepare. In 1732, nearly a decade after beginning to clear the land, Ambrose rejoiced in finally moving his family to their new home, in a location that would soon become a beautiful plantation.

Ambrose Madison's Death

Mere months after the move, Ambrose became very sick. Frances was horrified when his illness progressed, without any medical means of dealing with it. To the shock of his family, Ambrose died on August 27, 1732. Accusations that Ambrose had been poisoned began to surface, together with largely circumstantial proof that those accusations were true. After holding a trial, three slaves—Pompey, Dido, and Turk— were found guilty of murder. The court determined that Pompey, a slave leased from a neighbor planter, was the ringleader and sentenced him to death by hanging. It is likely that Pompey, a proud man, was justifiably angry about being transported across the sea, under inhumane circumstances, and enslaved in a foreign land, sold and moving from one master to another. It is not altogether surprising that Pompey took it out on his new master. Ambrose may have borne some fault for Pompey's actions. This was, nevertheless, the first instance in Virginia of hanging a slave found to be guilty of murdering his master. Some historians believe that evidence presented established that Pompey used a method of poisoning common within his native tribe in Africa. The two other alleged accomplices, Turk and Dido, each received a sentence of twenty-nine lashes. The court held that they were mere accomplices in the plot to poison Ambrose. After suffering their punishment, Turk, a male, and Dido, a female, returned to serving Ambrose's widow, Frances, and the Madison family.

At his death, Ambrose willed twenty-nine slaves to Frances, including ten male slaves who provided much of the initial labor necessary to run the property. Frances apparently treated the slaves with more compassion than her husband had. When the Madison family first came to Virginia, slavery was nonexistent. With the westward movement, the demise of the system of indentured servitude, and the labor-intensive nature and rising value of tobacco as a commodity, the need for lower cost laborers increased. Virginia, like many other states, tragically turned to slavery as their primary source of labor. Slavery, in a sense, was a government-imposed subsidy provided to the wealthier elements of colonial society. Using slave labor increased the profitability of their plantations at a very high cost, the treatment of men, women, and children as slaves. It also freed owners to lead a life in which they were, in some measure, freed to seek education and serve publicly.

The Madison family never disclosed the cause of Ambrose's death and declined to discuss it publicly. Some historians argue that the family did not openly talk about the poisoning of Ambrose, because such an acknowledgment would undermine a myth held among slave owners, including the Madison family, that their slaves were happy serving kindly masters. Another reason they may have kept silent could have been because it would also have raised concerns regarding how Ambrose treated his slaves and may have been an unpleasant memory that they considered better off buried with him.

After Ambrose's death, and under the wise leadership and understanding of Frances, the Madison family developed a reputation for treating their slaves better than was the norm in Virginia and the south generally. Frances was a woman known for her compassion and surely felt the pull of conscience to treat the slaves better, although not to the extent of freeing them, an act forbidden by law at that time in colonial Virginia. From the time of Frances forward, in their correspondence and daily living, the Madison family often referred to the slaves as family and with genuine endearment, although never with true equality. Some of their slaves earned money and paid for their freedom, but the Madison family freed no slaves. Excavations near Montpelier have disclosed that the slaves had access to many of the amenities enjoyed by the Madison family, such as china dinnerware. Their quarters appear to have been meager but livable, better than housing provided to many slaves in Virginia and elsewhere.

Frances Madison:
Widow, Mother, and Planter

With the death of Ambrose, Frances found herself thrust fully into the work of providing for her young family. In inspiring ways, she proved to be capable of doing so, without ever remarrying. At the time of his death, Ambrose left three children, the eldest of whom was James Sr., who was only nine years old and carried the given name of Frances's father, James Taylor.

Ambrose's final will and testament was woefully deficient. It wisely left management of his lands in the hands of Frances until their son James reached eighteen, the age of majority, at which time he had legal claim to run the property. Ambrose, however, left one important matter undone—he failed to divide the patent for the lands transferred by his father-in-law, James Taylor II, to his family. At his death, title to the land was held jointly with his brother-in-law, Thomas Chew. The acreage given to Ambrose by his father-in-law, therefore, passed fully to Chew and out of the hands of Frances and her children. This could well have left Frances and her family completely dependent on the Taylor family, but when Chew died not long thereafter, the property passed, by his will, as a life estate to Frances, which passed on her death to her son, James.

In these difficult circumstances, Frances focused on providing for her family and fully understood the importance of property as a means of securing her family's future. Frances and her children had not lived long at Mount Pleasant, but it was home and she was determined to keep as much of it as possible to meet the needs of her family.

Frances was relieved to receive full control of the land, thereby securing a home and livelihood for her family, although she knew well that running the plantation would not be easy. She may have previously worked closely with Ambrose in running the plantation, because the transition proved to be natural. Frances managed the plantation successfully until her son James Sr. assumed managerial responsibilities.

Frances raised her three children at Mount Pleasant, in a tiny home of about 400 square feet, an area smaller than some living rooms today. She inherited the job of caring for a young family and overseeing the further development of the land and making sure it was sufficiently productive to care for her family and the slaves who worked the land. This was no simple task.

Nevertheless, particularly in the early years after Ambrose's death and despite some assistance from family members, Frances and hardworking slaves largely shouldered the weight of responsibility for caring for the Madison family and others who depended on the land being productive year after year. Frances's character found its way into the hearts and minds of her family.

James Madison Sr.

Despite the difficulty of her family's circumstances, as an educated woman, Frances was personally committed to learning. She remained devoted to providing a quality, basic education for her children. Therefore, in addition to running the plantation, the burden of formally educating her children ultimately fell squarely on Frances. She, like many of her era, found herself naturally in the role of a homeschooler. As further evidence of her commitment to education, Frances and Ambrose used precious funds to acquire a functional library, consisting of twenty-eight books regarding religion, the operation of a plantation, and basic medical matters. At age nine, young James had already become useful around the plantation. There were daily chores that he was expected to complete. Nevertheless, Frances insisted that he continue with his education. He was studious, and it paid dividends.

Under the guiding hand of his mother, James's writing became clear. Throughout his lifetime his correspondence was grammatically sound, largely free from the phonetic spelling that was common at that time among many plantation owners. He also was adept at basic math, as evidenced by how well he ran the plantation later in life. Despite the daily demands that attended the running of the plantation, James was quite literate for his time, a trait that speaks to his mother's tenacity and his ever-willing work ethic and love of learning. Thanks to the slaves who did much of the hard work of planting, cultivating, and preparing the plantation products, largely tobacco, for sale, James and his siblings were given time to pursue their education. In the process, Frances instilled in James a lifelong desire to learn and an appreciation for the value of education, traits James passed on to his children, particularly his namesake and oldest son, James II, the focus of this biography.

Under the able tutelage of his mother, James began at an early age to acquaint himself with the business side of running a plantation. Well before he was eighteen, the age at which he was to assume primary legal responsibility for the property according to Thomas Chew's will, James helped his mother as she fulfilled her responsibility to maintain and expand the productivity of the plantation.

Throughout his life, James Sr. enthusiastically studied the latest trends in agriculture, rotating his crops as often as was necessary. Like his mother and his progenitors, James was frugal. He eschewed the extravagance typical of many plantation owners. His effort to avoid undue credit enabled him to operate a profitable plantation for well over a generation and to acquire additional land and avoid the threat of bankruptcy. Perhaps his greatest indulgence was the education of his son and namesake, James Jr. James Sr. refused to pamper his son, which occasionally caused young James to feel uncared for or ignored by his busy father. On occasion, for example, young James would write home from college to ask for a little more money to live on, with protestations that he was going hungry and was otherwise suffering deprivation of basic needs. Lessons in provident living were a good thing, principles that continue to be important to the present day. Throughout his lifetime, James Jr. respected his father greatly, always referring to him as "Honored sir" or "Mr. Madison" in their correspondence, just as wife of James Jr., Dolley, referred to her husband as "Mr. Madison," even in intimate communications. Young James knew his father had his best interests in mind, but he also knew his father bore the heavy responsibility of providing for many who were dependent on the plantation.

James Sr. toiled daily to manage the plantation well into his seventies, which freed young James to pursue higher education and a life of service to his country. The slaves owned by the Madison family, in turn, provided much of the backbreaking labor that made development of the fertile lands on the plantation possible.

James Sr. and Nelly Madison

Frances also provided a model for a wife. Her example was not lost on her son, James Sr., when it came time to begin to think about marrying and beginning a family of his own. His courtship and marrying of Nelly Conway played a critical role in the formation of the character of their son. Nelly was attractive and a fitting spouse for an enterprising young planter.

James Sr. and Nelly Madison

One of the tasks James Sr. had to perform as the manager of the family plantation was bringing the crops to market, which generally entailed a trip east to the Tidewater region. It may well have been on such a trip that he first became acquainted with Nelly Conway, who soon captivated his heart. Nelly's father, Francis Conway, was a trusted friend of the Madison family and had even served as executor of Ambrose Madison's will.

Francis was also a successful merchant and landowner. Sadly, a member of one of the nearby tribes killed him. He died in one of the many skirmishes that continued to plague the native tribes and the colonists. Nelly's mother, Rebecca, did what was common in that era: she remarried. Nelly's stepfather, John Moore, was also successful in his own right and was very good to Nelly, which lessened the impact of the loss of her birth father. Nelly's sisters also married into the Taylor family, and Nelly's brother Francis Jr. became a good friend of James Sr. It is not surprising, therefore, that James Sr. met and, in time, came to fall in love with Nelly. Frances Madison also knew Nelly, which helped make her an appealing choice for James Sr.

At the time that James Sr. began to court Nelly, she was a young woman of about seventeen, with many potential suitors. James Sr. learned that there were other suitors during his trips to the Tidewater region of eastern Virginia. He was determined, nevertheless, to gain her hand in marriage. When he came east to sell his tobacco at Port Royal, he must have thought often of Nelly. Just across the river from the market for tobacco was Nelly's home, Belle Grove, a beautiful plantation. Although we know little of the details of their romance, on one of those trips west, James Sr. made his intentions known to Nelly. Her warmth and friendly nature and her innate kindness, together with the grace that attended a solid education, contributed to Nelly's attractiveness as a potential wife and companion. These traits are often used to describe Nelly throughout her lifetime, which spanned nine decades, and were surely captivating to a young man in search of a companion to join in the challenge of raising a family and running a plantation in the west.

James Sr. had time for little else than work and courting young Nelly during this period of his life. His focus, work ethic, determination, keen intellect, and reputation as a young man of character made him the first among many suitors. In fact, one of his close friends complained that James failed to hold up his end of what had previously been a regular communication between the two of them. His friend, nevertheless, acknowledged that courtship and marriage was an appropriate course for James at that time in his life. That courtship soon led to marriage between the twenty-six-year-old James and the seventeen-year-old Nelly. James and Nelly understood the responsibility of managing a large estate and providing for a family.

As excited as she was about the prospect of marrying a highly respected young man of great promise, and of raising a family, she knew she would miss her own family and home at Belle Grove. She felt a measure of trepidation at the thought of moving westward to a land that was more rugged than her present home and offered few of the cultural enticements of the more developed Tidewater region.

James Madison Jr. Is Born

Just eighteen months after her marriage to James Sr., Eleanor (Nelly) Conway Madison gave birth to her first of many children, a son, James Jr. As was true when Rebecca Madison gave birth to Isaac "the Immigrant" Madison, women in the mid-eighteenth century feared the birthing process, realizing that it often drew mothers into the proverbial "valley of the shadow of death." Mortality rates were stark, with one in eight mothers dying in childbirth. Women feared for their own lives in childbirth. They also were apprehensive that the baby would not survive. Nelly and James Sr. became well acquainted with the sorrows that attended the death of a child in infancy, losing two children in infancy and other children before maturity. Young James, their firstborn, was old enough to suffer with his mother on the loss of two siblings as newborns. Those were dark days for the Madison family, but Nelly and the family were resilient.

With each pregnancy and with James Sr.'s encouragement, Nelly would travel east, where she could receive better care in the form of an accomplished midwife and support from her mother and the Conway family. She was in the comfortable confines of the home where she grew up. Freed from her daily responsibilities at Mount Pleasant, Nelly rested. At that time, women were encouraged to remain in bed after their delivery, which was often the one time they had a respite from the heavy responsibilities that characterized colonial life. Time for necessary rest from the burdens of helping to supervise a growing plantation, and proximity to family, familiar environs, and better medical care all coalesced to make the trip eastward a wise choice.

Despite the comforts of being home with the Conway family and childhood friends, the prospect of childbirth was particularly difficult for Nelly, who was by nature sickly and susceptible to the many illnesses that were generally uncared for during her lifetime. Some historians have gone so far as to refer to her as a hypochondriac, although those findings are more than outweighed by the number of children she bore and raised, as well as strong evidence of her active role in managing the plantation work. Nelly's susceptibility to illness was shared with her firstborn, James Jr., who struggled with health issues all his life, in part due to his willingness to work from early in the morning until late at night.

While there is little written about Nelly's feelings regarding the birth, we know that James Jr. was delivered late at night, about midnight. As the night wore on and Nelly faced the final hours of labor, she felt the excruciating pain that accompanies childbirth. As was the custom at that time, groaning, crying out, or make undue noise was discouraged, to avoid disturbing or worrying family members or others nearby. As the candlelight flickered on and as evening passed into the dark of night, Nelly found herself deep in the throes of childbirth, ultimately giving birth to James as one day passed into the next.

She felt gratitude and peace as she held her newborn son in her arms for the first time, realizing she survived the death that so often accompanied childbirth. Nelly's reward for her courage in giving birth to her first of many children, under difficult circumstances, was the birth of a baby boy who quickly evidenced a strong intellect. He became a source of loving comfort to Nelly throughout her lifetime. Baby James was healthy, a source of joy to his young mother and her family and friends.

Reverend William Davis, who served as rector of the Hanover Church in King George's County baptized baby James, just two weeks after his birth. Throughout his childhood, and later among old friends, James Jr. was affectionately known as Jemmy. The rectory was where Nelly attended church as a child and was close to her stepfather's home. The Conway family and many friends attended, delighting in the baptism of a healthy baby. It is unlikely that James Sr. was present at the baptism, given the time of the year and the attendant difficulty of traveling such distances. It was a joyous time, nevertheless. None in attendance could have known that the precious little baby boy on whom so much attention was being lavished would soon change a nation that had not yet been formed and a world that desperately awaited rule by constitutionally based law. He would also do much to ensure that families could continue to exercise their conscience, freed from government meddling.

Nelly lingered at Belle Grove Plantation in Port Conway, the home of her mother and grandmother, for days that must have seemed an eternity for her husband. She was unable to return to Mount Pleasant because the Rappahannock River was flowing vigorously, as it often does in March. Road and weather conditions made travel west impractical and even dangerous. It was necessary for Nelly and little Jemmy to stay with her family for a few months before returning to the Madison plantation. She enjoyed being with family, but also was anxious to return to her husband and home, praying for a time when the difficult fifty miles west to Mount Pleasant could be safely traversed. James Sr. and Frances anxiously awaited the arrival of little Jemmy and his courageous, young mother, Nelly.

Nelly was a remarkable woman. She gave birth to twelve children, attending to many of their needs, including education, while managing the domestic responsibilities of a growing plantation. House slaves, who worked and occasionally lived in the homes of their masters, often performed most family duties, including caring for the children of their masters.

Nelly was somewhat sickly, perhaps even a bit of a hypochondriac, throughout her lifetime, a trait she would share with her son, James, even though she lived into her nineties and James lived into his eighties.

Nevertheless, she was hard-working. Nelly assumed her responsibilities with a maturity beyond her age. She was well prepared, educated in the fullest sense of the word, as a daughter of one of the foremost families in Virginia. Assuming such responsibility was a given for young Nelly, which she welcomed and assumed with sincere delight throughout her lengthy lifetime. Nelly was also determined to bring much of the sense of culture and education that she enjoyed at Belle Grove to Mount Pleasant and her children.

The Madison Family's Commitment to Learning

It is not surprising that shortly after they were married, James Sr. and Nelly wanted to invest coveted family resources in an expansion to the family library. They did so by following the example of Frances, Ambrose, and the Conway families by investing hard-earned plantation income in the purchase of a four-volume commentary on the Epistles of Paul, two volumes of *The Guardian*, and the very popular eight-volume set of *The Spectator*. *The Spectator* and *The Guardian* were a collection of periodicals known for their moral content and provided access to the beginnings of a classical or liberal education for their readers. James Sr. enjoyed his expanded library, as did Nelly, but they fully understood that their children, particularly their eldest son, James, would be the ultimate beneficiaries of an improved library and increased educational opportunities.

With the growth and increasing economic success of the plantation, James Sr. and Nelly eventually went a step further and decided to provide young James with a far costlier formal education. His father had not enjoyed this luxury, but that only made James Sr. more determined to provide it for his own children.

James Sr. had learned to read primarily from the King James Version of the Bible. Reading from the Bible was common in families, and the Madison family was no exception. Perusing the pages of other volumes in the family library, as time permitted, also enhanced young James's reading skills and love of learning. The Bible and the other volumes were either moralistic or practical, and related to working a plantation. Such reading provided an opportunity to grasp proper language and moral concepts in a single act. It also fanned the flame of an independence of faith.

It would be a grave error to understate the influence that two very strong women—James's grandmother Frances and his mother, Nelly—had on his life and the shaping of his character. Each of them, together with his wife, Dolley, influenced the man that James Madison became. His mother and grandmother taught more than reading, writing, and sound moral principles to young James. As members of the Taylor and Conway families, with their strong family commitment to public service, they also joined the Madison family in emphasizing the importance of public service and personal integrity. They sought to shape young James into a "gentleman." The term "gentleman" in the Madison family was akin to the Jewish concept of a *Mensch*, a person of integrity and honor, a person of propriety. James Sr., by way of example and teaching, also provided his son James with a commitment to service above self, an allegiance to conscience and a strong personal ethical compass.

James's parents, like their parents before them, were quick to accept personal responsibility. They were people who endeavored to live in accordance with their strong faith in God. They were also committed to individual liberty and public service. From the arrival of Captain Isaac Madison to Virginia through the birth of young James Madison, the forging of the Madison character was developed in the refining crucible of frontier danger, sickness, and other physical challenges attending taming a wild land. Amidst this storm of constant challenges, James Madison's grandmother, mother, and his father, together with other family members, taught the importance of service to the broader community, by word and deed. Family members regularly served in local government and as lay members in the vestry or Church affairs. Indeed, Richard Taylor, Frances's father, was the only individual in the history of the United States to have two great-grandchildren, James Madison and Zachary Taylor, to serve as president of the United States. There was a related and strong sense that responsibility and liberty were a defining part of a person's identity. Hard work and an enterprising spirit also characterized the Madison family.

The influence of prior generations, including Isaac the Immigrant, and young James's faithful great-great-great-great grandmother, Rebecca, instilled in the young and promising James a legacy of strength and faithfulness.

A Nurturing Environment for Young James

James Sr., Nelly, Frances, and other relatives also emphasized the value of family. Raised in an environment characterized by love and commitment, James Jr. learned much of quiet kindness and concern for others, a character trait he valued deeply despite his often shy and reserved nature. These qualities served James Jr. well in his interactions with others, particularly in the courtship of the love of his life, Dolley Payne.

Serving and caring for others and being faithful to one's God were also traits taught in the Madison home. Young James naturally accepted the duty he owed to others and his nation. Part of what binds all those traits, and their underlying values, together is a sense of conscience, a belief in duty to God, family, and country. James Jr. embraced a deeply seated belief that one's own best self is a product of service. He struggled all his days to live up to a conscience that helped shape the person he was ever striving to become. He occasionally failed, as was the case with slavery, but in every area of his life he endeavored to live up to his conscience.

Conscience and the Abomination of Slavery

The Madison family shared the grievous national sins of exploitation of the native population and of slavery, in poignant and personal ways. Slavery, which James referred to as an abomination, and the colonial mistreatment of the native population also became a darker and defining part of the Madison family identity and the culture that James Jr. was born into and wrestled with throughout his lifetime. Isaac the Immigrant, the first Madison to come to the Virginia colony, played a role in the displacement of the native tribal population from their ancestral lands. The life-blood and labor of slaves, in turn, largely freed James Jr. to pursue a life of service. In some respects, though, the family paid a price for their sins. Young James's paternal grandfather died of poisoning at the hands of three of his own slaves and James's maternal grandfather died fighting in a skirmish with the native tribal population. The payment in the form of the lives of his grandfathers could not absolve the Madison family of their failures of conscience, but they are evidence that such failures come at cost to all involved.

It is easy to judge James and other early Virginians for their weaknesses, and from our historical perspective those weaknesses are quite evident. Perhaps it is best to acknowledge, however, that even good men and women often become captive to the mores and social demands of their culture. James Jr. spent a lifetime battling against such captivity by employing his conscience, the duty owed to his Creator, the Author of liberty. He considered this his most sacred property. He was also painfully aware of the weakness or broken nature of humankind. As he later put it, "Government is the greatest of all reflections on human nature. If men were angels, no government would be necessary."[5]

Young James learned at the knees of loving parents, from an early age, to live in accordance with his conscience. Like all who strive to lead a life of conscience, however, James fell short, occasionally missing the mark. He came to understand, sometimes from his own painful experience, that men and women of conscience, alike, are in a continual struggle to become their own best selves, as children of God. Although Madison's struggles with conscience were occasionally short of the high mark he set for himself, his commitment to conscience did pay great dividends in a life of public service that contributed mightily to the adoption and ratification of the Constitution and the Bill of Rights, and to so much more. Madison would surely agree with the words of Heber J. Grant, "I would sooner have the approval of my own conscience and know that I had done my duty than to have the praise of all the world and not have the approval of my own conscience. A man's own conscience, when he is living as he should live, is the finest monitor and the best judge in all the world."[6]

---

5. James Madison, *The Federalist* No. 51 (1788).
6. Heber J. Grant, *Gospel Standards,* 186, accessed October 8, 2018, http://mormonmedia network.com/quotes/conscience.

Chapter Two

The Early Education
of James Madison

"The dream begins with a teacher who believes in you,
who tugs and pushes and leads you to the next plateau,
sometimes poking you with a sharp stick called 'truth.'"[1]

Dan Rather

"From his lessons at the elbows of his fierce Scottish mentors, Donald
Robertson and John Witherspoon, Madison never wavered from
the gravitational pull of his conscience. The almost physical impulse
of his sense of right and wrong drove his political decisions as a
magnet pulls a compass's needle. By a conscience inspired by general
matters of right and wrong, he brought tremendous conviction
to his arguments about policy, at the same time illuminating
the motives of politicians as selfish and short-sighted."[2]

Michael Signer

Nelly Conway Madison and James's two grandmothers had a significant early role in his upbringing, devotedly nurturing and loving him. Young Jemmy was the beneficiary of a loving extended family living under a single roof. Nelly Conway was born to a prominent Virginia family at the Belle Grove Plantation in Port Conway. Port Conway carried her family's name. Young James, due

---

1. "Quotes about Teaching," accessed October 8, 2018, http://www.nea.org/grants/55158.htm.
2. Michael Signer, *Becoming Madison* (New York: Public Affairs, 2015), 138.

in part to health concerns, spent a good deal of time at his maternal grandmother's home. His maternal grandmother, Rebecca Conway, played a major role in the education of young James, both by word and force of example.

Nelly's prominent roots, which could have given her reason to feel she was better than others, never changed her kindness or her tenderness with her young son. She had suffered too much and worked too hard to be uppity. Though sickly, like so many colonial women of her generation, Nelly became a strong frontier woman. Among friends and acquaintances, Nelly was pious and unassuming, traits that made her pleasant to be with. Her piety contributed to her reputation as a woman of conscience and integrity, even though, for her, religion was private and sacred that she was never ostentatious in expressing her abiding faith. She was by nature a mother committed to raising a family with strong moral convictions untainted by airs or self-congratulation. Nelly's lack of pretentiousness naturally flowed from her innate humility. Throughout a lifetime that spanned nine decades, Nelly was always gracious and enjoyed a simple life, focused on her family.

Indeed, Nelly was humble in the richest sense of that word. Her humility translated into a love of the simple things in life and commitment to family and complemented her strong moral sensitivity. Her morality was based on a deep faith, a duty to God, and a commitment to serve others. It is not surprising that Jemmy came to embrace these traits.

Nelly earned the love and respect of family and others who knew her, including a growing number of slaves working on a plantation over which she was a matriarch. As those slaves aged and became unable to work, Nelly and James Sr. continued to care for them, often referring to them with great tenderness, a tenderness usually reserved for family, although the slaves were ever aware of their status. Because there was genuine warmth shared with the family slaves, Nelly never fully understood or empathized with their plight. Her husband, James, was devoted to her, as were her children, particularly Jemmy. This was especially true as he grew older and assumed responsibility for care of the plantation and all who lived thereon. As another a testament to Nelly's humility and warmth, later in life she also had a close, even affectionate, relationship with her daughter-in-law, Dolley. Nelly continued to reside with James and Dolley until her death, which occurred well after James Madison's retirement from public life. She witnessed his successes and trials as a leader with a mother's pride. Nelly and Dolley's relationship benefitted from the spaciousness of Montpelier, which was much larger than Mount Pleasant and provided two strong women with much-needed individual space.

During the earliest years of their marriage, James Sr. and Nelly resided with their growing family in cramped quarters at Mount Pleasant. Their home at Mount Pleasant was small, essentially the same four hundred square feet James Sr. had lived in as a boy. Nelly's willingness to accept such confined quarters, after having grown up at the much more lavish Belle Grove Plantation, is further evidence of her unpretentiousness and willingness to sacrifice. One can almost hear the noise of children and adults resounding through a home that was only twenty feet by twenty feet, what today we might refer to as a "tiny house."

From Mount Pleasant to Montpelier

James Sr. was not oblivious to the need to expand the residence to meet the needs of a quickly growing family. He directed and worked with the slaves and others as they built a new plantation complex, including a much larger two-story Georgian-style house, about half a mile southeast of their much humbler abode at Mount Pleasant. The new home featured two formal and symmetrical entries or façades that gave both sides of the mansion a certain majestic and welcoming feel. After passing through the striking front façade, one entered a parlor and dining room. These reception rooms included carved sandstone mantels that evidenced the Madison's commitment to elegance. A bedchamber was also included on the first floor. Slaves prepared food in a kitchen separate from the mansion, as was often the case in colonial Virginia. There were additional rooms upstairs. It was, in short, a major upgrade from the family's existing four hundred square foot residence.

Jemmy was young when the family moved from Mount Pleasant to their larger residence. Nevertheless, even when he had grown old, James fondly remembered helping with the move from Mount Pleasant to their new residence. In his later years, he named the new family home and plantation "Montpelier," which he spelled Montpellier, after the French city of the same name, a city with a storied religious history. This was an exciting time in the lives of the entire family. They, and all associated with the plantation, had worked hard to make the move possible.

In 1797, after James Jr. returned from his service in Congress, and again in 1809, after his election as the fourth president of the United States, Montpelier underwent further expansion. At that time, James Jr. expanded each side of the mansion to provide for additional living space, including independent living quarters for his mother and ample space for himself and Dolley. Given an increase in visitors after James's service, another expansion helped accommodate guests that came regularly when James retired from public service.

The first recorded use of the name, Montpelier, comes from a letter written by James Jr., in 1781, when he was thirty-one years old. James understood the word to mean "mount of the Pilgrim," which certainly was fitting, given that he would often return home to receive inspiration for some new task he was called to perform in the building of a new nation, conceived in liberty and law. The word *pilgrim* has long meant, "one who travels to a shrine or holy place as a devotee"[3] Madison spent much of his time in office away from his beloved and inspiring Montpelier. Each time he neared Montpelier, he felt like a pilgrim returning home to a sacred place, as the simple grandeur of the plantation unfolded to the eye. James never fully escaped the weight of his civic responsibilities, but he was able to leave the frantic pace of those public responsibilities long enough to make the journey or pilgrimage, returning to a special place where he could reflect, study, renew, and fuel the fires of inspiration he so desperately needed in his service.

---

3. *Merriam-Webster,* s.v., "pilgrim," accessed October 8, 2018, https://www.merriam-webster.com/dictionary/pilgrim.

It was at Montpelier that Madison often prepared for the great work he felt called to do. He generally worked at a desk on the second story. It was quite warm and sometimes unbearably hot during the humid summer months, made all the worse by the fact that James insisted on dressing formally. The family opened doors on each side of the mansion to facilitate the circulation of air through the home, but it hardly sufficed. Nevertheless, James cherished the opportunity for study and a measure of relaxation that he found at home. It is not surprising that it came to be the location where so much meaningful work occurred, a place where the pilgrim could feed his soul. Madison also loved to ride or walk around the plantation, enjoying moments full of reflection, captivated by the beauty around him. It was a special place of peace for a man who carried a prominent portion of the weight of a new nation upon his shoulders. Sadly, due to economic reverses that began later in Madison's life, Montpelier slipped out of the hands of his widow, Dolley.

By 1790, with the inclusion of thousands of new acres made possible by the industriousness of the elder James Madison, Montpelier was transformed into the largest plantation in Orange County, Virginia. The demands of providing for a family, in what could still accurately be referred to as the western frontier, contributed to making James Sr. a loving but strong-willed and demanding, perhaps even occasionally stern, father. James Jr. understood that his father had high expectations and always tried to avoid disappointing him.

Learning from Parental Example

James Sr. was an ever-frugal executive, which caused him to continue to travel west with some regularity, as he had done from the time he met and courted Nelly. As the plantation grew, and after James Sr. had moved his family to the beautiful Montpelier, James Sr. was able to follow in the Madison family tradition of public service set by Captain Isaac Madison. His fellow parishioners selected him to serve as a vestryman in the local parish. At a time when there was little local government, the parish played a quasi-governmental role, and selection as a vestryman represented a vote of confidence. James Sr.'s willingness to serve also evidenced his commitment to his religion and church and all who worshipped there. Local residents also elected James Sr. to serve as a sheriff and road surveyor.

James Sr. was significantly involved in military affairs, like his forbearers, serving as a colonel in the militia. In the years prior to and during the Revolutionary War, James Sr. also became a wholly committed patriot, heartily supporting the revolutionary cause, opposing British rule without fair representation, adopting the call of "no taxation without representation." For him, service in the cause was a matter of conscience and entailed increasing risk, as the British took umbrage at the early stages of a rising rebellion in their colony. His love of liberty was genuine, as was the case with so many who had been involved in taking personal responsibility to build a future for their families. Taming a wild land had a way of building a special spirit of independence, and it certainly did just that in the case of James Sr.

Like Nelly, James Sr. earned a reputation for honesty. The Madison name became the family's bond. Much of James Madison's commitment to conscience developed in his early years, as he came to value a sense of duty and belief in a cause greater than one's self interest. His growing commitment to conscience was attributable, in part, to his acceptance of the high standards set by his parents and the Taylor and Conway families.

James Jr.'s parents were concerned with his religious upbringing from his birth. They were church-going people and attended the Brick Church, an Anglican house of worship, each week. The chapel was on his great uncle's, James Taylor, property, which meant that extended family and neighbors would gather as a faith community each week. Young James delighted in seeing his cousins and worshipping with his extended family. The trip could take as many as four hours, round-trip, but the excitement of seeing family and the worshipping together was worth the sacrifice. Indeed, it was the grand culminating event of the week, a time that all looked forward to with anticipation. Family gathered after services, eating a meal and enjoying visiting with one another. It all seemed natural, the blending of faith and family, and it laid the foundation for a lifelong journey of faith for the ever-thoughtful James.

Madison Receives Religious and Ethical Teaching at an Early Age

Political and family news complemented the religious services held each Sunday. Religion, morality, and public service, all of which were a part of these Sunday gatherings, characterized the Madison family ethos, creating a remarkable sense of duty, both religious and public. As a vestryman, James Sr. used his ample managerial talents to help watch over the economic affairs of the parish. He also had special responsibilities to oversee efforts to maintain order in the broader community, provide for the needy, and act as a censor of activities considered immoral by the church and local citizens. He helped collect taxes to support the local Anglican parish, which was a part of what was then the established Church in the Virginia Colony and, as such, received tax revenues to assist with their operations. The local parishes were conduits to assist in performing many roles in the community. Much of the work that was done at the parish level is today the responsibility of local government.

Government support for the Anglican Church establishment in Virginia was broadly accepted until after the Revolutionary War, when what was then referred to as the Church of England or the Anglican Church was associated with the loyalist or English cause. Persecution of religious minorities influenced the Madison family transition away from unwavering support for the Anglican establishment. They came to oppose state financial support for a state established religion, believing that preference for the majority religion infringed on the rights of minority religions. In a matter of decades, James Jr. came to be a leader in opposition to the establishment of the Anglican Church, even though his father had served as a new breed of vestryman. His father was always open to other religious views, often inviting clergymen of other faiths to speak at the church. He was also later a party to the selection of a Presbyterian to serve as rector of the local church. James Jr.'s efforts reflected this transition and later proved critical in achieving the dismantling of the Anglican establishment. In the process, James became increasingly sensitive to persecuted minorities, particularly Baptists, and the need to treat people of all faiths equally and thereby avoid government support for a specific sect or religious establishment.

Young James, like his parents before him, also learned to read, in part, from the pages of the Bible. There are copies of his notes written in the margins of his personal Bible that establish that James Jr. read from it regularly. Jemmy also benefited from his father's expansion of the family library to include various books, religious and otherwise. One of his favorites was the *Spectator*, which was written to "enliven morality and wit, and to temper wit with morality,"[4] all of which appealed to Jemmy, a young and impressionable reader. When he grew older, James Jr. sent Richard D. Cutts, one of his favorite nephews on Dolley's side, a copy of the *Spectator* with a note indicating that he had read it as a boy and strongly recommended it for its capacity to instruct young readers with "a taste for Learning, and a lively sense of the duties, the virtues, and the proprieties of life."[5] James was known for his wit. This note is revealing because it makes it clear that, from his childhood and throughout his life, he valued duty and associated it with living a life of virtue and propriety, imbued with a pleasant sense of wit, or good humor, that occasionally carried with it a mild tone of irreverence.

Sadly, people today rarely speak of propriety, which the *Oxford Dictionary* defines as, "The condition of being right, appropriate, or fitting." Interestingly, according to the *Oxford Dictionary* "propriety" has its roots in "Late Middle English (in the sense 'peculiarity, essential quality')" and the "Old French propriete, from Latin proprietas (see property)." Propriety included a strong sense of personal integrity and respect, even reverence and was viewed by Madison as a part of who he was, a form of personal property. It also reflected the kind of man he wanted to grow up to become. Exercising propriety was important to Madison throughout his lifetime and was an expectation of the broader culture for a public servant or a "gentleman," the term used during that era. This commitment to propriety and a heightened sense of personal responsibility or duty imbued James's service with added

---

4. "The Spectator," *Encyclopedia Britannica,* accessed October 8, 2018, https://www.britannica.com/topic/The-Spectator-British-periodical-1711-1712.

5. James Madison to Richard Cutts, 4 January 1829, *Founders Online,* accessed October 8, 2018, https://founders.archives.gov/documents/Madison/99-02-02-1662.

meaning. From an early age, James set high standards for himself and strived to live up to them in inspiring ways. He counted it a blessing to learn at the feet of a religious, virtuous, successful, hardworking, patriotic father and a strong, gracious, and pious mother and grandmother.

Life as a Young Boy on the Plantation

Jemmy led an active childhood, accustomed both to hard work and enthusiastic play. Nevertheless, from his childhood and throughout his lifetime, James was subject to ill health, like his mother. Later in life, James's health often improved when he was in the pleasant environs of Montpelier and deteriorated when he was in positions of responsibility that required long hours of work, day after day. The most debilitating infirmity he occasionally suffered was what he referred to as epilepsy. He also suffered from common maladies that characterized colonial Virginia, including dysentery and fevers.

Jemmy, however, avoided some of the more life-threatening illnesses common to his day: diphtheria, smallpox, yellow fever, and malaria. Madison's health challenges, whatever their source, sometimes rendered him unable to fulfill his public duties. During those times, he also experienced depression. When he was not feeling ill as a child, Jemmy took full advantage of the breadth of the plantation, to play and seek out adventure. Jemmy was short and slight of build, perhaps even a bit frail; nevertheless, he was active and always appeared to enjoy walking and riding a horse. His frail appearance would last into adulthood, but it could be deceiving, because he generally led a vigorous life. Even after he was well into his sixties, he loved the friendly competition of racing his beloved Dolley back to the mansion after a hearty walk. Nelly was inclined, however, to use her ill health and her son's frailty as an excuse to visit her family to the east, for medicinal purposes. Nelly believed the eastern part of Virginia to be a healthier environment, although it is not clear that this was, in fact, the case.

Almost as soon as he could walk, Jemmy learned to ride a horse. Riding a horse was a necessary means of transportation during Madison's lifetime. Jemmy used his horse for practical riding and work, but he also enjoyed his time riding around the growing plantation during his formative and later years. Riding was a source of relaxation for him. Later in life, James rode a much-loved horse, which he had named Liberty, often using Liberty to carry him on his daily rides around the plantation and to Thomas Jefferson's home, Monticello, which was located in Albemarle County, a ride of some distance. When Liberty could no longer carry James on long trips, Madison retired his beloved horse to the plantation and refused to permit him to be fenced in. Liberty wandered the plantation at will and became the brunt of excuses on the part of plantation workers for any damage done around Montpelier. Liberty was an easy target and earned the blame for almost everything that was out of sorts on the plantation.

Jemmy learned to love his mount as a young boy, in part because he often associated riding with some personal time spent with his father. When they rode around the plantation or into town, young James and his father would talk. Those times together provided opportunities for instruction in the operations of the plantation, but they also provided opportunities to talk about both personal and educational matters. Those were cherished times for both Jameses and helped contribute to their collective love of agricultural science.

Play was the one area where some semblance of equality prevailed on the Montpelier plantation. The interaction of the children of slaves and plantation owners was common for children growing up on plantations in Virginia. During his youth in early Virginia, it is doubtful that Jemmy gave much thought to the awful predicament of his daily playmates, who would soon toil to serve him and the plantation as slaves, subject to enslavement unless they purchased their freedom. Those close relationships contributed to James's efforts, later in life, to try to do something to rectify the clear injustice of the institution of slavery that was a dominant force in southern culture. He was unsuccessful in those efforts, which clearly tried his conscience when he was older and realized what he referred to as the "abomination" of slavery. He and Dolley also permitted their slaves to use their talents to earn money working for others, after they finished their work for the Madison family. That additional work permitted some slaves to purchase their freedom. Since many slaves had family living on the plantation, however, they often declined to purchase their own freedom, which would divide their family and leave precious family members enslaved. Others purchased their freedom, and lived frugally, saving the dollars necessary to purchase the freedom of their enslaved family members.

By June 1762, when Jemmy was only eleven years old, and two years after the death of his grandmother, it became evident that he had outgrown the educational opportunities available at Montpelier, including instruction from outside teachers or tutors paid for by his parents. His parents, grandmother, and teachers in the area came to recognize his intellectual capacity and knew that Jemmy needed the benefits of education at the hands of better-educated teachers who could focus more time and energy on him. In what turned out to be a providential act, James and Nelly sent Jemmy to learn at the feet of Donald Robertson, who had earned the reputation as one of the finest teachers in Virginia at the time. This entailed substantial cost and sacrifice on the part of all who remained on the plantation. Jemmy left his parents and Montpelier to learn from a teacher, who, like educational manna, was sent to nourish his young pupil for a life of service to his fellow man.

Donald Robertson: The Man

Donald Robertson was born in Scotland, and was the son of Charles Robertson, a respected and reasonably wealthy person, known for his good character. Like Jemmy, his new teacher grew up in a household committed to virtue and propriety. Robertson graduated from the University of Edinburgh, where he learned from the thought of the leaders of the Scottish Enlightenment, which provided the basis for his deep faith, rooted in Presbyterianism and enlightenment thought.

To better understand the profound influence Robertson had on Madison, it is important to get a feel for Robertson's intellectual and personal development. In 1752, Scotland was in the throes of unrest, including religious and intellectual persecution. Robertson joined a steady flow of independent thinkers who refused to yield as to matters of conscience. They often left Scotland coming to the colonies in search of freedom and opportunity. Robertson was among the group of independent thinkers who came to Virginia. Other more prominent figures, including John Witherspoon, a later teacher of Madison and a signer of the Declaration of Independence, and James Wilson, perhaps the leading proponent of a democratic republic at the Constitutional Convention in 1787, also came to the northern colonies. Collectively, they were part of that generation's immigrants who crossed the ocean to settle in America seeking freedom. These Scottish Enlightenment thinkers embraced the rich philosophical teaching of that period, which centered on liberty, primarily the liberty of conscience. Given rising unrest in the colonies, these thinkers and teachers were destined to have a profound impact on the founding of America.

Robertson became a minister after graduating from the University of Edinburgh. Not long after assuming his pastoral role, he faced a life-changing choice. Charles Edward Stuart, known as Bonnie Prince Charles, invaded Scotland. Donald Robertson was a patriot to the Scottish cause. His father, on the other hand, supported Prince Charles, which contributed to some disaffection within the family. Robertson's father died at the Battle of Culloden. That battle put a bloody end to a war that pitted the Jacobites, who favored the restoration of Roman Catholicism, against the Protestant forces. Robertson sided, as a matter of conscience, with the Protestants, while his father had sided with the Roman Catholics. The Robertson family and the nation of Scotland were divided, with individuals on both sides driven by a strong commitment to conscience, rooted in a duty to their God. The death of Donald's father, a weak economy, and a desire for a new start in a new land free from religious wars contributed to Robertson's decision to migrate to the colonies.

Of necessity, Robertson reluctantly left his wife, Henrietta, behind in Scotland, as he crossed the sea in search of employment and a suitable home. Sadly, another family tragedy followed quickly on the heels of his father's death. Robertson's wife died, leaving him to raise his children alone in the new world. These personal losses tried Robertson's faith and eventually contributed to his decision to cease serving as a minister. Robertson reflected on death and sorrowed at the thought of the end of his relationship with Henrietta. Gordon Allport, a psychologist known for his study of the development of personality, wisely teaches that, "The mature religious sentiment is ordinarily fashioned in the workshop of doubt."[6]

Doubt proved to play just such a role in Donald Robertson's life and would later likewise influence Madison's deepening faith, a faith full of questions and occasional doubts. Madison sharpened his faith in the crucible of doubt, and accelerated his search for answers, for meaning. Robertson's challenges contributed to making him a stronger and more empathetic teacher. He became an independent and compassionate thinker, with a capacity for understanding and warmth. His intellectual discipline, coupled with his empathy, contributed to his being an able teacher, who served as just the kind of model young Jemmy needed.

Robertson took a job in the Americas as a tutor to the Baylor family in the northern part of King and Queen County in Virginia. John Baylor III was a wealthy planter and breeder of thoroughbred horses. Baylor served in the House of Burgesses during the time that Robertson tutored his children. In just a few years, Robertson's reputation grew to the point that he opened his own secondary school on his 150-acre farm in the area. The Robertson school became an attractive option for able young children of leading families in Virginia.

Donald Robertson: Teaching Madison

It was not surprising that the Madison family soon learned of Robertson's reputation as a teacher and person of strong moral fiber, someone fit to teach their son. Consequently, they arranged for James to be admitted to Robertson's school. After gaining admission, James joined some of his Taylor cousins and the children of many other prominent Virginia families at Robertson's school. Many of Robertson's students went on to gain prominence in Virginia and the nation. None, however, grew to be as influential as little James Madison, who soon won a special

---

6. C. W. Allport, *The nature of personality: selected papers* (Beading, Mass.: Addison-Wesley, 1950), 73,

place in Robertson's heart. Jamie (as Robertson affectionately called him), in turn, idolized his teacher, for the breadth and depth of his intellect and for his kindness. The bond between teacher and student was powerful.

Jamie remained under Robertson's tutelage for approximately five years. Later in life, he emphasized the value of those five years under the guidance of Robertson, one of the ablest teachers in the colonies, when he stated, "All that I have been in life I owe largely to [Robertson]."[7] Given that Madison was disinclined to offer effusive or unwarranted praise, the accolades directed toward Robertson were genuine. In turn, Madison earned the respect of a demanding and caring teacher.

In his first year of instruction with Robertson, Madison refined his use of the English language. That rigorous early training helped Madison later pen even the most challenging principles and concepts with a clarity that was critical to the founding of our republic. We do not know whether Madison was behind in the area when he arrived at Robertson school, or whether Robertson simply wanted to emphasize the importance of writing as a foundation for the remainder of James's instruction. Madison came to love words and learned that reading and writing with care provide a solid base, which establishes the gateway through which great ideas are illuminated, and he became enthralled by language, history, and philosophy. Through rigorous training under a superb teacher, Madison learned that sloppy reading and writing often obscure even simple ideas. Given that, in time, James Madison became known for the lucidity, depth, and breadth of his writing and thinking, this formative learning experience with Robertson clearly helped shape a life of public service that was founded in language, ideas, and a rich understanding of history.

During subsequent years of instruction with Robertson, Jamie took courses that included ancient languages and civilizations, which became another arrow in his powerful intellectual quiver. The histories of Rome, England, and other great nations provided exposure to a wide range of thinkers, including Cicero, Horace, Justinian, Tacitus, and Virgil, captivating students that were hungering to learn.

---

7. Ralph Ketchum, *James Madison* (Charlottesville, VA, 1990), 21.

Despite his youth, Jamie read these great works in Latin. He also refined his Greek, as well, by studying Plato, Herodotus, Plutarch, and Thucydides. Students, Jamie included, gained further stimulation from the more contemporary thought of Enlightenment thinkers, including Locke, Milton, Montaigne, and Montesquieu. As a willing pupil, Jamie became enthralled with history and ideas. Robertson's students felt transported from the quiet confines of Virginia to a world full of wonder and opportunity.

The works of Locke, Montesquieu, as well as a collection of Scottish and French Enlightenment thinkers, were complemented with a growing understanding of Greek and Roman history and philosophy. He also received basic instruction in other topics including mathematics, literature, and modern languages. Robertson taught with discipline but also with a real excitement for what he was teaching. These teaching skills appealed to young James, who was one of thirty to forty students. It was a rich education, which had a significant influence on Madison's thought, giving birth to an insatiable desire to learn on his part. One can imagine a dynamic, demanding, caring teacher and a bright student filled with a love of learning using challenging materials of this nature in ways that enlivened learning and helped shape the future thought of his able pupil.

After five years under the wise tutelage of Donald Robertson, young Jamie returned to Montpelier, leaving his beloved teacher and friends, and his affectionate name, Jamie, behind. He was pleased to see family, but he left Robertson's school with sadness. James was sixteen and could have gone directly to college. James, however, came home where he continued his education under the tutelage of Reverend Thomas Martin, who had recently accepted employment as rector of the Brick Church, the Madison family's place of worship. Martin lived with the Madison family, serving them as a "family teacher." The choice to have James return reflected financial needs and a desire to consolidate the education of all the Madison children and some of the neighborhood children. James's family anticipated that his younger siblings could learn from him.

Returning Home and Learning
from Thomas Martin

The return home would turn out to be yet another providential moment in James's life. Waiting two years before attending the College of New Jersey would cause James to attend the college shortly after the arrival of John Witherspoon, who would assume major administrative and teaching responsibilities and have a stabilizing influence at the college. Witherspoon was destined to become another great teacher in James's life. He prepared him well for a life of prominent public service and further imbued him with a life-long commitment to the right of conscience.

Prior to his attending the College of New Jersey, James was the oldest student at the school at the Brick Church, where he was a strong role model and tutor to the other students. Reverend Martin noticed, as did others, that his new pupil was exceptional and, in many ways, his intellectual superior.

Martin was carefully selected, both to serve as rector and as the tutor for the Madison family. James Sr. played a major role in the selection process and had confidence in Martin, in part because he was not the typical Anglican clergyman. Most parsons were Tories, with strong allegiance to the Anglican Church and Great Britain, a fact that troubled James Sr. Martin insisted on more independence of thought and support of the growing revolutionary cause and liberty generally, which James Sr. embraced. Martin was Scotch-Irish and a graduate of the College of New Jersey, where James would soon attend, operated by New Light Presbyterians, who believed in the light of conscience emanating from God. As such, Martin was a supporter of the liberty of conscience, religious freedom, and the thought of the Scottish Enlightenment. He was also a man of deep faith. Martin's teachings, therefore, were quite congenial to his eldest pupil, James. He was an apt successor to Robertson.

Madison was less effusive in his praise for Martin than he was for Robertson, but he respected his new teacher. During his two years with Martin, James continued to pursue his studies with vigor and independence, as evidenced by his later success in college. His preparation, under Robertson and Martin, was such that he passed entrance exams at the College of New Jersey at a very high level, permitting him to entering as a sophomore and facilitating his graduating in only two years, an unprecedented feat. James came to believe that the condensing of his undergraduate education into two exceedingly demanding years took a further toll on his already fragile health. Sometimes his body simply shut down for a period of time in response to over-work.

Madison's return home also found him in a changed world. James Sr. was concerned about British actions limiting the liberty of the colonies, and these worries had a profound impact on his son. The times and seasons were changing rapidly, and James Sr. and his son were being swept up in the revolutionary cause. Preservation of the gains from that cause consumed Madison's time and talents for a lifetime.

In addition to using his skills as a teacher, Reverend Martin also influenced the Madison family's choice of a college for James, who was now eighteen years old. The custom for many Virginia families, including the Jefferson and Monroe families who lived nearby, was to send their sons to the College of William and Mary, an institution affiliated with the Anglican Church and imbued with pro-British, or Tory, sentiments. Reverend Martin's brother Alexander visited Martin and the Madison family at the time that they were making a college decision for young James. Martin and Alexander were graduates of the College of New Jersey. They were articulate proponents and living examples of the value of a College of New Jersey education. Martin and Alexander were not hesitant to make their educational preference known to James and especially to his father. Donald Robertson shared those sentiments. Collectively, they persuaded James Jr. and the rest of the Madisons that the wisest course would be for James to attend the College of New Jersey and eschew education at William and Mary.

The College of New Jersey and New Friendships

The Madison family was concerned about stories that they had heard regarding serious problems with faculty at William and Mary. The faculty there were reputed to be found drunk in public on a regular basis. Moreover, according to rumor, they did little to engage their students. Martin extolled the virtues of his teachers at the College of New Jersey, the predecessor to Princeton University, as a contrast to the less vibrant educational environment at William

James Madison

and Mary. William and Mary's affiliation with the Anglican Church was also troublesome to James Sr., given that the Anglican hierarchy in Virginia were loyalists and reluctant to support the revolutionary cause of liberty. Troubled by his church's support for the English, James Sr. also respected Samuel Davies, a former president of the College of New Jersey and a famous dissenting clergyman in Virginia. Nelly agreed that James should attend the College of New Jersey believing that the New Jersey climate was more conducive to his good health than the climate in Williamsburg, and she worried about her son's physical well-being.

Regardless of the reasons behind the decision for James to attend the College of New Jersey may have been, the choice had a profound impact on the refinement of Madison's thinking and his commitment to conscience, personally and conceptually—particularly with John Witherspoon's recent arrival on campus.

Witherspoon was a Presbyterian minister and was thrilled to accept the call to serve as a member of the clergy and as a public servant. He also brought new and exciting extracurricular activities, including literary clubs, to the campus. Witherspoon believed it was important for his students to develop friendships by interacting with and learning from each other. The friendships forged in and the lessons learned from other students in these clubs were an important part of Madison's education at the College of New Jersey, as they are at many fine colleges and universities today. When done well, such activities provide a means for students with differing backgrounds and beliefs to learn from each other and forge lasting friendships. This was the case for Madison and other students at the college, with many going on to assume leadership roles in the arts, literature, law, medicine, the clergy, journalism, and public service. Those friends who often disagreed with each other in a civil manner also helped fashion the very compromises that made the Constitution and Bill of Rights possible.

Reverend Martin and his brother Alexander accompanied James on the trip to New Jersey. Sawney, a younger family slave, also joined them and stayed for weeks, sleeping on a pallet, as Madison made the transition to college. Nelly often entrusted James into Sawney's trusted care. On the way to the college, the entourage stopped in Philadelphia and stayed at the London Coffee House, owned by the Bradford family. The Bradfords were excited to learn that James was going to the College of New Jersey and told James about their son, William, who was also attending the college. This chance stop helped facilitate William and James meeting and becoming dear friends.

Philadelphia was a growing city, nearing a population of 20,000 at the time James passed through on his way to New Jersey. It was also vibrant, although sewage problems caused a permanent and pervasive odor to fill the air. Philadelphia was a city that would later become the site of Madison's great contribution to the work of the adoption of the Constitution. James was simultaneously excited and apprehensive about the prospect of starting college and was awestruck by the majesty of Nassau Hall, a relatively new and imposing three-story facility that housed the operations of the college. He felt a deep sense of responsibility and drive to do well, to ensure that his family's sacrifice in making his education possible was appropriately rewarded. He was determined to excel and graduate in only two years to warrant the investment his family was making. James was pleased to, once again, be pursuing knowledge on a full-time basis. Words written later in

Madison's life reflect how serious he was about the pursuit of knowledge. After years of public service, he reasoned, "Knowledge will forever govern ignorance; and a people who mean to be their own governors must arm themselves with the power which knowledge gives."[8]

Nassau Hall (Princeton University)

At the time of Madison's arrival in New Jersey, the college did not look like the Princeton campus of today. It, nevertheless, was an imposing sight to a young, impressionable student like James. Nassau Hall, which essentially contained the entire college, included rooms for students and faculty, classrooms, a library, and a chapel. Madison felt a special blend of anxiety and awe as he entered what would be his home for more than two years. It came to hold a special place in James's heart. On this first day, however, it was overwhelming.

His time at the College of New Jersey was intense and long, with days starting before morning light, at about 5:00 a.m., and ending, in a formal sense, around 9:00 p.m., when students had to be in their rooms. Many students wrote letters to family at night, after the imposition of curfew. They also used those hours for further study. James and his fellow students ignored the curfew on occasion, surreptitiously using this time to play pranks on one another and to enjoy being adolescents.

---

8. James Madison to W. T. Berry, 4 Aug. 1822, *The Founders' Constitution* (University of Chicago) , accessed October 8, 2018 http://press-pubs.uchicago.edu/founders/documents/v1ch18s35.html.

Madison and his roommate, Joseph Ross, joined in a commitment to complete the arduous curriculum in two rather than the generally prescribed period of three to four years. They studied late into the night, often leaving them with less than five hours of sleep. In fact, together they experimented, testing their physical and mental stamina to determine how little sleep was necessary to optimize performance. It was a taxing and rewarding process for two roommates engaged in rigorous study in an academically challenging environment. They occasionally took time to talk of aspirations and less studious materials.

Another roommate and close friend was Philip Freneau, who earned the title of "Poet of the American Revolution." During his senior year, Freneau collaborated with another College of New Jersey student, Philip Breckenridge, in writing a poem of epic proportions, "The Rising Glory of America," which is often deemed the greatest poem of the era. In that poem, Freneau and Breckenridge captured feelings shared by Madison, feelings that reflect the optimism of youth and a deep belief that America was a special place, a beacon of freedom. Early in the poem, Freneau sees the colonization of America as providential, with divine intervention that those who come to the land may be blessed with freedom:

> *This might we do, if warmed by that bright coal*
> *Snatch'd from the altar of cherubic fire*
> *Which touched Isaiah's lips—or if the spirit*
> *Of Jeremy and Amos, prophets old,*
> *Might swell the heaving breast—I see, I see*
> *Freedom's establish'd reign; cities, and men,*
> *Numerous as sands upon the ocean shore,*
> *And empires rising where the suns descend.*[9]

These words of these two young muses of the American Revolution expressed sentiments held by Madison, as well, and are reflective of what many call American exceptionalism, the belief that the United States of America has a special role to play in the world. If so, it is a vision that recognizes the worst in its people—"the fiercer passions of the human breast"—but also the best—a people free to overcome,

---

9. Philip Freneau, "A Poem, on the Rising Glory of America" (Philadelphia: Printed by Joseph Crukshank, 1772).

with providential assistance, "perpetual war with man" and obtain "universal peace . . . [a]nd future years of bliss."[10] They raise an anthem to America near the close of their epic poem:

> *This is thy praise America thy pow'r*
> *Thou best of climes by science visited*
> *By freedom blest and richly stor'd with all*
> *The luxuries of life. Hail happy land*
> *The seat of empire the abode of kings,*
> *The final stage where time shall introduce*
> *Renowned characters, and glorious works*
> *Of high invention and of wond'rous art . . .*[11]

Madison prized his friendship with his roommates and friends at the College. He learned much from his interactions with those dear to him. C. S. Lewis captures the kind of friendship they enjoyed with these words, "Friendship . . . is born at the moment when one man says to another 'What! You too? I thought that no one but myself' . . .'"[12] How often Madison and his friends exulted in just those sentiments—they found friendship as they worked, learned, and played together.

Learning at the Feet of John Witherspoon

Each day was full. After rising at 5:00 a.m., often with little sleep, Madison, his roommates, and other students began preparations for the day. By 6:00 a.m., the students were in morning prayers. The school's rector, John Witherspoon, as part of a period of devotion, led prayers. Witherspoon was an imposing figure who spoke with precision and stood erect, almost stiffened by his desire to exude

John Witherspoon

---

10. Ibid.
11. Ibid.
12. C. S. Lewis, *The Four Loves*, repr. (New York: Harcourt, Brace, 1960; Orlando: Harcourt, Brace & Company, 1991), 78.

propriety, portraying a captivating sense of dignity that reminded the students of the importance of their studies. Madison, though short and frail of stature, and other students, sought to emulate their teacher's serious demeanor. To begin one's day with such a charismatic figure, who possessed the capacity seemingly to fill any room in which he entered, had a profound impact on Madison and his fellow students. Many of Witherspoon's students reflected on their collegiate experience, noting that they were deeply impressed upon meeting Witherspoon for the first time. Their feelings for President Witherspoon were a blend of reverence and growing warmth, bred of an awareness that they were worthy of such a strong figure's very best efforts as a teacher and role model.

Witherspoon was married and had fourteen children, one of whom died in infancy. Twelve of his children were born to John's first wife, Elizabeth Montgomery Witherspoon, who died in 1789, at the age 67. After Elizabeth died, John married Anne Marshall. John and Anne had two children. At the time Madison attended the college, the voices of children, whose parents were at the college, were common, providing students a comforting sense of being at home. As the eldest sibling of a large family, James found such voices to be a source of comfort and, no doubt, at times a bother, an intrusion on the quiet time he coveted for his studies.

Witherspoon's devotionals and any discussions that followed often focused on a careful examination of a single verse of scripture from the Bible. Those morning devotionals contributed to Madison's own capacity, later in life, to analyze Biblical verses or phrases in meticulous detail, relishing insights drawn from careful study. Witherspoon believed that religious understanding came from diligent study, not a mere reading of chapters and books. It also helped shape Madison's careful choice of the words he used to clarify complex concepts and bring them to life. Such early training, at the hands of master teachers, helped make Madison a worthy wordsmith and a superb drafter. It is hard to declare James's exposure to a series of great teachers as simply a matter of pure coincidence.

After the morning devotional, students had more time to study before beginning their formal classes. It was not until 9:00 a.m., four hours after rising, that Madison and his fellow students were fed breakfast. Before eating breakfast, the students feasted intellectually and spiritually. Scheduling breakfast for later in the morning was intentional, so that the pangs of physical hunger might remind students to hunger first after things of the soul. The students were famished by the time they sat down to breakfast, but they learned discipline and a measure of stoicism in the process. After breakfast, they had more time for study and classroom instruction, followed by lunch at 1:00 p.m. After the midday meal, students exercised and interacted in less formal academic ways with one another, talking, studying, and preparing together. After this brief respite, a time for social interaction, the students engaged in further study and instruction. Evening devotionals and prayers were held at 5:00 p.m. Dinner followed at 7:00 p.m. This regimen was followed religiously day after day, providing the students with a sense of order and discipline.

The rules of the college—what we today would refer to as an honor code—made it clear that the students were to bridle their liberty to avoid the corruption of their morals. They were also to be respectful and civil in all their interactions. Such codes were common in that era and helped contribute to a sense of decorum or propriety and duty, bred of sound instruction and a commitment to moral conscience. The college's commitment to moral rectitude and the encouragement of civil discourse and independence of mind, under the able leadership of John Witherspoon, nevertheless, provided latitude and encouragement for students to develop and exercise their own conscience.

Madison proved to be a typical student in most respects. He enjoyed moments of frivolity and what some may have even deemed to be questionable behavior, including his love of penning bawdy lyrics. Ever aware of the sacrifices of his family to permit him to attend the college, however, James felt a need to keep such frivolity circumscribed within a carefully cultivated moral conscience. Nevertheless, to the end of his life, Madison indulged in the occasional telling of a slightly off-color or suggestive anecdote.

Madison and other students regularly attended chapel and religious services, including daily devotionals. On Sundays, they attended formal worship services. President Witherspoon generally led the

Sabbath services. These gatherings merged religious and moral training and were a significant part of the learning experience offered by the college. James and the other students saw their rector (college president) as a minister, teacher, and exemplar. Students accepted assignments to speak on assigned topics, which enhanced their religious understanding and helped students gain analytical, rhetorical, and public speaking skills. Witherspoon and other faculty expected much of their students. Witherspoon cultivated his students' capacity to engage in theological and philosophical discussions under his scrutinizing eye. Some of the students became strong speakers, but they knew Witherspoon was more concerned with substance than mere delivery. Unlike many of his fellow students, whose rhetoric was captivating, Madison's prowess as a speaker was unimpressive. He spoke in a whisper and those listening had to focus directly on each word that fell so quietly from his lips. Those who strained to listen reaped a substantial benefit. What Madison lacked in rhetorical flourish, he made up for in substance. Madison's failing in this regard may have been attributable, in part, to the stress he felt as a student, when it was his turn to speak. His lack of public speaking skills may also simply have been an instance of an area in which he lacked talent. At any rate, his careful use of language earned praise from Witherspoon and the respect of other students. Substance always trumped delivery for Madison.

During their first year, at the College students read Latin and Greek, studied Roman and Greek history and language, and rhetoric and the effective use of language. During their second year, students continued the study of the languages, geography, the first principles of philosophy, and the elements of mathematics. The third focused less on language and history, focusing rather on mathematics and natural philosophy. During their final year, students read the so-called higher classics, beginning with mathematics and natural philosophy, culminating in a rigorous course in moral philosophy. President Witherspoon gave lectures to the juniors and seniors, that initially emphasized history, and later turned to the study of composition and criticism.

After evening prayers, first, second and third year students offered what were referred to as orations on a stage erected for that purpose in the hall. Those student speeches were designed to develop presence of mind, together with proper pronunciation and the use of gestures in public speaking. For their part, every five or six weeks, the seniors offered original lectures, to an audience of student and other persons, who were invited to attend.

Madison was invigorated and often mesmerized by his studies and interactions with the faculty and his fellow students, making it easier for him to excel as student.

To enhance the students' speaking and writing ability, Witherspoon gave a series of Lectures on Eloquence, which complemented the students' intense study of Greek, Latin, and English, to which Madison later added Hebrew. In his third lecture, for example, Witherspoon offered lectures in eloquence, emphasizing grammar, spelling, and punctuation of the English language. Witherspoon emphasized that students must carefully avoid the "blemish" of using unnecessary words. In his book, *The Classical Education of our Founding Fathers*, Martin Cothran summarized the breadth of Madison's education at the College of New Jersey by correctly observing that James and his fellow students were "expected to be able to 'write Latin prose, translate Virgil, Cicero, and the Greek gospels and [to demonstrate] a commensurate knowledge of Latin and Greek grammar.' Even before he entered, however, [Madison] already read Virgil, Horace, Justinian, Nepos, Caesar, Tacitus, Lucretius, Eutropius, Phaedrus, Herodotus, Thucydides, and Plato."[13] With a growing command of languages, and an understanding of history and philosophy, Madison began to demonstrate excellence in the use of language, in cogent analysis. This love of language and command of English grammar helped make him the greatest legal draftsman in the framing era.

Whatever the reason may have been for his weakness in public speaking, James had to make many speeches throughout his generation-long life of public service. He even learned to use the faintness of his speech to his advantage, forcing listeners to pay close attention to his arguments. His desire to persuade and engage those involved in making significant policy choices overcame his weaknesses as a

---

13. Martin Cothran, "The Classical Education of the Founding Fathers," April 15, 2017, accessed October 8, 2018, https://www.memoriapress.com/articles/classical-education -founding-fathers.

speaker. His thinking was always impressive, and those who listened to what he said discovered that what he had to say was of vital importance, albeit quiet. Madison's detractors liked to belittle his speaking, but from his college days onward, he earned the respect of all who valued substance over delivery. Not surprisingly, while he was a weak speaker in large groups, he was effective when conversing one-on-one or in small groups. He was repeatedly reported to be charming in those more personal interactions, in part because he listened carefully and respectfully to others.

Shortly after arriving at the college, Madison wrote home extolling the value of what he was learning in the classroom and the chapel. Reminiscent of his days with Robertson, Madison was again in his element, learning with relish from substantive material that engaged his nimble mind. He also thoroughly enjoyed living with bright students who shared his exuberance for learning. In such an environment, it is not surprising that James was developing lifelong friendships and bonds with fellow students, many of whom went on to become leaders in government and other fields. Madison found great joy in his love of learning, which he shared with his closest friends. The stress of his drive to learn apparently needed an outlet, however. Like youth of all ages, James willingly engaged in harmless pranks and frivolity that helped relieve the pressure of his studies and endeared him to his friends.

Many of his fellow graduates would soon join Madison as delegates to the Constitutional Convention and in future public service. Ever an example to his students, Witherspoon followed his conscience and placed his very life at risk as a signer the Declaration of Independence. His fellow patriot, President John Adams, praised Witherspoon in the following terms, "[Witherspoon] is as high a Son of Liberty, as any man in America."[14]

---

14. John Adams, diary entry of August 27, 1774, in *The Diary and Autobiography of John Adams*, ed. L. H. Butterfield, 4 vols (Cambridge, MA: Harvard University Press, 1961), 2:112. Jeffrey H. Morrison, *John Witherspoon and the Founding of the American Republic* (Notre Dame, Indiana: University of Notre Dame, 2005), 1.

Learning from Friends and Classmates

Like many students today, Madison learned much, as well, from his friends and fellow students. Two of Madison's friends, Phillip Freneau and Hugh Henry Breckenridge, for example, gained renown for their literary talents. They helped Madison further hone his writing skills and love of language. As friends, they often collaborated in writing projects and helped to improve their ability to write clearly and persuasively.

Madison, Freneau, and Breckenridge wrote for the American Whig Society, a student literary club formed at the college. The Whigs were committed to liberty and supported the growing revolutionary cause. Most of the Whigs were from Pennsylvania and the southern colonies. They directed their comments, which were often a bit scurrilous, to the Cliosophians (Clios), another literary club made of students who largely resided in New England and were somewhat less enamored with the revolutionary cause. As evidenced by the record left of the Whigs and their correspondence with the Clios, Madison and his fellow students were not free from the playfulness to the point of being a bit risqué, an oft-repeated characteristic of college students for centuries. That frivolity included some rather suggestive poetry written by Madison, poking fun at his archrivals, the Clios. Madison's poetry deserves little praise for its structure or substantive content. Madison directed his doggerel to the "lecherous rascal[s]" (the Clios):

> *The lecherous rascal there will find*
> *A place just suited to his mind*
> *May whore & pimp & drink & swear*
> *Nor more the garb of christians wear*
> *And free Nassau from such a pest*
> *A dunce a fool an ass at best.*[15]

Such verse is hardly the work of a poetic genius. The archrival and adolescent Clios accepted such verse with good nature and replied in kind, much to the delight of the equally adolescent Whigs. In smaller groups throughout his lifetime, Madison occasionally reverted to his

---

15. See Ralph Ketcham, *James Madison* (Charlottesville, VA: University of Virginia Press), 1990, 36.

wit and somewhat bawdy side, evidencing his sense of humor. Though his sense of humor could be a bit risqué at times, friends and foes generally agreed that Madison was a man of integrity and decency, even when some vehemently disliked his policies and manner. Witherspoon, who knew of the antics of his students, nevertheless praised James for his talent and virtue. Madison's youthful frivolity was offset by his general sense of propriety and decorum.

When circumstances required it, as a young student, Madison could be very serious, even courageous. His classmate and friend, Phillip Freneau, recounted one such instance. One of their friends and classmates amassed a significant bill at a local shop that sold cake and beer. The owner of the shop became incensed with the boy, who was unable to pay his debt, and imprisoned him to force someone to come forward and pay the debt. Freneau, Madison, and some other boys determined to come to rescue their classmate. When the shop owner discovered that they wanted the boy's freedom but were unable to pay the debt, his wrath only increased. Wielding an axe, he threatened the cowering group of young students. Freneau writes that, at this very time a young, even a man of small stature stepped forward and declared, "You villain, would you dare strike any of us with that axe?" The shop owner recoiled, astounded by the temerity of young James Madison, and relented, putting down the axe and released the boy to his friends, without the payment of his debt. Even during his college years, Madison was both courageous and eloquent, despite his lack of physical presence.

One of Madison's closest friends at the college, and thereafter, was William Bradford. Bradford was a member of a respected Philadelphia family, in whose lodgings Madison had stayed on his initial trip to the college. William, like James, was a Whig. The two spent hours talking about a broad range of topics, including the classic texts and lectures they studied with exuberance and their growing allegiance to the revolutionary cause, the cause of liberty.

After graduating from the College of New Jersey, Madison and Bradford maintained a correspondence that revealed both the depth of their friendship and a glimpse into the kinds of issues that were of concern to them. These two young leaders in the making were engaged in discussions regarding personal matters, including their possible future vocations. They also regularly discussed political matters, which were increasingly of concern to these young men and had helped knit them together as Whigs at the College. It is in those letters, as well, that we obtain significant glimpses of Madison's growing interest regarding the liberty of conscience. Those letters reflect the substance of their college education at work, as theory began to take practical shape in their daily lives.

Madison's Professors and the
Influence of John Witherspoon

As important as friends were to Madison's education, James clearly owed the most to his professors. President Witherspoon handpicked instructors to teach at the College of New Jersey. Though the faculty was small, they engaged their students in demanding yet personal ways. Given the relatively small size of the student body, faculty individually tutored students. Faculty were not merely talking heads in a large lecture hall—they were involved in the very lives of their students inside and outside the classroom. The fact that the students and faculty lived together helped create a genuine learning community. During Witherspoon's twenty-six-year tenure at the College of New Jersey, the faculty never exceeded five in number, teaching a small number of engaged students. Witherspoon also taught courses and led the students in devotionals and Sabbath instruction. The quality of the teaching and the learning environment at the college were exceptional.

Witherspoon's style characterized the faculty generally. A student wrote,

> Witherspoon is always perfectly clear. No ambiguity clouds his style. He knows the subject thoroughly and is familiar with all the literature of it. The lectures abound with quotations and references to other writers and are lighted with pleasing illustrations. . . . The lecture as given by him was not a droning deliverance, the students nervously taking notes as were possible. It was rather a free conversation, the lecturer first stating his subject and his opinion of

it, the students afterwards questing him at their pleasure and being in their turn questioned by him.[16]

This engaging method of teaching helped refine the thinking of the students. It also ensured that they were prepared for class each day. The educational experience at the College of New Jersey enabled Madison to thrive.

One of the ways in which Witherspoon profoundly influenced Madison was in helping to develop his wholehearted commitment to liberty of conscience. This becomes clear when one examines the substance of Witherspoon's lectures and Madison's later work in the area. Madison found Witherspoon's teaching to be edifying, laying the initial foundation for Madison's thinking and engagement in a life as a public servant. After graduating in only two years, achieving his personal goal, Madison returned home. Once home, he missed the College of New Jersey, and Witherspoon, a great deal. It is not surprising, therefore, that he quickly found his way back to the college to study directly with his mentor. As a graduate student, Madison focused his study on Hebrew, which enhanced his capacity to use words with care and that they can have multiple and sometimes antithetical meanings. The desire to study Hebrew was also motivated by Madison's desire to understand scripture, as he pursued his lifelong journey of faith. His return to the College of New Jersey was also strongly influenced by his admiration for Witherspoon.

Madison, who was not inclined to providing effusive compliments to others, thought highly of Witherspoon's character, referring to it as at "once strong and gentle," virtues that Madison emulated. To understand fully the impact of Witherspoon on Madison, it is necessary to examine Witherspoon's own educational development. Witherspoon, like Donald Robertson, was a student of the Scottish Enlightenment, with a rich and thoughtful commitment to liberty. The Scottish Enlightenment, therefore, naturally provided a justification for the founding a new nation conceived in liberty.

---

16. David Walker Woods Jr., *John Witherspoon* (New York: Fleming H. Revell Company, 1906), 108–9.

John Witherspoon: The Man

Like Madison and so many of his students, Witherspoon developed intellectual curiosity at a young age, fueled by an independence of thought and depth of faith that reflected the teachings of his early instructors. He also quickly developed a heightened sense of conscience, a duty owed to God to use his talents and learning to bring the fruits of liberty to others. Witherspoon was only fourteen when he entered the University of Edinburgh, an academically challenging university that emphasized the teachings of the Scottish Enlightenment. He related well to the experiences of young boys attending the college. After graduating from the University of Edinburgh, Witherspoon entered the ministry, a profession that permitted him to meld his spiritual and intellectual sides.

As a newly called minister, Witherspoon found himself in the middle of a major church controversy. Powerful patrons of the church supported, selected, and retained clergy, without consulting with or permitting the membership of their congregations to confirm the appointment. Ministers were subservient to the patron, who could mete out the discipline and governance of the established church of his native land, the Church of Scotland. Witherspoon joined a group opposed to these practices and became the "Popular Party."

The popular party raised the right of conscience in defense of their position that "God alone is the Lord of conscience." Witherspoon and the Popular Party, however, also made it clear that they were not seeking to undermine the authority of the Church of Scotland; rather, they were seeking to ensure that the Church respected the right of conscience on the part of its members. Indeed, members of the Popular Party believed the practice of recognizing the liberty of conscience would strengthen and not weaken the Church, or any church that was worthy of being called Christian. Witherspoon's early experience within the church, coupled with his instruction in the Scottish Enlightenment, helped shape and provide a practical foundation for his future teaching regarding the pre-eminence of the right of conscience. His concern for the sanctity of the individual right of religious conscience became a central tenet of all that he taught his students, because it was so deeply ingrained in his character. His work with the Popular Party also contributed to his growing reputation within Presbyterian circles.

When the presidency (rector's position) at the College of New Jersey came open, it is not surprising that the trustees recruited Witherspoon. He was relatively young, which would add vitality to the economically troubled college, but had earned a reputation that spanned both continents. He was already a well-respected church and intellectual leader. He was also a man of courage and conviction, suffering imprisonment and torture as a young man for participating directly in opposing the tyranny of the British monarch, Prince Charles. His opposition to the king and support for the cause of liberty was a conviction he shared with Donald Robertson and James Madison Sr. Witherspoon, like Robertson, tired of incessant political battles with intransigent church leaders and patrons over issues of governance and the fighting of a civil war against the King Charles and his forces. He was ready for a change. His desire to move to a land of opportunity led him to accept the offer to serve as president at the College of New Jersey.

Upon his arrival at the College of New Jersey, Witherspoon found an institution that was underfunded and in need of energetic leadership. After reflecting on the costs and benefits of immigrating to the colonies, he accepted the call to serve. Serving at the college placed Witherspoon in an environment where his talents blessed the lives of a generation of students and the cause of liberty. John was coming to a nation that was on the cusp of a battle over liberty with Britain, a battle that would transcend the effort in Scotland to obtain a measure of freedom from King Charles and Britain. Witherspoon quickly warmed to that cause, as evidenced by the college's awarding patriots like John Hancock honorary degrees shortly after Witherspoon took the helm of the struggling college. He also was an ideal leader to encourage students to learn and support the principles of liberty and the freedom of conscience, as part of the natural law given by God to His children. Based on their correspondence, British visitors to the campus, during Witherspoon's early years, viewed Witherspoon as a rebel, believing that he was fomenting the cause of revolution among his students. To others he was a patriot. To all, he was formidable.

Witherspoon was surely pleased to find a group of enthusiastic and intellectually capable students committed to serving their fellow men and living virtuous lives. He discovered students who were also anxious to put their learning to practical use. He, more than any other teacher at the college, influenced the students by word and deed. Throughout their lives, many former students, including Madison, sought Witherspoon's wise counsel. They went out of their way to visit their mentor and teacher on the campus they had come to love, as a place that had flamed their desire to become better men, intellectually and spiritually.

President Witherspoon was equal to the challenge of teaching such talented and enterprising students. The combination of great teaching with able and willing students led one commentator to refer to Witherspoon as "one of the most influential professor in American history."[17] Though still young himself, Witherspoon's former students quickly became leaders in the revolutionary and founding era. They enthusiastically followed the example of their mentor and teacher, who served in the New Jersey legislature and the Continental Congress. He was also the only clergyman who signed the Declaration of Independence. He worked long hours, in many capacities, ever-driven by his own conscience, a trait he passed on to many of his students, not the least of which was James Madison.

Students who attended the College of New Jersey that were deeply influenced by Witherspoon's leadership, teaching, and example included a president (Madison) and vice-president of the United States (Aaron Burr, Jr.), nine cabinet members, twenty-one senators, thirty-nine members of the House of Representatives, three justices of the Supreme Court, and twelve state governors. Many graduates of the College of New Jersey served as influential delegates to the Constitutional Convention of 1787. Others played a critical role in the adoption and ratification of the Bill of Rights. They mirrored Witherspoon's personal emphasis on learning and then acting. They learned to understand all sides of issues and to be free thinkers,

---

17. Wayne S. Moss, "Witherspoon, Madison, Moral Philosophy, and the Constitution," *Princeton Alumni Weekly*, accessed October 8, 2018, https://paw.princeton.edu/article /essay-witherspoon-madison-moral-philosophy-and-constitution.

followers of their own respective consciences. Though they often disagreed, compromise could always be found because they generally shared a commitment to making a difference in the life of the new nation, on the battlefield, in government, in the clergy, in law, and in literature. They thought deeply and acted conscientiously and usually with civility. Witherspoon stood as an example worthy of emulation. He was a leader in the revolutionary cause, an influential member of the Continental Congress, a minister, and a teacher, and combined a deep understanding of the material taught with an allegiance to his conscience and a love of his students. He also embraced humility of the kind noted in the margin of Madison's own Bible, where James defined humility as the better a man becomes, the less he thinks of himself. Witherspoon's students willingly emulated his sense of duty above self. He was, in so many ways, a leader-servant.

John Witherspoon:
A Clergyman and Patriot

His students were aware that Witherspoon embraced the revolutionary cause. The college conferred honorary degrees on supporters of the revolution and provided them with opportunities to address the students. Nevertheless, Witherspoon encouraged his students to speak out on all sides of the issues of the day, even and perhaps especially when their views differed from his own position regarding the revolution. He was, however, pleased when a group of students, including Madison, formed a politically motivated procession at the tolling of the college bell. They burned a letter from northern merchants who had urged other merchants to violate the non-importation agreement supported by proponents of the revolution. With a hint of pride and knowing his father's sentiments favoring the revolutionary cause, James wrote home describing the event on campus. On July 23, 1770, James noted, with a tinge of pride, "We have no publick news but the base conduct of the Merchants in N. York in breaking through their spirited resolutions not to import, a distinct account of which I suppose will be in the Virginia Gazette before this [letter] arrives. Their letter to the Merchants in Philadelphia requesting their concurrence was lately burnt by students of this place in the college yard, all of them appearing in their black Gowns & the bell Tolling."[18] James, Sr., the ardent patriot, must have smiled with some delight when he received this enthusiastic report from his son.

Before turning to the substance of Witherspoon's teachings, it is worthwhile to examine Witherspoon's views regarding service and political activity by religious leaders, views that clearly influenced Madison. As previously noted, as a clergyman, Witherspoon served in the state legislature and Continental Congress and was a signer and major proponent of the Declaration of Independence. He clearly believed that his voice, his religious conscience, should be a part of the dialogue that influenced public policy. Like many great religious leaders after him, including the likes of Dr. Martin Luther King, Jr., John Witherspoon believed that the muzzling of religious conscience in public dialogue was a cause for alarm. Indeed, he felt he was duty-bound as a matter of conscience, religious and otherwise, to speak out and ultimately serve in public office. His students, including Madison, joined in Witherspoon's belief that no legitimate government should preclude him or other religious leaders from addressing public issues. To limit their role in public life would be an unacceptable limit on the right of conscience and would deprive the broader populous of the important and influential voice of leaders who spoke from religious as well as public conviction. Witherspoon believed the voice of conscience should open, not end, the debate. The views of a clergyman, like Witherspoon, should not be dispositive in the public square simply because they have their basis in religious conscience. They added a much-needed dimension to the dialogue.

Witherspoon, together with Madison and so many other dedicated patriots of the founding generation, firmly believed that the voices of religious conscience from clergy and the faithful should be encouraged as a part of the public dialogue, because they often contribute significantly to wise policymaking. Not surprisingly, Witherspoon strongly opposed limits on participation by clergy in government. In

---

18. Letter from James Madison to James Madison, Sr., 23 July 1770, *Founder's Online (National Archives)*, accessed October 9, 2018, https://founders.archives.gov/documents/Madison/01-01-02-0008

one such effort to limit religious voices in the public square, legislators in Georgia sought to adopt a constitutional limitation on public service by clergy by forbidding clergy from serving in the General Assembly. Witherspoon openly and vigorously opposed this limitation and other related efforts to limit religiously motivated voices, the voice of conscience, in the public square.

Madison learned this lesson well. After Madison graduated from the College of New Jersey and assumed the responsibilities attendant with public life, he faced a similar issue. Thomas Jefferson had recommended that the new Virginia Constitution bar the clergy from holding public office. Madison found his friend's idea to be appalling. Thinking of the example of his former teacher and other examples, as well as the principle of liberty of conscience itself, James wrote Jefferson: "Does not the exclusion of Ministers of the Gospel as such violate a fundamental principle of liberty by punishing a religious profession with the privation of a civil right? Does it [not] violate another article of the plan itself which exempts religion from the cognizance of Civil power? Does it not violate justice by at once taking away a right and prohibiting a compensation for it."[19] Madison believed that taking the right of clergy in this manner was a non-compensable taking of a sacred right. Ultimately persuaded, Jefferson relented, although he maintained a lifelong apprehension regarding the role of religious voices in the public sphere, a view Madison did not necessarily share. Madison's strict allegiance to the right of conscience was reflective of the view of his able teacher, John Witherspoon.

Witherspoon, together with prominent members of the founding generation, including Adams and Madison and an ever-reluctant Jefferson, were supportive of people with strong religious views entering the political fray and speaking as a matter of conscience. They were particularly pleased when those "ministers" represented a minority sect or served as a voice of conscience in a political world often dominated by mere expediency and the currying of public favor. Madison and other founding leaders understood that the voice of religious

---

19. James Madison, "Observations on Jefferson's Draft of a Constitution for Virginia," 15 Oct. 1788, Founders Online (National Archives), accessed October 9, 2018, https://founders.archives.gov/documents/Madison/01-11-02-0216.

conscience would come in the form of moral arguments designed to persuade those who were of other faiths or no faith at all. This was particularly true at the national level, where no single religion commanded a majority. That practical limitation sufficed, in terms of permitting religious voices to enter the political dialogue. Madison wisely believed a truth that he emphasized throughout his lifetime of service, that many factions and sects engaged in vigorous discourse, including religious factions, temper tyrannical government power, and promote wise policy. Multiple factions were a blessing, not an impediment, to liberty. In a complementary sense, Madison and Jefferson remained vigilant in their efforts to ensure that the possibility of any single sect commandeering the political process to their own sectarian ends was unlawful.

Witherspoon's Teachings

A brief study of the substance of Witherspoon's teachings at the college is also instructive in helping the reader understand how Witherspoon instructed and ultimately influenced his students, particularly Madison. It is best to read these words in the precise form delivered, which requires including some lengthy quotes.

In his moral philosophy course, Witherspoon emphasized the role of "common sense." For Witherspoon, common sense or judgment based on morality and time-tested traditions, values, and social virtue brings order to human relationships. We see this form of common sense reflected repeatedly in Madison's public and private life.

In his *Lectures on Moral Philosophy*, Witherspoon taught his students that belief in God, in some form, was also a universal dictate of common sense. Early in his lectures on moral philosophy, and regularly in his weekly sermons, President Witherspoon emphasized moral duty and obligation. He taught that the principles of duty and moral obligation are drawn from the very nature of man. Witherspoon added that it follows that if we can understand man, as formed by his Maker, we can certainly ascertain what man ought to be.

One's identity, or self, has its base in human nature. Thoughtfully examining how God made man illuminates the true nature of man.

His view, in this regard, is reminiscent of a Hebrew word for *atonement* (becoming one with God and one's own self), *teshuva*, which roughly translated, means that the purpose of this life is to "return to God and one's own true self." In a subsequent lecture, Witherspoon rejected moral relativism. He emphatically declared,

> The moral sense implies also a sense of obligation, that such and such things are right and others wrong, that we are bound in duty to do the one, and that our conduct is hateful, blamable, and deserving of punishment if we do the contrary; and there is also in the moral sense or conscience an apprehension or belief that reward and punishment will follow according as we shall act in the one way or the other.[20]

For Witherspoon, the moral sense was what in scripture and common language we have come to call conscience—the law written by our Maker on our hearts. Conscience, as such, enforces duty, which is itself previous to human reasoning. Witherspoon also emphasized that duty or moral obligation derives from an individual's conscience and is prior and superior to choices made solely through reasoning, unaided by inspiration. Indeed, reason, the use of analysis alone, was incomplete without inspiration, or personal revelation. He did not disparage the use of reason, but he believed it to be insufficient standing alone. He believed that if one was acting according to an inspired sense of duty or moral obligation, reason is useful in articulating reasons for that duty. He taught that God is perfect in His use of reason. We, as mere mortals, at best dimly understand God's will, in part due to the limitations on the capacity of human understanding and the insufficiency of language to describe the thoughts of God. These teachings find their way into James Madison's character and thought.

Witherspoon taught that justice requires a person to live in accordance with his or her conscience or sense of moral obligation. If we fail to live in accordance with our conscience, then we are accountable for our failure to abide by a moral obligation rooted in that conscience. Conscience necessarily creates duty—a duty to God and one's self—a moral obligation. Liberty is not merely a license to do as we please—it

---

20. Thomas Miller, ed., *The Selected Writings of John Witherspoon* (Carbondale, Southern Illinois University Press, 1990), 163.

is an obligation or duty to do what we know to be right. For religious believers this duty is sacred, rooted in the word of God. As such, moral obligation may be viewed as part of the price of liberty. We are free to choose, but we are also accountable for those choices. In turn, it follows that no just government may force a person to violate his or her conscience, thereby intruding on a person's most sacred of all obligations, not to self or to government, but to God. If a government does so, even in the pursuit of what the majority considers a public good, it has unjustly violated that person's right. The government may intervene only when a person in pursuing his or her conscience violates the equal right of conscience, or moral obligation, of another. In such a case, according to Witherspoon, it is appropriate to limit a right, but only to an extent necessary to salvage or protect the right of conscience of another person. For example, one may not use the right of conscience to justify the killing of another, because to do so would deprive the slain person of life and with it the opportunity to exercise his or her right of conscience.

Witherspoon understood that morality, justice, and conscience are connected. This position is all too foreign today, when so many are inclined to believe that rights involve license (the opportunity to do something) and not duty (the right and attendant responsibility to act in accord with that right of conscience). Witherspoon and Madison believed that their conscience was sacred, a duty to God, and to living by a higher law. As will become evident, Madison and Witherspoon shared the view that God endowed His children with the liberty of conscience so that they might use their God-given agency to choose what is morally right and act responsibly as they progressed, becoming better persons. This process of obedience to conscience permitted individuals to gain dignity and improve as a person, not simply to frolic in an unbridled freedom.

This teaching makes great sense. Loving parents often give their children choices with consequences so that the child may grow and develop. If there is no expectation or accountability for performance for one's acts, the child's growth is stifled, remaining little more than a slave to his or her appetite. In a world without duty and justice, a world of license, there is only licentiousness—moving from one momentary pleasure to the next. In such a world, there is little room for moral growth. When a person disobeys higher law and violates his or her conscience, in a just world there must be consequences. Children learn and grow when there are consequences that attend disobedience. Personal responsibility of this sort, which is essential to the exercise of conscience, is therefore a blessing and not a punishment, even though accepting consequences in the short term may be difficult. A child learns from mistakes and is then encouraged (mercy has a role here) to improve and try anew to live up to a refined conscience. Such a world of justice and judgment dignifies humanity—it raises individuals from being little more than brute creatures in search of personal gratification to becoming moral agents. In the words of Eliza R. Snow, a poet and religious leader, "How great, how glorious, how complete, redemptions grand design, where justice, love, and mercy meet in harmony divine."[21] Witherspoon taught moral responsibility, justice, and mercy in ways that Madison understood well, treating each as a true and complimentary principle.

Despite the broad latitude given to one's natural right of conscience, Witherspoon taught that examining that which promotes the general good is helpful in deciding close cases. Nevertheless, he urged care, fearing that determinations of what may seem to promote the general good is never permitted to displace principles of individual duty rooted in conscience. In his words, "True virtue certainly promotes the general good, and this may be made use of as an argument in doubtful cases to determine whether a principle is right or wrong, but to make the good of the whole our immediate principle of action is putting ourselves in God's place and actually superseding the necessity and the use of the particular principles of duty which he hath impressed upon the conscience."[22]

In a succeeding lecture, his fourth, Witherspoon summarized his thinking regarding duty and the obligation to act according to one's moral duty or conscience, in a manner consistent with the will of God. He asserted, "The result of the whole is that we ought to take

21. Eliza R. Snow, "How Great the Wisdom and the Love," verse 5, accessed October 9, 2018, http://mldb.byu.edu/ersnow1.htm.

22. Thomas Miller, ed., *The Selected Writings of John Witherspoon* (Carbondale, Southern Illinois University Press, 1990), 167–68.

the rule of duty from conscience enlightened by reason, experience, and every way by which we can be supposed to learn the will of our Maker and his intention in creating us such as we are. And we ought to believe that it is as deeply founded as the nature of God himself, being a transcript of his moral excellence, and that it is productive of the greatest good."[23] He believed and taught that conscience is the primary source of moral excellence and is ultimately that which is most productive of the greatest good in society. He essentially taught his students that religious conscience is inviolate and insulated from other senses of the general good. The protection and furtherance of religious conscience is, as such, critical to the achievement of the greatest good. Witherspoon taught a truth that Madison later echoed in his work that an individual's conscience is one's most sacred property, that property which is least within the reach or the touch of government.

During his studies at the College of New Jersey, under the tutelage of Witherspoon, Madison learned the following line of reasoning regarding to the sanctity of the natural or God-given right of conscience:

1. The principles of moral duty and obligation are reflective of the divine nature of man, as the creation of God, and man's relationship to God;
2. This sense of moral duty is what may be termed "conscience," which is written upon our hearts by our Maker;
3. Duty to God is precedent to reason, although reason refines conscience, and perfect reason originates with God;
4. As a matter of action, following one's God-given and inspired religious conscience results in true virtue, which in turn is the source of the greatest public good;
5. Religious conscience, as such, is a foundational or natural right, a right given from God; and
6. Given that conscience is a foundational or natural right and the source of the greatest public good, general conceptions of the public good derived from other sources, including the will of a political majority may legitimately infringe on the right

---

23. Ibid., 168.

of conscience only when necessary to protect another's equal right of conscience.

These teachings regarding the natural right of conscience, our most sacred property and right, deeply influenced Madison and found their way into his work regarding religious liberty, Madison was naturally inclined to accept such teachings, which echoed the teachings of Donald Robertson, who influenced young James during his most impressionable years. It is clear, as well, that Madison found such thinking to be congenial, reflective of the person he desired to become. Persuaded, James later sought to include a vibrant right of conscience in constitutional documents designed to secure that liberty. Madison and Witherspoon agreed that religiously based conscience, derived from the very nature of God, is distinguishable from other forms of belief or non-religiously based conscience. Religious conscience defines the person who holds it in sacred ways—ways that should not have to yield to the public good defined by the majority except under the extreme cases. Taking such property is not like the taking of real property. It is possible to compensate for the taking of real property, but it is never possible to compensate for a loss of the right of conscience, because obedience to one's conscience, a duty to God, defines the very soul of its holder. To limit religious conscience deprives a believer of a part of his or her soul, a deprivation appropriately beyond the reach of a just government.

Witherspoon's views and teaching regarding what we now have come to term the non-establishment value or principle were not well developed. He did not expound on government establishments. He focused on the right of conscience itself. For Witherspoon, non-establishment was a value subsumed in the right of religious conscience. Under such a view, public establishment of a given religious sect, or dominance by a religion, would violate the individual right of conscience of those who did not belong to that sect. That may have contributed to the expectation at the College of New Jersey that students live in accord with their own sense of religious conscience or moral obligation. Unlike most other religious institutions of higher learning at the time, the College of New Jersey did not require students to adhere to the views of any specified sect. The college encouraged those of differing faiths to learn to respect one another, in a culture committed to generalized moral values—values shared by most religions. Madison came to see great power in this concept of the unifying force of broadly shared moral values that denigrated no religious sect, preferring to lift them collectively.

Witherspoon was apprehensive about the possibility that the power of government might be wrested by any individual sect or group of religious sects, in furtherance of that group's own sectarian ends. Such a move would clearly violate the right of religious conscience. We can see the roots of this thinking, by analogy, in Witherspoon's opposition to the Church of Scotland's forcing individual members and congregations to comply with centralized Church governance, without an opportunity to participate in some manner in the decisions of the Church. For Witherspoon, to protect the right of conscience, commandeering the electoral process by a religious group, to impose its sectarian will on others (who do not share those views as a matter of conscience) violates the individual conscience of those in the minority. No group nor majority, under Witherspoon's thinking, may use government to control the conscience of others. Conscience must be exempted from any such law, whatever its origin, except when an equivalent right of conscience is in jeopardy. To fail to exempt those who oppose an act of the majority on the ground of religious conscience constituted the tyranny of the majority over the most sacred right or property held by man, the right of conscience, one's duty to God and one's own true self. Such tyranny would certainly be present in an instance in which a sect or group of sects wrested control of government in furtherance of its exclusive sectarian agenda.

The Pilgrims and Puritans

Madison had observed the violation of these principles in his daily life, as one who was also well versed in colonial history. He understood the often-rocky role of conscience in the founding of the colonies. He knew the Pilgrims came to New England, seeking to find a refuge where they could practice their religion, in its pure and undefiled form.

The Puritans traced their roots to the mid-sixteenth century, when a religious sect began to form, as followers of John Calvin. They believed human nature was fallen or depraved. They also sought to purify the Church of England from the influence of Roman Catholicism, a sect Puritans pejoratively referred to as Papists. They were seeking the true faith and believed that fallen men and women had to follow the doctrine or law of the Bible with exactness. They believed in salvation by works. "Puritans" was the general name given to this group, a name they considered vile or offensive.

The Pilgrims were the first sect within the Puritan movement to come to the Americas, founding the Plymouth Colony or Plantation. Pilgrims believed that the Church of England was corrupt and that, as Christians, they must separate from the Church of England or face damnation. Saints, as they called themselves, must separate from sinners. This desire to separate from unbelievers resulted in their moving to Holland and then North America. The Pilgrims were Separatists.

The Pilgrims arrived in New England in 1620, although they were initially bound for the Colony of Virginia. The Mayflower Compact, which provided a social contract under which they agreed to live, became their governing document. The Compact provided, in part:

> Having undertaken, for the Glory of God, and advancements of the Christian faith and honor of our King and Country, a voyage to plant the first colony in the Northern parts of Virginia, do by these presents, solemnly and mutually, in the presence of God, and one another, covenant and combine ourselves together into a civil body politic; for our better ordering, and preservation and furtherance of the ends aforesaid; and by virtue hereof to enact, constitute, and frame, such just and equal laws, ordinances, acts, constitutions, and offices, from time to time, as shall be thought most meet and convenient for the general good of the colony; unto which we promise all due submission and obedience.[24]

The Pilgrims were seeking to form a separate community, in fulfillment of their collective desire to practice their religion, a religion purified from the Church of England, the Roman Catholic Church, and

---

24. "The Mayflower Compact," Pilgrim Hall Museum, accessed October 9, 2018, https//www.pilgrimhallmuseum.org/mayflower_compact_text.htm.

all other impure Christian sects. They were also combining themselves into a political body. For them, there was no distinction between their community of faith and the government. Both, working in unison, furthered the true Christian faith.

Another group of Puritans came to America in 1630, after the founding of the Plymouth Colony. This group included approximately 1,000 colonists, led by John Winthrop. John Winthrop became governor of the Massachusetts Bay Colony. He distinguished himself and his group from the Pilgrims or separatists. They wanted to purify the Church, but they did not want to separate from it. They were determined to establish a "City upon a Hill," a colony capable of lighting the world with Christianity in its purest form. To do so, they had to purge themselves of all ungodliness, individually and collectively.

The Puritans came to the Americas to purify themselves. Soon, as Madison understood, dissident members of the colony were subject to purging or purification. Therefore, church leaders tried those acting in accordance with their conscience in ways deemed disruptive of the pure form of Christianity embraced by the community and its leaders for heresy. Anne Hutchinson and Roger Williams were two leaders who found themselves in the role of dissenters, and ultimately outcasts from the Colony.

Anne Hutchinson and Roger Williams

Anne Marbury Hutchinson believed that God revealed to her that the churches of her day were unfaithful, failing to preach the Lord in truth. She became embroiled in the antinomianism controversy. Sides were drawn between those who believed salvation is a matter of works based on Biblical doctrine (Governor Winthrop and the leaders of the colony believed this) and those who believed in salvation, at least in part, by grace through a personal relationship with Jesus Christ (Hutchinson). The Puritans believed that the enforcement of Biblical doctrine within the community was a common good. The faith community must purify itself from all ungodliness. Anne was an unexpected dissenting and disruptive voice, a voice that threatened the faithfulness and purity of the colony.

Anne Hutchinson was a devoted mother of fifteen children. Based on personal revelation, which she defined as, "the voice of his own spirit to my soul,"[25] and a careful study of the scriptures, she believed she must follow the path dictated by her religious conscience. She held meetings in her home with others who shared an interest in or affinity for such beliefs. A church court, made up of male leaders or elders of the religious sect, tried her for heresy and disrupting the peace with her heretical views. They found her guilty, after a lengthy trial. The guilty verdict resulted in banishment from the colony for Anne, her family, and followers. She responded to the painful decision with these words: "Now, if you condemn me for speaking what in my conscience I know to be the truth, I must commit myself to the Lord."[26] She believed duty-bound to God to follow the "inward light," the light of conscience.

Anne was commanded to repent and "honor her fathers," the leaders of the colony. She refused, emphasizing that God and her family wanted her to remain true to her conscience. She knew her family wanted her to be true to her faith. Her father, Francis Marbury, provided Anne with an example of allegiance to one's conscience. Francis was a teacher, tried years before in England, as a heretic for his views. He responded to the charges much as Anne did during her trial. He humbly stated he would give up everything for God.

Anne Marbury Hutchinson before her accusers

Francis responded to the charges against him by avowing that he feared God, not man. Interestingly, one of Francis Marbury's students was a young boy, John Smith, who later played a significant founding role in building Jamestown and the Virginia colony. Anne, like her father

---

25. See Eve LaPlante, *American Jezebel* (New York: HarperCollins 2004), 119.
26. Ibid. 118,

before her, wanted to remain a part of the faith but refused to deny or act against her religious conscience. She also knew that failing to live in accordance with her conscience was a breach of a duty owed to God, a part of the very essence of her soul. Roger Williams understood the importance of religious conscience and duty. He suffered earlier expulsion from the Massachusetts Bay Colony and welcomed Anne and her family to come join in building the Providence Plantation.

Williams founded the First Baptist Church in America. He deserves credit for his significant role in providing meaning for the religious liberty protected by the First Amendment. Anne and the extended Hutchinson family joined the Providence Colony, playing an influential role in its early development, even though they shortly relocated to New York to live among the Dutch. It was initially a good union—Williams and Hutchinson—two individuals devoted to the right of conscience. The colony soon adopted the Charter of Rhode Island and Providence Plantations. That Charter secured the right of conscience. It stated that, "No person within said colony, at any time hereafter shall be any wise molested, punished, disquieted, or called in question, for any differences in opinion in matters of religion, and do not actually disturb the civil peace . . . but that . . . every person [may] fully and freely enjoy his and their own judgments and consciences in matters of religious concernments, throughout the tract of land hereafter mentioned."[27]

Like Anne Hutchinson, Roger Williams was a supporter of the Native Americans, taking a position that was uncommon in the colonies. Too many colonists viewed the native tribes as unequal unless they converted to Christianity, as the colonists practiced it. If tribal members failed to convert, in the eyes of the Pilgrims, Puritans, and other colonists, they proved that they were less than fully human. However, Williams wrote a book regarding native language, in which he disclosed his belief that members of native tribes were his equal, as children of God. Many Puritans disparaged Anne for her views regarding nearby tribal members. As one Edward Johnson put it,

---

27. "Charter of Rhode Island and Providence Plantations," 15 July 1663, The Avalon Project (Yale Law School), accessed October 9, 2018, http://avalon.law.yale.edu/17th_century/ri04.asp.

"Being amongst a multitude of Indians [Hutchinson] boasted they were become all one Indian."[28]

Sadly, due to a failure to communicate, the Siwanoy, members of a native tribe, responded to a brutal killing by settlers of eighty native men, women, and children by scalping and killing Anne, five of her children, and other family members and associates. The Siwanoy had warned the Dutch settlers to leave, which they did, but Anne refused to heed the warnings, believing that her faith and Christian understanding would prevail and prevent her death at the hands of the natives, whom she counted as her brothers and sisters, children of God.

The experiences of Anne Hutchinson and Roger Williams, as dissenters from the Pilgrim majority, helped inform and shape Madison's growing concern with regard to religious persecution in any form. His views were also deeply influenced by William Penn.

William Penn

William Penn, a Quaker and founder of the Commonwealth of Pennsylvania, referred to as the Province of Pennsylvania, was an inspiration to Madison. In 1681, Penn obtained an extensive grant of land from King Charles II, in payment for a debt owed William's father. That land grant was extensive and provided William, and many others, refuge from religious persecution. Penn was also founder of the City of Philadelphia, which later served as the home for the

William Penn

Constitutional Convention. Philadelphia continues to carry the title of the City of Brotherly Love, a direct reference to its Quaker roots.

William converted to the Quaker faith as a young man, a decision that had negative implications for his personal and political future—an

---

28. See, Eve LaPlante, *American Jezebel* (New York: HarperCollins), 233.

act that essentially led to exile. In fact, his commitment to his religious conscience, and his faith, resulted in imprisonment on more than one occasion and sadly created a rift with his father. His father initially disowned William, upon learning that he had converted to become a Quaker. As a Quaker, William was seeking to live according to his light of conscience, his sense of duty to God. Rejected by his own father, William went to live with the Quakers, which further solidified his faith. While William never fully reconciled as to matters of faith with his father, his father eventually came to understand his son's sincerity. Later in life, William Penn Sr. counseled his son and namesake that integrity demanded that he never be tempted to act against his God-given conscience. During one imprisonment, William's father sought to pay his son's fine. Believing the law under which he was imprisoned to be a violation of his conscience, William entreated his father to not purchase his liberty, believing that it was better that he pay the price of conscience.

On yet another occasion, the Bishop of London orchestrated Penn's imprisonment in the Tower of London for blasphemy. The bishop wanted to hold Penn until he recanted his "blasphemous" words and heretical views. Penn responded to claims that he was acting in a manner that disrupted the community peace by seeking to demonstrate that he was not a Puritan. He simply wanted to follow his conscience and practice his religion, free from the heavy hand of the established religion. He did not intend to be disruptive or to harm the public peace. William believed in Primitive Christianity and embraced the Quaker belief in individual revelation or inspiration from God. The light of conscience ignited young William, and that light never went out. His pursuit of conscience brought persecution in its wake, but it also helped form Penn's commitment to religious toleration and the right of conscience, values that he put into action in the Province of Pennsylvania.

During one of his six major imprisonments, Penn wrote an essay entitled, "The Great Case of Liberty of Conscience." That essay influenced Madison, Jefferson, and others. Penn posed the following lengthy question, "Whether imposition, restraint, and persecution, upon persons for exercising such a liberty of conscience as is before expressed, and so circumstantiated, be not to impeach the honour of God, the meekness of the Christian religion, the authority of Scripture, the privilege of nature, the principles of common reason, the well-being of government, and apprehensions of the greatest personages of former and latter ages?" His powerful and historic response to this questioned echoed the teachings of his friend John Locke. Penn declared, "Imposition, Restraint, and Persecution, for matters relating to conscience, directly invade the divine prerogative, and divest the Almighty of a due, proper to none besides himself."[29] His commitment to religious toleration and conscience was amplified in these words,

> If we do allow the honour of our creation due to God only, and that no other besides himself has endowed us with those excellent gifts of Understanding, Reason, Judgment, and Faith, and consequently that he only is the object, as well as the author, both of our Faith, Worship, and Service; then whosoever shall interpose their authority to enact faith and worship in a way that seems not to us congruous with what he has discovered to us to be faith and worship (whose alone property it is to do it) or to restrain us from what we are persuaded is our indispensable duty, they evidently usurp this authority, and invade his incommunicable right of government over conscience: "For the Inspiration of the Almighty gives understanding: And Faith is the gift of God," says the divine writ.[30]

Penn's reference to conscience, the duty owed one's God, as a form of property beyond the rightful reach of government, helped fashion Madison's belief that the most sacred of all property is conscience. Government can compensate for the loss of physical property, but it cannot compensate for the taking of one's conscience or soul. No rightful government may intervene between God and a person's conscience.

When given the power to create a charter and government for the Province of Pennsylvania, Penn provided for a right of conscience and toleration of the beliefs of others. He declared:

---

29. "The Great Case of Liberty of Conscience," The Pluralism Project (Harvard University), accessed October 9, 2018, http://pluralism.org/document/the-great-case-of-liberty-of-conscience.
30. Ibid.

[N]o people can be truly happy, though under the greatest enjoyment of civil liberties, if abridged of the freedom of their consciences as to their religious profession and worship. And Almighty God being the only lord of conscience, father of light and spirits, and the author as well as object of all divine knowledge, faith, and worship, who only does enlighten the minds and persuade and convince the understandings of people, I do hereby grant and declare that no person or persons inhabiting in this province or territories, who shall confess and acknowledge one almighty God, the creator, upholder and ruler of the world; and profess him or themselves obliged to live quietly under the civil government, shall be in any case molested or prejudiced in his or their person or estate because of his or their conscientious persuasion or practice, nor be compelled to frequent or maintain any religious worship, place, or ministry contrary to his or their mind, or to do or suffer any other act or thing contrary to their religious persuasion.[31]

Penn believed that individuals receive revelation or inspiration from God and are duty-bound to follow God, not man. Government must tolerate such differences in religious conscience. Permitting others to exercise their right of conscience was, therefore, a duty Penn believed he owed to God, the author of such light or revelation.

William became a lifelong advocate of religious toleration and his Province was a beacon for such rights. The French philosopher, Voltaire, who also supported religious toleration, wrote that, "William Penn might, with reason, boast of having brought down upon earth the Golden Age, which in all probability, never had any real existence but in his dominions."[32]

For Penn, that government which is most likely to be lasting is one that respects the right of conscience of its people.

Jim Powell, a Senior Fellow at the Cato Institute, said this of William Penn, "William Penn was the first great hero of American liberty. During the late seventeenth century, when Protestants persecuted Catholics, Catholics persecuted Protestants, and both

---

31. William Penn, "Charter of Privileges for the Province of Pennsylvania," 1701, Treasures of the APS, accessed October 9, 2018, https://www.amphilsoc.org/exhibits/treasures/charter.htm.
32. See, Jim Powell, "William Penn, America's First Great Champion for Liberty and Peace," accessed October 9, 2018, http://quaker.org/legacy/wmpenn.html.

persecuted Quakers and Jews, Penn established an American sanctuary which protected freedom of conscience."[33] Powell added that Penn practiced his religion and sought to treat everyone, including members of native tribes with brotherly kindness: "Almost everywhere else, colonists stole land from the Indians, but Penn traveled unarmed among the Indians and negotiated peaceful purchases. He insisted that women deserved equal rights with men."[34] The native tribes sensed both the sincerity with which Penn held his beliefs and his respect for their beliefs. Respecting the right of conscience, therefore, brings peace, where sectarian or tribal conflict fosters misunderstanding, lack of respect, and conflict. Powell noted further that Penn "gave Pennsylvania a written constitution which limited the power of government, provided a humane penal code, and guaranteed many fundamental liberties."[35]

These historical figures had an influence on Madison, particularly William Penn who put the teachings of his friend, John Locke, into practice. They were both victims of opposition to the right of conscience, a victimization that contributed to their friendship and thinking. Locke's thought, in turn, profoundly influenced James Madison, Thomas Jefferson, Thomas Paine, George Mason, Benjamin Franklin, James Wilson, and many other members of the founding generation. Locke's thinking provided the basis for the Declaration of Independence, as largely penned by Thomas Jefferson. His influence on Madison, however, proved to be the most influential.

John Locke

John Locke contributed to the emphasis on rights and limited government that first found its way into the Virginia Declaration of Rights, and later into the Constitution and the Bill of Rights. The careful study of Locke's writings, particularly his *Second Treatise Concerning Civil Government, A Letter Concerning Toleration*, and *An Essay Concerning Human Understanding*, in concert with the able instruction of Don

---

33. Ibid.
34. Ibid.
35. Ibid.

Robertson and John Witherspoon, provided an inspired foundation that Madison built upon in his role as the principal author of the Constitution and Bill of Rights.

Locke was tall and thin. Madison, in turn, was short and thin to the point of appearing to be frail. They both had a prodigious work ethic and an impressive intellect. Ideas for Locke and Madison were a matter of hard work followed by insights and inspiration. Yet, putting that inspiration into words required painstaking clarity. Voltaire appropriately praised Locke for his wisdom. Locke's thought was foundational, and Madison's amplification on and application of that thought gave it life, in a political sense.

John Locke, like Madison, was a man of faith. He believed that, "The Bible is one of the greatest blessings bestowed by God on the children of men. It has God for its author; salvation for its end, and truth without any mixture for its matter. It is all pure."[36] He never, however, sought to use government to impose his beliefs on others. Indeed, he believed that all men have an equal right to believe, without being subject to the authority of another man. Locke also believed, "Every man has a property in his own person. This nobody has a right to, but himself."[37] Rights for Locke and later Madison were reflective of a right one has to one's own person. Taking a right, therefore, was akin to taking property, although rights, unlike property, cannot be translated into a monetary value and are therefore not compensable. The right of conscience, tied as it is to the soul of the individual exercising it, is certainly non-compensable. Like his friend Penn, Locke believed that the most important property held by a person is the right of conscience. That right, for Locke, was a natural right, placed largely beyond the reach of government. Locke, nevertheless, permitted government to intervene to secure an equal right. Government, he maintained, may also intervene when the exercise of conscience became a threat to public peace and security.

---

36. See "John Locke—Christian Theologian," Virtue, Liberty, and Independence, accessed October 9, 2018, http://liberty-virtue-independence.blogspot.com/2012/04/john-locke-christian-theologian.html.

37. See John Locke, "Second Treatise," Property, Founders' Constitution (University of Chicago), accessed October 8, 2018, http://press-pubs.uchicago.edu/founders/documents/v1ch16s3.html.

Beginning with his proposed amendment to the Virginia Declaration of Rights, Madison refined and circumscribed each of Locke's limitations in ways precisely designed to secure the full and free exercise of conscience, the most sacred of all property. For the present, it is sufficient to note that Locke's thinking had a profound impact on Madison, and through Madison, the Constitution, and particularly the right of conscience in the First Amendment.

Madison's education at the College of New Jersey introduced him to the great thinkers of antiquity. It also exposed him more fully to more contemporary thinkers, including Locke, and to great figures in American history, including Williams, Hutchinson, and Penn. As a student of history, and a strong supporter of the right of conscience, Madison accepted much of the thought of dissenters like Hutchinson, Williams, and Penn. Some in Madison's generation, however, attacked Roger Williams and the Rhode Island experience in their zeal to support their preferred religion. Opponents of the right of religious conscience often favor an established religion or belief. They argue that beliefs that contradict the norm are disruptive.

The belief that the public welfare is enhanced by eliminating dissenting forms of conscience was as true during Penn's day as it is today. Penn's detractors argued that religious toleration produced public disorder and asserted that dissidents should be forced to comply with established, majoritarian norms, even, and perhaps especially, when they were rooted in religious conscience. Penn's detractors believed dissenting religious voices undercut the religious establishment and disrupted the community. They believed that a single, established religion, based on adherence to the pure religious faith of the majority secured peace. Madison saw such an imposed peace as illusory and simply wrong, as an anecdotal and theoretical matter. Madison's support for a strong right of religious conscience later endeared him to Baptists and members of other minority religious sects in Virginia, precisely because he respected their right of religious liberty. Those groups, in turn, supported the right of religious conscience and played a crucial role in electing Madison in multiple significant elections, permitting him to become the leading voice for and framer of the right of conscience in the United States.

Madison left the College of New Jersey with a rich education that profoundly influenced his views regarding the right of conscience and helped shape all aspects of his life. Professor Ketcham summarized James's education at the College of New Jersey, by noting that it "furnished him, from the wisdom of Greece and Rome, a lifelong realism about human nature, a comprehensive concept of political obligation, and an instinctive admiration of patience, prudence, and moderation. From the Christian tradition, he inherited a sense of the prime importance of conscience, a strict personal morality, an understanding of human dignity as well as depravity, and a conviction that vital religion could contribute to the general welfare."[38] Reflecting on the influence of Donald Robertson, Thomas Martin, and John Witherspoon on their prize pupil, James Madison, Professor Ketcham observed, "it is not possible to understand the purpose and earnestness of Madison's public life without seeing its connection with the Christian atmosphere in which he was raised."[39] Madison also left an ardent supporter of individual liberty and the right to exercise one's conscience. As he interacted with challenging faculty members and student friends, Madison also learned to respect, as sacred, the conscience of others, particularly when it differed from his own personal form of faith or religious commitment.

Upon returning to Montpelier, after his post-graduate experience, Madison was shocked to see serious issues regarding religious conscience arising in his own neighborhood. Those fierce disputes soon drew Madison into their swirling vortex. As he confronted this tumult of belief and opinion, his instruction at college soon found a practical application. Before turning directly to Madison's involvement in public issues involving the right of conscience, however, it is important to understand a variety of personal and related issues James faced upon his return home, as a newly minted but unemployed graduate.

Madison returned to Montpelier uncertain about his future. In fact, his return was not fully on his own terms. His father had called him home to assume responsibilities related to the plantation,

---

38. Ralph Ketcham, *James Madison* (Charlottesville, VA: University of Virginia Press, 1990), 50.
39. Ibid. 48.

including the tutoring of his younger brothers and sisters, a task that Madison accepted but never quite embraced. As he traveled home, he felt a deep mix of emotions like those experienced by most students returning home, transitioning from academia to participation in the workplace. His immediate future was clear: he was to tutor his siblings, and assume increased responsibilities related to operation of the plantation. Yet, his long-term future remained uncertain. Madison was distraught, not knowing which profession he would claim and uncertain as to how he could find fulfillment applying what he had learned. Madison was desperate to find ways in which he could make a difference in an increasingly troubled world, a world consumed by a revolution against Britain, the most powerful nation in the world. Madison was well prepared in theory, but he was not at all certain as to how he would apply that theory in a chosen profession. This he would learn in time, as he learned everything else in his lifetime, line upon line, like the unfolding of a beautiful piece of music, guided by the hand of providence.

Chapter Three

Madison's Return to Virginia and His Call to Public Service

"You can not divorce religious belief and public service. I've never detected any conflict between God's will and my political duty. If you violate one, you violate the other."[1]

President Jimmy Carter

"Tears shed for self are tears of weakness, but tears shed for others are a sign of strength."[2]

Reverend Billy Graham

U pon returning home to Montpelier after his advanced study with President Witherspoon, Madison spent much of his time serving as a tutor to his siblings and working with his father on the plantation. During this time, James continued his study and reinforced some of what he had learned in teaching his siblings. It was clear from his correspondence, nevertheless, that he did not find the work to be satisfying. He certainly took some pleasure in encouraging his young brothers and sisters in their studies and also enjoyed learning more about the operation of the plantation from his father. But he yearned for more. While young James never found the same high degree of meaning from the land and managing the plantation, as his

---

1. See AZ Quotes, accessed October 9, 2018, https://www.azquotes.com/author/2561-Jimmy _Carter/tag/belief.
2. Billy Graham, *Twitter*, January 19, 2018, accessed October 9, 2018, https://twitter.com /BillyGraham/status/954525649682751488.

father had, he did feel a peculiar attachment to the land and became known later in life for his scientific approach to agriculture.

Correspondence with William Bradford

With the loss of his roommate James Ross, James rekindled his friendship and correspondence with William Bradford Jr. of Philadelphia. That renewed friendship, together with physical activity, became his source of solace in difficult times. True friendship, for James and for many of us, provided the comfort that aided him in dealing with difficult times.

Unable to shake those dark moments when he felt deep discontent, James wrestled to find himself,

William Bradford

to obtain direction in his life. He knew he should be happy, given the nature of the many blessings he enjoyed in his life, but such happiness seemed fleeting, just beyond his grasp. A series of troubling losses compounded this lack of meaning and direction in his life. James sorrowed to learn of the untimely passing of his dear friend and roommate, Joseph Ross. The loss of a younger brother and sister from the all too common scourge of dysentery also contributed to making life seem fragile. Those deaths and his yearning for direction in his life contributed to a high level of anxiety and doubt. As the stress intensified, James became seriously, perhaps clinically, depressed. He wrote Bradford that he was "too dull and infirm to look out for any extraordinary things in this world, for I think my sensations for many months have intimated to me not to expect a long or healthy life."[3] He added, that he had "little spirit or elasticity to set about anything that is acquiring, and useless in

---

3. Letter From James Madison to William Bradford, 9 November 1772, Founders Online (National Archives), accessed October 9, 2018, https://founders.archives.gov/documents /Madison/01-01-02-0015

possessing after one has exchanged time for eternity."[4] Darkness and a sense of aimlessness had displaced the engagement, effervescence, and friendship he experienced in life at Nassau Hall.

James's depression began to manifest itself in physiological ways. He became lethargic and suffered from epileptic-like seizures. During such a seizure, Madison would become immobile, unable to perform the simplest tasks. Some historians believe that James suffered from epileptoid or epileptic hysteria, which is a psychosomatic condition. One suffering such a condition is believed to deal with the frustrations of life through converting that anxiety and frustration into a physical disability. In Madison's time, the general standard of care was to bleed the patient. Most doctors believed that taking a few pints of James's blood would rid him of the so-called bile of melancholia. Fortunately, James did not have to suffer the archaic treatment of bleeding. The Madison family doctor wisely tried to lift James's spirits by prescribing exercise—riding and walking—two things that Madison always enjoyed and found invigorating. His doctor also sent James to Warm Springs in West Virginia to provide a change of climate and the "medicinal" benefits of that area. Whether the springs were medicinal or not, they were clearly therapeutic in nature, and Madison began to rebound.

Madison's thoughts, nevertheless, remained fixed on his professional future, on his personal studies, and on his possible role in the growing revolutionary cause. Madison faced a dilemma common to many new graduates of his age: What shall I do with my life? What vocation or profession should I pursue to provide meaning in my life? The trials of depression and the lack of direction shook James to the core, worrying his friends and family. James and his family, particularly his mother, believed that his return home contributed to his infirmities. James noted that one reason why he stayed longer at the College of New Jersey and was very reluctant to return home was his fear that being home would leave him adrift and would eventually destroy his already fragile health. This fear of ill health then associated with Montpelier was unsurprising, given the persistent protestations of his mother and grandmother that Montpelier was a less healthy environment than New Jersey. Young James also mourned the loss of security

---

4. Ibid.

he found at the College of New Jersey, surrounded by his many friends and teachers, all of whom were collectively engrossed in learning.

Bradford was a handsome, slender young man, with penetrating eyes that revealed his thoughtfulness and sense of duty or conscience, characteristics that appealed to Madison. Upon arriving home from the College of New Jersey, William began work as a printer in his family's business. His father was a distinguished printer, the first official printer of Congress, and served with distinction as a Colonel in the Pennsylvania Militia and revolutionary forces. Like young James, William Jr. was dissatisfied working in the family business. He felt increasingly drawn, even called, to the law, as revealed in his correspondence with Madison. Heeding that call, Bradford read the law, working in the law office of Edward Shippen, which was the common route to licensure in law during that era. Law was something he became passionate about and it allowed him to use his intellect to serve others and the new nation.

Like Madison, William was also unwavering in his support of the developing revolutionary cause. As soon as the Pennsylvania militia formed to do battle with the British in 1776, William volunteered to serve as a private. His commitment and talent quickly caught the eye of his superiors, notably Daniel Roberdeau, who served the militia as Pennsylvania's first brigadier general. Roberdeau selected William to serve directly on his staff. By the time his service in the militia ended, William had earned the rank of captain. When William's service in the militia concluded, he promptly joined the Continental Army, serving initially as a captain. He was company commander of a regiment and was involved in the Battle of Trenton. By April 1777, he had risen in rank and was serving as a lieutenant colonel. As the year ended, William was a part of the forces encamped at Valley Forge. By early 1778, Bradford's health had weakened, and he had to resign from the military, return home, and find other ways to serve.

Upon returning home, Bradford resumed his practice of law and a decade later, in 1784, married Susan Vergereau Boudinot, the only daughter of Elias Boudinot, who had served as president of the Continental Congress and as a member of the United States House of Representatives. By the time of their marriage, William was steadily earning acclaim for his work as a lawyer. He became a distinguished attorney, arguing the first case to be heard by the United States Supreme Court, albeit on the losing side. William also served as Attorney General of Pennsylvania for more than a decade and thereafter served as a Justice on the Supreme Court of the Commonwealth of Pennsylvania. Early in 1794, President Washington nominated William to succeed Edmund Randolph as our nation's second Attorney General. William's life of service sadly ended abruptly in 1795, when he died just a month shy of his fortieth birthday. Regrettably, once again, Madison faced the premature loss of a friend. Our nation also lost an able public servant.

Years prior to Bradford's death, William and James trusted and sought counsel from each other as then-recent graduates from the College of New Jersey. Madison had returned to Montpelier and Bradford to Philadelphia. The early letters that passed between James and William reveal a warm friendship between these two extraordinary young men. That correspondence disclosed their respective hopes, aspirations, and doubts, providing a revealing glimpse into Madison's thinking as he slowly transitioned from the College of New Jersey to a life of public service.

In his correspondence with Bradford, Madison generally referred to William as "My dear Billy" and Bradford referred to Madison with equal affection as "My dear Jemmy." In an early letter, Bradford expressed his sadness at having to leave the College of New Jersey, noting that if collegiate life "is a state of bondage, then . . . I am in love with my chains."[5] Madison clearly shared this sentiment, but both were coming to the realization that they were entering a new phase in their life at a momentous time. It is not surprising, therefore, that much of their correspondence focused on the difficult decision regarding their respective choices of profession, current events, and general happenings in their lives.

In his earliest letter to Bradford, written in 1772, Madison expressed concern regarding health issues and his fear of an early

---

5. Letter to James Madison from William Bradford, 13 October 1772, Founders Online (National Archive), accessed October 9, 2018, https://founders.archives.gov/documents /Madison/01-01-02-0014.

death. Over the course of the early years of his life, Madison often revealed his fear that he would die at an early age. It was a fear with little prophetic force, as he outlived almost all other major figures in the nation's founding.

Facing sudden personal losses and his own health issues may have seemed Job-like to young James, leading him to reflect in more depth on religious matters. Madison engaged in some religious reflection in his early correspondence with William. Those writings provide insight into his thinking at this stage in his life. Madison wrote that a "watchful eye must be kept on ourselves lest we are building ideal monuments of Renown and Bliss here we neglect to have our names enrolled in the Annals of Heaven."[6] He prized his treasure in heaven more than earthly mammon. Throughout their correspondence, Madison and Bradford referred in positive ways to religious or spiritual matters. Echoing the teachings of Witherspoon, they often alluded to the importance of moral virtue and its source, religious conscience. Madison's concerns were more than personal, however. He also wrote increasingly about his growing uneasiness regarding the deprivation of the right of conscience in Virginia and the pernicious role of the existing established Anglican Church. He was particularly concerned regarding persecution of the Baptists, and a smattering of Presbyterians and other minority faiths, by the leaders of the Anglican Establishment.

Madison and Bradford each spoke positively about the ministry as a possible vocation and consistently referred to the importance of continuing the study of Divinity and theological matters. Bradford suggested that he might enter the ministry if he felt qualified to do so, because such service "may be the most useful." He added that a clergyman may well be the most "happy member of society."

Madison responded at some length to his friend's decision not to enter the ministry. He began by indicating that he was saddened that the Church was losing "a fine Genius and persuasive orator." James then offered the following friendly advice: "Always keep the Ministry

---

6. Letter from James Madison to William Bradford, 9 November 1772, Founders Online (National Archive), accessed October 9, 2018, https://founders.archives.gov/documents /Madison/01-01-02-0015.

obliquely in View whatever your profession be. This will lead you to cultivate an acquaintance with the most sublime of all Sciences and will qualify you for a change of public character if you should hereafter desire it." Madison then concluded that part of his earliest letter to Bradford, with a strong religious witness, when reflected, "I have sometimes thought there could not be a stronger testimony in favor of Religion or against temporal Enjoyments . . . than for men who occupy the most honorable and gainful departments and are rising in reputation and wealth, publicly to declare their unsatisfactoriness by becoming fervent Advocates in the cause of Christ."[7] It is clear that as a young man and recent graduate, Madison took his Christian faith and commitment to the cause of Christ seriously. Indeed, in the intimate context of a dear friendship, a world in which the most closely guarded sentiments of heart are occasionally revealed, Madison declared his faith in Christ in ways that he rarely did in more public settings, believing that such professions of his faith were of the most sacred and private nature, not to be trifled with in public discourse. Throughout his life, Madison endeavored to find a sect that met the needs of his personal form of faith.

Many of Madison's and Bradford's classmates from the College of New Jersey entered the ministry. Some of these classmates came to visit Montpelier during these formative years. When visiting, they accepted invitations to preach at the Brick Church, the Anglican Church the Madison family regularly attended. They were encouraged to do so even though some were of non-Anglican faiths, generally Presbyterians. Madison and his family viewed their preaching in a positive light.

In his December 1, 1773, letter to Bradford, Madison reflected on his friend's decision to enter the law by musing, "I hope you had better reasons for chusing [law] than I could suggest. I intend myself to read the Law occasionally and have procured books for that purpose so that you need not fear offending me by Allusions to that science." Madison added, "The principles & Modes of Government are too important to be disregarded by an Inquisitive mind and I think are [worthy of] a critical examination by all students that have health & Leisure. I should be well pleased with a sketch of [the] plan you have fixed upon

---

7. Ibid.

for your studies, the books & the order you intend to read them in."[8] At a time when James was searching for his life's profession, he followed in his friend's footsteps and spent a few weeks working in a successful law office, exploring it as a possible profession. He found that the day-to-day practice to be uninspiring and marked it off his list, a list that was very thin with the omission of two of the major learned professions of the time: the ministry and law. The study of legal matters and the practice of lawmaking, however, became a lifelong endeavor for Madison. It is fair to say that he became America's greatest lawmaker, even though he initially shunned the practice. Throughout his life, Madison also continued to study religion and theology, believing such matters to be of great importance.

In that December 1st letter to Bradford, Madison turned to an issue that was increasingly on his mind. He requested information from Bradford regarding the right of conscience and ecclesiastical establishments in Pennsylvania. Madison asked the following favor of his friend: "[W]hen you have obtained sufficient insight into the [Pennsylvania Constitution] and can make it an amusement to yourself send me a draught of its Origin & fundamental principles of Legislation; particularly the extent of your religious Toleration."[9] His reference to "religious Toleration" was, in part, a reference to William Penn's contributions to religious toleration and the liberty of conscience. James asked the following more pointed questions of William: "Is an Ecclesiastical Establishment absolutely necessary to support civil society in a supreme Government? & how far it is hurtful to a dependent State?"[10] These queries were the product of Madison's increasing concern regarding matters of religious conscience in colonial Virginia, based on his developing opposition to excesses on the part of the Anglican Establishment.

In some fashion, these inquiries and Madison's rising concern of religious freedom were beginning to provide new direction in his life. Madison was being inexorably drawn into a life of public service, a life

---

8. Letter From James Madison to William Bradford, 1 December 1773, Founders Online (National Archives), accessed October 9, 2018, https://founders.archives.gov/documents /Madison/01-01-02-0027.

9. Ibid.

10. Ibid.

that would ultimately provide him with the direction and meaning he was seeking. He wanted a life that would satisfy his conscience, while blending service with his insatiable desire to learn.

The request by Madison for a list of readings, in that December 1st letter, became a common occurrence in correspondence between friends, although it was more common for Bradford to request readings from Madison, which may have been an understandable act of deference on William's part. During this early period, Madison was also in correspondence with his teacher, John Witherspoon, requesting a list of books to enhance his studies. Later, as Madison's friendship blossomed with Thomas Jefferson, the habit of sharing books and readings became a centerpiece of that friendship. Even at the time of this early correspondence with Bradford, Madison was continuing to be an exceedingly diligent student with a voracious desire to learn. His formal study, therefore, was but a gateway to a life of continuing education. Indeed, the true evidence of a quality education is that it continues long after one has graduated. Those early letters between friends also reveal that Madison's interests and intellectual curiosity were increasingly turning to government and a growing concern regarding the status of the liberty of conscience in Virginia.

Bradford, at one point in his continuing correspondence with Madison, reminded his friend that his intense studies may have contributed to his ill health while at the College of New Jersey and thereafter. Madison agreed, noting that his doctor had emphasized the need for him to seek some worthy diversions and avoid spending so much time in his studies. Madison added that he was taking the advice, but he could never quite quench his thirst for study and learning.

James seldom wandered far from his studies. Increasingly swept up in issues of the day, he gave much attention to the religious persecution of Baptists and minority religionists by the Anglican Establishment. He was observing this disturbing persecution firsthand and it was having a profound personal impact.

In the fall of 1773, in response to a summons issued in August 1772, Nathaniel Saunders—a Baptist pastor of the Mountain Run Church in Orange County, Madison's home county—was arrested and convicted of sedition and unlawful preaching by the Culpepper

County Court. Many believed that preaching by a Baptist was a seditious act. Indeed, after a brief trial in September, Saunders was found guilty. With that verdict in hand, the court set a hefty bond of 200 pounds to prevent Saunders from repeating his crime of preaching without a license. Saunders was unable or unwilling to pay such a fine and found himself confined in the county jail.

Only months later, in November 1773, Joseph Spencer, who later became a strong political supporter of Madison's, was arrested and imprisoned in Orange County on similar grounds. Spencer was charged with a breach of the peace for teaching and preaching without a license as a Baptist minister. Madison's father was a member of the court at that time but was not in attendance on the day of the trial. The seven other justices found Spencer guilty and ordered him to post bond in the amount 100 pounds, which was also a stiff penalty in a time when land cost little more than a few pounds per acre. Spencer, like Nathaniel Saunders, was either unable or unwilling to pay, resulting in his confinement in the Orange County jail.

Spencer's incarceration in a small jail cell lasted for almost a month. On November 25, the court granted Spencer's petition and allowed him to live within the larger and freer confines of the courthouse, provided he agreed to make restitution for any damage he might cause to the courthouse. The next day, buoyed no doubt by the success of his first petition, Spencer sought a reduction in his bond to twenty pounds, together with two securities of ten pounds each, with the bond forfeited if he violated the order again.

James Sr. soon thereafter became involved in the matter, expressing his dissatisfaction with the initial decision. James Sr. returned to the court on November 25 and 26, the precise days when Spencer reappeared to argue for his new petition.

In a January 1774 letter to Bradford, James Jr. congratulated William for the "heroic proceedings in Philada with regard to the Tea [referring to support for the principles of the Boston Tea Party]."[11] Madison quickly turned, however, to his concerns regarding liberty

---

11. Letter From James Madison to William Bradford, 24 January 1774, Founders Online (National Archives), accessed October 9, 2018, https://founders.archives.gov/documents/Madison/01-01-02-0029.

of conscience and the darkening cloud of the Anglican Establishment in Virginia. James observed that, "If the Church of England had been the established and general Religion in all the Northern Colonies as it has been [in Virginia] . . . [i]t is clear to me that slavery and Subjection might and would have been gradually insinuated among us."[12] This allusion to the institution of slavery is interesting and aptly depicts James's strong aversion to violations of the right of conscience, including the consciences of slaves. Madison concluded his expression of a rising concern regarding state ecclesiastical establishments by adding, "Union of Religious Sentiments begets a surprising confidence and Ecclesiastical Establishments tend to great ignorance and Corruption all of which facilitate the Execution of mischievous Projects."[13]

James turned to that which "vexed" him most: "I have indeed as good an Atmosphere at home as the climate will allow; but have nothing to brag of as to the State and Liberty in my Country. Poverty and Luxury prevail among all sects: Pride ignorance and Knavery among the Priesthood and Vice and Wickedness among the Laity."[14] After noting that, as if this was bad enough, Madison turned to the worst that he had to share with his friend when he declared, "That diabolical Hell conceived principle of persecution rages [among some people living in his area] and to their eternal Infamy the Clergy can furnish their Quota of Imps for such business. This vexes me the most of anything whatever."[15] Madison then clarified his concerns by noting that there were "5 or 6 well meaning men confined to jail in his area for publishing their Sentiments which in the main are very orthodox."[16] Leaving no doubt regarding the magnitude of vexation he felt continually over the state of conscience in Virginia generally and Orange County specifically, Madison concluded, "I have neither the patience to hear talk or think of anything relative to this matter, for I have squabbled and scolded abused and ridiculed so long about it, to so little purpose that I am without common patience. So I

12. Ibid.
13. Ibid.
14. Ibid.
15. Ibid.
16. Ibid.

leave you to pity me and pray for Liberty of Conscience to revive among us."[17]

By the relatively tender age of twenty-two, Madison had found a cause that would consume him for years to come, as he became a strong advocate of the "Liberty of Conscience," and an unyielding opponent of the persecution of conscience in any form or under any pretext, a topic that he had studied at the College of New Jersey and was now personally observing firsthand. He was fast concluding that religious establishments, like the establishment of the Church of England (Anglican) in Virginia could momentarily create peace or unite sentiments, but in the long run could only lead to mischief. These themes remained lifelong concerns of the highest order for Madison. In his autobiography written when he was over eighty years old, Madison stressed that he was "under very early and strong impressions in favor of liberty both Civil and Religious."[18] In that reminiscence, James added that he had "spared no exertion"[19] in his effort to save Baptist preachers from the persecution that was raging in the counties surrounding Montpelier.

In an April 1774 letter to Bradford, James continued on this theme by expressing his hope that the Virginia Assembly would respond to petitions of the Baptists and Presbyterians seeking "greater liberty in matters of Religion." He was not optimistic, however, because of the zeal and power of some prominent public figures, led by the powerful Anglican Establishment. He concluded with a somber language revealing his fervor and depth of his commitment to the cause of conscience: "Religious bondage shackles and debilitates the mind and unfits it for every noble enterprise, every extended prospect."[20]

As Madison expressed his concerns for the right of conscience in this correspondence with Bradford, it is easy to sense that his ill health was giving way to a cause of consuming force. Little did Madison know that he would soon find himself leading the legislative effort to

---

17. Ibid.
18. James Madison: Autobiography, December 1830, Founders Online (National Archives), accessed October 9, 2018, https://founders.archives.gov/documents/Madison/99-02-02-2226.
19. Ibid.
20. Letter from James Madison to William Bradford, 1 April 1774, Founders Online (National Archives), accessed October 9, 2018, https://founders.archives.gov/documents/Madison/01-01-02-0031

eliminate the shackles of religious bondage through his advocacy for the liberty of conscience, together with his fervid opposition to the Anglican Establishment as it then existed in the Virginia Colony. His first step in the direction of public service came with his selection to serve on the Orange County Committee on Safety on December 12, 1774. At last, he had a forum in which to serve and begin to express his strong political sentiments.

As a member of the Committee on Safety, Madison dealt with incidents that involved religious matters. In the first matter involving the rights of conscience and expression, Madison revealed that his thinking was still at a formative stage in its development. In that first decision, James did not oppose the punishment of Reverend John Wingate, who served as rector of the St. Thomas Parish in the county, for refusing to surrender seditious pamphlets that were in the reverend's possession. The committee, with Madison's approval, seized and burned the materials. At this time, he was persuaded that the revolutionary cause, the larger liberty issue, warranted limiting the right of conscience and expression of a pro-British clergyman.

James's understandable zeal for the revolutionary cause continued unabated, but in time he came to see that the liberty of conscience was at the heart of what he was fighting for. He came to see that conscience as a support for, not a reason for opposing, the revolutionary cause of liberty. With this unification, Madison reconsidered his early actions regarding the Committee on Safety's efforts to deal strongly with religiously based opposition to the war. Whatever his reasons for supporting earlier decisions by the Orange County Committee on Safety in regulating the rights of conscience and expression, Madison was finding meaning in public service, as an outlet for his special brand of faith. He was increasingly committed to building a new nation on the foundation liberty and natural rights.

Unlike his friend William Bradford, however, Madison was not able to fulfill his desire to serve as a soldier in the revolutionary forces. Despite having trained to serve with a Virginia rifle company, and having learned to shoot with some proficiency, James's persistent health issues rendered him incapable of serving with the company. This caused James much heartache. Nevertheless, he earned a commission as a colonel in the Orange County Militia and was able to find ways to serve the cause. From that time forward, citizens of Orange County often respectfully referred to James Jr. as Colonel Madison, even after his service as president of the United States. He became an ardent supporter of the Revolutionary cause at a distance from the battle lines. He used his notable talents, working tirelessly and with substantial effectiveness in fulfilling another, perhaps more significant responsibility, obtaining enough supplies for Washington's troops then suffering mightily at Valley Forge. Madison's inability to serve in battle troubled his conscience throughout his life, but it also may have aided his determination to demonstrate courage in other areas of his life, areas where his ill health did not preclude him from serving.

On April 25, 1776, just months prior to the signing of the Declaration of Independence, the voters (freeholders or landowners) of Orange County gathered at the Courthouse to select two delegates to represent the citizens of the county at a constitutional convention to be held in Williamsburg. Those who were to select the delegates well understood that they were electing delegates to serve in a significant capacity—the newly elected delegates were being selected to help frame a new government and constitution for Virginia. The voters selected James, who had recently turned twenty-five, and his uncle to serve them in this significant responsibility. These two men were selected, in part, because of their commitment to the revolutionary cause. The Baptists who supported James believed they were choosing a delegate committed to the liberty of conscience. It did not take much time for Madison to demonstrate his commitment to both causes, quickly earning the trust of the electorate and the respect of fellow delegates, many of whom he would serve with during his lifetime of public service.

Despite his young age, Madison quickly demonstrated his capacity as a legal draftsman, as a framer. On May 15, 1776, the Virginia Constitutional Convention unanimously directed its delegates for the Continental Congress to support a declaration of independence at the national level. They also worked on preparing a Declaration of Rights for the Commonwealth. George Mason was the primary author of Virginia's Declaration of Rights.

George Mason

Some refer to Mason as the "reluctant or forgotten" founder, given his nuanced opposition to the ratification of the Constitution. At the time Virginia was developing a Declaration of Rights, however, his credentials as a patriot to the revolutionary cause and the cause of liberty was unquestioned. Madison worked closely with Mason and learned to respect him, even though these two great men often differed on aspects of public policy.

George Mason

Many years after the ratification of the Constitution, Mason expressed some concern to Thomas Jefferson regarding Madison's opinion of his service. Mason also was concerned later in life that, despite a friendship that stretched back to their youth, President Washington thought less of him due to his eventual opposition to ratification.

Irrespective of their disagreements, however, Madison and Washington viewed Mason as a patriot and a man of conscience. Mason was, indeed, a distinguished leader nationally and in Virginia. Madison admired Mason for acting courageously and in accordance with his conscience, even though they differed as to matters that sometimes were of great moment. Indeed, James may have concurred in the assertion that George Mason was reluctant in initially supporting the Constitution but may well have earned the title, "Forgotten Founder," given his strong support for a Declaration of Rights in Virginia and his persistent demand that the Constitution include a Bill of Rights.

Mason was also active participant in the Constitutional Convention of 1787. Admirably, he acted against interest in supporting efforts to eliminate slavery and include a Bill of Rights. Mason departed two weeks prior to the completion of the work of the convention, refusing to support the final document. Mason's views regarding the abolition of slavery and the inclusion of a Bill of Rights explains Madison's view that two of them were often closer as to ends than some who professed to agree with their respective and differing means for accomplishing these ends. Even though he enjoyed much success as a public figure, including his support for natural rights, Mason became disgruntled and sadly withdrew from public life in 1780. Thankfully, Mason's tragic withdrawal from public life came after his valiant stand in support of human rights.

During the Virginia Convention, as previously noted, Mason and not Madison assumed the responsibility of serving as principal drafter of the Virginia Declaration of Rights. This assignment reflects the high regard that Mason earned in the eyes of his fellow delegates. Mason's willingness to accept the conscientious views of Madison, despite his youth, also made it easy for James later to accept Mason's contrarian views regarding ratification of the Constitution. At the Virginia Convention, with some trepidation, but with a clear sense of purpose, a young Madison offered a significant and somewhat audacious amendment to Mason's proposed provision in the Declaration of Rights dealing with the liberty of conscience. In doing so, Madison began to establish himself as a conscientious intellectual and the leading voice for the right of conscience. His thoughtful views also earned him a lifelong role as a political force in Virginia politics.

George Mason was asked to draft the Declaration of Rights with good reason. He had served for many years as a respected legislator and had developed a strong reputation as an excellent draftsman. His devotion to the revolutionary cause was also unquestioned. In 1765, he had drafted a strong letter in opposition to the Stamp Act, which he shared with merchants in London to persuade them of the justice of the cause of the colonists. Later, he drafted the Fairfax Resolves, which set the constitutional basis for opposition to the Boston Port Act. Not surprisingly, therefore, Mason's colleagues assigned him the heavy responsibility of preparing the first draft of what would become Virginia's Declaration of Rights, which was in many respects a substantive model for the Declaration of Independence and the Bill of Rights.

Madison, the youthful delegate, was driven by his commitment to the principles of religious conscience by responding to Mason, the senior statesman. Drawing from that commitment, Madison marshaled the courage to offer his own proposal.

Madison's Amendment to the Declaration of Rights

To best understand Madison's view regarding the right of conscience, and his response to Mason's draft of a Declaration of Rights, it is necessary to examine carefully Mason's proposed draft and Madison's response or amended draft. Both drafts were written with great care and warrant careful attention, to clarify points of agreement and disagreement. Madison's response also provided the earliest elaboration of his theory of conscience. Mason's original proposed provision regarding religious liberty provided:

> That religion, or the duty which we owe to our Creator, and the manner of discharging it, can be directed only by reason and conviction, not by force or violence; and, therefore, that all men should enjoy the fullest toleration in the exercise of religion, according to the dictates of conscience, unpunished and unrestrained by the magistrate, unless under color of religion any man disturb the peace, the happiness, or safety of society, and that it is the mutual duty of all to practice Christian forbearance, love and charity toward each other.[21]

Madison's education at the feet of Witherspoon at the College of New Jersey and his recent "vexing" experiences regarding the rights of minority religionists, including the Baptists, contributed to his strong support for the right of religious conscience and provided the basis for his response to Mason's proposal. Madison believed Mason's proposal was far too weak. However, he understood that he needed to formulate his own thoughtful amendment with care. Madison's proposal is reflective of the position that James supported throughout his lifetime:

> That religion, or the duty which we owe to our Creator, and the manner of discharging it, being under the direction of reason and conviction only, not of violence, or compulsion, all men are

---

21. As cited in M. Malbin, *Religion and Politics: The Intentions of the Authors of the First Amendment* (Washington, D.C.: Aei Press, 1978), 21.

entitled to the full and free exercise of it according to the dictates of conscience; and therefore no man or class of men ought on account of religion to be invested with particular emoluments or privileges, nor subjected to any penalties or disabilities, unless under color of religion the preservation of equal liberty, and the existence of the State be manifestly endangered.[22]

Even a cursory glance reveals that Madison's amendment differed substantially from the proposal offered by Mason.

Young and lacking seniority, as a delegate who was largely expected to learn by quietly listening to his senior delegates, Madison's role in the legislative process at the Convention was limited but influential, foreshadowing his future service in powerful ways. Rules prevented him from proposing his amendment in person on the floor. It was important to James, however, that his views be considered. He felt compelled to enlist the help of a person equal in stature to George Mason at the time, Patrick Henry, who agreed to bring Madison's pro-posal amendment to the floor. Henry appeared to be a good choice, because he had represented some Baptists as part of his thriving law practice and was a respected advocate, orator, and delegate. His will-ingness to offer the amendment in Madison's behalf also ensured that other delegates would give it serious consideration. Henry's advocacy of Madison's strong form of the right of conscience was, in truth, lukewarm at best. Henry was not supportive of Madison's libertarian views regarding disestablishment of Virginia's Anglican establishment nor of Madison's version of a vibrant right of religious conscience, which placed religious exercise largely beyond the regulatory reach of the state. Indeed, Henry was a proponent of the existing church establishment in Virginia and was a proponent of moderate tolera-tion of the rights of minority sects. Not surprisingly, Patrick Henry and Madison would soon clash over these issues and ratification of the Constitution. Henry later did all that was in his power to ensure that the Constitution would not be ratified and to oppose Madison's election as a delegate and later as a member of Congress. Nevertheless, for the present, Henry's support of Madison's proffered amendment to the Declaration of Rights was helpful and resulted in garnering

---

22. Ibid.

a measure of support for Madison's amendment. That support was insufficient to get the entire amendment adopted, but it did result in strengthening the final version in ways suggested by Madison. Patrick also played a significant, and endearing role, in Madison's life, when he took the Payne family, including Dolley, into his home and care at a time of need.

A close reading of Madison's proposed draft reveals that James went much further than Mason in protecting the right of conscience. They agreed on some crucial points, however. The primary point on which they agreed was their assertion that the right of conscience was a natural right, originating in one's duty to God and was not the creation of man or of government. As such, it had an existence independent of the state. This was a point on which all delegates seemed to agree.

Mason and Madison differed, however, regarding how far the natural right extended in protecting religious liberty. Madison believed the natural right of conscience went much further than Mason was willing to concede. Madison asserted that religious conscience was a natural right that any just government may not legitimately limit by violence (exercise of government power or might) or compulsion. *Any* governmental limitation of the right of conscience would violate an individual's highest duty, the duty one owed to God. This commitment on Madison's part to a right based on a higher duty is reminiscent of Witherspoon's teachings. It evidenced Madison's view that the right of religious conscience should remain carefully secured, beyond the reach of government, except in limited circumstances, which Madison later sets forth in his draft. For Madison, men are entitled to the "full and free exercise" of the duties or obligations owed their Creator, according to the "dictates of conscience," or the light that is within them.

The use of the terms *full* and *exercise* are quite significant and differ substantially from Mason's more tepid view that merely tolerated religious exercise. *Exercise* clearly protects more than belief. It entails acting upon one's religious conscience or duty to God. Exercise and not mere belief must be "full[y]" protected, under Madison's draft. His inclusion of the term *full* was indicative of the extent to which the government may not regulate the exercise of religion. This fulsome version of the free exercise right later found its way into Madison's draft and the final version of the First Amendment to the Constitution of the United States.

Madison was even more precise to make it clear that the "full and free exercise" of religious conscience was placed safely beyond the reach of the government. He was willing to recognize only two limits on the "full and free exercise" of religious conscience: (1) "no man or class of men ought on account of religion [may] be invested with particular emoluments or privileges"; and (2) no man or class of men may be "subjected to any penalties or disabilities, unless under color of religion the preservation of equal liberty, and the existence of the State be manifestly endangered." Any other limitations infringed directly on the natural right of conscience and were unjust and unacceptable.

Madison's first proposed limit on the right of conscience does not permit any man or class of men to be invested with "particular emoluments or privileges" because of their religion. In the Cambridge Dictionary, emolument means "a payment in money or some other form for work that has been done." This term evidences Madison's opposition to government support for the payment of ministers. It also reflects his opposition to the Anglican or any other religious establishment. Privileges connoted special benefits given to people based solely on their religious beliefs. Madison later clarified this concern by emphasizing an equality or nonpreferential model of a right of conscience. He was intent on ensuring equal treatment, or non-preference, as to matters of religion. One religion or religionist was not to be favored over another. This limitation on receiving salaries or fees paid from public funds or other public emoluments or privileges conferred based on religion was a precursor to our establishment clause, and was designed to limit the receipt of special or preferential public benefits by religious individuals or sects.

The second limit referred directly to the otherwise full and free exercise of religion. It provided that no man or class of men may be penalized or disabled in the exercise of religious conscience unless the "equal liberty" of another is infringed and the existence of the state is "manifestly endangered." With this language, Madison dramatically abandoned Mason's much weaker terminology. Mason would permit religious conscience to be limited by government in the interests of preserving public peace, happiness, or safety. Such a standard, espoused by Mason and Jefferson after him, would, in Madison's mind, open the door widely for the majority to tyrannize the minority, by giving government—a tyrannical majority—the capacity to limit the full and free exercise of one's religious conscience in the interests of some broadly conceived public good. To permit the majority to limit the individual right of conscience in the interests of some generally conceived good was tantamount to the tyranny of the majority, an imposition of majority will in the most sacred of all areas, the right of conscience. Madison's proposal rejected the public good limitation and called for much stronger protection for the exercise of religious conscience, protection consistent with the vibrant, full, and free exercise of conscience. This debate continues today.

Madison proposed a liberty-maximizing principle under which government could only intervene in matters touching or infringing upon the full and free exercise of one's conscience or religious conviction when it did so "under the color of religion the preservation of equal liberty, and the existence of the state be manifestly endangered." This standard far exceeded the public good standard as a means of protecting the right of conscience. Only something of the magnitude of actual sedition or the denial of the equal liberty of another was sufficient to permit the government to limit religious conscience. For Madison, if the right of conscience is a duty to God, then that right should be left between the person and God, demanding that great care is due to avoid its limitation by a tyrannical majority.

For Madison, when the majority directly or indirectly acted to infringe the religious conscience of minority religionists, it was violating a natural right of the highest order. The majority would never have to face such a threat, because they naturally wielded the power in a democratic system. Only the most defenseless and least respected forms of religious conscience (sects like the Baptists in Virginia in his day, Catholics, and members of The Church of Jesus Christ of Latter-day Saints in the latter part of the eighteenth century, or Muslims today) that had any need to fear that a majority would interfere with their right to practice (or exercise) their right of religious conscience.

To deprive an individual or minority group who were unable to muster sufficient support to obtain an exemption from the majority controlling the legislature of the protection of their most sacred right, the right of religious conscience, was a reprehensible act in Madison's eyes.

James firmly believed that government could limit conscience when one party's right of religious conscience, or duty to God, came into conflict with another's equal right of religious conscience. Government, under Madison's view, could also limit religious conscience if, and only if, the interests of the state were "manifestly endangered." Madison understood that if protecting the right of religious conscience endangered the existence of the state, all rights of conscience would be of little worth, because there would be no governmental means left to enforce those rights.

These views, which Madison so ably articulated were not adopted in their entirety by the delegates, but they clearly became the basis of the First Amendment and were the foundation of his lifetime commitment to protecting the liberty of conscience. Madison's amendment, nevertheless, was a subject for deliberation and ultimately influenced the final version of a right of conscience that appeared in the Declaration of Rights:

> That religion, or the duty which we owe to our Creator, and the manner of discharging it, can be directed only by reason and conviction, not by force or violence; and therefore all men are equally entitled to the free exercise of religion, according to the dictates of conscience; and that it is the mutual duty of all to practice Christian forbearance, love, and charity toward each other.[23]

Madison had persuaded Mason and his fellow delegates that the term *toleration* was too weak and they replaced it with "all men are equally entitled" to the free exercise of religion. They dropped the term *full* but retained the free exercise language. Madison was also able to persuade his fellow delegates to temper Mason's original draft with regard to limitations on the right. The final version dropped the language, "unpunished and unrestrained by the magistrate, unless under color of religion any man disturb the peace, the happiness, or safety of

---

23. Ibid., 22.

society." The issue of the standard under which government may limit free exercise of conscience remained open or undecided. These were major victories for Madison. Madison had been forced to compromise among clashing principles, something that would become commonplace in his career as a public servant.

Thomas Jefferson: Friendship and Collaboration

Given the growing respect earned by Madison, in October 1776, James was selected to serve a member of the Virginia House of Delegates, which had been established by the new state constitution. Madison's early role in this capacity was limited. For example, he deferred to Thomas Jefferson, who led the effort to limit state aid to religion and the state establishment.

Madison supported Jefferson and his efforts. Given that he largely agreed with Jefferson, his deference to Jefferson, a more senior statesman, was well placed. Just months before, Jefferson had served as the primary drafter, inspired in significant measure by Locke, of the Declaration of Independence and was held in high esteem by most of the delegates. In the process, Madison began to earn the respect of Jefferson, who became a dear friend and ally. Madison's role

Thomas Jefferson, portrait by Gilbert Stuart

regarding the dismantling of the Anglican establishment may have been less influential than that of Thomas Jefferson, during this legislative session, but Madison soon became the leader of the disestablishment effort in Virginia and nationally.

After a series of successes in public life, Madison suffered a debilitating political setback in 1777. The electorate refused to select him to serve in the House of Delegates. In his autobiography, written in the third person, Madison gives this account of his defeat: "[As was the case in England, voters expected candidates] to recommend themselves to the voters, not only by personal solicitation, but by the corrupting influence of spirituous liquors, and other treats having a like tendency. Regarding these as equally inconsistent with the purity of moral and of republican principles, and anxious to promote, by his example, the proper reform, he trusted to the new views of the subject which he hoped would prevail with the people; whilst his competitors adhered to the old practice."[24] The consequence of Madison's zeal in support of his principles "was that the election went against him: his abstinence being represented as the effect of pride or parsimony."[25] Madison's supporters sought to set aside the electoral result, but their efforts were unavailing. Madison found himself in the predicament of being out of public service.

He had little time to despair, however. The House of Delegates selected Madison to serve on the Virginia Council of State. This selection by his former peers reflected the esteem they held for Madison as a person of integrity and as an able public servant. The electorate soon recognized their folly in not electing him. In 1778, the voters in Orange County again elected Madison to serve as a delegate. Acting responsibly, James declined, preferring to fulfill his obligation by completing his work on the Virginia Council of State.

Virginia voters selected Thomas Jefferson as the next governor of Virginia. Madison and Jefferson continued to develop a strong friendship, built on mutual respect and their commitment to the new nation. In December 1779, in part due to a plea from George Washington that Virginia send her "able and best men to Congress," Madison earned a seat, at the national level, in the Continental Congress. He continued to serve at the national level in the Continental Congress until 1783, when he returned home once again to serve in the Virginia House of Delegates, having been elected in part due to support from religious dissenters, including the Baptists who were a growing force in Orange County. The electorate came to prize his talents, as someone capable of getting things—good things—accomplished.

---

24. James Madison: Autobiography (1830), Founders Early Access, accessed October 9, 2018, https://rotunda.upress.virginia.edu/founders/default.xqy?keys=FOEA-print-02-02-02-2226.
25. Ibid.

The Assessment Bill

Madison's return to Virginia was momentous, even providential, in terms of his work regarding the right of conscience. In December 1784, James returned to discover that leaders in the House of Delegates were trying to strengthen the Episcopal (formerly Anglican or Church of England) establishment. These proponents of the Anglican Establishment previously scored a success within the House of Delegates by passing a bill that provided special corporate privileges to the established Episcopal Church. Swayed by the moving rhetoric of Patrick Henry, proponents of the establishment had become concerned about the undue weakening of the Anglican establishment, during the Revolutionary War. They were determined to restore its strength at the commonwealth or state level. The pro-establishment forces were buoyed by Henry's words and by the fact that they believed they had momentum within the House. Proponents of the pro-establishment legislation were ready to flex their legislative muscles to enact the General Assessment Bill of 1784. The bill was formally entitled a "Bill establishing a Provision for Teachers of the Christian Religion," and preferred the Episcopal establishment, a fact that was not lost on Baptists and other dissenters.

Madison opposed this Assessment Bill with vigor, born of his long-standing commitment to the right of conscience. He found himself once again deeply troubled by the efforts of legislative leaders to restore the Commonwealth's pre-war established religion, the Anglican or Episcopal establishment. His involvement in this controversy adds further light to his views regarding the establishment issue.

Madison's strong opposition to the Assessment Bill was initially unavailing. Given the powerful rhetoric of the pro-establishment forces, the House voted 47–32 to pass the Bill. The House initially passed a resolution that declared, "The people of the Commonwealth, according to their respective abilities, ought to pay a moderate tax or contribution [to] the support of the Christian religion, or of some Christian church, denomination, or communion of Christians, or of some form of worship."[26] Madison was prepared to fight anew for his

---

26. William C. Rives, *History of the Life and Times of James Madison* (Boston: Little, Brown, and Company, 1859), 600.

principles, not with the flourish of moving speeches but by the power of his substantive arguments.

William Rives, Madison's friend and early biographer, reproduced the outline of Madison's argument, "written on the back of a letter, in a very condensed hand and with many abbreviations,"[27] that he offered in opposition to the bill. Rives summarized those arguments as follows: "We learn from it that Mr. Madison contended, first, that the regulation of religion was not within the province of civil power, and that every attempt of the kind tended necessarily to ultimate projects of compulsory uniformity." According to Rives, "Madison then showed that, as the benefits of the proposed provision were to be limited to Christian societies and churches, it would devolve upon the courts of law to determine what constitutes Christianity, and thus, amid the great diversity of creeds and sects, to set up by their fiat a standard of orthodoxy on the one hand and of heresy on the other, which would be destructive of the rights of private conscience."[28]

Madison's arguments were powerful and persuasive. James understood that, despite the broad language of the bill, the Episcopal majority likely would apply it in a preferential manner. To favor Christianity, as the proponents suggested, might lead to disfavoring those whose theological conceptions of Christianity differed, much as the majority Christian forces at the time of Constantine disfavored and persecuted anthropomorphic views of Christianity. Constantine believed that public peace or the general welfare justified restricting the conscience of those who believed in a manner contrary to the state's established version of Christianity. He went so far as to threaten the lives of members of sects who rejected the Trinitarian Doctrine declared in the Nicaean Council. Heretics and foes of the state were penalized for their belief that Christ was a separate being, a God of body, parts, and passions. Non-adherents to the state-imposed form of Christianity found themselves persecuted and severely punished. Madison feared Christian orthodoxy, understanding that it often gives birth to persecution. He had seen this with Baptists imprisoned for preaching the wrong form of Christianity.

---

27. Ibid., 603.
28. Ibid.

Rives further notes that Madison "argued, finally that the proposition dishonored Christianity by resting it upon a basis of mercenary support and concluded with vindicating its holy character from such a reproach, contending that its true and best support was in the principles of universal and perfect liberty established by the [Virginia Declaration of Rights], and which was alone in consonance with its own pure and elevated precepts."[29] A grave consternation and even vexation to Madison was the persecution and unfair treatment of the Baptists and his sense that many who favored the establishment did not consider the Baptists and other dissenting sects to be "Christian" in their doctrine. Madison believed that providing special benefits to "Christian" religions is "destructive of the rights of private conscience." Madison believed legislators and judges will "set up by their fiat a standard of orthodoxy." For James, the government lacks the legitimacy or competency to determine whether a sect was in fact Christian. Madison understood that Christianity, or any religion claiming to be of God, and a true religion needs nothing more than a level playing field—God needs nothing more than equality for truth to win out. Indeed, Madison knew, by sad experience, that assessments favoring an established religion violated the natural and *equal* right of religious conscience—he had seen, firsthand, the results of the tyranny of the majority regarding religious establishments.

Madison's powerful arguments caused many delegates to rethink their initial support for the bill. Nevertheless, despite Madison's continuing and often effective efforts to derail the bill, it passed again on second reading by a mere 44–42 margin, a significant reduction of the 47–32 margin originally supporting the assessment resolution. With this shifting momentum, Madison and opponents of the bill were heartened and mustered the support necessary to postpone a third and final reading and passage of the bill until the next session of the House of Delegates, which gave them time to go back to build support within the citizenry.

During that interval, between the postponement and the planned reconsideration of the Assessment Bill in the next legislative session, petitions circulated throughout the commonwealth opposing the effort

---

29. Ibid., 604–5.

to provide special support to the "Christian" religion. Madison's arguments gained ascendancy, finding their way into many petitions. This petition effort ultimately undercut public support for the assessment and helped prevent its passage.

Madison personally drafted a petition opposing the Assessment Bill, which was labeled as a "Memorial and Remonstrance against Religious Assessments." James's petition was anonymous, and he insisted that it remain so. He trusted that his Memorial would rise or fall on its own terms, and he was reluctant to use his name, fearing that some partisans might oppose it simply because he had authored it. He also realized that he had to work with opponents of the bill in the future and did not want to curry their disfavor. Madison's Memorial and Remonstrance is one of the great documents in our nation's history. It has regularly been cited by justices on the United States Supreme Court, as an aid in understanding the principle of the right of conscience and the meaning of the establishment limitation included in the First Amendment.

Madison opened his Memorial and Remonstrance with strong rights of conscience language: "The religion, then, of every man must be left to the conviction and conscience of every man; and it is the right of every man to exercise it as these may dictate. This right is, in its nature, an inalienable right."[30] In doing so, he clarified why the right was by its nature inalienable. Madison, once again, returned to the right of conscience and its foundation in a duty to God or Creator. He reasoned, "It is inalienable, because the opinions of men, depending only on the evidence contemplated by their own minds cannot follow the dictates of other men; it is inalienable also, because what is here a right towards men is a duty towards the Creator."[31] This opening explanation closely mirrors the teachings of Witherspoon regarding the inalienable nature of the right of conscience and the language of Madison's amendment to the Virginia Declaration of Rights.

Madison next emphasized that this duty to honor the Creator "is precedent both in order of time and in degree of obligation, to the

---

30. Ibid., 635. See also "Memorial and Remonstrance Against Religious Assessments," [CA. 20 June] 1785, Founders Online (National Archives), accessed October 9, 2018, https://founders.archives.gov/documents/Madison/01-08-02-0163.

31. Ibid.

claims of Civil Society."[32] He added, "We maintain therefore that, in matters of religion, no man's right is abridged by the institution of civil society, and that Religion is wholly exempt from its cognizance."[33] Madison's use of the language "wholly exempt from [the] cognizance [of civil authority," evidencing his belief that the right of conscience is, by its nature, exempt from direct or indirect government action. James was clearly unwilling to subject the right of conscience to the majority will, even in furtherance of some public good. The proponents to the bill believed it ensured peace and tranquility, a sense of Christian unity within the state. This argument was unpersuasive to Madison and an increasing number of Virginians. They had observed firsthand the results of such efforts to enforce religious unity in the form of persecution of Baptists and other minority religionists in Virginia. Patriots fought in the Revolutionary War to secure liberty, rendering efforts like the Assessment Bill to restrain liberty unacceptable to most Virginians.

In Madison's eyes, the bill violated the principle of equality, a principle that undergirds the rule of law—the principle that all are equal before the law. He argued, "Who does not see that the authority which can establish Christianity, in exclusion of all other Religions may establish with the same ease any particular sect of Christians, in exclusion of all other Sects? That same authority which can force a citizen to contribute threepence only of his property for the support of any one establishment, may force him to conform to any other establishment in all cases whatsoever."[34] This statement is often misread to imply that any aid to religion was unacceptable to Madison. In other words, Madison's primary fear was that the bill would be preferential or unequal in its enforcement and that it opened the door to the state defining what is and what is not Christian. Madison's form of Christianity was personal, even intimate, and generally idiosyncratic and nonsectarian, hardly part of the Anglican mainstream in Virginia. On its face, the bill also discriminated against non-Christian

---

32. Ibid.
33. Ibid.
34. Ibid., 636.

faiths. The message of the bill as whole was antithetical to everything Madison believed.

Madison further developed this equality argument when he stated, "Because the bill violates that equality which ought to be the basis of every law, and which is more indispensable, in proportion as the validity or expediency of any law is more liable to be impeached. . . . Above all are men to be considered as retaining an 'equal title to the free exercise of Religion according to the dictates of conscience.'"[35] Madison understood what so many ignore: the rule of law itself insures equality under the law. After making a general rule of law argument, that just laws must be applied equally to all, Madison emphasized that the Assessment Bill itself violated the non-establishment principle and the liberty of conscience of which it was supposedly intended to promote. Madison added, "Whilst we assert for ourselves a freedom to embrace, to profess and to observe the religion which we believe to be of divine origin, we cannot deny an equal freedom to those whose minds have not yet yielded to the evidence which has convinced us."[36]

James elaborated further on his commitment to equality and non-preference by making an argument designed to appeal to Christians, of all sects. He observed, "The first wish of those who enjoy this precious gift [of Christianity] ought to be that it may be imparted to the whole race of mankind."[37] This was a premise no Christian at that time disagreed with. Madison then argued that the Assessment Bill "at once discourages those who are strangers to the light of [Christian] revelation from coming into the region of it [Christianity], and countenances by example the nations who continue in darkness [nonbelief in Christianity], in shutting out those who might convey it [the Christian faith] to them."[38] In short, Madison argued that Christians must shun preferential treatment from government. He argued strongly for a level playing field, an equal opportunity for Christianity and nothing more. Christianity, if the true faith, which Madison believed it to be, would flourish in a world of equal treatment. Preference, on the other

---

35. Ibid.
36. Ibid.
37. Ibid., 639.
38. Ibid.

hand, intimated that God needed special treatment to draw His children to the faith. For Madison, truth in religious matters needed no special support from the civil authority. This statement makes it clear that Madison believed the bill was not equal as to religious sects. It failed the non-preference principle, which was of critical importance to Madison.

Madison's arguments in the Memorial and Remonstrance clarify his views regarding the scope of the inalienable right of religious conscience and the need for equal liberty (non-preference) as to matters of religious conscience. These were complementary principles: full and free exercise of conscience (what we today refer to as free exercise) and non-preference and equality (non-establishment). Christians should oppose the Assessment Bill on prudential as well as principled grounds—Christianity benefits most from a world in which the equal liberty of conscience is recognized and there is free and open dialogue among all religious groups. For Madison, truth benefits from equality and is susceptible to harm by governmental preference.

The Baptists and other dissenting groups strongly supported Madison's Memorial and Remonstrance. They made their views clear, from the pulpit and otherwise. Madison, the Baptists, and other minority sects joined forces as allies, an enduring alliance built on mutual respect and shared political objectives. Thanks to the efforts of the Baptists, religious dissenters, and members of the Episcopal Church who sought nothing more than a level playing field, the Assessment Bill never became the law of the Commonwealth. Rives reports that the "table of the House of Delegates almost sunk under the weight of accumulated copies of the memorial sent forward from different counties."[39] The Assessment Bill's proponents did not reintroduce it, and the Bill suffered a quiet death. Madison's arguments, so lucidly stated in the Memorial and Remonstrance, had won the day. Madison's success in the battle over the Assessment Bill made it clear that he was the leading voice for religious freedom and equality in Virginia—a leadership that would soon become national in scope. His commitment to the right of religious conscience would yet facilitate placing Madison in positions of political consequence.

---

39. Ibid., 632.

Madison made one other noteworthy contribution to the cause of the liberty of conscience during his service as a delegate in the Virginia Assembly. In 1779, Jefferson authored a Bill for Religious Freedom, but it languished in the legislature for many years. Given the successful effort to oppose the preferential nature of the Assessment Bill, the timing was right for the introduction of Jefferson's statute. Madison played an instrumental role in shepherding his friend's bill through the Assembly. The substance of the bill provided that: "No man shall be compelled to frequent or support any religious worship, place, or ministry whatsoever, nor shall be enforced, restrained, molested, or burdened in his body or goods, nor shall otherwise suffer on account of his religious opinions or beliefs, but that all men shall be free to profess, and by argument to maintain their opinions in matters of religion, and that the same shall in no wise diminish, enlarge, or affect their civil capacities."[40]

A recital to the bill added that it is improper for the "magistrate to restrain the profession or propagation of principles, on the supposition of their ill-tendency." Jefferson was responding to the persecution that had been rampant in Virginia in 1779. In keeping with the tenor of the time when it was drafted, Jefferson added a further recital stating, "It is time enough for the rightful purposes of civil government for its officers to interfere when principles break out into overt acts against peace and good order."[41] Madison personally went much further than Jefferson did in his efforts to secure a vibrant right of conscience. Jefferson's peace and good order standard was far less protective of the right of conscience than was Madison's "manifestly endangered standard." Madison, nevertheless, supported the statute as a step in the right direction and as a token of his respect for its primary author, Thomas Jefferson.

Madison was a strong advocate of the full and free exercise of religion, whereas Jefferson distinguished between protected beliefs and action or exercise, as to which government was given border power to limit, particularly when those actions threaten "peace and good

---

40. Thomas Jefferson, *A Bill for Establishing Religious Freedom,* 18 June 1779, Founders Online (National Archives), accessed October 9, 2018, https://founders.archives.gov /documents/Jefferson/01-02-02-0132-0004-0082.

41. Ibid.

order." Madison did not accept Jefferson's belief-action dichotomy or his "public good order" test. James believed in the full and free *exercise* of the right of conscience, limiting that right only when the interests of the state were "manifestly endangered" or the "equal liberty [of conscience]" of another is infringed. It is an error, therefore, to read too much into the substance of Madison's support for each word in Jefferson's statute. Madison did not agree with every word of Jefferson's bill, but he did see it as a further and appropriate expansion of the right of conscience at the state level. James wanted more protection for the right of conscience, but he was pleased that the statute actually made certain violations of the right of conscience illegal.

In less than a decade, Madison positioned himself as the leading advocate of a vibrant right of conscience during a critical time in Virginia. His support of religious liberty in Virginia predominated, as he articulated his position with clarity. His education at the College of New Jersey and his decade working at the state level were about to influence his actions in a storied life of service at the national level. His talents were soon to be displayed on a larger stage, as the fledgling nation confronted financial and other challenges associated with the Articles of Confederation, which provided for a mere confederation of the states, a national government of powers so limited that it was not clear whether the nation could survive. Madison understood that a weak nation presented a serious threat to liberty and national independence. Madison was about to become a leader in the effort to form a new and stronger constitutional government and he took his commitment to conscience with him.

Chapter Four

The Adoption of the Constitution

"It appears to me, then, little short of a miracle that the delegates from so many different states (which states you know are also different from each other in their manners, circumstances, and prejudices) should unite in forming a system of national Government, so little liable to well-founded objections."[1]

George Washington in a 1788 letter to Lafayette

"Don't interfere with anything in the Constitution. That must be maintained, for it is the only safeguard of our liberties."[2]

Abraham Lincoln

Within a decade after a miraculous victory over the British in the Revolutionary War, the new nation found itself on the brink of collapse. The Articles of Confederation were just that—a set of articles that provided for a weak confederation of states. The individual states retained almost complete power, including the power of the purse, which left the confederation at the national level unable to pay debts and function. The national government had to requisition the states for funds, which was an ineffectual means of financing the basic operations of government at the national

---

1. Letter from George Washington to Lafayette, 7 February 1788, Founders Online (National Archives), accessed 18 October 2018, https://founders.archives.gov/documents/Washington/04-06-02-0079.

2. Speech at Kalamazoo, Michigan, August 27, 1856, *Collected Works of Abraham Lincoln*, Volume 2, 366, accessed October 9, 2018, https://quod.lib.umich.edu/l/lincoln/lincoln2/1:391?rgn=div1;view=fulltext.

level. The national government also lacked executive or judicial authority and exercised only limited legislative power. Many legislative acts, particularly those dealing with financial matters, required the affirmative vote of at least nine of the thirteen original states. Without sufficient power at the national level, the confederation of states faced threats from other nations seeking claims to lands in the Americas, dissension between mercantile and agrarian interests within the states, unpaid claims from increasingly restless soldiers who had fought in the Revolutionary War, and disagreements in a wide variety of areas among states with differing interests and cultures. It was increasingly clear that the national government needed increased power to accomplish the demands of nationhood and provide a viable government for the states.

By 1785, Madison and many others were growing increasingly concerned regarding the unwillingness of the states to deal with pressing economic issues. During his three years of service in the Continental Congress, which ended in 1783, Madison became convinced that the lack of power at the national level threatened the preservation of the nation that had been formed with the blood and the sacrifices attending the Revolutionary War. Hard-earned liberty was also in jeopardy. Madison's service in the Virginia legislature prior to 1780 and after 1783 further contributed to related fears that the states were incapable of dealing with pressing international threats. In short, many of the critical issues faced by the new nation were national in scope and could not be resolved at the local or state level. The Continental Congress, however, was not equipped to meet those issues.

State governments were also too parochial, too prone to influence groups or sects with selfish, short-term interests. That parochialism rendered the states incapable of dealing with economic issues of the day and precluded them from dealing with increasing threats from European nations. Individual states were prone to control by individual groups and sects, which were inclined to limit the liberty of those who did not belong to the controlling groups. Madison knew that only a stronger and more diverse national government could solve those pressing problems. Without a strong central government, the liberty earned in a prolonged war of attrition with the British government had to be preserved, and that required a strengthened national government. Madison was also convinced that the right of conscience was poorly protected at the state level, where individual sects tended to predominate.

The challenges faced by the young nation demonstrated why Madison concluded that survival of the nation and liberty demanded a stronger national government. In virtually every speech he gave at that time, Madison also emphasized the need to deal with pressing economic issues. Those issues, together with instability of the national government, consumed Madison. He could think or talk of little else.

European nations, as well, were like ravenous animals sensing a weakened prey in the confederation of states. Britain, France, and Spain had serious and often conflicting interests in the colonies and the lands surrounding them. Those claims included the right to travel and engage in commerce along the nation's major internal trading and travel route, the Mississippi River. The Treaty of Paris, negotiated with Britain to end the Revolutionary War, awarded the new nation land all the way west to the Mississippi River. Ownership granted through a treaty between Britain and the new nation did not, however, translate into the power to control shipping on the Mississippi, nor did it resolve growing claims to portions of that land on the part of France and Spain. If left unchecked, skirmishes related to those claims would soon lead to another war. Preventing and, if necessary, fighting another war would require a stronger and economically viable national government for defensive purposes.

Economically, Madison was troubled by the failure of the states and nation to meet their debts in an equitable manner. Unpaid debts, particularly to veterans of the Revolutionary War, contributed to growing distrust of the national government. Additionally, the rise of the use of overvalued paper money was leading to rampant inflation. Debts were paid, if at all, with pennies on the dollar in the form of inflated currency. Failure to meet these obligations, or to meet them with highly inflated currency, was a grave concern. Madison was justifiably convinced that failure to meet the nation's obligations would soon lead to distrust of the economic system, which, in turn, would make investment in the new nation problematic, at best. The failure to recognize legitimate debts also denigrated the rule of law, which James knew was essential to the survival of the Republic. Madison's opponents, however, misconstrued his strong vocal support for solid currency and for full payment of debts. Debtors, who tended to be poorer, mistrusted Madison, believing that he was little more than a pawn of the interests of wealthy creditors. Those differences led some partisans to argue that Madison was really working to make the rich richer and the poor poorer. As a well-to-do plantation owner, James was an easy target, as were others who took up the cause of economic stability.

Opposition on the part of debtors, however, was understandable. Creditors within the states were seeking to use the power of their state and local governments to imprison debtors or to foreclose on properties, leaving them destitute and angry. The imprisonment of debtors, coupled with the foreclosing on or taking of property, was fomenting rebellion within the states, pitting debtors against creditors. The nation was suffering from a significant national recession. Hardworking farmers, many of who had fought valiantly in the Revolutionary War, found themselves imprisoned for their debts. They were losing their lands, which were being foreclosed on to satisfy those debts in many states, placing their livelihood and the needs of their families in a precarious state. Hopelessness and poverty were displacing the promise of land and opportunity.

Shays' Rebellion

This came to a symbolic head in Pennsylvania, where Daniel Shays led the "Shays' Rebellion." Shays was the father of six. He had a strong war record, having fought valiantly in the Battle of Bunker Hill, the Battle of Lexington, and the Battle of Saratoga. His courage and ability earned Shays the rank

Home of Captain Shays

of captain. He ultimately suffered a debilitating wound that forced him to resign from military service. General Lafayette awarded Shays with an ornamental sword in recognition of his service. Sadly, like other veterans, Shays received no other payment and had to sell the sword simply to put food on the table for his family. His fellow service members ridiculed Daniel for selling the sword, which further contributed to Shays's anger. When he returned to his farm in western Massachusetts, he was not greeted with a celebratory parade. Rather, like many other Revolutionary soldiers, his courageous efforts were rewarded with a summons to appear before the local judge to pay his debts or be imprisoned and lose his property.

Efforts of struggling farmers to resolve matters peaceably proved to be unsuccessful. General Shepherd and others who supported the creditors, demanded payment with little appreciation for the plight of the debtors. After exerting efforts to redress their grievances in more acceptable ways, as many as one thousand debtors joined Shays in marching, with petitions in hand, to the courthouse. The petitions sought to prevent foreclosure on their lands.

The farmers demanded due process in the form of a hearing for the airing of their grievances. They also sought the right to pay debts in paper money. The march of angry debtors was threatening to creditors and their supporters. Local judges and commercial interests were alarmed. They called on the army to disperse the growing crowd of protesters. The army dispersed the debtors, only to see the angry crowd begin to gather anew. The army was then directed to respond by arresting the protesters, to put an end to the rebellion. This solution worked in the short term, but imprisonment of patriotic soldiers raised concerns that rippled among sympathetic supporters in many states. Debtors everywhere, and there were many of them, were concerned. They feared losing their homes and being left destitute, without the capacity to care for their families. Distrust increased daily, as each side questioned the fairness of the other.

Some historians argue that Shays' Rebellion was of little significance. Whether that is true, Shays' Rebellion became a symbol that fueled concerns among debtors, throughout the states, who found themselves in circumstances like those faced by Daniel Shays. Many creditors, in turn, believed the debtors were rabble, disreputable people or deadbeats who refused to pay their loans. Madison saw clearly that debtors were largely patriots without the wherewithal to pay their debts. He also understood that creditors were simply seeking payment on lawful agreements. The threat symbolized by Shays' Rebellion was real. Even John Adams expressed a measure of sympathy and support for the debtors. The standoff between the debtors and creditors crossed state lines and was a threat that the respective state governments seemed unable or unwilling to deal with in an effective manner.

Equal liberty was also in serious jeopardy. Partisans were controlling the states, resulting in the deprivation of liberty to individuals and minority groups. Madison understood that man was, by nature, self-interested. That self-interest manifested itself in the form of factions or sects, combinations of individuals sharing similar beliefs. Individuals with similar interests often joined forces, thereby gaining control of the smaller and occasionally even larger state and local governments. This resulted in the tyrannizing and threatening of the liberty of minorities. Madison had seen this firsthand in Virginia, and he knew from correspondence with friends that the situation was even worse in some states with strongly entrenched established churches. A major structural cure for this malady of self-interested individuals and sects was a multiplicity of sects, with none being large enough to commandeer the government to their sectarian ends. That cure could only be found at the national level, where no single sect predominated. Those sects, in turn, would constantly be vying for power. Since no faction or sect could retain power over time, all factions must be solicitous of the liberty of others to avoid persecution when they were out of power. Equality, not preference, would prevail.

Alexander Hamilton: The Man

Alexander Hamilton, a young leader from New York was even quicker to understand the economic threat to the nation than Madison. Hamilton was becoming a powerful voice for a strong national government. As early as July 1783, Hamilton was working on a resolution in the Congress of the Confederation and called for a convention to amend the Articles of Confederation. Those amendments could recommend changes to the Articles that would increase national power in a manner equal to the economic challenges the nation was facing.

Because of Lin-Manuel Miranda's recent hit musical, *Hamilton*, Alexander Hamilton is increasingly well known and admired, within the United States and abroad. Together with John Adams, whose life was chronicled in an excellent recent biography and miniseries, George Washington, who has been an appropriate focus of study for school children since the founding, and Thomas Jefferson, who is credited with authoring the Declaration of Independence, Alexander Hamilton may today be among the most recognizable figures of the founding generation. Madison remains less well known, perhaps in part because he was less colorful than his counterparts—particularly Hamilton, who was born in the West Indies under difficult circumstances. In many ways, his life is an example of the promise of America. He rose from humble beginnings to be a leader in the Revolution and the building of a constitutional republic.

Alexander Hamilton

Hamilton held adamant nationalist views and had a shaky relationship with Jefferson. Although Hamilton supported Jefferson's effort to remove Aaron Burr from his party's presidential ticket, his relationship with James Madison was weak. Nevertheless, as members of the Continental Congress, Madison and Hamilton became strong allies, an alliance that proved critical to the adoption and ratification of the Constitution. The collaboration of two unlikely allies in supporting the Constitution is one of the many small miracles that contributed to the "Miracle of Philadelphia"—the Constitution.

As a fellow member of the Continental Congress, Madison opposed Hamilton's first resolution calling for a convention to consider the effectiveness of the government under the Articles of

Confederation. Madison initially believed that a convention would fan jealousies among the states. He worried, as well, that a convention could be used to cause more harm than good, dividing rather than unifying the states. As problems intensified at the national level and within the states, however, Madison's views on the issue changed. Ever one open to the ideas of others, and in characteristic fashion, Madison offered a more moderate proposal than the one offered by Hamilton, in an effort to retain much of the good that had been done at the state level, including the Declarations of Rights that had been adopted by Virginia and many other states. Madison's proposal called for a convention designed to focus on commercial issues. Hamilton, in turn, became persuaded that Madison's moderate proposal had more likelihood of success. It was a bridge that brought Hamilton and Madison together. They became formidable allies in a concerted effort to reform the Articles of Confederation, even though Hamilton clearly wanted to go further than Madison in strengthening the national government.

Annapolis Convention

Early in 1786, with urging from Hamilton and Madison, the Continental Congress voted to approve the holding of a convention in Annapolis, Maryland, to deal with economic issues. Not surprisingly, both Madison and Hamilton were selected to serve as delegates to the convention. In communicating with his friend, James Monroe, Madison took a nuanced position. He supported the holding of a convention but was "not in general an advocate of temporizing or partial remedies. But rigor in this respect, if pushed too far may hazard everything."[3]

During the summer of 1786, Madison returned to Montpelier, where he prepared exhaustively for the convention to be held in Annapolis, even though he was dubious that it would achieve much. His preparation included re-reading the classics, to better understand

---

3. Letter From James Madison to James Monroe, 19 March 1786, Founders Online (National Archives), accessed October 9, 2018, https://founders.archives.gov/documents/Madison/01-08-02-0269.

the history of confederations and to determine what light that study might cast on the work of the delegates to the convention. In characteristic fashion, Madison was determined to be prepared and developed over forty pages of notes at Montpelier before leaving for Annapolis.

As was his habit, Madison arrived early at Annapolis to prepare further for the convention and to ease the wear of a fatiguing journey on his fragile health. Only eleven delegates from a mere five states followed Madison and Hamilton to Annapolis. Most states, including the host, Maryland, did not send delegates, leaving the convention without a working quorum. The chairman of this failed convention was the major author of the Articles of Confederation, John Dickinson of Delaware. Madison, Hamilton, and Dickinson were joined by Edmund Randolph from Virginia and a handful of other delegates. As it turned out, Madison's belief that the convention would achieve little proved to be as prophetic as it was discouraging. Nothing of merit materialized in the convention, with one exception.

Not to be entirely derailed, at the end of the convention, Madison joined Hamilton in successfully recommending a subsequent convention that would deal with all the defects of the weak government under the Articles of Confederation, or as Madison was inclined to say, the "vices" of the current ineffectual federal system. The persistence of Hamilton and Madison would yet bear fruit.

In Madison's and Hamilton's minds, the weakening of the fabric of the new nation demanded that the next convention be successful. That required bringing able representatives from all or nearly all states together to find ways to deal with the defects of the Articles and thereby secure nationhood and liberty, the sacrifices of the Revolution. Leaders in the states, however, remained divided regarding the value of holding such a convention.

In Madison's home state of Virginia, Patrick Henry—who later became Madison's nemesis in the battle for the ratification of the Constitution—led the opposition to such a convention and to any major change on the national level. Henry expressed willingness to support breaking the nation into three regions, but he largely wanted power to continue to remain in the states. He was particularly resolute regarding the rights of the states. Patrick was concerned that a union of the states might weaken Virginia's claim to control over travel on the Mississippi. To offset the strong opposition in Virginia to any diminution of state power, Madison fully understood that delegates of the stature of General George Washington would have to be recruited to support the effort.

George Washington

George Washington

With good reason, more has been written regarding the contributions of George Washington to the creation and sustaining of the new nation than any other individual. There would be no United States of America without him. He was a remarkable leader. He was the general charged with assuming the near-impossible task of defeating the greatest military power in the world, with an army of patriotic but largely untrained soldiers and militia. Later, he was called upon to preside over a weakly connected group of states under an untried Constitution. President Washington proved to be a deliberative leader, who relied on the power of counseling with wise individuals who held differing views. He had a unique capacity to attract talent and to use that talent to a good end. As President Ronald Reagan once wisely noted, "The greatest leader is not necessarily the one who does the greatest things. He is the one who gets the people to do the greatest things."[4] Washington was just such a leader. He was tall and impressive in appearance, inspiring confidence in all around him. His

---

4. Cited in Gilbert A. Robinson, *Reagan Remembered* (New York: Beaufort Books 2015), Course Hero, accessed October 9, 2018, https://www.coursehero.com/file/11078287 /ginapower.

commitment to the cause of liberty and the United States of America was unequaled.

Soldiers wanted to follow Washington, as a general. One can imagine the force of these words, which he offered in an address to his troops before the Battle of Long Island: "The time is now near at hand which must probably determine whether Americans are to be freemen or slaves; whether they are to have any property they can call their own; whether their houses and farms are to be pillaged and destroyed, and themselves consigned to a state of wretchedness from which no human efforts will deliver them. The fate of unborn millions will now depend, under God, on the courage and conduct of this army."[5] Through severe deprivation and despite an often-inattentive Continental Congress, which was ever reluctant to provide necessary support for General Washington and his army, Washington and his forces remained determined to courageously serve and, in time, defeat the British. Washington, nevertheless, remained well aware of the ineffectiveness of the weak confederation of states under the Articles of Confederation.

The people regularly entrusted Washington with the power to lead a new nation, first in war and then in peace. Washington served with strength, but also with grace and humility. He was driven by a humble yet resolute faith in God and the cause of the revolution, in assuming the reigns of military and political leadership in securing the future of the new nation. Washington regularly confessed his and our nation's debt to God. Washington once noted, "Providence, to whom we are infinitely more indebted than we are to our own wisdom, or our own exertions, has always displayed its power and goodness, when clouds and thick darkness seemed ready to overwhelm us."[6]

In one of the most inspiring events during the Revolutionary Era, on the morning of March 15, 1783, General Washington surprised an assembly of army officers meeting in Newburgh, New York. The

---

5. George Washington, General Orders, 2 July 1776, Founders Online (National Archives), accessed 18 October 2018, https://founders.archives.gov/documents/Washington/03-05-02 -0117.
6. Letter From George Washington to Lund Washington, 19 May 1780, Founders Online (National Archives), accessed October 9, 2018, https://founders.archives.gov/documents /Washington/99-01-02-01806.

officers had gathered to discuss how to deal with the failure of the Continental Congress to honor the promises made to pay them and for failing to settle other accounts for food and clothing due members of the revolutionary army. The officers were discontent over mistreatment by a government that appeared oblivious to their sacrifices. There were even calls for outright rebellion against Congress, a coup.

When Washington entered, they respectfully granted him the opportunity to address the assembled officers. As he prepared to read a letter to the officers, Washington hesitated for a moment as he fumbled to retrieve his spectacles from his pocket. Gaining his composure, Washington almost apologetically but dramatically declared, "Gentlemen, you must pardon me. I have grown old in the service of my country and now find I am growing blind."[7] He then read his carefully drafted letter with visible emotion. Those present responded spontaneously, some in tears, realizing that Washington had sacrificed as much, or more, than they had, and did so without complaint. Moments later, the officers voted unanimously to express their confidence in the new government. In his First Inaugural Address, Washington later remarked, "I was summoned by my country, whose voice I can never hear but with veneration and love."[8] Patriots, members of the revolutionary forces, including the officer assembled in Newburgh, felt the same kind of veneration and love for their leader. Washington was trusted as no other American and had the capacity to elicit the best in those around him.

After winning the war against the British, Washington knew that the newly conceived nation was losing the battle against its own worst enemy: itself. Something had to be done, and that something was to build union within a weak confederation of states in America, with a national government capable of dealing with threats from abroad and within. That required a strong Constitution, but that task, like the Revolutionary War itself, seemed impossible in a nation of states prone to act only in their self-interest. Madison knew it would be impossible

7. This Day in History, March 15, 1783, "Washington puts an end to the Newburgh Conspiracy," History, accessed October 9, 2018, https://www.history.com/this-day-in-history/washington-puts-an-end-to-the-newburgh-conspiracy.
8. First Inaugural Address of George Washington, April 30, 1789, The Avalon Project (Yale Law School), http://avalon.law.yale.edu/18th_century/wash1.asp.

to hold a successful convention and create a viable Constitution without George Washington's highly visible support. Washington's imprimatur in the new nation was like no other, and the lack of his support at this precarious moment in the new nation's history would have doomed the Convention to failure. Madison, therefore, vigorously sought to persuade Washington to participate in the convention to be held in Philadelphia.

In addition to the need for attendance at the convention by George Washington and other respected delegates from all, or nearly all, of the states, success at the convention required a clear enumeration of the vices of the Articles of Confederation and a viable plan for strengthening the national or federal government. The national government's vices were generally well known, but differences existed regarding their magnitude and there was little agreement regarding how to rectify these vices. The development of a viable plan capable of receiving the support of a sufficient majority of the delegates, therefore, was a daunting task. There were simply too many diverse, and often adverse, views regarding the utility and nature of any new national government. Achieving success at the Convention would be no easy task. Indeed, if the past was a prologue, the lesser task of simply obtaining a quorum might itself prove to be nothing short of a miracle.

Undaunted, Madison went to work on both fronts. He repeatedly sought to find ways to persuade George Washington to attend the convention, even though Washington doubted that it would be successful. Washington was understandably hesitant. General Washington had tired of service and wanted nothing more than to retire to his beloved Mount Vernon. In his eyes, it was time for the rising generation to take their turn in securing the future of the new nation. General Washington also understood that a failed constitutional convention, over which he presided, would do considerable harm to his reputation. Washington, like Hamilton and Madison, was keenly aware of the need for a stronger national government to secure the continuation of the nation and liberty that he had done so much to secure, but he remained unpersuaded that he was duty bound to participate.

Madison persisted in seeking to persuade General Washington that preservation of the nation required that Washington attend and thereby legitimize the Convention. After six months of repeated efforts, through letters and visits, Madison helped persuade Washington to participate in the Convention, In doing so, Washington was again agreeing to serve his beloved nation , in yet another effort fraught with risk. Washington's commitment to attend, accept the responsibility to preside over the convention, and ultimately support its final product, the Constitution, was an act of moral courage. It gave others courage to take the risks attending participation in the convention. Without his attendance and support, the Constitution would never have been adopted. He did not actively participate in debates at the convention, but his daily presence presiding over the proceedings helped the delegates remain fixed on the greater need—the survival of the nation—and less on more provincial yet powerful political positions at the state level that divided them in significant ways. As long as Washington remained, presiding over the convention, his very presence was a powerful reminder that each delegate must stay the course, even when disagreements appeared inseparable. Leaving the convention prematurely would be an act of moral cowardice, the abandonment of a faithful general in the field of battle. Washington's presence and ultimate support for the Constitution helped assure its adoption and ratification.

The Virginia Delegation

George Mason and Edmund Randolph, who was then serving as governor of Virginia, were two of the other delegates from Virginia. John Blair, James McClurg, and George Wythe joined them, and together they collectively constituted the Virginia delegation to serve at the Convention. That delegation became a major force in the convention. Virginians had selected delegates from among their most respected leaders, an act that

Edmund Randolph

helped legitimize the convention within Virginia. Other states also sent well-respected leaders, which increased confidence that the second proposed convention might be successful. To their credit, all of the delegates realized that attendance was a risk to their political and personal reputation. They also knew that the likelihood of success remained seriously in question.

George Mason ultimately refused to sign the Constitution and argued against its ratification for three primary reasons:

1. It provided too much power to the national government (he was reluctant to weaken the Commonwealth of Virginia's sovereignty).
2. It did not include a Bill of Rights to secure the people against the national power included in the Constitution.
3. It did not adequately address the issue of slavery, which even though he was himself a slaveholder Mason considered to be "disgraceful to mankind."

Mason was active in the debates; but, in the end, his conscience would not permit him to sign the document.

Randolph also played a significant role in the deliberations, including his introduction of the Virginia Plan, but he also ultimately followed in Mason's footsteps and declined to sign the Constitution. Edmund believed strongly that the Constitution deviated from the "Republican propositions" of the Virginia Plan, which he proposed. William Pierce, of Georgia, who attended much of the convention, described Randolph as a "gentleman in whom unite all the accomplishments of the Scholar, and the Statesman. He came forward with the postulata, or first principles, on which the Convention acted, he supported them with a force of eloquence and reasoning that did him great honor."[9] Pierce added that Randolph was "a most harmonious voice, a fine person [with] striking manners."[10]

Like Mason, however, Randolph was concerned that the Constitution as adopted and presented for ratification in the states

---

9. William Pierce, The Framers of the Constitution, U.S. Constitution, accessed October 9, 2018, https://www.usconstitution.net/constframe.html.
10. Ibid.

was seriously deficient. He refused to sign the Constitution believing it was a threat to Virginia's sovereignty and to liberty, particularly the right of religious conscience. In time, Randolph yielded to Madison's persuasion and supported ratification of the Constitution. Edmund later explained his change from his refusal to sign the document before leaving Philadelphia to his eventual support of the Constitution in the ratification convention in Virginia. His change of position was directly related to his belief that the right of religious conscience would be protected. In now supporting the Constitution, Randolph declared, "Freedom of religion is said to be in danger. I will candidly say, I once thought that it was, and felt great repugnance to the constitution for that reason."[11] He added, however, that he was "willing to acknowledge my apprehensions removed—and I will inform you by what process of reasoning I did remove them."[12] He found solace in the fact that "no power is given expressly to congress over religion. . . . It puts all sects on the same footing."[13] Echoing Madison's view, Randolph noted, "I am a friend to a variety of sects, because they keep one another in order. . . . [T]here are so many now in the United States that they will prevent the establishment of any one sect in prejudice to another . . . and will forever oppose all attempts to infringe religious liberty."[14] He concluded that if the national government ever sought to prefer one religion over another or deny any individual of religious liberty, the government would "run the risk of exciting the resentment of all, or most of the religious sects in America."[15] He envisioned that the wide variety of sects at the national level would band together, as brothers of faith, to vigorously oppose any effort by any branch of the national government to deprive the people of their natural and equal right of conscience.

Many Virginians, Mason included, remained unpersuaded, and demanded a Bill of Rights, to expressly protect the right of

---

11. Edmund Randolph, Virginia Ratifying Convention, 10 June 1788, Elliott 3:204, The Founders' Constitution (University of Chicago), accessed October 9, 2018, http://press-pubs .uchicago.edu/founders/documents/a6_3s24.html.

12. Ibid.

13. Ibid.

14. Ibid.

15. Ibid.

conscience. While Mason and Randolph initially declined to sign the Constitution, with Randolph later changing his mind, Washington and Madison signed the final document on behalf of the Virginia delegation. Even that division was providential. Virginia sent some of its greatest leaders to serve as delegates to the convention, but they returned divided. That division was itself providential in that it helped ensure the adoption of the Bill of Rights in the first Congress. Other states sent their luminaries to the convention as well, despite the belief on the part of so many that the effort to amend the Articles was doomed from the start. The task of unifying the country seemed futile, but many among the greatest members of the founding generation were willing to take the risk.

As stated before, Madison arrived early in Philadelphia to finish preparations for the convention and begin discussing issues with the other delegates. One such delegate proved to be an ally at the Convention and in the ratification process. His name was James Wilson. Wilson lived in Philadelphia and was a highly respected delegate from Pennsylvania. Wilson probably did more than any other single delegate to help democratize the Republic. His sharp intellect was intent on finding a balance between democracy and representative government, resulting in a Democratic Republic. Some go so far as to assert that the final substantive draft of the Constitution is written in Wilson's handwriting and give him credit as the primary draftsman of the Constitution. Madison, however, asserted that if any single individual deserves credit as primary draftsman of the Constitution, it is Gouverneur Morris, who served as a member of the Committee on Style and was given authority by members of the Committee for wordsmithing the final draft.

In truth, the ideas captured in the Constitution belonged to many of the delegates, and most would have taken umbrage at the assertion that any one of them deserves full credit for the final product. Indeed, there were nearly three thousand individual decisions made during the convention, many of which involved conflicting values or principles, requiring compromise, and all of which collectively led to the Constitution as adopted. Wilson was, nevertheless, among the leading delegates involved in fashioning the Constitution.

James Wilson

James Wilson was from Scotland, a product of the Scottish Enlightenment. As such, he would have had much, in an intellectual sense, in common with Madison. James Wilson studied at St. Andrews, Edinburgh, and Glasgow, and was also a devotee of Scottish Enlightenment thought, including the primacy of liberty and the right of the people to select their own leaders.

James Wilson

Like Madison, in keeping with Enlightenment teachings, Wilson believed in natural rights. In a lecture to his law students at the University of Pennsylvania, Wilson taught, "Government, in my humble opinion, should be formed to secure and to enlarge the exercise of the natural rights of its members; and every government, which has not this in view, as its principal object, is not a government of the legitimate kind."[16] He did much to democratize the republic, as well, by providing for popular representation at all levels. In his words, "The extension of the theory and practice of representation through all the different departments of the state is another very important acquisition made, by the Americans, in the science of jurisprudence and government. To the ancients, this theory and practice seem to have been altogether unknown."[17] He acknowledged the unique nature of American democracy when he noted, "To this moment, the representation of the people is not the sole principle of any government in Europe. . . . The American States enjoy the glory and happiness of diffusing this vital

---

16. Steve Straub, "James Wilson, Lectures on Law, 1791," The Federalist Papers, accessed October 9, 2018, https://thefederalistpapers.org/founders/james-wilson/james-wilson-lectures-on-law-1791.

17. James Wilson, Lectures 1790–91, Founding Fathers Quotes, accessed October 9, 2018, http://www.foundingfatherquotes.com/father/id/56.

principle throughout all the different divisions and departments of the government."

James Wilson was also a tireless advocate of the constitutional rule of law. He understood what so many forget in all ages, including our own, that the rule of law does more to secure liberty than any other principle or theory. He declared, "How prevalent even among enlightened writers, is the mistaken opinion, that government is subversive of equality and nature! Is it necessarily so? By no means. When I speak thus, I speak confidently, because I speak from principle fortified by fact. Let the constitution of the United States . . . be examined from the beginning to the end. No right is conferred, no obligation is laid on any, which is not laid or conferred on every, citizen of the commonwealth or Union—I think I may defy the world to produce a single exception to the truth of this remark. [T]he original equality of mankind consists in an equality of their duties and rights."[18] Wilson wisely taught that equality is founded primarily on the rule of law. It is not so much a matter of identity, as it is a matter of law, with everyone being treated equally under the law. The just rule of law, in turn, is rooted in rights and duties. Rights, for Wilson, entailed duty. That duty included respect for the rights of others and obedience to the dictates of our conscience.

As previously noted, some argue that Wilson was the primary drafter of the Constitution, based on his work as a significant member of the Committee of Detail, which was tasked with putting all that had been agreed to in the Constitutional Convention into a single document. That final document, the report of the Committee of Detail, is written in Wilson's pen. It is also clear that he had a major influence within the Committee. He was largely responsible for adding the "necessary and proper" clause, which provided a means to expand the enumerated rights of the national government. Enumerated rights were viewed as a limit on national power. Providing the national government with the power to do all that is necessary and proper to effectuate an enumerated power clearly increased the power of the national government. He also helped tailor the "supremacy clause," making the

---

18. James Wilson, "Of Natural Rights of Individuals, 1790-91, Founding Fathers Quotes, accessed October 9, 2018, http://www.foundingfatherquotes.com/father/id/56.

Constitution the supreme or highest law of the land in the United States of America. Without question, Wilson was one of the most powerful and respected delegates to the Constitutional Convention. The Pennsylvania delegation, like the Virginia delegation, played a primary role in the work of the Convention.

Wilson was also a committed patriot and a distinguished lawyer, who later lectured at what is today the law school at the University of Pennsylvania. He was deeply respected as a lawyer, and that respect resulted in President Washington selecting him to serve as one of the first justices on the United States Supreme Court. Sadly, like Hamilton and Burr before him, Wilson died an ignominious death as the victim and sometimes perpetrator of a series of highly speculative and failed investments in land. That speculation and the unanticipated failures that followed left many pointing their finger at Wilson. To escape creditors, he fled to North Carolina, where he died in poverty and disrepute. It was well over a century after his death before his remains were finally returned to rest in his native state of Pennsylvania, where he was finally recognized for the highly significant contributions he made in the Constitutional Convention and as a member of the founding generation.

It is tragic that Wilson's contributions to the adoption and ratification of the Constitution have been forgotten by so many. He, as much as any other delegate, was the equal of Madison, intellectually and as an advocate of liberty. Benjamin Rush, a signer of the Declaration of Independence and Surgeon General during the American Revolution described Wilson well when he stated, "[Wilson] spoke often in Congress, and his eloquence was of the most commanding kind. . . . His mind, while he spoke, was one blaze of light. Not a word ever fell from his lips out of time, or out of place, nor could a word be taken from or added to his speeches without injuring them."[19] James Wilson's commitment to the constitutional rule of law (equality through the rule of law) and liberty (natural rights, including the right of self-governance) is written all over the Constitution. Wilson's "blazing light," to use

19. "Delegates Discussions: Benjamin Rush Characters," James Wilson, Declaration Resources Project (Harvard University), accessed October 9, 2018, https://declaration.fas. harvard.edu/blog/dd-rush.

Rush's term, continues to bless the lives of all who bask in the light of the blessings made possible by the Constitution.

Benjamin Franklin

In addition to spending time with Wilson, Madison also dined early and regularly with the eighty-one-year-old elder statesman Benjamin Franklin, who agreed to serve as a delegate to the Convention. Franklin's commitment to the cause of the Convention was evidenced by the fact that he attended every session, even though he was suffering ill health and often had to ask others to speak on his behalf, a duty generally delegated to James Wilson. Like Washington,

Benjamin Franklin

Franklin—a senior statesman and patriot—added legitimacy in the eyes of the American public to the convention. Without the presence of General Washington and Benjamin Franklin, it is likely that others would not have participated, leaving the convention without a quorum, as had been the case with the failed Annapolis Convention. Franklin had gained the respect of the American people for his courageous voice supporting the revolutionary cause and many accomplishments, including his critical role as an emissary in France during the Revolution. His diplomacy in France proved critical in securing an ally, on the part of France, against the world's greatest military power at that time, Britain. Franklin was also deeply respected by Madison, a respect that was clearly mutual. Franklin also had a wonderful capacity of conciliation, the ability to remind delegates with strongly divergent views that the cause of the nation was more important than personal political beliefs or allegiances.

At a particularly difficult time during the deliberations of the delegates to the Convention, as the heat of summer and lack of progress on the drafting of the Constitution frayed tempers and increased acrimony among all present, Franklin exhorted his colleagues, reminding them of the need for prayer as a force for unity. The words were written by Franklin but offered by his friend and fellow delegate from Pennsylvania, James Wilson. Franklin's admonition, as Madison recorded it at the time, began on a worrisome note, "The small progress we have made after four or five weeks close attendance & continual reasonings with each other-our different sentiments on almost every question, several of the last producing as many noes as ays, is methinks a melancholy proof of the imperfection of the Human Understanding. We indeed seem to feel our own want of political wisdom, since we have been running about in search of it."[20] He then inquired, "In this situation of this Assembly, groping as it were in the dark to find political truth, and scarce able to distinguish it when presented to us, how has it happened, Sir, that we have not hitherto once thought of humbly applying to the Father of lights to illuminate our understandings?"[21]

At a time when, despite incessant wrangling, the framers had managed to agree on only a few words of text, Franklin's humble recognition of the need for heavenly aid was heartfelt. In acknowledging the need for providential assistance, Franklin reverted to the experience of the Revolution, "All of us who were engaged in the struggle must have observed frequent instances of a superintending providence in our favor. To that kind providence we owe this happy opportunity of consulting in peace on the means of establishing our future national felicity." Franklin then rebuked all present with these powerful words of faith, "Have we now forgotten that powerful friend? or do we imagine that we no longer need his assistance?" He answered his own largely rhetorical question by raising another, "I have lived, Sir, a long time, and the longer I live, the more convincing proofs I see of this truth—that God Governs in the affairs of men. And if a sparrow cannot fall to the ground without his notice, is it probable that an empire can rise without his aid?"

---

20. James Madison's Notes of the Constitutional Convention (June 28, 1787), ConSource, accessed October 9, 2018, https://www.consource.org/document/james-madisons-notes-of-the -constitutional-convention-1787-6-28.
21. Ibid.

Citing the scripture, "Except the Lord build the House they labour in vain that build it," Franklin "firmly" declared that, "[W]ithout [the] concurring aid [of Providence] we shall succeed in this political building no better, than the Builders of Babel: We shall be divided by our little partial local interests; our projects will be confounded, and we ourselves shall become a reproach and bye word down to future ages."

He concluded by declaring and proposing that, "[W]hat is worse, mankind may hereafter from this unfortunate instance, despair of establishing Governments by Human wisdom and leave it to chance, war and conquest. I therefore beg leave to move—that henceforth prayers imploring the assistance of Heaven, and its blessings on our deliberations, be held in this Assembly every morning before we proceed to business, and that one or more of the Clergy of this City be requested to officiate in that Service."

A silence fell for a moment over those present, as they searched their own hearts and souls. Ultimately, Franklin's motion failed, but his words had their intended effect, reminding all present of the sacred nature of the work of the convention and reminding all present of the need for humility in such an important work. In his notes, Madison reported that the delegates adjourned "without a vote on the matter," but where animosity had been on the rise, it was now replaced with humility and a determination that all present would put petty differences aside and come to a common accord.

Many years later, Madison offered three reasons why Franklin's stirring motion failed: "The Quaker usage, never discontinued in the State & the place where the Convention held its sittings, might not have been without an influence [in the delegate's decision to table the motion] as might also, the discord of religious opinions within the Convention, as well as among the Clergy." Madison makes it clear that the delegates were not opposed to prayer, but they feared that the offering of prayers might become sectarian, adding to, rather than limiting, discord within the convention. For Madison and others, a vocal prayer offered by a sectarian clergyman would violate the principle of equality or non-preference among religions and religious voices in the public square. The delegates were also concerned about whether it was appropriate to compensate a chaplain.

Prayers, nevertheless, were surely offered silently and in the morning before gathering and in the evening when delegates retired to the quiet of their own rooms. Inspired by Franklin's admonition, the discord that was threatening the convention lessened, and the great compromise between the large and small states followed not long thereafter. With gratitude, Franklin signed the Constitution. His words at the close of the convention have been immortalized. Speaking of the sun carved in the chair in which George Washington sat as he quietly, but with great dignity, presiding over the proceedings, Franklin reflected that he had "often looked at [President Washington's chair] without being able to tell whether it was a rising or setting [sun]. But now I . . . know that it is a rising . . . sun." Franklin's presence at the convention, his consultations with Madison and others, and his wisdom proved critical to the enterprise of the adoption and ratification of the Constitution. His reminder that without the aid of Providence the convention was doomed also lingered and was a significant reminder of a truth that President Abraham Lincoln would utter at another crucial time in American history, "I have been driven many times upon my knees by the overwhelming conviction that I had no where else to go. My own wisdom and that of all about me seemed insufficient for the day."

In addition to meeting with Franklin and early arriving delegates, Madison took time to enjoy Philadelphia, the City of Brotherly Love. Ever seeking to learn more about various faiths, he attended Mass at a Roman Catholic Church. Over the course of his lifetime, Madison attended services of a wide variety of sects, thereby gaining an understanding of and appreciation for a multiplicity of faith traditions. This practice of seeking to attend and understand various sects also reflected the yearning of a soul in search of a sect he could believe in. As part of his preparation, Madison studied and prepared lengthy notes supporting arguments that he knew he would have to make and met with important delegates prior to the arrival of a quorum. He completed his preparations and waited for the arrival of the delegates. Ever anxious, Madison feared that a full quorum might not materialize, remembering well the failure of the Annapolis Convention.

Madison was increasingly heartened as delegates slowly began to trickle into Philadelphia. Washington arrived receiving applause from crowds lining the streets. It was another token of the respect he earned from the citizens of the City of Brotherly Love and the newly formed nation. Washington's arrival was a source of joy to Madison. Washington's presence made the ever-anxious Madison more confident that the quorum would, in fact, materialize; but it was the third week of May before a significant number of delegates began to arrive.

Constitutional Convention

By May 25, eleven days after the scheduled start date for the convention, twenty-nine delegates gathered in Constitution Hall, a name later placed upon the building as a tribute to the work of the delegates. At last, they had a quorum, and the near-impossible task of unifying the nation lay before them. Delegates came and went, during the convention, with fifty-five attending at one time or another. Nevertheless, they maintained the necessary quorum throughout the months of the convention. Delegations attended from twelve of the thirteen states. Rhode Island was the only state that failed to send representatives.

The first order of business was the formality of electing George Washington as president of the convention. The delegates next adopted a series of procedural rules, including a rule that provided for secrecy. The delegates made the proceedings confidential, so they could deliberate openly and confidentially, without fear of the political consequences of having to respond to external inquiries from the press and prematurely alarmed partisans. It is amazing how faithful the delegates were in keeping this promise of secrecy. In today's world, one can imagine that the participants would make multiple anonymous leaks to the press to weaken opposing forces. The willingness of the delegates to keep their promise to maintain confidentiality is a tribute to their integrity. A few disaffected delegates left the convention early and tried to raise alarm regarding what was being done in secret in the convention.

Citizens in Virginia and elsewhere were concerned about the lack of information regarding the proceedings at the convention. There was considerable pressure on Madison and other delegates to share information regarding the proceedings. Their refusal to do so maintained a cloak of confidentiality and resulted in transparency and candor among delegates. The commitment to confidentially facilitated honest dialogue and promoted understanding. With time, this open dialogue led to the many compromises that were necessary to create a viable Constitution. In some sense, each compromise was a tender mercy, a small miracle. The result was adoption of a collaborative and negotiated document, the Constitution.

The Virginia Plan

Just four days after the opening session of the Convention, on May 29, Edmund Randolph presented the Virginia Plan. It was a wise move. Randolph and Madison understood that there is real power in presenting the first substantive draft in any deliberation—that first draft set the substantive tone for all that would follow. Not all provisions of the plan would be adopted, but the plan remained prominent. That plan included fifteen resolutions, which were in Madison's handwriting and were largely his handiwork. Those resolutions provided the basis for a much stronger national government than the one that existed at the time under the Articles of Confederation. The first resolution stated that, "the Articles of Confederation ought to be so corrected & enlarged as to accomplish the objects proposed by their institution; namely, common defense, security of liberty and general welfare."[22] These three areas or vices were also indicative of the three necessary cures or purposes of that any proposed constitution would have to embody. There was a growing consensus that the new national government must have the power to provide for the common defense. Madison, Randolph, Hamilton, and others were deeply troubled by threats from Britain, Spain, and other nations. There was also concern regarding internal unrest within the states, as symbolized by Shays' Rebellion.

---

22. *The Virginia Plan*, 29 May 1787, Founders Online (National Archives), accessed October 14, 2018, https://founders.archives.gov/documents/Madison/01-10-02-0005.

Above all, most of the delegates, Madison included, knew that the cause of liberty hung in the balance. Madison understood that it was urgent to protect the liberty that had been earned at such great cost. To protect freedom, he believed that, unless the national government had enough power to deal with external and internal threats, it was doomed to fail. Defeat by an external power could lead to a diminution or deprivation of the liberty of the people, including externally imposed limitations on the right of conscience. Without a stronger national government, a government with enumerated powers designed to permit it to act in specific areas of concern, the new nation would soon find itself in battles with other nations. Any such battle threatened division and perhaps even overt conflict among states and regions within the fledgling nation. To fail to provide the national government with limited power to deal with continual threats from external and internal sources would prove fatal to the nation's survival in the eyes of Madison and others.

The states often divided by region, with the north seeking to protect their manufacturing interests and the south seeking to secure their agricultural interests. Within the states, there were also concerns that strong factions, including religious establishments, might wrest and then seek to exercise power in ways that would lead to deprivations of liberty. Madison was also particularly concerned about restraints on the right of expression and habeas corpus within the states. James and Edmund Randolph, as evidenced by the Virginia Plan, wanted a stronger national government to maintain the general welfare, including peace within the states and the promotion of interstate commerce, which was a source of economic well-being. They also wanted to secure a more democratic form of government throughout a nation that was conceived in a commitment to liberty. The last of these concerns, ensuring liberty including the right of self-governance, presented a serious obstacle to adoption of a constitution, given the small states' concern that they would experience a loss of power under such any plan that weighed each individual vote equally.

To achieve these necessary ends, the Virginia Plan offered a series of other resolutions. The second resolution provided for a democratic form of government: "The rights of suffrage in the National Legislature ought to be proportioned to the Quotas of contribution, or to the number of free inhabitants, as the one or the other rule may seem best in different cases."[23] Free inhabitants would select members of Congress, the National Legislature. This proposal was objectionable to delegates representing the small states, which would have fewer votes under such a system. Delegates from the smaller states were opposed to "one person one vote." They rightly feared that a national legislature, selected primarily from citizens in the larger states, would have the power to deprive the citizens of smaller states of their rights and role in the national government. Opponents of a purely democratic system understood that human nature was such that the large states, and their voters, would use the system to increase their power and decrease the power of smaller states.

The next four resolutions in the Virginia Plan provided additional details regarding the nature of the national legislative body, including two houses. Those details were designed to diffuse and check the power of any single branch of government, thereby further securing the nation against tyranny by the majority. The ideas presented in the Virginia Plan, however, did little to satisfy the concerns of delegates from the smaller states. In time, that division into branches, however, would provide a critical area for a compromise between those favoring one-person-one-vote and those committed to the power of individual states.

The resolutions in the Virginia Plan proposed the requirement that, "the National Legislature ought to consist of two branches." Two branches, with differing modes of election, would serve as limitations, or checks, on each other. The threat of tyranny by a single elected branch of government was common in many governments throughout history. While the existence of two branches provided for checks and balances, moderating the power of the majority, proponents of the Virginia Plan also believed that more checks on power needed to be in place. Chief Justice Roberts extolled this virtue of checked power when, over two centuries after the adoption of the Constitution, he declared, "By ensuring that no one in government has too much

---

23. Ibid.

power, the Constitution helps protect ordinary Americans every day against abuse of power by those in authority."[24]

In furtherance of this principle of checked or limited government, Madison and other proponents of the Virginia Plan sought to require that "members of the first branch of the National Legislature . . . be elected by the people"[25] for a period of years to be decided by the delegates present. This provision provided further that elected representatives were to receive "liberal stipends by which they may be compensated for the devotion of their time to public service [and] be ineligible to any office established by a particular State, or under the authority of the United States, except those peculiarly belonging to the functions of the [legislature], during the term of service."[26] This provision was designed to ensure that legislators at the national level could focus on service in the national legislature, without distraction.

The Virginia Plan also provided for term limits. Members of the national legislative bodies would "be incapable of reelection for the space of [__ years] after the expiration of their term of service, and to be subject to recall."[27] The term limit provision was designed to ensure that no members of the national legislative bodies would become too powerful. Interestingly, various term limit recommendations were defeated on seven separate occasions during the convention. The Virginia Plan, as penned by Madison and presented by Randolph, sought to subject legislators to re-election on a regular basis and to limit their tenure, with the intent to limit the power that could be exercise by any individual legislator or group of legislators. On seven occasions, delegates would consider term limits, refusing to adopt them in each instance.

The resolutions in the Virginia Plan also provided that "members of the second branch of the National Legislature ought to be elected by those of the first, out of a proper number of persons nominated by the individual Legislatures, to be of the age of __ years at least."[28] These representatives, in turn, were "to hold their offices

---

24. Ibid.
25. Ibid.
26. Ibid.
27. Ibid.
28. Ibid.

for a term sufficient to ensure their independency; to receive liberal stipends, by which they may be compensated for the devotion of their time to public service."[29] They were also "ineligible to [serve in] any office established by a particular State, or under the authority of the United States, except those peculiarly belonging to the functions of the second branch, during the term of service, and for the space of after the expiration thereof."[30] Thus, the people would directly elect the first legislative body, the House of Representatives, and the members of that first house, would in turn, select members of the second legislative body, the Senate. Once again, we see a desire to limit the potential for a majority of the electorate to obtain too much unchecked power.

The Virginia Plan further "resolved that each branch ought to possess the right of originating Acts; that the National Legislature ought to be impowered to enjoy the Legislative Rights vested in Congress . . . & moreover to legislate in all cases to which the separate States are incompetent, or in which the harmony of the United States may be interrupted by the exercise of individual Legislation."[31] Madison had observed the need for the national government to have sufficient legislative power to deal with issues that the states had been unable to address. In joining Randolph in preparing the Virginia Plan, Madison went further, giving the national legislature the power "to negative all laws passed by the several States, contravening in the opinion of the National Legislature the articles of Union . . . and to call forth the force of the Union [against] any member of the Union failing to fulfill its duty under the articles thereof."[32] With this provision, we see Madison struggling to provide the national legislative bodies with enough power to help secure the common defense, liberty, and the general or collective welfare of the nation, while also seeking to ensure that the national legislative body not be given power to limit liberty or tyrannize the minority.

---

29. Ibid.
30. Ibid.
31. Ibid.
32. Ibid.

The Virginia Plan turned next to the power of the executive branch of government. The chief executive was to be "chosen by the National Legislature for a [specified] term of years."[33] The executive was also to receive "a fixed compensation . . . and to be ineligible a second time."[34] The Virginia Plan thus provided for an Executive who would be sufficiently independent and powerful to do the work necessary at the national level. That Legislature and not the people directly, in turn, were given the authority to select the executive, thereby insulating the national government in some measure from the kinds of populist demagogues that could occasionally gain favor among the less-informed electorate. To ensure that the Executive did not have too much power, the Virginia Plan provided further that the Executive would serve a single term, another effort at term limits that would ultimately fail to be adopted. The requirement of fixed compensation also provided for independence, prohibiting the Legislature from using compensation as a means of unduly influencing the work of the Executive.

The Virginia Plan addressed the power of the courts at the national level: "A National Judiciary be established to consist of one or more supreme tribunals, and of inferior tribunals to be chosen by the National Legislature, to hold their offices during good behaviour; and to receive punctually at stated times fixed compensation for their services."[35] The judicial branch, in turn, included "inferior tribunals" which were "to hear and determine [cases] in the first instance."[36] They also provided for a supreme tribunal "to hear and determine in the [final] resort, all piracies & felonies on the high seas, captures from an enemy; cases in which foreigners or citizens of other States applying to such jurisdictions may be interested, or which respect the collection of the National revenue; impeachments of any National officers, and questions which may involve the national peace and harmony."[37] Thus, the national government was to include a third branch of government, the judiciary, with powers to hear an array of cases, including

---

33. Ibid.
34. Ibid.
35. Ibid.
36. Ibid.
37. Ibid.

the broad power to hear cases that "may involve the national peace and harmony."[38]

In one of its more controversial resolutions, the Virginia Plan provided for a Council of Revision. That council was to be given the power to revise national legislation: "The Executive and a convenient number of the National Judiciary, ought to compose a Council of revision with authority to examine every act of the National Legislature before it shall operate, & every act of a particular Legislature before a Negative thereon shall be final; and that the dissent of the said Council shall amount to a rejection, unless the Act of the National Legislature be again passed, or that of a particular Legislature be again negatived by the members of each branch."[39] This resolution, once again, showed Madison's desire to place carefully limited power in the hands of the national government to do the necessary work of the union. At the same time, the Virginia Plan was designed to enhance dialogue among the branches of government by shared powers that further checked the power of any branch of government. As such, while the Virginia Plan did not emphasize efficiency, it did provide for effective national governance.

The Virginia Plan also anticipated the growth of the union over time and provided for a means of admitting additional states. It further insured that a "Republican [form] of Government" would "be guaranteed by the United States to each State."[40] This provision anticipated a democratic and republican (representative democracy) form of government at the national and state levels. The Virginia Plan further provided for a transition from the Continental Congress, under the Articles of Confederation, to a more vibrant national form of government. It also provided for change over time, by recommending a liberal means of amending the Articles of Union, "provision ought to be made for the amendment of the Articles of Union whensover it shall seem necessary, and that the assent of the National Legislature ought not to be required thereto."[41] The details of the amendment provision were

---

38. Ibid.
39. Ibid.
40. Ibid.
41. Ibid.

not included in the Virginia Plan, but it did envision the need for a national government that could change in fundamental ways over time through some form of amendment or addition.

In another effort to limit the largely unrestricted power of the states, the Virginia Plan resolved that "the Legislative Executive & Judiciary powers within the several States ought to be bound by oath to support the articles of Union."[42] Madison feared greatly that demagogues within the states would simply ignore the power of the national government in a ploy to augment their own power and authority. He believed the most effective manner of dealing with those excesses, and with other accretions of power within the state governments, was to bind state officials by oath, at a time when integrity and personal honesty was largely a given.

The fifteenth and final resolution provided that, after receiving Congressional approval, the changes to the Articles of Confederation would be "submitted to an assembly or assemblies of Representatives, recommended by the several Legislatures to be expressly chosen by the people, to consider & decide thereon."[43] The Virginia Plan placed the power to select delegates to ratify the plan adopted in the convention in the hands of the state legislatures and not directly with the people. Madison believed that the state legislatures would wisely select honorable and able delegates who would be more inclined to put country before self. Madison retained his fear that demagogues could sway the general electorate.

In introducing the Virginia Plan early in the convention, Madison and Randolph gained a major advantage. By introducing their plan at the outset, the Virginians provided the framework for further discussions and deliberations. In doing so, they delegated other major plans, including the New Jersey Plan to a secondary status. By the time those other plans were offered, the Virginia Plan had set the general substance and tone.

The delegates were quick to react to the provisions of the Virginia Plan. Delegates from the smaller states led the charge against the Virginia Plan, which they believed favored the power of the larger states

---

42. Ibid.
43. Ibid.

at the expense of smaller states. On May 29, 1787, Charles Cotesworth Pinckney of South Carolina offered his own carefully drafted set of proposals, a series of proposals that would have an influence on the work of the convention equal to that of the Virginia Plan.

Charles Cotesworth Pinckney

Charles Cotesworth Pinckney enlisted in the Continental Army to serve under the leadership of General Washington. He served first as a captain leading the famed Grenadiers of South Carolina. After fighting in many important battles, Charles rose to the rank of major general and was recognized for his distinguished record of military service. Pinckney later served as Minister to France in the Washington administration. He was the Federalist nominee selected to run in a campaign against Jefferson in 1804. Charles and the Federalists ran a minimal campaign. They understood the effort was sure to be futile, given Jefferson's popularity. Charles later changed his allegiance to the Democratic Republican party.

Like Madison, Pinckney was an ardent supporter of religious liberty. He recommended that the following language be included in the Constitution: "The legislature of the United States shall pass no law on the subject of religion." That language was referred to the Committee on Detail but was never adopted. He was, however, able to secure adoption of the following language: "No religious test shall ever be required as a qualification to any office or public trust under the United States." His views regarding religious liberty later gained new life in debates in the First Congress regarding the Bill of Rights.

Pinckney was respected and drew the attention of the delegates when he spoke. His epitaph reads, "One of the founders of the American Republic. In war he was a companion in arms and friend of Washington. In peace he enjoyed his unchanging confidence."[44] Charles was a major slave owner, with about 250 slaves. He gave fifty slaves to a daughter when she married. Pinckney was in the group of Southerners who believed slavery was necessary to maintain the

---

44. See Charles Cotesworth Pinckney, Find A Grave, accessed October 14, 2018, https://www.findagrave.com/memorial/816/charles-cotesworth-pinckney.

economy of that region of the country. In initially defending the lack of a written Bill of Rights in the Constitution, Pinckney observed that a Bill of Rights would declare all men to be free, undercutting slavery as an institution.

The respect of the delegates for Pinckney on other issues, however, insured that his views would be taken seriously. Pinckney's role in the Constitutional Convention was of such significance that many considered him to be the Father of the Constitution. He surely was one of the leading framers. For some unknown reason, Madison's generally copious notes of the Convention failed to include the substance of Pinckney's remarks in support of his plan, offered as a substitute for in the Virginia Plan. Pinckney's plan included twenty-five major points. In many respects, the Pinckney Plan was an elaboration of the Virginia Plan, given concerns regarding the survival of the nation under the Articles of Confederation. Charles, however, strongly differed with Madison regarding the rights of smaller states. The Pinckney Plan included a significant additional provision regarding state power, a precursor to the tenth Amendment: "Each State retains its Rights not expressly delegated."

The stage was set for a vigorous debate regarding the rights of states. Pre-existing disagreement and parochial interests threatened the adoption of any document. Even Madison, who normally was a leading voice for compromise, was caught up in fierce disagreement over the large and small state issue. The small states and advocates of limited changes to the Articles of Confederation were emboldened. They could almost taste victory over those, including Madison, favoring a stronger national government. Without some form of compromise, the Convention was seemingly doomed to failure.

William Paterson of New Jersey offered an alternative to the Virginia Plan that fueled the debate, even though little of Paterson's plan was ultimately adopted. Paterson's plan is generally referred to as the New Jersey Plan or "the small state plan." It proved to be far less influential than the Virginia Plan or the Pinckney Plan.

William Paterson

Paterson had a distinguished military record in the Revolutionary War and went on to practice law. He studied law under Richard Stockton, who was a signer of the Declaration of Independence. William was an influential delegate to the Constitutional Convention and later served with distinction in New Jersey as attorney general and governor. His later national service was also noteworthy. As a senator, he played an instrumental role in the adoption of the

William Paterson

Judiciary Act in the First Congress. George Washington also appointed him to serve as a Justice on the United States Supreme Court, where he served for thirteen years. Paterson aspired to be named Chief Justice of the Supreme Court, but his hopes were dashed when John Marshall received that appointment. Paterson had a serious accident in 1803 and died three years later in 1806.

Paterson and his fellow College of New Jersey alumnus, Madison, may have both been "brothers," members of the Clios during college, but they soon clashed at the convention. Madison favored a stronger national government while Paterson offered a small state proposal, as an alternative to the Virginia Plan. The New Jersey Plan provided for limited modification of the Articles of Confederation, creating only a bit more power in the national government. Paterson's plan largely maintained the status quo of state representation and power (votes were to be allocated evenly among the states, as was the case in the Articles of Confederation).

Paterson did, nevertheless, offer an inkling of a willingness to recognize the supremacy of national power in some areas: "All acts of the United States in Congress made in pursuance of the powers hereby and by the articles of confederation vested in them, and all Treaties made and ratified under the authority of the United States shall be the supreme law of the respective States . . . and the Judiciary of the several States shall be bound thereby in their decisions, anything in the respective laws of the individual States to the contrary notwithstanding."[45]

Debate ensued, and tempers quickly flared regarding the substance of the plans. The stifling heat and humidity of a Philadelphia summer was beginning to take its toll on the delegates. To intensify the physical discomfort, the room was made stuffy by the necessity of closing the windows for the sake of confidentiality. The delegates were also tormented by flies that were common during this season of the year in Philadelphia. The stench of open sewers in the nation's largest city also contributed to making the environment exceedingly unpleasant. It was a setting that made heated disagreement likely.

The large and small state proponents took positions that appeared to be intractable. Madison and the large state contingent, in turn, were unwilling to compromise, asserting that democratic values and the effectiveness of the national government were threatened by principles articulated in the New Jersey Plan. Paterson and his allies were adamant that smaller states needed additional power to avoid being overwhelmed and left powerless by the control of the larger states. Paterson and supporters of his plan demanded that the interests of the small states not be made subservient to the special interests of the larger states. Strong allegiances to state governments, coupled with fear of a strong national government, persisted among many delegates. Paterson's Plan helped frame the debate but few of its provisions ultimately became part of the final Constitution.

On June 18, matters were complicated further. A disgruntled Alexander Hamilton offered what is known as the British plan, envisioning a system of government like that found in Britain. The British form of government appealed to Hamilton, a leader in the Federalist and nationalist cause. Hamilton's plan called for a governor who was to hold powers that, although not necessarily hereditary, were clearly akin to those held by the king:

"The supreme Executive authority of the United States to be vested in a Governor to be elected to serve during good behavior—the

---

45. "The New Jersey Plan," Constitutional Convention, June 15, 1787, U.S. Constitution, accessed October 14, 2018, https://usconstitution.net/plan_nj.html.

election to be made by Electors chosen by the people in the Election Districts aforesaid. The authorities and functions of the Executive to be as follows: to have a negative on all laws about to be passed, and the execution of all laws passed, to have the direction of war when authorized or begun; to have with the advice and approbation of the Senate the power of making all treaties; to have the sole appointment of the heads or chief officers of the departments of Finance, War and Foreign Affairs; to have the nomination of all other officers (Ambassadors to foreign Nations included) subject to the approbation or rejection of the Senate; to have the power of pardoning all offenses except Treason; which he shall not pardon without the approbation of the Senate."[46]

Not surprisingly, the Hamilton Plan did not muster much support. Nevertheless, raising the specter of a British form of government—with a powerful executive—served to increase the palpable tension that filled the hall. Seemingly interminable debates wore on with rising rancor on both sides and with little movement toward compromise. The delegates managed to reach agreement on some lesser points, but the issue of how to handle the allocation power between the large and small states persisted and threatened the success of the convention.

The Convention Reaches a Low Point

Madison and many others were exceedingly fearful that their efforts to secure a more stable union were failing. It was at this dark time, late in June, after a two-day rambling and uninspiring monologue by Luther Martin of Delaware, that Benjamin Franklin offered his stirring reminder of the need to seek providential assistance in the form of prayer. As noted previously, his proposal was never voted on, but it reminded the delegates of the gravity of the task before them and of the need to put aside personal differences for the good of the union.

---

46. Constitutional Convention, Plan of Government, [18 June 1787], Founders Online (National Archives), accessed October 14, 2018, https://founders.archives.gov/documents /Hamilton/01-04-02-0099.

Despite Franklin's reminder, a few more days passed without much forward momentum.

Indeed, by June 30, the Convention reached what may have been its lowest point, when Gunning Bedford of Delaware demeaned his colleagues representing large states by questioning not just their policy preferences but also their integrity. Bedford exclaimed, with stinging vitriol, "We have been told with a dictatorial air that this is the last moment for a fair trial in favor of a Good Governmt. It will be the last indeed if the propositions reported from the Committee go forth to the people."[47] However offensive Bedford's comment was, it was another reminder of the importance and difficulty of agreeing on some form of compromise and of the need for humility. Through the Fourth of July holiday, reminded, as Franklin hoped they would be, of the sacrifices associated with the revolutionary cause, delegates began to put petty differences aside to work on a compromise. Persistence and perhaps much silent prayer was beginning to pay off. By July 16, 1787, a pivotal point in the work of the delegates, the momentum was swinging back in favor of dialogue and compromise of conflicting values.

The delegates had completed much of the easier lifting. One major issue remained unresolved: whether representation should be based on population, elected democratically based on one-person-one-vote, or simply be allocated equally by state. Delegates from the small states were insistent that all states be equally represented in both houses. The large states were equally inflexible, demanding that they should have greater representation than the small states in both houses. Proponents of the large states argued that, given their size, they would necessarily provide more of the resources required to run the government than the smaller states. This concern was a version of the no taxation without full representation argument that helped spawn the revolution. Some also argued that yielding to the small states' desires would dilute the votes of citizens in larger states and thereby violate democratic principles and the right of self-governance.

---

47. *James Madison's Notes of the Constitutional Convention* (June 30, 1787), ConSource, accessed October 14, 2018, https://www.consource.org/document/james-madisons-notes-of -the-constitutional-convention-1787-6-30/.

Two delegates from Connecticut, Roger Sherman and Oliver Ellsworth, stepped forward with an idea—a great compromise—that ultimately saved the day and the Constitution.

Roger Sherman

Roger Sherman was a senior statesman, who had earned the respect of other delegates with a life of committed service to his nation. Sherman was a self-made man, a living symbol of America as a land of opportunity. He was born to a poorer farming family in Massachusetts. In an effort to provide additional family income, Roger's father, William, worked as a cobbler, mending shoes. Roger also learned the cobbler's trade. He earnestly sought to gain an education

Roger Sherman

by personal study, while working on the farm and as a cobbler. After his father's death, Sherman moved with his brother to Connecticut, where he purchased a store and became involved in local politics. While serving in a variety of public capacities, Roger decided to read the law and become a lawyer, eventually serving as a judge. Sherman served for almost a decade in the Continental Congress. He earned the respect of other members, which led to his selection as a member of the committee tasked with drafting a Declaration of Independence, which he signed when it was completed.

Sherman's public service and the demands of raising a large family contributed to periodic economic setbacks. He was on the verge of insolvency when he was selected to serve as a delegate to the Constitutional Convention, representing Connecticut. He was a Federalist known for supporting efforts to strengthen the national government. Nevertheless, Sherman understood the concerns of those favoring greater state representation in the new government. It is believed that he helped Paterson draft the New Jersey Plan.

Sherman's commitment to strengthening the national government coupled with his understanding of the interests of smaller states uniquely qualified him to make what was probably his greatest act of public service—development of the Great Compromise that satisfied a majority of large and small state advocates at the convention. Sherman later fittingly served in the House of Representatives and the Senate, two bodies that he had helped design.

Oliver Ellsworth

Oliver Ellsworth was born in Windsor, Connecticut, to David and Jerusha Ellsworth. Raised in Connecticut, Oliver commenced his higher education at Yale. After a year at Yale, he transferred to the College of New Jersey, where he studied theology and was a founding or early member of the Cliosophic Society, with William Paterson, James Madison, and Aaron Burr. As a fellow Clio, he had strong personal ties to Madison, a leader who

Oliver Ellsworth

favored a stronger national government, and Paterson, the leading proponent of the small states. Madison, Paterson, and Ellsworth disagreed on major issues, but they largely trusted each other and shared a strong commitment to the cause of the new nation.

Like Madison and Bradford after him, upon graduation from the College of New Jersey, Ellsworth wrestled to discover what occupation best suited his talents and temperament. He decided to become a lawyer and, with time, developed a thriving practice. In 1772, he married Abigail Wolcott Ellsworth, with whom he had nine children. Many of the Ellsworth children made major contributions to the new nation, serving publicly and in business. Their son, William, served in the House of Representatives and as Governor of Connecticut, while another son, Henry, became the Commissioner of the Patent Office and president of the Aetna Life Insurance Company.

Ellsworth was selected to serve in the Continental Congress in 1777. He served with distinction, while also serving in a variety of legal capacities. Together with James Wilson, he was selected to serve on the Committee of Detail that prepared the first draft of the Constitution, as finally agreed to by delegates of large and small states. He left in August before the Constitution was formally signed, but he remained a strong supporter of the Constitution and a leader in the ratification effort in Connecticut. He also played a significant role in the subsequent adoption and ratification of the Bill of Rights.

Ellsworth favored a strong national government, but he was also sensitive to the interests of small states. That sensitivity helped make Sherman and Ellsworth able proponents of the "Great Compromise." Oliver is also credited with suggesting the name for the nation conceived under the Constitution—"the United States of America." While serving in the Senate, he joined Madison in supporting the Judiciary Act and was a major sponsor of the Bill of Rights in the Senate. He served effectively on the conference committee that ironed out the final version. He later served as the second Chief Justice of the United States, following John Jay.

Sherman and Ellsworth were the primary architects of what would come to be known as the Connecticut or Great Compromise. They recommended a system of dual representation, with members of the House being assigned seats in proportion to population. Members of the Senate, on the other hand, were assigned in equal numbers to each of the states, giving the small states equal representation in the Senate. Delegates from large states vigorously opposed "equal representation" on the part of the states in the Senate, preferring that members of the House and the Senate be directly elected by popular or majority vote.

Popular Election

Madison was one of the strongest proponents of popular election of members of both houses. In one of his most significant pieces of advocacy during the Convention, Madison argued for popular representation, noting that it was a clear principle in any free government. In support of this principle, Madison offered an argument that was central to his thinking and became a part of the genius of the new republic. Madison endeavored to respond to small state concerns regarding possible tyranny by the majority at the national level and a consequent diminution of state power. James argued that potential tyranny by a majority at the national level was ameliorated by enlarging "the sphere [of representation], thereby [dividing] the community into so great a number of interests and parties, that in the first place a majority will not be likely at the same moment to have a common interest separate from that of the whole or the minority; and in [the case that] they should have such an interest, they might not be apt to unite in pursuit of it."[48] It was, in Madison's words, "incumbent [that the delegates] try this remedy . . . with a view to frame a republican system on such a scale and in such a form as will control all evils which have been [heretofore] experienced."[49]

Madison sincerely believed that the small states had nothing to fear from a national government that was based on population and not on equal representation for the states. He also worried that powerful groups in smaller states would persist in threatening minorities at the state and the national levels. Madison's belief that the large states would not support such a system of dual representation proved incorrect. On July 16, 1787, the delegates voted by a single vote, the slimmest of majorities, to support the great compromise offered by Ellsworth and Sherman.

The battle over representation was not quite over, however. Members of the larger and some smaller states, perhaps led by Madison, met on the morning of July 16, 1787, to determine what could be done to revive full commitment to popular representation. In his notes, with an uncharacteristic air of exasperation, Madison noted, "The time was wasted in vague conversation on the subject, without any specific proposition or agreement. It appeared indeed that the opinions of the members who disliked the equality of votes differed so much as to the

---

48. James Madison, "Notes on the Convention," June 6, 1787, The Avalon Project (Yale Law School), accessed October 9, 2018, http://avalon.law.yale.edu/18th_century/debates_606.asp.
49. Ibid.

importance of that point, and as to the policy of risking a failure of any general act of the Convention, by inflexibly opposing it."[50] Several attendees, including Madison, believed that, "no good Govern[ment] could or would be built on that foundation, and that as a division of the Convention into two opinions was unavoidable; it would be better that the side comprising the principal States, and a majority of the people of America, should propose a scheme of Gov[ernment] to the States."[51] Other delegates present at this morning meeting "seemed inclined to yield to the smaller States, and to concur in such an act however imperfect & exceptionable, as might be agreed on by the Convention as a body, tho[ugh] decided by a bare majority of States and by a minority of the people of the U. States."[52]

A week later, on Monday, July 23, proponents of popular representation, including Madison, made one last effort to preserve the principle of popular representation. Delegates King and Morris moved that senators be permitted to vote individually and not as a block. The Congress under the Articles of Confederation had required voting by block. The King and Morris motion passed. This appealed to Madison, who believed that senators could then vote their individual consciences rather than being forced to vote as a block. This motion may have helped persuade Madison ultimately to support the great compromise, as contained in the Constitution.

The Committee of Detail and the Committee of Style

On July 24, the Committee of Detail was given the task of putting the various provisions that had been debated and adopted into a single, coherent document. That proved to be a challenging task. It also presented an opportunity to change some of the provisions. One development in that committee is particularly worthy of note. As a delegate

---

50. J. Madison, Notes on the Constitution, July 16, 1787, Addendum, The Avalon Project (Yale Law School), accessed October 9, 2018, http://avalon.law.yale.edu/18th_century /debates_716.asp.
51. Ibid.
52. Ibid.

from the large state of Pennsylvania, James Wilson, a powerful voice in the committee and the convention, strengthened the national government by adding the "necessary and proper" and "supremacy" clauses.

The necessary and proper clause modified the national government's enumerated powers, permitting the government to do whatever was necessary and proper to effectuate the enumerated powers. This clause has been interpreted as providing the national government with extensive power. The supremacy clause made the Constitution the supreme law of the land, providing the national government with final constitutional authority. These additions helped create a balance between the national and state governments that became part of the final document.

The convention did, nevertheless, retain dual-sovereignty between nation and state as recommended by Rutledge and Wilson. The Committee of Detail's final draft became the first actual draft of the Constitution, an amalgam of the various points agreed to over the course of the Convention. Madison was not on the committee, which adds to the case that he is not really the primary draftsman of the Constitution, even though his Virginia Plan helped focus the early discussion in the Convention and his comments were influential in providing substance to the Constitution. The Committee of Detail was the most powerful committee in the Convention and continued to meet after submitting their final draft.

On September 8, 1787, the Committee of Style, with different members than the Committee on Detail, was formed and charged with refining the actual text of the Constitution, to make it consistent as a matter of style. Gouverneur Morris chaired that committee, which put the final touches on the Constitution, causing Madison to note that the Constitution, in its final form, was primarily the stylistic work of Gouverneur Morris. The question of who deserves credit for drafting the Constitution is really resolved only by recognizing that it was a collaborative endeavor, a negotiation and collection of ideas and compromises made by delegates who were able, for a brief moment in history, to put most of their personal or provincial views aside and counsel together to form a more perfect union.

As evidenced by his skill in writing, Morris was well educated, a graduate of King's College, like Hamilton. Morris offered lengthy comments during deliberations at the convention, speaking more than any other delegate. His comments were often as lengthy as they were numerous. Thankfully, his style in drafting the Constitution did not evidence any such excess. Indeed, his skill in drafting led Hamilton to invite him to join in participating in the drafting of the *Federalist Papers*, a series of essays supporting the Constitution, but Morris declined. In fact, Morris played little role in the ratification process. Nevertheless, his penning of the final draft of the Constitution, which included a moving preamble that has been recited by school children in the United States for generations, merits acclaim. Despite his willingness to credit others, Madison's accolades of Morris were warranted, even though it is evident that Madison also played a major role in drafting the convention's final document—the Constitution—given his role in drafting the Virginia Plan, the first document discussed at the convention.

The Committee of Detail had to decide the way the Constitution would be ratified by the states. Some delegates argued that the state legislatures should act as the ratifying body. Other delegates believed that delegates representing the states should serve as state ratifying conventions. Madison argued in support of the latter view. He began by noting that the changes in the form of government included in the Constitution would "make essential inroads on the State Constitutions, and it would be a novel & dangerous doctrine that a Legislature could change the constitution under which it held its existence. There might indeed be some Constitutions within the Union, which had given a power to the Legislature to concur in alterations of the federal Compact. But there were certainly some which had not; and in the case of these, a ratification must of necessity be obtained from the people."[53] In an elaboration of this argument, Madison "considered the difference between a system founded on the Legislatures only, and one founded on the people, to be the true difference between a league

---

53. Method of Ratifying the Constitution, [23 July] 1787, Founders Online (National Archives), accessed October 9, 2018, https://founders.archives.gov/documents/Madison/01 -10-02-0070.

or treaty, and a Constitution."[54] He concluded, "all the considerations which recommended this Convention in preference to Congress for proposing the reform were in favor of State Conventions in preference to the Legislatures for examining and adopting it."[55]

Madison's argument prevailed, and the Constitution was submitted to state ratifying conventions, not state legislatures or assemblies. Given their provincial interests, Madison wisely understood that state legislative bodies were highly politicized and unwilling to act against present interests to achieve a greater good. In short, delegates to a state ratifying convention would be more inclined to act according to conscience. Morris and other delegates, including Madison, had served in state legislative assemblies and had observed firsthand the effectiveness of conventions as opposed to legislative bodies in acting for the collective good. This decision was providential for two reasons. First, it is unlikely that the state assemblies would have voted to support the Constitution given opposition to the Constitution based on provincial, statewide interests. Second, Madison was elected to serve in the state ratifying convention, but he would not have been selected at the state legislative level, where opponents of the Constitution, including Patrick Henry, were in power and vigorously opposed Madison.

The final document was an imperfect, yet miraculous, amalgam of major compromises. Madison and the large state proponents were forced to compromise, but so were the small states. Indeed, advocates of a variety of strongly held opinions were willing to yield their private interests to a greater common good. The final task left to the delegates was signing the document.

On September 17, 1787, the final draft of the Constitution was presented to the delegates. At this momentous time, as a final vote neared, James Wilson read words written by the convention's senior statesman, Benjamin Franklin, who moved adoption of the Constitution. Franklin openly and humbly confessed that "there are several parts of this constitution which I do not at present approve, but I am not sure I shall never approve them: For having lived long, I have experienced many instances of being obliged by better information, or fuller

---

54. Ibid.
55. Ibid.

consideration, to change opinions even on important subjects, which I once thought right, but found to be otherwise."[56] He added, "The older I grow, the more apt I am to doubt my own judgment, and to pay more respect to the judgment of others."[57] Franklin reflected further, "When you assemble a number of men to have the advantage of their joint wisdom, you inevitably assemble with those men, all their prejudices, their passions, their errors of opinion, their local interests, and their selfish views. From such an assembly can a perfect production be expected?"[58] Answering his own question, Franklin alluded to the Tower of Babel and declared that it "astonishes me, Sir (referring to General Washington, who presided over the Convention), to find this system approaching so near to perfection as it does; and I think it will astonish our enemies, who are waiting with confidence to hear that our councils are confounded like those of the Builders of Babel; and that our States are on the point of separation, only to meet hereafter for the purpose of cutting one another's throats. Thus I consent, Sir, to this Constitution because I expect no better, and because I am not sure, that it is not the best."[59] With that, the wise statesman concluded, "On the whole, Sir, I cannot help expressing a wish that every member of the Convention who may still have objections to it, would with me, on this occasion doubt a little of his own infallibility, and to make manifest our unanimity, put his name to this instrument." With that, Franklin offered the following formal motion: "Done in Convention by the unanimous consent of the States present the 17th of September 1787. In Witness whereof we have hereunto subscribed our names."[60] The response was not unanimous, as Franklin had hoped, but the vote for the adoption of the Constitution was substantial.

As Madison signed the Constitution, Franklin's words pulled anew on his heartstrings and pricked his conscience. He was surely struck by Franklin's statements regarding "fallibility" and his assessment that the Constitution was the best imaginable under the circumstances,

---

56. J. Madison, *Notes on the Convention*, September 17, 1787, U.S. Constitution, accessed October 9, 2018, https://www.usconstitution.net/franklin.html.

57. Ibid.

58. Ibid.

59. Ibid.

60. Ibid.

a veritable miracle. Throughout the convention James Madison had joined others in falling prey to his biases, failing to weigh competing values and becoming a party to near-fatal disagreements. He had learned much about humility and was coming to better understand his own fallibility and the need for compromise between competing values, two keys to learning and wisdom that helped shape his own career as a statesman. Like Franklin, Madison knew that the Constitution was imperfect, failing to deal with major issues, but he was also painfully aware that it was the best that could be hoped for at the hands of the mortal men who shaped the document.

Three-Fifths Compromise

The failure to resolve the slavery issue would hang over the nation, but that failure is understandable, if not fully forgivable. In July, to get the votes necessary to support the Connecticut or Great Compromise, it was necessary to obtain votes from the small states, most of which were in the south. Many of the delegates came to support the three-fifths compromise, which was fashioned to placate the smaller southern states. The southern states demanded that slaves be counted for electoral purposes, even though they could not vote. In one of the major compromises agreed to during the convention, a majority of the delegates agree that slaves should be treated as three-fifths of a person for the purposes of determining the number of representatives in the House of Representatives, the popularly elected branch of government, even though they were not permitted to vote and remained enslaved. This maybe helped legitimize slavery. Without this compromise, however, it is likely that the convention would have remained deadlocked.

The slavery issue proved to be intractable, even though many delegates opposed it as a wicked or abominable institution. On June 6, 1787, early in the convention, Madison argued a theme he would return to regularly—that liberty can best be protected by a government large enough to prevent any particular sect from securing power and tyrannizing minority sects or groups. He reflected that even "conscience . . . is known to be inadequate in individuals; in large numbers, little is to be expected from it. Besides, religion itself may become a motive to persecution and oppression."[61] For Madison, the highest form of conscience was that conscience which is driven by a duty to God. With clear disappointment, he concluded that not even conscience, the right he treasured over all others, was enough to secure liberty in a world filled with imperfect human beings, in a world that had long embraced slavery. In his remarks on June 5, Madison concluded by using slavery as an illustration of the inadequacy of even conscience, the greatest power for good, in resolving all issues of grave importance at a given point in time. Sadly, he reflected, "We have seen the mere distinction of color made, in the most enlightened period of time, a ground of the most oppressive dominion ever exercised by man over man."[62]

Counting slaves as three-fifths of a person to secure the votes of delegates from the smaller southern states became a critical piece of the grand, yet imperfect, compromise. Slavery was vehemently argued in the convention, particularly during the month of August, when the Committee on the Slave Trade presented its proposal that would prohibit interference with the slave trade until 1800. The provision was later amended to extend the period until 1808.

On August 25, Madison stood to argue for a shorter term and offered his opposition the slave importation provision stating, "Twenty years will produce all the mischief that can be apprehended from the liberty to import slaves. So long a term will be more dishonorable to the National character than to say nothing about it in the Constitution."[63] In short, Madison believed that the convention should do nothing to prohibit the national government from dealing with or prohibiting slavery. Madison believed that the national government would rise above the influence of the slave states and find a means of freeing the slaves and compensating the slave owners. The 1808 clause was, therefore, reprehensible to Madison, who legitimately feared that the momentum gained in the convention would be lost as the slave trade continued.

---

61. J. Madison, Notes on the Convention, June 6, 1787, The Avalon Project (Yale Law School), accessed October 9, 2018, http://avalon.law.yale.edu/18th_century/debates_606.asp.

62. Ibid.

63. J. Madison, *Notes on the Convention*, August 25, 1787, The Avalon Project (Yale Law School), accessed October 9, 2018, http://avalon.law.yale.edu/18th_century/debates_825.asp.

Madison's fellow Virginian, George Mason, was more emphatic. On August 22, 1787, Mason fumed that the "infernal traffic [in slaves] originated in the avarice of British merchants [who] constantly checked the attempts of Virginia to put a stop to it."[64] Mason referred prudentially to the great costs to the entire nation related to insurrection on the part of slaves and then turned moralistic in arguing that, "Every master of slaves is born a petty tyrant. They bring the judgment of heaven on a Country."[65] He lamented, "As nations cannot be rewarded or punished in the next world they must be in this. By an inevitable chain of causes & effects providence punishes national sins, by national calamities."[66] Mason concluded that it was "essential in every point of view that the General Government should have power to prevent the increase of slavery."[67] Mason was a more prophetic and powerful voice than Madison in opposing the 1808 slave trade clause. They both shared the belief that a new national government would find a way to eliminate slavery, rising above petty regional interests and powerful voices fueled by economic self-interests tied to the slave trade, but Madison was not willing to jettison the entire Constitution to eliminate the abomination of slavery. He reluctantly agreed to the compromise, while Mason did not.

As it turned out, the 1808 slave trade and the three-fifths clauses were, indeed, necessary to maintain the slim and ever-fragile majority of delegates necessary to secure adoption of the Constitution in the convention. Some anti-slavery delegates, including Madison, nevertheless, harbored a hope that the 1808 clause might portend the end of slavery, if not too much "mischief" was done in the interim. Madison and others were saddened by the failure of the convention to deal with slavery, but they refused to give up hope. Having been part of one miracle, the miracle of adoption of a Constitution against seemingly insurmountable odds, Madison remained convinced that right would peaceably prevail and the most "oppressive dominion ever exercised by man over man" would be ended. In the end, opponents of slavery,

---

64. J. Madison, Notes on the Constitution, August 22, 1787, The Avalon Project (Yale Law School), accessed October 9, 2018, http://avalon.law.yale.edu/18th_century/debates_822.asp.
65. Ibid.
66. Ibid.
67. Ibid.

including Madison, had to content themselves with two limited victories: (1) slaves were being recognized, at least in part, as persons, and (2) the delegates had given the national government the power to address the slavery issue by ending or limiting the slave trade, and perhaps slavery itself, within two decades.

The delegates fell grievously short on the issue of slavery. It was their greatest failure, but without it the Constitution would never have been adopted, given the strong sentiments regarding slavery in the southern and even some of the northern states. The economic interests of the southern states tied to slavery, coupled with the unwillingness of the northern states to assist in finding a way to compensate slave owners and provide reparations to the slaves, doomed efforts to end slavery at the convention to failure. The failure to address slavery ultimately led the new nation to a brutal and bloody Civil War. The losses incurred in the bloodiest war in the history of the United States were a high cost to pay for failing to address slavery.

Despite the evident imperfections in the Constitution, James Madison, who seldom was effusive, offered the following assessment of supporters of the Constitution in the preface to his notes on the Constitutional Convention: "There never was an assembly of men, charged with a great and arduous trust, who were more pure in their motives, or more exclusively or anxiously devoted to the object committed to them."[68] He later added, "The happy Union of these states is a wonder; their Constitution a miracle, their example the hope of liberty throughout the world."[69]

Elbridge Gerry

Not all the delegates supported the final document. Thirteen delegates left before the signing, and many of them returned home to warn people and to begin preparations to oppose the ratification of the Constitution. Others remained but refused to sign the final document.

---

68. J. Madison, Preface to Debates in the Convention, Constitution Society, accessed October 9, 2018, http://www.constitution.org/dfc/dfc_0001.htm.

69. James Madison, Outline, September 1829, The Founders' Constitution (University of Chicago), accessed October 9, 2018, http://press-pubs.uchicago.edu/founders/documents/v1ch7s27.html.

Two distinguished delegates from Virginia, George Mason and Edmund Randolph, joined with Elbridge Gerry of Massachusetts in refusing to sign the Constitution.

Elbridge Gerry

Gerry, who had an aristocratic air, was an active participant in the proceedings of the Convention. He chaired the committee that drafted the Great Compromise, which he ultimately opposed. Nevertheless, even though he was a vocal participant in the Constitutional Convention, Gerry objected to the final document. Gerry believed the final product, the Constitution as adopted, to be full of vices, including unequal representation and ill-defined and potentially excessive legislative and judicial power. He became a leader in the effort to oppose ratification in Massachusetts, unless the Constitution was amended in significant ways. Gerry also typified the pro-amendment forces, arguing for addition of a Bill of Rights and modification of many other provisions. Having already reached many compromises, members of the convention were resistant to efforts to add a Bill of Rights. Some believed it to be unnecessary and almost all believed that drafting such a Bill or Declaration of Rights would be difficult, given the major differences in existing declarations of rights at the state level. Despite Gerry's persistent opposition, the Constitution was adopted by the delegates.

Religious Liberty in Constitution

At this point, it is important to note that the Constitutional Convention of 1787 was characterized by the general absence of discussions regarding religious liberty. Only one clause involving religion appeared in the final draft of the Constitution. The "no religious test" provision was supported by Madison and was added to the Constitution in part at the insistence of minority religious groups. It provides that "no religious Test shall ever be required as a Qualification to any Office of public Trust under the United States."

Participants at the convention did on occasion seek to include references to religion in the Constitution. One effort initiated by Charles Pinckney and James Madison, two strong advocates of the right of conscience, proposed a national university "in which no preference or distinction should be allowed on account of religion." This "no preference" language was clearly reminiscent of Madison's earlier work in Virginia and was reflected in his subsequent understanding of the establishment limitation in the Bill of Rights. While this provision for a national university, without religious preference or distinction, found some support among influential delegates to the convention, including Gouverneur Morris and James Wilson, it was defeated. The proposal failed ultimately because of indifference to the idea of creating and funding a national university, not because it included the "no preference" language. It was an idea Madison continued to propose throughout his lifetime.

Pinckney also advocated what he believed to be a guarantee of religious liberty. He proposed addition of a provision stating that "the legislature of the United States shall pass no law on the subject of religion." This proposal was referred to the Committee on Detail at the Convention, where it languished and ultimately died for lack of support. Madison saw no need to include a provision like this in the Constitution. He went so far as to oppose adding a more complete Bill or Declaration of Rights. Madison claimed that the government had no legitimate right to interfere with an individual's inalienable right to religious liberty. Such a right or privilege was, by its nature, immune from the government action. In Madison's opinion, there was no reason to include a specific provision securing religious liberty, because the right of conscience and all other inalienable rights were properly beyond the reach of any legitimate or just government regulation. Perhaps based on his experience in dealing with the Virginia Declaration of Rights, Madison also feared that efforts to enumerate a right of religious conscience would lead to a pernicious result. Given weaknesses in expression and the proclivity of government to limit rights, adoption of language designed to protect the right of conscience might be read restrictively. He feared that placing such a right in the form of general language would imply that government had the capacity to create or limit a right that he believed to be inalienable, a natural right beyond the reach of any just government.

There were a few other efforts to bring religious matters before the delegates. Benjamin Franklin's effort to institute prayer is one such example. As previously noted, while the failure of Franklin's motion seems to imply an aversion to religious exercise in the public square, it is largely conceded that no such antipathy existed. The framers were overwhelmingly religious, men of faith.

There was another effort made to raise a religious issue at the convention. Isaac Backus was a Baptist who had gained significant notoriety for having refused to pay five dollars in tax for the support of the Congregationalist Church in Massachusetts. He argued before the delegates that a provision should be added to protect religious freedom. He sought protection against potential taxation demands of a state church. Madison certainly was inclined to support such a proposal, as he had done in Virginia, but he remained fearful that the placement of such a provision into words might provide for the limitation and not the protection of that right. Even though Backus's recommendation did not lead to the inclusion of a provision securing the right of conscience in the Constitution, it is unlikely that such inactivity in any way implied opposition to the proposal on the part of Madison or most of the delegates.

There are many possible reasons for the refusal of the delegates to include a provision for religious liberty in the Constitution. Perhaps the weakest of these proffered reasons was Hamilton's assertion that the delegates merely forgot to do so in their efforts to deal with weightier matters. This is a view that Madison clearly did not share, based on his previous efforts to do all that he could to secure such a right in Virginia. The ends of a continuum representing the views held by the delegates regarding reasons for not including a provision securing the right of conscience are largely represented by the Hamilton and Madison views. Hamilton believed that religious liberty was not important enough to be included in the Constitution and further feared that the effort to include it might become divisive, derailing the effort to adopt the Constitution. Madison, in turn, believed that religious liberty or conscience was so important that efforts to include it would be more likely to limit it and might even imply that the right was given by government as a privilege and not by God, as a natural right. In the middle of the continuum are a significant number of delegates who believed the Constitution was appropriately silent as to the issue of national power regarding religious matters. For that group, the power in government to regulate these activities, if any, remained solely with the states. For them it was a states' rights issue, and they believed that the states were protecting the right.

It must also be emphasized that Madison clearly felt he and the other delegates had done the single most effective thing necessary to secure the right of conscience by creating an enlarged national government of enumerated powers. In a larger national government, in which no religious group could predominate and become tyrannical, he believed that persecution of individual religious minorities would be less likely, given that no sect could retain a majority at the national level. For Madison, those structural protections were much more effective than "parchment barriers" (words) in keeping the right of conscience beyond the reach of government. As a capable wordsmith, Madison also knew that language could easily be manipulated or interpreted to constrain rather than secure rights, and he feared that some would believe that a grant of such a right might imply that government retained the right to limit it.

Having earned the respect of his fellow delegates, Madison was given responsibility for transmitting the Constitution and a letter to the Continental Congress. The letter noted that, "The Constitution, which we now present, is the result of a spirit of amity, and of mutual deference and concession which the peculiarity of our political situation rendered indispensable."[70] Madison surely hoped a similar "spirit of amity" would prevail in the ratification debates. Nevertheless, he was practical enough to know that this was unlikely and was surely gratified

---

70. The letter presenting the Constitution, September 17, 2018, American History, accessed October 9, 2018, http://www.let.rug.nl/usa/documents/1786-1800/the-letter-presenting-the-constitution.php.

when, on September 28, 1787, the Continental Congress unanimously resolved that the Constitution should be transmitted to the several legislatures and calling for a convention of Delegates to be chosen in each state by the people. Much had been accomplished, but perhaps the most significant obstacle of all remained—ratification by the states.

An Exhausted Delegate Facing an Unclear Future

The fact that two prominent Virginians refused to sign the Constitution signaled an uphill battle in Virginia and other states to ratify the Constitution. While the delegates toiled in secrecy in Philadelphia, opponents of the Constitution were working openly and with great earnestness to ensure that the proposed Constitution never be ratified. In Virginia, Patrick Henry, a force to be reckoned with, was actively marshalling forces in opposition to the Constitution.

Madison was exhausted when he returned home. He was weakened by long days in the various meetings associated with the Convention and hours of work at night by candlelight. He also had a trying journey home. He had earned a respite, but the welcome home for Madison was more of an invitation to renewed labor than a reason for celebrating the fruits of his efforts and the efforts of the delegates, who had often ignored self-interest to salvage what they viewed to be the crumbling fabric of the national government under the Articles of Confederation. A ratification battle loomed—a battle that would soon require the best Madison and others had to offer. The fate of the Constitution once again hung in the balance.

Opposition was broad, stretching across the thirteen states of the Confederation, and deep, extending into strong insular interests and prejudices peculiar to the various states.

Chapter Five

Ratification of the Constitution

*"Miracles are a retelling in small letters of the very
same story which is written across the whole world
in letters too large for some of us to see."*[1]

C. S. Lewis

*"The happy Union of these States is a wonder; their Constitution a
miracle; their example the hope of Liberty throughout the world."*[2]

James Madison

Madison and the other delegates who had signed the Constitution returned home to face another monumental challenge—securing the ratification of the Constitution in an increasingly skeptical political climate. Without ratification, the Constitution would be of no legal force. The delegates in Philadelphia provided a special process for ratification under Article VII of the proposed Constitution. This ratification process differed from the process already in place for amending the Articles of Confederation. Amendment of the Articles of Confederation required that *all* states agree to any change. Article VII of the Constitution set forth the requirements for ratification: "The Ratification of the Conventions of nine States, shall be sufficient for the Establishment of this Constitution

---

1. C. S. Lewis, *God in the Dock* (Grand Rapids: Wm. B. Eerdmans, 2014), 13.
2. James Madison, Outline, September 1829, The Founders' Constitution (University of Chicago), accessed October 9, 2018, http://press-pubs.uchicago.edu/founders/documents /v1ch7s27.html.

between the States so ratifying the Same." Thus, nine of the thirteen states (slightly less than 70 percent), through ratifying conventions, were required to ratify the Constitution before it became the supreme law of the land. The specially designed Article VII ratification process, for final approval of the Constitution, also differs from the amendment process in the Constitution itself. Article V applies to amendments to the Constitution and requires ratification by three-fourths (75 percent) of the states for an amendment to become the law of the land.

Securing the approval of only nine of the thirteen state ratifying conventions, without amendment, was easier than obtaining unanimous agreement as required under the Articles of Confederation. It was also easier than ratification of an amendment under Article V of the Constitution. But the true picture was much bleaker. Rhode Island had refused to send delegates to convention and could be counted on to oppose ratification. John Lansing and Robert Yates, delegates from New York, had joined forces with Governor George Clinton in opposing the Constitution in their home state. There was also substantial fear that North Carolina and South Carolina might not ratify, because of continuing concerns regarding the slavery issue—the prevailing sentiment in those states seemed to be that the Constitution, as adopted, did not do enough to secure the "institution of slavery." Indeed, their fear was Madison's hope—that the Constitution was a first step toward dismantling slavery.

It was even unclear whether Madison's home state of Virginia would ratify the Constitution as adopted in Philadelphia. Opposition was growing. That opposition initially included powerful opponents and was led by Patrick Henry. George Mason, and John Randolph were influential Virginia delegates who had refused to sign the Constitution. They were counted among those who were likely to provide powerful opposition to efforts to ratify the Constitution in Virginia. Randolph later changed his mind and came to support ratification, but George Mason maintained his vigorous opposition, perhaps due to a perceived slight or act of disrespect he experienced during the convention.

George Mason shared his objections to the Constitution in written form. In that document, Mason argued, "There is no Declaration of Rights, and the laws of the general government being paramount to the laws and constitution of the several States, the Declarations of Rights in the separate States are no security. Nor are the people secured even in the enjoyment of the benefit of the common law."[3] He also attacked the three branches of government and added his fear that the enumerated powers of the government were effectively boundless due to the necessary and proper clause. He concluded his attack by noting, "[The government under the new Constitution] will set out a moderate aristocracy: it is at present impossible to foresee whether it will, in its operation, produce a monarchy, or a corrupt, tyrannical aristocracy; it will most probably vibrate some years between the two, and then terminate in the one or the other."[4] Mason also believed he was personally mistreated in the concluding days of the convention, when the decision was made to permit voting by states in the ratification process. Mason wanted to offer a formal dissent but was prevented from doing so. He later wrote Thomas Jefferson that he was discouraged from dissenting "by the precipitate & intemperate, not to say indecent Manner in which the Business was conducted during the last week of the Convention, after the Patrons of the new plan found they had a decided majority in their favor."[5] Smarting under what he perceived to be a personal slight, Mason proceeded to attack the proponents of ratification of the Constitution personally.

In a stump speech supporting his own candidacy, Mason railed against the delegates who supported the Constitution as adopted,, arguing that the delegates to the convention were at best vain and conceited and at worst fools. Mason soon allied with another prominent Virginian, Patrick Henry, in arguing against ratifying the Constitution and in indulging in personal attacks directed against those who favored ratification.

Patrick Henry became the leader of the Anti-Federalist effort to prevent ratification of the Constitution in Virginia. Henry was the first governor of the Commonwealth of Virginia and was legendary for

---

3. "George Mason's Objections to the Constitution," November 22, 1787, Constitution Society, accessed October 10, 2018, http://constitution.org/gmason/objections.html.
4. Ibid.
5. Letter to Thomas Jefferson from George Mason, 26 May 1788, Founders Online (National Archives), accessed October 10, 2018, https://founders.archives.gov/documents /Jefferson/01-13-02-0117.

his moving rhetoric and capacity to persuade. Spencer Roane, a judge and member of the House of Delegates, described Patrick Henry's eloquence as follows, "I myself have heard some Touches of Eloquence which would almost disgrace Cicero or Demosthenes."[6] The historian, Gordon S. Wood, put it this way, "Like the evangelical preachers he listened to as a youth, Henry was the master of the oral culture in which most ordinary people lived."[7] Wood adds, ""To . . . Henry fancy words and learned citations no longer mattered as much as honesty and sincerity and the natural revelation of feeling."[8] Patrick Henry proved to be a tenacious rival to any who stood in the way of what he deemed to be just. He became a natural nemesis, but not an enemy, to Madison personally and to the effort to form a more perfect union, under the Constitution.

Patrick Henry

Patrick Henry was a man of faith and a committed father, with seventeen children, born of two wives. His first wife, Sarah Parks Henry, died tragically of mental illness, which was a severe blow to her loving husband. Henry so cherished his time with his second wife, Dorothea "Dolly" Winston, that later in life he declined offers to serve in high offices in the government, including the Supreme

Patrick Henry

Court, preferring to be with Dolly and his family. He was a person of conscience and great ability. As a deeply religious person, Henry reportedly spent an hour in prayer during the evening on a daily basis. In some sense, his opposition to the Constitution and the Bill

6. See, Henry Mayer, *A Son of Thunder: Patrick Henry and the American Republic* (New York: Grove Press, 1991), 437.

7. Gordon S. Wood, *Revolutionary Characters* (New York: The Penguin Press, 2006), 258.

8. Ibid.

of Rights may be viewed, through the lens of time, as salutary to Madison's cause of securing a nation dedicated to liberty. Henry's initial opposition to the Constitution helped push supporters of the Constitution, including Madison, to first consider and later embrace the addition of a written bill of rights as the very first amendments to the Constitution. Despite being an ardent supporter of rights, Henry eventually opposed even the ratification of the Bill of Rights, claiming all rights would be diminished by exertions of national power. He was apprehensive that a powerful national government would be inimical to rights and was, therefore, a strong supporter of the rights of states. The efforts of Madison and others to allay the concerns of many, including Patrick Henry, provide helpful evidence of the intent behind the Bill of Rights—to secure self-evident rights to their fullest extent, placing them beyond the reach of the tyranny of the majority at the national level.

Henry's eloquence and political acumen were such that supporters of ratification hoped he would side with them. Immediately after returning to Virginia from the Constitutional Convention in Philadelphia, George Washington wrote Patrick Henry a letter seeking Henry's support for the Constitution. General Washington had heard rumors that Henry was in the early stages of building opposition to the Constitution. Washington wanted to win Henry to the side of the Constitution and wrote, "I wish the Constitution [was] more perfect, but I sincerely believe it is the best that could be obtained at this time—and as a constitutional door is opened for amendment hereafter—the adoption of it under the present circumstances of the Union is in my opinion desirable."[9] The General added, "The political concerns of the country are . . . suspended by a thread. If nothing had been agreed upon . . . the seeds [of anarchy would have been planted deep in the soil]."[10]

Henry's response made it clear that he was not going to support ratification of the Constitution: "I . . . lament that I cannot bring my

---

9. Letter from George Washington to Patrick Henry, September 24, 1787, Teaching American History, accessed October 10, 2018, http://teachingamericanhistory.org/library /document/letter-to-patrick-henry.

10. Ibid.

Mind in accord with the proposed Constitution."[11] Patrick added, "The Concern I feel on this Account is really greater than I am able to express, perhaps mature Reflection may furnish me Reasons to change my present Sentiments into a conformity with the opinion of those personages for whom I have the highest Reverence."[12] His somewhat terse but respectful response to the substance of Washington's letter made it clear that Henry was no supporter of the Constitution. It soon became evident to all that he was, in fact, a determined opponent of the effort to ratify the Constitution in Virginia.

A major battle was brewing between the Anti-Federalists, led by Patrick Henry, and supporters of the Constitution, led by James Madison. Madison and Henry were odd foes—Madison was short and spoke in a voice that all present had to strain to hear while Henry stood erect and spoke with fervor and eloquence. Madison's arguments were dignified and powerful, while Henry's eloquence was deeply moving and powerful in its own right. Two great figures in American history were battling, with the Constitution hanging in the balance, and they were joined by able partisans on both sides. The stage was, indeed, set for a battle between two different but equally able advocates. The decision, however, remained uncertain to the end.

Patrick Henry, together with other opponents of the new Constitution, raised strong arguments. Complaints surfaced in many states regarding the lack of a written bill of rights. Patrick Henry raised such arguments in a powerful, yet personal, way. He called on Madison to find a time when liberty prevailed when the people entrusted government with military power and the power of the purse., "Let Mr. Madison tell me when did liberty ever exist when the sword and purse were given up from the people? Unless a miracle shall interpose, no nation ever did." This would become a rallying cry for the Constitution's opponents. Patrick Henry and his fellow opponents of the Constitution also feared that the national government would unduly limit the sovereignty of the states. Contingents in the small and large states were uncomfortable with the Great Compromise, believing

11. Letter to George Washington from Patrick Henry, 19 October 1787, Founders Online (National Archives), accessed October 10, 2018, https://founders.archives.gov/documents /Washington/04-05-02-0350.
12. Ibid.

that the small states had been given too much or too little. Momentum seemed to be growing in favor of the opponents in Virginia, who were generally referred to as the Anti-Federalists.

The supporters of the Constitution clearly had their work cut out for them. The task of obtaining ratification in nine of the states was daunting, but even nine states would, as a practical matter, be insufficient, if Virginia failed to ratify the Constitution.

For many, ratification seemed unlikely. Indeed, without another series of miracles, it simply would not have materialized. Realizing that they faced an uphill battle, proponents of the newly adopted and hotly contested Constitution went to work quickly to secure the election of delegates to the state ratifying conventions who would either support or, at a minimum, be open to supporting the new Constitution. Opponents to all or part of the Constitution were equally determined to ride a wave of momentum that increasingly favored opposition to the Constitution. Sadly, it is often much easier to oppose a major change than to garner support for it.

Proponents had to persuade the Virginia delegates to support the Constitution, without amendment. The challenge was threefold: (1) elect a slate of delegates to the ratifying conventions who supported or were open to supporting the Constitution, in the face of strong opposition; (2) persuade a majority of the delegates to support the Constitution; and (3) avoid any efforts to amend the document.

Amendments would be fatal to the ratifying process because it was likely that each state would word its respective amendments differently. If states adopted amendments that differed as a substantive matter or if they adopted amendments that were substantively consistent but worded differently, the Constitution would be doomed. Similarly, if they called for a new convention to resolve which changes should be made, the work of the delegates to the convention, the Constitution, would be for naught, given the difficulty of garnering support for a new document. Survival of the new nation hung in the balance.

Anti-Federalists and other opponents to the Constitution, as drafted, had long been preparing for a battle. They were rallying opposition to the Constitution before it was finally adopted, and they were fully prepared to use every argument and procedural device available to them to derail the Constitution. Delegates and Constitution supporters, on the other hand, had spent four long months simply trying to negotiate a document that might save the nation. Proponents were only beginning to strategize as to how to secure ratification in such a perilous climate. The stage was set for an epic battle, a battle that would draw deeply on the talents of James Madison and other leaders of the ratification effort.

The first task was to get the supportive delegates elected. Madison initially declined to seek election to the Virginia Convention because he believed the issue of ratification should be handled by men who were not involved directly in its adoption. Supporters of the Constitution and Madison's personal friends, however, earnestly sought to persuade him that his voice and vote were critically necessary in the Virginia Convention. In time, Madison reluctantly agreed to stand for election. Even though he also believed it was unbecoming to run for office by soliciting votes, he became a reluctant but powerful candidate.

It initially appeared that Madison's election was secure, given the respect that he had earned with those who knew him best. As a result, he felt no need to return to Virginia to campaign. There was, however, an ominous development in the county—the Baptists, who had historically been among Madison's strongest supporters, were deeply concerned that the Constitution did not include protection for religious conscience in the form of a bill of rights. As such, they were initially inclined to oppose the Constitution.

While Madison lingered in New York working on a set of essays explaining why the Constitution should be ratified, opposition to his candidacy mounted. The other candidate on the Federalist slate in Orange County, James Gordon Jr., joined Madison's friends and family, including General Washington and Madison's father, in writing to Madison, pleading with him to return home to campaign and stand for election. Gordon captured the feelings of those who were anxious for Madison to return when he wrote Madison slowly became persuaded that he should return home and seek election as a delegate to the Virginia ratifying convention. In doing so, he soon crossed paths with John Leland, a man of powerful faith and a leader among the Baptists in Orange County, where Montpelier was located.

John Leland

John Leland had recently moved to Virginia from Massachusetts and was becoming a formidable voice among Baptists in Orange County and throughout the region. Like Madison, Leland had earned a reputation as one of the foremost proponents of religious liberty in the new nation. Leland was born in 1754, not far from Boston, in Grafton, Massachusetts. Like so many in Massachusetts, as a boy, Leland

John Leland

loosely affiliated with the established Congregationalist Church. At the age of eighteen, however, he had a religious experience that caused him to begin to associate with the Baptists. As a man of conscience, Leland took the better part of two more years praying and studying before he finally was convinced that God wanted him to accept baptism. He quickly became a powerful preacher, a person of great influence within the growing Baptist faith.

Once again, Providence played a role that influenced Madison and the new nation—Leland was inspired to move to Virginia with his wife, Sarah, in 1776, where the couple's two children, Sally and Betsy, were born. In 1778, John, Sarah, and Betsy moved to Orange County, where the family lived for thirteen years. His powerful preaching and commitment to liberty, supporting a vibrant right of conscience free from government limitation, earned Leland great respect wherever he preached. Madison was persuaded that Leland and other Baptists in Orange County had to be swayed to the cause of the Constitution.

Joseph Spencer, another prominent Baptist minister and friend of Madison's, urged James to meet with Leland on his way back to Montpelier from Philadelphia. Spencer believed the meeting would enable Madison to allay Leland's and his fellow Baptists' concern that religious liberty was unprotected in the Constitution. It appears evident that Madison took Spencer's advice and met with Leland, as he did with many other Baptists. Over time, Leland was persuaded that Madison remained wholly committed to the right of conscience and that the Constitution did no harm in limiting the right and, in fact, did some good in furthering the cause of religious liberty, by creating a large nation made up of many diverse sects. Leland's support strengthened Madison's candidacy in the Baptist community.

Once persuaded, Leland helped obtain support from fellow Baptists to elect Madison as a delegate to the Virginia Ratifying Convention. Leland reported that he voted for Madison, adding that he voted for someone he considered to be a dear personal friend and a friend of the cause of religious liberty. The warm friendship, borne of a commitment to religious liberty, among Madison, Leland, and other Baptists and minority religionists generally became a strong part of the base that collectively supported Madison in election after election. This alliance, for example, would later prove invaluable when James had to seek election to the First Congress, in which he would fulfill a promise he had made to the Baptists and others. Madison came to agree with the other minority sects that the Constitution could be improved by addition of a strong bill of rights, including a vibrant right of conscience.

With support from many Baptists and minority religionists, and others who respected him, Madison was elected as a delegate from Orange County, joining James Gordon, the other Federalist candidate in the county as representatives to serve in the Virginia Ratifying Convention. They were both elected, defeating the two Anti-Federalist candidates by significant margins. Once he was convinced that he needed to seek election as a delegate, Madison became a strong candidate, receiving approximately 80 percent of the vote.

Supporters of the Constitution throughout Virginia and in other states were also being elected, but their numbers were not sufficient to ensure ratification. In fact, very able Anti-Federalists were also being elected, leaving the fate of the Constitution uncertain. It was clear that debates would be animated, and the cause of the Constitution would be dependent upon the capacity of the Federalists to persuade the undecided and, in some instances, sway Anti-Federalists to their side. Speaking of the deliberations in the ratifying conventions and the parties to them, Madison mused, "The diversity of opinion on so interesting a subject among men of equal integrity and discernment is at once melancholy proof of the fallibility of human judgment and of the imperfect progress yet made in the Science of government."[13] Given human nature, Madison recognized that "unanimity is not to be expected [on such a] great political question."[14]

Unanimity was, in fact, lacking. Neither the Federalists nor the Anti-Federalists could be assured of the final result, in Virginia or in any of the other twelve states. The nation was sorely divided. Delegates had to be persuaded to accept the Constitution, as drafted, resisting the urge to alter it, given its acknowledged imperfections, the kind of imperfections that accompany any negotiated document. Madison knew he had to persuade others to support the cause. He also needed allies to make cogent arguments and develop effective strategies as to how those ideas could best be disseminated at the state and national levels. That is why Madison followed what had become his modus operandi in any such battle—he focused much of his time in New York, before returning to Virginia, on study, writing, counseling with others, and developing arguments to support ratification.

Other supporters of the Constitution were working to achieve the same end. Despite his support for a strong central government built on the British model, Alexander Hamilton fully understood that the Constitution was the best hope for those who wanted a stronger national government. Like Madison, he had to yield on some significant issues during the Constitutional Convention, but he had come to support the ratification cause with a tireless commitment. Hamilton soon became a leader in the fight for ratification in his home state of New York, battling against Governor Clinton and former convention delegates Yates and Lansing, who had walked out of the convention to build opposition to the Constitution. The battle in New York, like Virginia, was critical and difficult.

Part of Hamilton's ratification strategy was to write a series of substantive essays supporting the Constitution. Hamilton enlisted the support of another prominent and highly respected New Yorker, John

---

13. Letter from James Madison to Archibald Stuart, 30 October 1787, Founders Online (National Archives), accessed October 10, 2018, https://founders.archives.gov/documents/Madison/01-10-02-0161.
14. Ibid.

Jay, who had served as president of the Continental Congress and as an accomplished diplomat. Jay agreed to join Hamilton in writing several essays designed to persuade New Yorkers. Those essays would also be disseminated outside New York and was used to influence residents of other states that the Constitution should be ratified.

John Jay

John Jay

Among the illustrious group of founders of the United States, John Jay may have been the most deeply religious, in a traditional sense. He believed the Bible to be the word of God and served two terms as president of the American Bible Society. A decade before his death, his daughter, Nancy, wrote of his undying faith noting, "His continued peace of mind and habitual trust in overruling Providence....more strongly recommends the blessings of religion, than volumes written in its praise."[15] In his last will and testament, Jay expressed his abiding gratitude to [16]God for providing him with "excellent parents, with a virtuous wife, and with worthy children." He also expressed his gratitude to God for "His protection [that] has accompanied me through many eventful years, faithfully employed in the service of my country, and His providence has not only conducted me to this tranquil situation, but also given me abundant reason to be thankful."[17] Jay concluded his will with a bequest that reveals his Christian faith, asking that funds that might otherwise be spent on finery in his funeral service be given "to any one poor deserving widow or orphan of this town, whom my children shall select."[18]

---

15. Walter Stahr, *John Jay* (New York: Hambledon & Continuum 2006), 368.
16. Ibid., 383.
17. Ibid.
18. Ibid.

On May 2, 1781, writing on behalf of Congress, Madison praised Jay, who was negotiating with Spain, noting that Jay displayed the "utmost . . . discernment . . . necessary to reconcile . . . the dignity of the United States.[19] Later in life, however, in an interview with Jared Sparks at Montpelier, , however, Madison reflected that Jay had a propensity to be suspicious, even to the point of "bigotry," regarding other religions.[20] In that interview, Madison used the example of Jay's unyielding opposition to the French Revolution, in part due to French ties to Catholicism.[21] In 1788, as further evidence of his anti-Catholicism, Jay endeavored to get the New York Legislature to prevent Catholics from holding public office. Madison viewed such acts as bigotry as an act of tyranny against a minority sect, even though many Americans shared Jay's sentiments regarding so-called Papists and Catholicism. For the present, however, Madison and Jay would be allies, in seeking to obtain ratification of the Constitution. Jay's commitment to his personal faith and family was, nevertheless, unquestioned.

Jay's faith found its way into the powerful words he penned in his first essay in *The Federalist Papers*: "This country and this people seem to have been made for each other, and it appears as if it was the design of Providence that an inheritance so proper and convenient for a band of brethren, united to each other by the strongest ties, should never split into a number of unsocial, Jealous and alien sovereignties."[22] Jay was also an able advocate as a delegate within the New York ratifying convention, which he was pleased to describe in a letter to his wife in the following terms: "[D]ebates have been temperate and inoffensive to either party. The opposition to the proposed Constitution seems formidable, though more so from numbers than other considerations."[23]

Jay previously had served as president of the Continental Congress and was fully committed to the revolutionary cause. He later earned respect as a diplomat, serving in Britain and in Spain. Jay was so

---

19. Report on Instructions to John Jay (prepared by Madison), [2 May] 1781, accessed October 10, 2018, Founders Online (National Archives), https://founders.archives.gov /documents/Madison/01-03-02-0050.
20. See, Ralph Ketcham, *The Madisons at Montpelier* (Charlottesville: University of Virginia Press, 2009), 103.
21. Ibid.
22. *The Federalist Papers*, No. 2 (New York: Dover Publications, 2014), 8.
23. Walter Stahr, *John Jay* (New York: Hambledon & Continuum, 2006), 257.

respected that he was named by President George Washington to serve as the first Chief Justice of the United States under the new Constitution he labored to support. The role of the Supreme Court was uncertain at that time. It was generally viewed as weaker than the supreme courts in the states. Even though the courtroom in the Exchange Building in New York City was full for the first hearing of the United States Supreme Court, for example, only three justices were in attendance, so no cases could be heard for lack of a quorum. Jay, nevertheless, helped create a procedural foundation for the court and heard a few significant early cases.

In 1794, while serving on the court, Jay negotiated what has come to be known as the Jay Treaty. The Jay Treaty is formally known as the Treaty of Amity Commerce and Navigation between the United States and Great Britain. It is credited with momentarily averting another war with Great Britain, even though Madison and others believed that it was little more than an act of appeasement. Jay resigned from the court in 1795 and returned to New York to serve as the state's second governor under the government formed by the Constitution.

President John Adams praised John Jay for his work in supporting the Constitution by declaring that Jay's efforts were "of more importance than any of the rest [of the founders], indeed almost as much weight as all the rest."[24] One of Jay's greatest contributions to the formation of the new nation came in the form of his commitment to ensure ratification of the Constitution, including his authorship of five essays in *The Federalist Papers* and his noteworthy contributions to securing ratification in the critical state of New York.

The Federalist Papers

Given his high regard for Madison's thinking and writing, Hamilton asked Madison to contribute to *The Federalist Papers*, as well, even though Madison was not a New Yorker. He agreed, which helped provide an effective medium for him to share his arguments supporting the Constitution on the national stage. Jay was suffering ill health at the time, so the burden of supporting the cause of ratification through

---

24. Ibid., 270.

the media of the day fell largely on Hamilton and Madison. The final product, consisting of eighty-five essays, was largely published between October 1787 and August 1788 in two primary newspapers—*The Independent Journal* and *The New York Packet*. The essays were shared broadly beyond the borders of New York, as well, and were helpful to delegates supporting the Constitution. This collection of essays was, at the time of its publication, referred to as *The Federalist*. Today, those essays are classics in political thought and are referred to as *The Federalist Papers*. The publication of these essays provided its authors with a significant opportunity to clarify their own thinking, as they sought to persuade others and provide substantive arguments for supporters of the Constitution.

Hamilton was the primary author. Madison's contributions were numerous and are among some of the best of the works. These essays reflect the depth and the breadth of the arguments raised in ratification debates and are reflective of the views of their authors. They help to explain the Federalist position supporting ratification. Madison raised similar arguments in the Virginia ratifying convention. George Washington placed his personal stamp of approval on the essays and assisted in distributing them to Virginia newspapers. Thomas Jefferson, in turn, referred to them as "the best commentary on the principles of government, which was ever written."[25] Winston Churchill added his praise for *The Federalist Papers* when he reflected, "The Federalist letters are among the classics of American literature. Their practical wisdom stands pre-eminent amid the stream of controversial writing at the time." To this day, *The Federalist Papers* are considered by lawyers, legal scholars, and legal jurists to be legally significant tools in determining the meaning of various provisions in the Constitution. They were first cited by the United States Supreme Court, in *Calder v. Bull* in 1798, and have since been cited hundreds of times by the court. Interestingly, the most often cited essay is number 78, written by Alexander Hamilton, which defines the role of the judiciary under the Constitution.

---

25. See, "Quotes Regarding the Federalist Papers," May 18, 2013, Washington, Jefferson & Madison Institute, accessed October 11, 2019, http://wjmi.blogspot.com/2013/05/quotes-concerning-federalist-papers.html.

Many delegates to the state conventions were concerned about the powers granted to the national government. They were particularly fearful that the national government envisioned in the Constitution would infringe on individual liberty and intrude unduly on state power. Those interrelated concerns echoed a common theme: the national government under the Constitution might become oppressive by aggressively exercising powers granted to it. In responding to those concerns, Madison and Hamilton began their collection of essays by arguing that the Articles of Confederation provided for a national government that was insufficient to protect the union. In essays 18–20, for example, the authors examined the history of confederations and found that they all proved inadequate to protect a union from threats from without, on the part of other nations, or within, on the part of rebellious groups or powerful sects within the states. A stronger national government was therefore necessary to protect against threats both internal and external.

Without an effective national government, the authors argued that the present confederation of states, like past confederations, would prove ineffective in protecting its people from the national and international threats.

In their essays, Hamilton and Madison turned logically from avoiding internal and external threats to responding to the Anti-Federalist argument that the national government was too powerful, intruding on the sovereignty of the states and thereby jeopardizing liberty within the states. Madison and Hamilton responded by arguing that a national government of enumerated powers was given no more power than necessary to maintain the union. By expressly enumerating the powers of the national government in the Constitution, the national government was carefully limited to those powers. The federal government was not permitted to intrude unduly on the actions of the states and, therefore, posed little, if any, threat to liberty. They pointed out that liberty was also secured from international threats under the Constitution, something that the individual states were unable to achieve. The Anti-Federalists understood, however, that the necessary and proper clause strengthened the enumerated powers of the national government in significant ways that could constitute a significant threat to state power and liberty. They argued that the national government could do anything that was necessary and proper to effectuate fully any enumerated power.

Hamilton and Madison argued that the Constitution limited national or federal power in other significant ways. The proposed Constitution provided for the separation of powers, between the legislative, executive, and judicial branches of government, which constituted a further limitation on the power of any branch of the national government. Each branch of government exercised separate and, on occasion, shared powers. By separating and in some instances sharing power, the Constitution protected liberty and the sovereignty of the states by enumerating the powers of each branch of government and then creating a set of checks and balances among the carefully circumscribed branches of government, thereby ensuring that none of them could become tyrannical. This separation of powers further ensured that any power granted to any branch of government would be moderated by requiring strong and multiple majorities in both houses of Congress and support of the executive branch before any decisive action could be taken. The judiciary would also check unconstitutional exercises of power by the legislative and executive branches of government.

Madison and Hamilton went on to argue for the wisdom of the bicameral legislative system created in the Great Compromise. Madison came to accept the large and small state compromise, providing the small states with more power in the Senate. That compromise provided for the House of Representatives to be elected directly by the citizens of each House district. Members of the Senate, two from each state, on the other hand, were originally selected by the state legislatures, providing small states with increased power to check excesses on the part of the national government. This Great Compromise, once again, helped provide protection to the states and secured another form of check on the power of the national government. Given that most legislation had to be supported in the two houses of Congress (the legislative branch) *and* the executive branch, the power of the national government was limited or checked. Legislation also had to be signed into law by the Executive.

The Executive could also veto acts of Congress that were believed to be excessive or unconstitutional. Finally, if there were questions of a constitutional magnitude regarding the legislation that had been adopted by both the House and the Senate and had been signed into law by the Executive, the Supreme Court could intervene and declare the legislation to be unconstitutional.

Madison also believed that the states should be active in preparing resolutions indicating why they believed some national laws to be excessive or breaches of the constitutional authority of the national government. Madison had seen such interposition by resolution or petition to be effective ways of drawing attention to issues and thereby checking the power of the national government, when his *Memorial and Remonstrance* influenced the Virginia legislature to decline to support a questionable legislative effort.

The limited form of government conceived under the Constitution provided only specified or enumerated powers to the national government, permitting the states to retain significant power. All power not specifically delegated to the national government by the states was to remain within the province of the state governments. This concept of federalism, as recognized by Madison, was designed to ensure that the states would continue to be more powerful than the national government. At the same time, the Constitution provided a means for recognizing differences between the states and maintain a system of government that offered wide latitude to the states to innovate and experiment, to act according to their own respective wills.

In short, Madison and Hamilton understood that the new government would provide sufficient protection against external and internal threats, while moderating the exercise of power at the national level through a series of structural limitations that were carefully designed to avoid undue accretion of power at the national level. Madison actually believed that these structural checks on the power of the government did more to avoid tyranny by any majority and thereby protect liberty than could be accomplished under a written bill or declaration of rights. As persuasive as Madison's arguments were, in this regard, concerns remained and there was a **strong** push afoot to include a bill of rights in the Constitution.

Failure to Include a Written Bill of Rights

Reflecting the general uneasiness of the citizenry, delegates in Virginia and other states remained hesitant to ratify the Constitution without some assurance, at a minimum, that a written bill of rights would be added. They feared that citizens were ceding their rights to a powerful national government. As an illustration of the nature of this concern, Thomas Jefferson wrote Madison to object strongly about the failure to include a bill of rights in the final draft. Jefferson's major objection to the substance of the Constitution, as proposed for ratification purposes, was the "omission of a bill of rights providing clearly & without the aid of sophisms for freedom of religion, freedom of the press, protection against standing armies, restriction against monopolies, the eternal & unremitting force of the habeas corpus laws, and trials by jury in all matters of fact triable by the laws of the land & not by the law of Nations."[26] Jefferson made it clear that he shared the sentiment of many Virginians and citizens from other states that no just government, state or federal, should refuse to secure rights in written form to its citizens. To ensure that this would occur, the rights of the people should be formally secured by a written declaration of those rights.

Many delegates in Virginia joined Jefferson in being deeply troubled by the lack of a written bill of rights in the Constitution. They insisted that the Constitution be amended to provide for a bill of rights, to secure the liberty of the people from government action at the national level. The nation was built on a revolution which was fought to secure liberty based on natural rights. Many had sacrificed much to secure that freedom, and they insisted that those natural rights be included in the Constitution in written form, as a declaration that the people were secure in their life, liberty, and pursuit of happiness, free from the heavy hand of government.

Madison had long been one of the strongest proponents of individual rights in Virginia. He agreed with Jefferson and others as a substantive matter, regarding the imperative to protect liberty and natural

---

26. Letter to James Madison from Thomas Jefferson, 20 December 1787, Founders Online (National Archives), accessed October 11, 2018, https://founders.archives.gov/documents/Madison/01-10-02-0210.

rights. Nevertheless, he sincerely believed that the Constitution did much structurally to secure such rights against actions at the national level. He also feared that efforts to draft such protections would be interpreted to limit rather than secure those natural rights, which he believed to be inalienable.

Madison offered four powerful arguments supporting his view that a including a written bill of rights in the Constitution was unnecessary and could do more harm than good:

1. As a structural matter, at the national level, it would be more difficult for a single group to tyrannize the rights of individuals and smaller groups than would be the case at the state level.
2. Given that such rights were by their very nature inalienable, the national government lacked any authority to interfere with such rights.
3. Rather than securing liberty, putting such rights into written form could ultimately lead to their dilution in the form of constrained interpretation.
4. Opening the amendment process to ensure inclusion of a bill of rights would provide a means for opponents to make or mandate changes that ultimately would have the effect of denigrating rights and defeating ratification of the Constitution.

James believed that rights were protected by a steady balance of power between the national and state governments. In fact, Madison feared state excesses more than he feared national ones, because the national government under the Constitution was limited in power and was structured in a manner that made it less, not more, likely that the rights of individuals and minorities would be tyrannized at the national level.

Each of these arguments warrants elaboration, because they help clarify Madison's view, making it clear that he strongly supported rights and limiting power at the national level to infringe on such rights. He merely disagreed with Jefferson and others as to how best to protect those rights. While Madison believed a stronger central or national government was necessary to preserve the fragile union of the states against internal and external threats, he did all that he could to help create a system or structure of government that by its very nature would be checked in the exercise of its power, thereby protecting rights.

Madison believed strongly that liberty can best be secured in larger republics where the multiplicity of interests and sects tend to minimize the power of any single interest or sect and the tyranny by any permanent majority. In "Federalist No. 10," one of the most cited essays included in *The Federalist Papers,* Madison clearly stated his fear of despotism and the limitation of liberty at the state level and reiterated his belief that the nature of the national government avoided some excesses that were likely at the state level. He argued that, "The influence of factious leaders may kindle a flame within their particular States but will be unable to spread a general conflagration through the other States. A religious sect may degenerate into a political faction in a part of the Confederacy; but the variety of sects dispersed over the entire face of it must secure the national councils against any danger from that source."[27] He added, "A rage . . . for any other improper or wicked project, will be less apt to pervade the whole body of the Union than a particular member of it, in the same proportion as such a malady is more likely to taint a particular country or district than an entire State."[28]

For Madison, the very size of the national government helped secure rights, because no single sect or group could gain a true majority. Any given majority at the national level would be made up of several smaller groups. Those groups, in turn, would continually be vying for power. As a result, minority groups would coalesce into an ever-changing majority, moderating power and creating a sensitivity to the rights of groups that might be out of power for a time. Therefore, the system was dynamic, with minorities ever vying for a power that was in continual flux. In time, however, a new group of minority interests would coalesce and form a new majority. Since no minority could be confident that they would continue to retain power over time, there would be an incentive to treat minorities out of power with respect, knowing that the sitting majority would one day be out of power, ousted by that same minority group, perhaps. By contrast, Madison

27. *The Federalist Papers, No. 10* (Mineola: Dover Publications, 2914), 47.
28. Ibid.

noted that at the state level, a single sect or group could maintain its control and tyrannize minority sects or interests, because there were fewer minority groups or interests capable of coalescing and forming new majorities within an individual state than at the national level. At the national level there were multiple interests or factions from all states participating in governance, whereas at the state level fewer groups vied for power.

Sir William Blackstone:
Privileges and Immunities

Madison also argued that rights were prior to government or inalienable. He believed strongly in the concept of natural rights. In Madison's view, the national government lacked any legitimate authority to interfere with such rights, especially the right of conscience. He had long been familiar with and influence by the work of William Blackstone, an English jurist whose book, *Commentaries on the Laws of England*, was read widely in America. Even though he did not personally support the revolutionary

William Blackstone

cause, Blackstone's work, together with the work of John Locke and others, provided some of the legal basis for the revolution and the structure of the new government. Madison and his friend William Bradford discussed the substance of Blackstone's *Commentaries on the Laws of England*, which was also widely read by signers of the Constitution and the Declaration of Independence.

As early as 1773, Madison noted that he was very pleased with his experience reading Blackstone. A decade later, in 1783, James recommended that Blackstone's *Commentaries on the Law of England* be included on a list of books he deemed to be appropriate for use in Congress. Influenced by those teachings, Madison believed Congress was required to recognize natural rights or risk losing its legitimacy as a government. In every office he ever held, including service in Congress and as president, Madison understood that he had taken oath to abide by the Constitution. He also understood that the Supreme Court was a final arbiter in constitutional matters, but that did not absolve him of his own personal responsibility to maintain fidelity or remain faithful to the Constitution and the rights it preserved, even when he personally disagreed with that constitutional limitation or mandate.

Blackstone's legal scholarship also helped fuel what had become a successful legal practice and led to his serving as a respected judge. William also served as a member of Parliament. Despite his many other achievements, his *Commentaries on the Law of England* were his real gift to his generation and generations to come. In his introduction to the *Commentaries*, Blackstone wrote, in language reminiscent of Witherspoon's teachings on the morality of law, "Upon these two foundations, the law of nature and the law of revelation [from the Holy Scripture], depend all human laws; that is to say, no human laws should be suffered to contradict these."[29] In his *Commentaries*, Blackstone also provided strong legal or analytical support for the concept of natural rights. Blackstone summarized English law and argued that, "[R]ights themselves, thus defined by these several statutes, consist in a number of private immunities; which will appear to be indeed no other, than either that residuum of natural liberty, which is not required by the laws of society to be sacrificed to public convenience; or else those civil privileges, which society hath engaged to provide, in lieu of the natural liberties so given up by individuals."[30]

For Blackstone, therefore, the concept of "immunities" referred to natural rights retained by the people when they entered civil society. Citizens in any just and legitimate government, therefore, were to remain immune from government intrusion on those natural rights, which existed prior to the formation of the state. No government could

---

29. William Blackstone, *Commentaries on the Laws of England, Introduction, Section 2, "Of the Nature of Laws in General,"* accessed October 11, 2018, https://ebooks.adelaide.edu.au/b/blackstone/william/comment/introduction2.html.

30. "Blackstone on the Absolute Rights of Individuals (1753)," 129, Online Library of Liberty, accessed October 11, 2018, http://oll.libertyfund.org/pages/blackstone-on-the-absolute-rights-of-individuals-1753.

limit those immunities without undermining its own legitimacy and risking rebellion. In short, failing to recognize such natural rights constituted a breach of the contract between people and their government.

This very thought was captured beautifully in the Declaration of Independence: "We hold these truths to be self-evident, that all men are created equal, that they are endowed by their Creator with certain unalienable Rights, that among these are Life, Liberty and the pursuit of Happiness. That to secure these rights, Governments are instituted among Men, deriving their just powers from the consent of the governed, That whenever any Form of Government becomes destructive of these ends, it is the Right of the People to alter or to abolish it, and to institute new Government, laying its foundation on such principles and organizing its powers in such form, as to them shall seem most likely to effect their Safety and Happiness."[31] Thus, under the Declaration of Independence and in accordance with the views of Blackstone, Locke, Penn, Witherspoon, and others, citizens must be immune from actions on the part of any legitimate government seeking to limit the natural rights of the people. Immunities, therefore, are those natural rights that exist prior to the formation of government, rights inherent in humanity, gifts of God to His children.

The term "Privileges," on the other hand, refers to positive law, laws designed by government to grant a certain privilege to its citizens. Privileges, therefore, were given by government and could, in turn, be limited by government. Governments, however, had to grant those privileges equally to those within their borders under the rule of law. Today, many believe that rights and privileges are grants from government, not natural rights, individual rights originating in nature as a gift from a loving God.

Interestingly, Article IV, Section 2 of the Constitution sets forth a privileges and immunities clause: "The Citizens of each State shall be entitled to all Privileges and Immunities of Citizens in the several states." In "Federalist No. 42," Madison addressed this clause and noted, "[T]hose who come under the denomination of *free inhabitants* of a State, although not citizens of such State, are entitled, in every

---

31. "The Declaration of Indepndence," last accessed October 11, 2018, http://www.ushistory .org/Declaration/document.

other State, to all the privileges of *free citizens* of the latter; that is, to greater privileges than they may be entitled to in their own State."[32] Some refer to such a provision as providing for "comity" between the states—citizens of another are entitled to the privileges granted by that state to its own citizens. Thus, for example, a citizen of another state traveling through or residing in Virginia for a time would be entitled to enjoy the same privileges as citizens of Virginia.

Madison did not feel compelled to address the immunities portion of Article IV, Section 2. It was widely understood to protect natural rights. Madison, in fact, feared the inclusion of written rights in the Constitution. He said as much in a letter written in 1788 to Jefferson: "My own opinion has always been in favor of a bill of rights; provided it be so framed as not to imply powers not meant to be included in the enumeration. At the same time, I have never thought the omission a material defect, nor been anxious to supply it even by subsequent amendment, for any reason than it is anxiously desired by others."[33]

Fear That the Written Text of a Bill of Rights Would Be Read Restrictively

In "Federalist No. 37," Madison argued further that language by its very nature has the potential to foster limitations by government officials seeking to exercise and legitimize their own power. Madison began his argument by stating, "All new laws, though penned with the greatest technical skill, and passed on the fullest and most mature deliberation, are considered as more or less obscure and equivocal, until their meaning be liquidated and ascertained by a series of particular discussions and adjudications. Besides the obscurity arising from the complexity of objects, and the imperfection of the human faculties, the medium through which the conceptions of men are conveyed to

---

32. *The Federalist Papers* (Mineola: Dover Publications, Inc. 2014), 208.
33. Letter from James Madison to Thomas Jefferson, 17 October 1788, Founders Online (National Archives), accessed October 11, 2018, https://founders.archives.gov/documents /Madison/01-11-02-0218.

each other, adds a fresh embarrassment."[34] Madison understood that, by their nature, words are equivocal and demand careful clarification. He added, "The use of words is to express ideas. Perspicuity therefore requires not only that the ideas should be distinctly formed, but that they should be expressed by words distinctly and exclusively appropriated to them."[35] For Madison, it was incumbent that words be distinctly used to clarify ideas, even though the task is a daunting one. He mused, "But no language is so copious as to supply words and phrases for every complex idea, or so correct as not to include many equivocally denoting different ideas. Hence, it must happen, that however accurately objects may be discriminated in themselves, and however accurately the discrimination may be considered, the definition of them may be rendered inaccurate by the inaccuracy of the terms in which it is delivered."[36] He then added, "This unavoidable inaccuracy must be greater or less, according to the complexity and novelty of the objects defined."[37] Madison drives his point home by declaring, "When the Almighty himself condescends to address mankind in their own language, his meaning, luminous as it must be, is rendered dim and doubtful, by the cloudy medium through which it is communicated. Here then are three sources of vague and incorrect definitions; indistinctness of the object, imperfection of the organ of conception, inadequateness of the vehicle of ideas. Any one of these must produce a certain degree of obscurity."[38]

Put simply, Madison recognized the inadequacy of words as tools to describe and secure rights, particularly when expressing a natural right or immunity from government action. Based on his experience in the drafting of the Virginia Declaration of Rights, and his disagreement with George Mason and others, Madison had learned that declaring rights was a difficult and fearful business, because language itself is incapable of fully expressing the breadth and depth of such rights. For Madison, language was deficient and likely to be used by

---

34. *The Federalist Papers* (Mineola: Dover Publications, Inc. 2014, No. 42 at 172–73.
35. Ibid., 173.
36. Ibid.
37. Ibid.
38. Ibid.

those in control of government to limit the right through construction and increase their power thereby.

Madison also was apprehensive that a majority might use the guise of writing a bill of rights as a means of limiting those very rights. In some measure, even though his intentions had been good, Madison saw that Mason had used language to do exactly that, particularly regarding the right of conscience, in his draft of the Virginia Declaration of Rights. Rather than being accorded respect, religious conscience was only worthy of toleration by government, according to Mason.

The Virginia Ratifying Convention

As stated before, Madison was reluctant to even permit the well-intentioned effort in adopting a bill of rights. He recognized that opening the amendment process to ensure inclusion of a bill of rights would give opponents another opportunity to make changes that would have the ultimate effect of denigrating those rights that Madison believed men and women possessed independent of any government. In his mind, there was no assurance that rights would be secure under such an amendment process—some might be subject to exclusion and others could be limited by a restrictive reading of the language in any bill or declaration of rights. He also understood that the writing such a statement of rights seemed to imply that the enumerated rights were governmentally created, making them little more than privileges granted by government, and as such, subject to the whims of the government that granted them. In other words, if government was the source of such privileges, it also retained the capacity and right to limit them.

Despite the power of Madison's arguments, a storm was brewing over the issue of amendments, including the demands by the Anti-Federalists for a written bill of rights. Proponents of a written bill of rights in Virginia offered a series of rights that they believed should be expressly protected. The twentieth of those proposed amendments dealt with the issue of religious liberty and provided, "That religion, or the duty we owe to our Creator, and the manner of discharging it, can be directed only by reason and conviction, not by force or violence;

and therefore all men have an equal, natural, and unalienable right to the free exercise of religion, according to the dictates of conscience, and that no particular religious sect or society ought to be favored or established, by law, in preference to others." For Madison, this provision was reminiscent of Mason's language and did not go far enough in securing the right of conscience. Madison also saw similar deficiencies in other declarations of rights offered by the Anti-Federalists, none of which adequately protected the right it was designed to secure.

Delegates to other state conventions also demanded a bill of rights in some form, with many offering amendments addressing rights generally and the subject of religious liberty specifically. Delegates in North Carolina, for example, proposed an amendment that generally tracked the one offered in Virginia. The North Carolina proposal included the "free exercise" language used in Virginia Declaration of Rights. The New Hampshire convention, in turn, suggested the following proposal: "Congress shall make no laws touching religion or [infringing] the rights of conscience." The New York convention also considered a similar amendment.

The battle over whether to include amendments raged on in the Virginia Convention. The delegates slowly worked their way through each of the clauses of the Constitution, as Anti-Federalists pressed their arguments supporting written amendments. Madison and proponents of the Constitution had to explain, day after day, why the Constitution merited ratification as drafted. Serious differences remained late into the Virginia Ratifying Convention regarding the contentious issue of whether new amendments should be included in the Constitution.

Tempers often flared. Patrick Henry fumed, "Old as I am, it is probable that I may yet [be a rebel]. . . . As this government stands, I despise and abhor it."[39] Henry became increasingly personal in his invective, attacking even his friend John Randolph, arguing that Randolph had become a traitor to the cause. Randolph, who initially refused to sign the Constitution, had been persuaded by Madison and others to become a supporter of ratification. John declared his change of position with the following words, "The suffrage which I shall give

---

39. See *Lion of Liberty: Patrick Henry and the Call to a New Nation* (Cambridge: Da Capo Press, 2010), 222.

in favor of the Constitution will be ascribed, by malice, to motives unknown to my breast. But although for every other act of my life, I shall seek refuge in the mercy of God—for this I request his justice only."[40] He added, "Lest, however some future analyst should, in the spirit of party vengeance, deign to mention my name, let him recite these truths—that I went to the Federal convention, with the strongest affection for the union; that I acted there, in full conformity with this affection: that I refused to subscribe, because I had as I still have objections to the constitution, and wished a free enquiry into its merits, and that the accession of eight states [the other eight states that had already ratified the Constitution] reduced our deliberations to the single question of union or no union."[41]

Henry never accepted Randolph's reasons for a change of position, viewing that change to be a weakness of principle. Patrick may have come to believe that John accepted an inducement to change sides, implying that Randolph accepted a bribe to support ratification. Henry cried out, "It seems very strange and unaccountable that that which was the object of [Randolph's] execration should now receive his encomium. . . [S]omething extraordinary must have operated so great a change in his opinions."[42] Randolph recoiled, incensed by Henry's personal attack, and with firmness declared, "I find myself attacked, in the most illiberal manner, by the Honorable Gentleman. I disdain his aspersions and insinuations."[43] Randolph's voice rose to a crescendo as he declared that Henry's "asperity is warranted by no principle of parliamentary decency, nor compatible with the least shadow of friendship, and if our friendship must fall, Let it fall like Lucifer, never to rise again."[44] Finally, Randolph indulged in a rhetorical flourish equal to that of Henry in defending his integrity: "Sir, if I do not stand on the bottom of integrity, and pure love for Virginia, as much as those who

40. Edmund Randolph in the Virginia Convention (June 25,1788), ConSource, accessed October 11, 2018, https://www.consource.org/document/edmund-randolph-in-the-virginia-convention-1788-6-25.

41. Ibid.

42. See *Lion of Liberty: Patrick Henry and the Call to a New Nation* (Cambridge: Da Capo Press 2010), 226.

43. Ibid.

44. Ibid.

can most clamorous, I wish to resign my existence."[45] Patrick Henry was losing a friend and also feared that his majority was slipping away.

Late in the convention, in yet another effort to undercut ratification, Patrick Henry raised the issue of slavery. He declared slavery to be a state right beyond the reach of the power of the national government. For Henry, slavery served as an example of rights, in this case a property right on the part of slave owners. It was also a right the definition of which resided exclusively in the states. He asserted that the national government infringed on individual and state rights when it acted to limit slavery under the 1808 slave clause. Patrick asserted that "it would rejoice my very soul that every one of my fellow being was emancipated,"[46] but quickly added, "This is a local matter and I can see no propriety in subjecting it to Congress."[47]

When Madison tried to get the floor to speak in opposition to Henry's slavery argument, Patrick refused to yield. Rising to his full stature, Henry's voice filled the room, as he reached a crescendo, with his voice ringing through the hall:

> [Madison] tells you of important blessings, which he imagines will result to us and mankind in general from the adoption of this system. I see the awful immensity of the dangers with which it is pregnant.
>
> I see it! I feel it!
>
> I see beings of a higher order—anxious concerning our decision. When I see beyond the horizon [I see] those intelligent beings which inhabit the ethereal mansions, reviewing the political decisions and revolutions which in the progress of time will happen in America [and our] own happiness alone is not affected by the event. All nations are interested in the determination. We have it in our power to secure happiness of one half of the human race. [Ratification of the Constitution] may involve the misery of hemispheres.[48]

At that precise moment, lighting struck, and thunder caused the hall to shake. Using nature as a welcome prop and as a means of driving home his argument that the Constitution was an evil work, Patrick

---

45. Ibid.
46. Ibid., 230.
47. Ibid.
48. Ibid., 232.

cried anew: "I see it! I feel it!" As those final words fell from Patrick Henry's lips, lightning and thunder again shook the room, bringing chaos in its wake. Shaken delegates fell to the ground or rushed for the door. Many believed that the very elements had spoken. Some fled, and the business of the day concluded without formal adjournment.

For Patrick Henry and many of his fellow Anti-Federalists, the thunder and lightning were a heavenly sign, a divine imprimatur placed on their cause. Some Federalists responded in kind, however, asserting that Henry had resorted to conjuring up the black arts. Most Federalists, including Madison, were less convinced that Providence had intervened or that the black arts had been at play. Thunder and lightning, after all, were common during that time of year, and it was not surprising that Henry took advantage of a coincidence, treating it as a prop for his theatrics. Madison and most delegates simply wanted to get back to business and were unwilling to end the work of the convention that day on that thunderous note. They remained determined to find a compromise between legitimate Anti-Federalist concerns regarding liberty and state sovereignty and the need to provide for security in the form of a viable national government.

George Wythe was a respected delegate, a signer of the Declaration of Independence, former Speaker of the Assembly, and our nation's first law professor (the law school at William and Mary continues to bear his name). Together with some other delegates, he offered support for a compromise. That compromise was based on a similar effort that had proven successful in Massachusetts. Wythe recommended that the Committee of the Whole draft a set of amendments to be introduced in the new Congress. The following day, with delegates aware that the Ratifying Convention was about to close, members spoke, often quite eloquently, in favor and opposition to the Constitution and whether amendments should be mandated or simply proposed. Madison joined in supporting Wythe's compromise and personally promised the Virginia delegates that he would assist in developing a set of amendments for presentation in the First Congress.

James Innes was a prominent lawyer who was serving as Virginia's attorney general at that time. He joined in the effort to derail Anti-Federalists who insisted on mandating rather than merely proposing amendments. Innes expressed a concern of many present that mandating amendments would make ratification impossible and would result in a return to a nation governed by the ineffectual Articles of Confederation. Patrick Henry rose a final time to argue for the addition of amendments, but he seemed to realize that the time had come for a vote. In closing his final address, he noted, "I beg pardon of this House for having taken up more time than came to my share, and I thank them for the patience and polite attention with which I have been heard. If I shall be in the minority, I shall have those painful sensations, which arise from a conviction of being overpowered in a good cause."[49] Realizing that there were those who might seek to oppose ratification by violent means, in his final words, Henry declared, "Yet I will be a peaceable citizen—My head, my hand, and my heart shall be at liberty to retrieve the loss of liberty, and remove the defects of that system-in a constitutional way—I wish not to go to violence, but will wait with hopes that the spirit which predominated in the revolution, is not yet gone, nor the cause of those who are attached to the revolution yet lost-I shall therefore patiently wait in expectation of seeing that Government changed so as to be compatible with the safety, liberty and happiness of the people." Still stinging from prior questioning of his motives, Governor Randolph followed Henry and was the final speaker. He reflected, "The suffrage which I shall give in favor of the Constitution, will be ascribed by malice to motives unknown to my breast. But although for every other act of my life, I shall seek refuge in the mercy of God—for this I request his justice only."[50]

The time had come for a vote in the Virginia Ratifying Convention. The voting procedure was broken into parts. The delegates first had to decide the issue of whether to condition ratification on the inclusion of amendments and call for a new convention. Proponents of this strategy for derailing ratification offered the following resolution: "Resolved, That previous to the ratification of the new Constitution of Government recommended by the late Federal Convention, a declaration of rights asserting and securing from encroachment the great

49. "Journal Notes of the Virginia Ratifying Convention Proceedings (June 25, 1788)," ConSource, accessed October 11, 2018, https://www.consource.org/document/journal -notes-of-the-virginia-ratification-convention-proceedings-1788-6-25.
50. Ibid.

principles of civil and religious liberty, and the unalienable rights of the people, together with amendments to the most exceptional parts of the said Constitution of Government, ought to be referred by this Convention to the other States in the American confederacy for their consideration."[51] Tension and uncertainty filled the room as a vote was taken on this resolution that, if adopted, would effectively be fatal to ratification of the Constitution, as adopted in Philadelphia. By a very slim margin, 88–80, the delegates voted against the resolution. Amendments and changes were not mandated, in a manner requiring a new convention. The second issue to be decided was whether to ratify the Constitution. Again, by a slim margin, 89–79, the delegates voted to ratify the Constitution, picking up a sole vote in the process. Madison and proponents of ratification were relieved. Their perseverance and persuasiveness had prevailed.

In a mighty war of words and ideas, Madison and proponents of ratification had barely prevailed over Henry and the Anti-Federalists. Henry was a great orator, who touched the emotions of those who were privileged to listen to him speak on an issue of importance. Madison had a great power to persuade. In his excellent biography of Madison, David O. Stewart quoted a contemporary of Madison as saying, "[H]is whole soul is engaged . . . and it appeared to me he would have flashed conviction into every mind."[52] Later in his life, John Marshall, who served as a delegate to the Virginia Ratifying Convention and as Chief Justice of the United States Supreme Court was known to praise Henry as a truly great orator. He reserved even higher praise for Madison, a man that he often disagreed with: "Eloquence has been defined as the art of persuasion…. If it includes persuasion by convincing, Mr. Madison was the most eloquent man I ever heard."[53] Coming from a Chief Justice who regularly heard arguments from the leading advocates of that era that was high praise indeed

Wythe's compromise and Madison's convincing arguments helped win ratification, but the Federalist's greatest weapon may have been

---

51. Virginia Ratifying Convention, June 25, 1788, Constitution Society, accessed October 14, 2018, http://constitution.org/rc/rat_va_21.htm.

52. David O. Stewart, *Madison's Gift* (New York: Simon & Schuster 2015), 66.

53. William C. Rives, *History of the Life and Times of James Madison, Vol. II* (Boston: Little, Brown, and Company 1870), 612.

the quiet support that General George Washington offered in behalf of the Constitution, even though he did not participate as a delegate in the Virginia Ratifying Convention. James Monroe, an Anti-Federalist, expressed the sentiment of many on both sides, Federalists and Anti-Federalists alike, when he reflected, "Be assured. General Washington's influence carried this government."[54] Madison's persuasion was critical at the Virginia Ratifying Convention, but it is clear that Washington's support for the Constitution was ever-present and influenced the final vote in significant ways.

When Virginia finally ratified the Constitution, it was tenth in line, behind the states of Delaware, Pennsylvania, New Jersey, Georgia, Connecticut, Massachusetts, Maryland, South Carolina, and New Hampshire. The formation of the union was technically secure, when New Hampshire supplied the critical ninth vote to ratify the Constitution as drafted. The viability of the nation under the Constitution, however, remained unclear, even after New Hampshire's legally necessary ninth vote to ratify with two of the largest states, Virginia and New York, yet to sign. These two states were essential to the formation and survival of the nation. New York soon followed Virginia and nationhood under the new Constitution was secure. Only two less consequential states, North Carolina and Rhode Island remained as outliers, refusing to ratify. North Carolina had taken the course of refusing to sign the Constitution without the addition of a written bill of rights, a decision that Virginia had barely avoided. Rhode Island, in turn, was the only state that had refused to send delegates to the Convention, and it remained recalcitrant, refusing to ratify. In time, Rhode Island and North Carolina joined the union. They soon became convinced that they had to join the newly formed United States of America, under the Constitution, to secure their economic and political futures.

Madison was troubled by substance of many of the amendments proposed in Virginia. Nevertheless, he saw them as just that—recommendations. He particularly had strong objections to some of the

---

54. See "Presiding Over the Convention: The Indispensable Man," Mount Vernon, accessed October 11, 2018, https://www.mountvernon.org/george-washington/constitutional-convention/convention-president/.

structural amendments. What was important to Madison and other proponents of the Constitution was that Virginia had ratified and that New York followed suit.

Madison understood, however, that he could not bask too long in the moment. It was clear that the First Congress under the Constitution would have to address, in good faith, the various amendments proposed in the state ratifying conventions. To fail to do so would place the new government under intense and continuing pressure from Anti-Federalists and others. Patrick Henry had offered conciliatory remarks in the Virginia Convention, just prior to and after the final votes, but any peace was temporary and fragile. Henry and others remained resistant to the new Constitution and were likely to pursue ways to dismantle the government and thereby return power to the states. Others would not be satisfied until rights were secured in writing under the Constitution. The fate of the newly instituted government under the Constitution remained uncertain, as did the addition of amendments, including most significantly, a bill of rights.

Chapter Six

Adopting the Bill of Rights

"In Europe, charters of liberty have been granted by power. America has set the example . . . of charters of power granted by liberty. This revolution in the practice of the world, may, with an honest praise, be pronounced the most triumphant epoch of its history, and the most consoling presage of its happiness."[1]

James Madison

"Madison's careful drafting and skilled floor management of the Bill of Rights through Congress gives him just title to two great tributes—Father of the Constitution and Father of the Bill of Rights. The Founders deeply admired classical heroes. But no figure of antiquity—no Greek like Pericles or Solon, no Roman like Cicero or Cincinnatus—can claim an equal standing with Madison as lawgiver and champion of liberty."[2]

William J. Bennett

The preservation of the United States of America, as proposed under the newly ratified Constitution, continued to be seriously in question. Anti-Federalists were marshalling forces within the states to elect members to the Senate and House of Representatives who would oppose the newly ratified Constitution at

---

1. James Madison for the *National Gazette,* 18 January 1792, Founders Online (National Archives), accessed October 11, 2018, https://founders.archives.gov/documents/Madison /01-14-02-0172.
2. William J. Bennett, *America, the Last Best Hope,* Vol. 1: *From the Age of Discovery to a World at War* (Nashville: Thomas Nelson, 2006), 143.

every turn, with a desire to dismantle or change it in dramatic ways. The challenging work of instituting a constitutional fabric of government, including a written bill of rights, remained far from finished. Those elected to serve in the new government would make all the difference in securing the future of the United States, the Constitution, and the yet to be adopted Bill of Rights. At every turn, Madison was destined to play a pivotal role, but he was challenged repeatedly, as a candidate and an advocate.

At the time of the ratifying convention, it was clear that General George Washington, a friend of the Constitution, was destined to serve as the first president under the Constitution, provided he was willing to serve. Once he declared his willingness to leave the life at Mount Vernon that he coveted to reluctantly serve as president, the result of the first presidential election under the Constitution was certain. When the Electoral College votes were counted, all sixty-nine were cast in favor of General George Washington. It was not clear, however, that even George Washington could hold the United States together under the newly ratified Constitution. He needed strong support in the House and Senate to do so, particularly given that Congress (the legislative branch) was then believed to be the strongest branch of government under the Constitution.

Washington's First Inaugural Address

In his first inaugural address, largely written by James Madison, Washington alluded to the prospect of amending the Constitution and the concomitant challenge that must be faced in the first Congress. He addressed Article Five of the Constitution, which deals with the Amendment power, stating, "[I]t will remain with your [the people through their elected representatives] judgment to decide, how far an exercise of the occasional power delegated by the Fifth article of the Constitution is rendered expedient at the present juncture by the nature of objections which have been urged against the System, or by the degree of inquietude which has given birth to them."[3] Washington then wisely declined to enter the fray by stating,

---

3. "First Inaugural Address of George Washington," 30 April 1789, The Avalon Project (Yale

Instead of undertaking particular recommendations on this subject, in which I could be guided by no lights derived from official opportunities, I shall again give way to my entire confidence in your discernment and pursuit of the public good: For I assure myself that whilst you carefully avoid every alteration which might endanger the benefits of an United and effective Government, or which ought to await the future lessons of experience; a reverence for the characteristic rights of freemen, and a regard for the public harmony, will sufficiently influence your deliberations on the question how far the former can be more impregnably fortified, or the latter be safely and advantageously promoted.[4]

The president's reference to his "reverence for the characteristic rights of freemen" made clear his belief that natural and accepted rights needed to be "impregnably fortified."

President Washington closed his address with the following powerful benediction:

Having thus imported to you my sentiments, as they have been awakened by the occasion which brings us together, I shall take my present leave; but not without resorting once more to the benign parent of the human race, in humble supplication that since he has been pleased to favour the American people, with opportunities for deliberating in perfect tranquility, and dispositions for deciding with unparalleled unanimity on a form of Government, for the security of their Union, and the advancement of their happiness; so his divine blessing may be equally conspicuous in the enlarged views, the temperate consultations, and the wise measures on which the success of this Government must depend.[5]

Washington, Madison, and others who supported the cause of the Constitution, including rights "impregnably fortified" against government action, also understood well the perilous state of the new nation. They openly acknowledged the need for the new constitutional government to be blessed from on high. More providential aid was necessary that a nation conceived in liberty might be secured.

Law School), accessed October 11, 2018, http://avalon.law.yale.edu/18th_century/wash1.asp.
4. Ibid.
5. Ibid.

With the most significant step to forming a "more perfect union" out of the way, the next crucial step involved the selection of members of Congress. The nation's future depended on election of strong representatives willing to follow President Washington's example and committed to serving as supporters of the rule of law under the Constitution. State or provincial interests, personal pride, and partisanship were common, then as now, and the election of members of Congress who would put country before self was necessary but hardly assured. The newly elected members of the Senate and the House would need to deliberate, and when necessary compromise, in a joint effort to perpetuate a united government under the Constitution. They had to be committed to deliberating civilly, laying aside personal or provincial interests for the higher good, tasks that often ran directly against their immediate self or political interest. Madison was clearly such a man. His election to serve in the First Congress, tied as it was to the destiny of the United States under the Constitution, however, remained uncertain.

Still bristling over his defeat in the Virginia Ratifying Convention, Patrick Henry joined with other powerful Anti-Federalists in combining to ensure that opponents of the Constitution were elected to serve in Congress at this critical time. Henry focused his efforts, in significant measure, on preventing the single most powerful voice supporting the Constitution in Virginia, Madison, from serving in the First Congress.

The Anti-Federalists knew that if they could gain control over the government under the newly ratified Constitution, they might still prevail in their efforts to undermine the Constitution. They committed to fighting the battle on two fronts: (1) by electing a solid majority of members of Congress openly opposed to the Constitution; and (2) by joining in a temporary and secret alliance with some Federalists or supporters of the Constitution in opposing inclusion of a written bill of rights. The Anti-Federalists understood that if they prevented the First Congress from curing the major lingering objection to the Constitution among the citizenry—the addition of a bill of rights— the government under the Constitution would falter, facilitating the return of power to the states. If they could succeed on either front, the perpetuation of the Constitution was in jeopardy.

This realization provided the Anti-Federalists with confidence as they formed a new set of battle lines. George Mason and Patrick Henry, two of the most formidable and well-respected Anti-Federalist leaders in the Commonwealth of Virginia, were by no means alone. They were joined by another influential young politician, James Monroe. Despite his claim of civility at the close of the Virginia Ratifying Convention, Patrick Henry remained fully committed to using his political and rhetorical skills to ensure that Virginia elected only opponents to the new Constitution to serve in Congress.

Madison agreed to have his name included as a candidate for the Senate in the First Congress. The Virginia Assembly selected the Senators. Henry maintained firm control over most of the Virginia Assembly—a control that Madison referred to as "omnipotent." Exercising that power, Henry took great satisfaction in his effort to thwart Madison's election. In garnering support for his efforts, Henry claimed that Madison was a wholly unacceptable candidate because Madison refused to support structural and related amendments to the Constitution designed to secure the rights of the states and the people. Henry specifically declared that Madison believed that "not a letter of the Constitution could be spared."[6] To this questionable charge and in language unbecoming a statesman, Henry added that the election of Madison would result "in producing rivulets of blood throughout the land."[7] With such inflammatory rhetoric and careful deployment of his political power and skills, Patrick Henry succeeded in his efforts to persuade a majority of the Assembly to reject Madison and select two committed Anti-Federalists to serve as the first United States Senators from the Commonwealth of Virginia. The Assembly elected Richard Henry Lee, a member of an influential Virginia family known for his early support of the revolutionary effort, and William

---

6. See, "Did Madison Flip-Flop?," *Teaching American History*, accessed October 11, 2019, http://teachingamericanhistory.org/bor/themes/flip-flop.

7. Henry Lee Letter to James Madison, 19 November 1788, Founders Online (National Archives), accessed October 11, 2018, https://founders.archives.gov/documents/Madison /01-11-02-0258.

Grayson, another early patriot and Oxford educated lawyer who was also a cousin of James Monroe.

James Monroe v. James Madison

Having succeeded in keeping Madison out of the Senate, Henry and his fellow Anti-Federalists devised a two-fold political strategy to keep Madison out of the House of Representatives, as well. Henry began by persuading the Assembly to pass legislation of questionable constitutionality, which required candidates for the United States House of Representatives to be residents in their respective districts for a full year. Henry next persuaded the Assembly to create, or more accurately gerrymander, a district (including Madison's home county of Orange) intentionally designed to favor the Anti-Federalist candidate. If they successfully accomplished this dual strategy, the Anti-Federalists could keep Madison out of the First Congress. By gerrymandering the district, Henry and his supporters required that Madison run, if at all, in his home district against their preferred candidate, James Monroe, who had already declared his intention to run for the seat. The stage for a contested election between two able candidates was set.

In a letter to Thomas Jefferson, Madison later reminisced that it was his "misfortune to be thrown into a contest with our friend, Colonel Monroe."[8] Madison, however, noted that he had "no reason to doubt the distinction was duly kept in mind between political and personal views, and that it has saved our friendship from the smallest diminution."[9] Monroe and Madison engaged in one of the most hotly contested elections of the time. They differed dramatically on policies and as to the importance of the Constitution. Nevertheless, they often traveled together to campaign events. The campaign proved to be one of the most important in our nation's history. Despite opportunities for acrimony and personal attacks, at every stop on the campaign, the election remains a model of civility in public discourse and a lasting tribute to the greatness of Madison and Monroe.

---

8. Letter to Thomas Jefferson from James Madison, 29 March 1789, Founders Online (National Archives), accessed October 11, 2018, https://founders.archives.gov/documents /Jefferson/01-15-02-0004
9. Ibid.

James Monroe was seven years younger than Madison and rising in prominence as a political figure, a force to be reckoned with, in Virginia politics.

Thomas Jefferson knew Monroe well. Monroe became Jefferson's closest neighbor, living in a home designed by Jefferson. As evidence of his sense of humor, Jefferson designed Monroe's back door in a manner that made it necessary for him to stoop and bow to Monticello, Jefferson's home, each time he passed through the door. Jefferson said this of Monroe's character, "The scrupulousness of his honor will make you safe in the most confidential communications. A better man . . . cannot be."[10]

Monroe and Madison often worked together and occasionally opposed each other in seeking public office. Through it all, their friendship and mutual respect never diminished in any significant measure. Monroe was certainly a highly qualified and formidable candidate to run for the seat in the 5th District in Virginia against Madison. Interestingly, Monroe's uncle Joseph Jones, who was not a proponent of the Constitution, tried to discourage his nephew from running against Madison. Against the wise advice of his uncle, Monroe decided to run, believing that the issues that separated him from his friend made it imperative that he provide the electorate with a choice.

Despite being younger, Monroe was about eight inches taller and much broader of shoulder than Madison. He had a commanding presence and was a war hero, who tended to favor the Anti-Federalist cause. He threw himself fully into the campaign with characteristic vigor. Together with Madison, Monroe worked hard to shape with clarity the issues that separated the candidates. The electorate would have to decide between two good men with very different visions for the future of America.

Perhaps disheartened by his defeat as a candidate for the Senate, Madison was initially reluctant to become a candidate for the House seat in his home district. He did not relish running in an uphill race against James Monroe, and he was also inclined to remain in New

---

10. Letter From Thomas Jefferson to James Madison, 8 May 1784, Founders Online (National Archives), accessed October 11, 2018, https://founders.archives.gov/documents /Jefferson/01-07-02-0179.

York, far away from the distasteful task of campaigning for office. At the time, Madison was also suffering from a severe bout of piles (hemorrhoids). A dreaded long ride on bumpy roads, in an uncomfortable carriage, presented an unpleasant prospect for Madison. His friends, nevertheless, continued to believe Madison could win the seat in the House and refused to be quieted in their persistent efforts to get Madison to be a serious candidate. They were fearful that Madison was falling into his pattern of reluctance to campaign actively for a seat. Madison's initial unwillingness to return and subject himself to the rigors of campaigning, something he intensely disliked doing, was further compounded by the fact that it was winter. He may also have continued to harbor the hope of being elected from a distance, based on his past record, without having to campaign. Monroe's candidacy, however, made it clear that Madison would have to run in the carefully gerrymandered district or be foreclosed from participation in the First Congress.

With insistent urging from friends and supporters, Madison finally agreed to actively seek election to the House of Representatives in the First Congress. On his return trip to Montpelier to campaign, James stopped for a week at Mount Vernon to visit with George Washington. It was the Christmas season and Madison knew that the stop would help him prepare, physically and emotionally, to mount a strong campaign. Madison was quite aware of the significant obstacles that he faced in seeking election to the House. He understood that the district was created to favor Monroe and disfavor his candidacy. Madison also knew of Monroe's strengths as a candidate. Madison realized, however, that the issues at stake were significant and that he and Monroe could help frame them. These two patriots initially differed on two major issues: (1) possible amendment of the Constitution to include a bill of rights and possible major structural changes to the government; and (2) taxation to fund debts and the future of the government.

The electorate was fearful that the national government had been designed in a manner that would have the effect of limiting their rights. It was evident to his allies, therefore, that for Madison to have any chance of prevailing in such an uphill electoral battle, he would need to support adding a bill of rights and was already beginning to show signs of changing his view regarding this. Even if he changed his view, however, he would have to make it clear to the electorate that his support was genuine, given his past statements to the contrary.

Madison had political reasons for changing his position, even author, a written bill of rights to the Constitution. Some historians argue that he changed his position on the issue solely as a matter of political expediency. There was, however, more to Madison's shift from initially opposing a written bill of rights to becoming its primary advocate and author in the First Congress. Madison was often willing to act out of political expediency, but only if he was convinced that it was likely to lead to a greater good. In this instance, Madison had to be convinced of the utility of a written bill of rights—it had to be more than a meaningless parchment barrier. It had to be more than a matter of political expediency but also as a matter of principle. Given his openness to new ideas, and his humble and teachable nature, Madison was susceptible to persuasive arguments that might cause him to change his position. His friends acknowledged the reasons for his hesitancy and were ready to supply him with some highly persuasive arguments to support of a written bill of rights.

Thomas Jefferson, and to a lesser extent other friends, persisted in persuading Madison to change his mind and support the addition of a written bill of rights to the newly ratified Constitution. Jefferson's correspondence with Madison, during this crucial period, was a dialogue between two great minds and dear friends, each of whom was committed to the perpetuation of a united government conceived in liberty under the Constitution. Those letters reflect how teachable Madison was. Jefferson believed that "a bill of rights is what the people are entitled to against every government on earth."[11] Madison responded in October 1788, just prior to the gerrymandering of the House of Representatives districts in the Assembly under Henry's leadership. Madison acknowledged that many believed such a written enumeration of rights to be unnecessary. He noted, however, that his "opinion has always been in favor of a bill of rights; provided that it be so framed

---

11. Letter from Thomas Jefferson to James Madison, 20 December 1787, Founders Online (National Archives), accessed October 11, 2018, https://founders.archives.gov/documents/Madison/01-10-02-0210.

as not to imply powers not meant to be included in the enumeration."[12] He added that he had "never thought the omission [of a bill of rights in the Constitution] a material defect, nor [was he] anxious to supply it by subsequent amendment, for any other reason that it is anxiously desired by others."

In that revealing letter of October 17, 1788 to Jefferson, Madison offered reasons supporting his belief that the omission of a written bill of rights from the Constitution was not a material defect. In an oft-quoted argument, Madison noted that "repeated violations of these parchment barriers [written Declarations or Bills of Rights] have been committed by overbearing majorities in every State." He added that he had "seen the bill of rights violated in every instance [in Virginia] where it has been opposed to a popular current."[13] Again, he cited the denial of the right of conscience or religious liberty by "overbearing majorities" as an example of the ease with which government infringed on written rights. Nevertheless, Madison acknowledged to Jefferson that he was coming to believe that written amendments should be included in the Constitution. At a minimum, Madison was beginning to be persuaded that if such a written bill was ably drafted, it might constitute an affirmation that such rights exist, an aspiration that could prove to be helpful to the cause of liberty.

In responding, Jefferson persisted in arguing that "[even though a written bill of rights] is not absolutely efficacious under all circumstances, it is of great potency always, and rarely inefficacious."[14] He also responded to Madison's fear that overbearing majorities would limit such rights in furtherance of their self-interested policy objectives (their view of the public good). In making this argument, Jefferson conceded that the majority might be inclined to limit such rights but stressed that Madison had failed to consider the helpful role of the one non-majoritarian branch of government, the judiciary. Jefferson

---

12. Letter from James Madison to Thomas Jefferson, 17 October 1787, Founders Online (National Archives), accessed October 11, 2018, https://founders.archives.gov/documents /Madison/01-11-02-0218.

13. Ibid.

14. Letter From Thomas Jefferson to James Madison, 15 March 1789, Founders Online (National Archives), accessed October 11, 2018, https://founders.archives.gov/documents /Jefferson/01-14-02-0410.

stressed, "In the arguments in favor of a declaration of rights, you omit one which has great weight with me, the legal check which it puts in the hands of the judiciary. This is a body, which if rendered independent, & kept strictly to their own department merits great confidence for their learning and integrity."[15] This argument in favor of an independent judiciary, which could protect minority rights from the excesses of the majority, had a significant influence on Madison's thinking, as evidenced by the fact that he later embraced that very position in support of judicial protection of rights. This correspondence also demonstrates that Jefferson, at this early juncture, understood that the judiciary, the Supreme Court under Article III of the Constitution, was intentionally designed to act with independence to protect rights against infringement at the national or state level. It was a nonelected body specially founded to protect liberty and the rule of law.

Madison was beginning to understand that a written bill of rights might, in fact, be the best way to protect rights and preserve the Constitution. By the time that he was actively running for a seat in the House of Representatives, Madison was transformed, through sound argument, and became a strong advocate for adding a written bill of rights. To ensure the broad and clear statement of such rights, Madison pledged to be directly involved in drafting and securing adoption of those amendments. His commitment to rights and limiting the capacity of a majority in the government to infringe upon or tyrannize the rights of individuals and groups or sects was widely known. As such, Madison was an ideal candidate for those who sincerely supported a strong bill of rights. His longstanding support of such rights and his special capacity for drafting with precision made Madison a uniquely capable champion of the bill of rights.

In later introducing the Bill of Rights in the First Congress, Madison clarified the reasons that dictated his change of mind. He declared, "It may be thought all paper barriers against the power of the community are too weak to be worthy of attention . . . yet, as they have a tendency to impress some degree of respect for them, to establish the public opinion in their favor, and rouse the attention of the whole community, it may be one means to control the majority

---

15. Ibid.

from those acts to which they might be otherwise inclined."[16] Madison understood that a written bill of rights should be embraced by the people and their representatives, but he also acknowledged that a written bill of rights standing alone was not enough to secure the cause of liberty. He had a record of fighting to secure rights and believed broad rights enshrined in clear written form were worthy of his support, as a bulwark against momentary impulses of ever-changing majorities at the national level. Madison knew that no single faction would always retain power in a large and diverse nation. Therefore, he was hopeful that all factions would learn to support the rights, as written, as an assurance against occasions when they might be out of power. Madison was now convinced that three constitutional forces working together were best designed to protect rights in an optimal fashion. Those three forces—(1) the structure of a limited government with checks and balances among the branches, (2) the multiplicity of factions and ever-changing majority coalitions at the national level, and (3) a written bill of rights duly approved in the form of carefully written amendments to the Constitution—combined to protect rights against the tyranny of any transitory majority.

In today's political climate, such a change in position on the part of a candidate would be suspect, perhaps even fatal, in the eyes of an increasingly distrustful electorate. The openly fallible candidate in our age is often viewed as unprincipled, shifting his or her view for purely political reasons. That was somewhat less true during Madison's era, particularly when the political figure was otherwise known for his integrity and commitment to principle. Madison was just such a candidate. He had a reputation who understood that politics is not about splitting a static pie—politics does not have to be a zero-sum game with winners and losers. All can often win, and the pie can become bigger, when parties talk openly, respectfully, and with a genuine desire to leave the discussion a better and wiser person, having learned from the other side. In that spirit, Madison embraced fallibility and the thoughtful changing of his position as a transformative strength, not a weakness.

---

16. James Madison, House of Representative, 8 June 1789, The Founders Constitution (University of Chicago), accessed October 11, 2018, http://press-pubs.uchicago.edu/founders/documents/v1ch14s50.html.

The electorate, in turn, knew and trusted Madison. His integrity was unquestioned. He had a strong record of supporting rights, particularly the right of conscience. At a critical juncture in the campaign, George Eve, a Baptist minister who served many small congregations in the district, with a combined membership in the hundreds, received a letter from Madison assuring him of the sincerity of his support for a written bill of rights and for the right of conscience. Eve trusted Madison and read regularly from that letter during the final month of the campaign. In that letter, Madison emphasized his "sincere opinion that the Constitution ought to be revised, and that the first Congress meeting under it, ought to prepare and recommend to the States, for ratification, the most satisfactory provisions for all essential rights, *particularly the rights of conscience in the fullest latitude*"[17] (emphasis added). Baptists, led by the preaching of John Leland, George Eve, and others, willingly threw their support to their long-time ally, Madison, as did members of other minority religious groups or sects living in the district, including Lutherans and Presbyterians. During his years of service in Virginia, Madison had earned the trust and support of minority religious groups by his genuine devotion to rights, particularly the right of these minorities to worship and exercise their religion as they pleased. Even his opponent, James Monroe, seemed reluctant to raise the issue of Madison's change or clarification of position regarding inclusion of a written bill of rights, other than to say that he had long supported the need for amendments in the form of a bill of rights. Madison's willingness to support a written bill of rights eliminated one of the major obstacles to his election to the House of Representatives in the First Congress.

Two obstacles remained. One was substantive, and the other was personal and practical for Madison, involving running a campaign during a frigid winter. The major substantive issue remaining was whether the federal government should be permitted to levy direct taxes. On this issue, the candidates strongly disagreed. Madison took the less enviable position, arguing that direct taxation at the national level

---

17. Letter from James Madison to George Eve, 2 January 1789, Founders Online (National Archives), accessed October 11, 2018, https://founders.archives.gov/documents /Madison/01-11-02-0297.

was necessary and more equitable than imposts or requisitions seeking largely voluntary payments from the states. He argued that direct taxation was, in fact, necessary to protect the national government. Direct taxes were also more equitable than import taxes or requisitions from the states. Madison used the failure of providing adequate funds to the troops in the Revolutionary War as an example of the necessity for direct taxation. Efforts during the war to requisition funds from the states failed miserably, leaving courageous troops underfunded, suffering, and even dying for lack of necessities. Madison added that, under those circumstances, the war would not have been won were it not for financial and related support from France. Relying on other nations for funding, however, was, at best, a precarious means of securing revenue for national defense.

As one who personally suffered for months at Valley Forge due to a lack of supplies and revenue to fund the cause fought for by patriots like himself, Monroe acknowledged the need for revenue to deal with international threats and challenges at the national level. He, however, believed that the best way to secure those necessary funds was through import taxes, selling of lands to the west, or requisitions from the states. At a minimum, he argued that requisitions should be tried before giving the national government the power to engage in direct taxation in any form. Monroe reflected Patrick Henry's concerns regarding increasing political power at the national level, arguing that a national government with the power to engage in direct taxation was an omnipresent threat to liberty. Monroe was in the enviable position of being the anti-tax candidate.

Given that Monroe agreed there was a need to provide revenue for national necessities, Madison began by carefully framing the remaining issue of how to best obtain that revenue. Madison fashioned a cogent and convincing response that favored direct taxation over other forms of taxation. He took a negative and turned it into a positive by arguing that direct taxation provided a stable source of revenue at the national level, which was more equitable than import or other forms of taxation and revenue generation. The electorate listened carefully as Madison explained his position in detail.

As to the use of import taxes, a position endorsed by Monroe, Madison argued Virginia and other southern states would suffer more than citizens in other states under such a system. Madison reminded Virginians that they consumed imported goods more than their northern counterparts and would bear the brunt of such taxation. As such, they would be subjected to an inequitable system of taxation, under Monroe's proposed taxation of imports. The electorate came to see that Madison seemed to have the better of the argument regarding the problems associated with the use of import taxes to meet national needs.

Madison continued with his equitable argument by asserting that direct taxation was also preferable to requisitions. In doing so, he drew on his experience with efforts to generate revenues through requisitions during the Revolutionary War. He framed the issue as whether requisitions or direct taxation are more equitable., By its nature, Madison argued that non-direct forms of taxation failed the test of reason. He emphasized that requisitions can never succeed, because some states are more willing to pay them than other states. The states that pay the requisitions therefore will bear an equal burden., While making his case for direct taxation in public gatherings, Madison's voice remained barely above a whisper. Nevertheless, his argument reached an intellectual crescendo when he eloquently warned that war was the likely result of requisitions. He argued that those who pay their requisitions will complain that they are being unfairly burdened, with ill-will leading to quarrels and ultimately perhaps even war. Under any circumstance, the natural inequity of requisitions will lead to disunity. Those present began to understand the full force of Madison's argument— an underfunded national government would be easy prey to stronger European nations and internal bickering. The fairest way to secure liberty and adequately fund the national government came in the form of direct taxation.

Monroe and the Ant-Federalists initially seemed to have the upper hand on the substantive arguments regarding Madison's prior opposition to a written bill of rights and his support of direct taxation. Madison, however, was equal to the task. Indeed, perhaps no one was better positioned to respond to substantive arguments than James Madison. But his arguments were sophisticated and required careful explanation. Therefore, one final obstacle had to be overcome: the electorate had to be convinced that Madison was the better candidate. That highly personal issue required that Madison do that which he disdained—actively campaign and seek votes, carefully explaining his complex positions before small gatherings throughout the district.

Madison was reluctant to campaign for yet another reason. His frail health made campaigning physically taxing and potentially debilitating. Nevertheless, he slowly came to understand that he had to campaign with vigor, traveling throughout the district during a brutally cold season of the year.

During the campaign, Madison and Monroe presented the issues with clarity and civility, a civility that enabled them to maintain a lifelong friendship. Jefferson used a scientific metaphor to describe the remarkable civility of the Madison v. Monroe campaign, a contest he witnessed firsthand, as a friend and neighbor of both candidates. Jefferson reflected that there was no ill-will between the candidates. Despite their respect for each other, however, they campaigned vigorously. They both worked hard to persuade the electorate, to win them over to their respective candidacies.

At an event at a Lutheran Church in Culpepper, the candidates attended services, which included music that lifted Madison's spirits. They then spent hours in the bitter cold, explaining their respective positions to voters. Those voters were critical to the success of either candidate. Culpepper was an Anti-Federalist stronghold, a county likely to vote for Monroe. It was also home to the Lutherans and other religious minorities, groups Madison had to win to be elected. The Lutherans tended to vote as a block, so winning that skirmish on the church grounds was extremely important to each candidate.

Monroe stood erect, nearly a head taller than Madison. He spoke with a powerful voice that carried and was easy to understand. He was an impressive candidate. Bound up in his dark, heavy coat, Madison appeared to be tiny in contrast to Monroe. The voters also had to gather into a close group to hear Madison's weak voice, each word coming in wispy clouds of Madison's breath as each newly formed syllable struck the freezing air. The Lutheran voters were warmed by their proximity to each other, as they closed ranks to hear Madison. They were also warmed by Madison's conviction and sound reasoning. They could feel the spirit of a great man of conscience, as Madison methodically offered sound arguments supporting each of his positions. He explained why a direct tax was equitable, which drew on the commitment to fairness of those present. He powerfully but quietly described his commitment to a written bill of rights, including the right of greatest importance to all present, the right of conscience. Each candidate was likeable, and each had his own form of charisma. Nearly all the voters left feeling positively about both candidates.

When Election Day arrived, however, Madison's capacity to convince proved victorious over the outward charisma of his friend, Monroe. Madison received 256 votes in Culpepper, clearly carrying its strong Lutheran community. Monroe, the favored Anti-Federalist, received only 103 votes.

The weather that night in Culpepper was severely cold, as each candidate spent lengthy periods of time articulating their respective positions. That evening, Madison suffered frostbite to the tip of his nose. Later in life, Madison wryly referred to that frostbite as a battle scar. To Madison, they became a token of the kind of zeal that was necessary to secure the future of the new nation, under a Constitution replete with a written bill of rights. The campaign was, indeed, a battle between two able candidates with views that differed in significant ways.

On February 2, 1789, the electorate throughout the district, joined electors in Culpepper County, and trudged through dangerous weather conditions to cast their votes. It took over a week to tally the votes from the eight counties in the district. It was not until February 12 that the results were announced. In an election characterized by an understandably low turnout, given the severity of the weather, Monroe won Amherst, a heavily Anti-Federalist county, where turnout was high at 74 percent. However, Monroe won by a much slimmer than anticipated margin of 246–145. Monroe also prevailed in the counties of Fluvanna, Goochland (by a margin of a single vote), and Spotsylvania, his home county. Even in Spotsylvania, Monroe's home county, Madison ran surprisingly well, with Monroe prevailing by a vote of 189–115. Madison won by substantial margins in Albemarle (Jefferson's home county), Culpepper, Louisa, and Orange counties.

Madison won his home district, Orange County, where he was known best, by a stunning vote of 216–9. When tallied, to the surprise of many, Madison won rather handily, with 1,308 votes compared to Monroe's 972. It is conceded by those who have studied the election closely that the Baptists and other minority religious sects, including the Lutherans in Culpepper, played a major role in securing Madison's election. Madison's commitment to conscience had warmed the hearts, satisfied the minds, and touched the spirits of those minority religionists. Once again, they helped place Madison in a position to influence the future of the United States of America.

Drafting the Bill of Rights

Madison had prevailed in a competitive and physically and emotionally taxing race. There was little time to rest, however. He had to prepare for the First Congress, where the Constitution was about to be tested. It was also necessary that Madison quickly assume what he knew to be a difficult task: putting natural rights, including an inviolable right of conscience, into a clear and coherent textual form. This was a task he took seriously. In the congenial environs of Montpelier, and the confines of the space where he worked ever so effectively, Madison commenced the trying labor associated with preparation for attendance at the First Congress, where his foremost goal was to obtain adoption of a viable bill of rights and thereby secure liberty and the constitutional rule of law.

Madison meticulously examined existing declarations of rights that had been adopted by the states and poured over the various suggestions in ratifying conventions in the states that recommended inclusion of a bill of rights, including Virginia. The difficulty of drafting such rights with a precision sufficient to minimize the capacity of future governments to limit rights given of God was daunting, requiring great care. He also understood that gaining support for a fulsome bill of rights presented a challenging political task. Doing what he always did extraordinarily well, Madison began the process of studying and brooding with care over the mass of material he had accumulated that would provide light and inspiration in his drafting efforts. His brooding was reflective of his humility and his acknowledgment of the need for providential inspiration.

Each word was agonized over as Madison carefully assumed the consuming task of drafting, a work that he had little time to perform. Congress was scheduled to convene on March 4 in New York City. Madison went right to work, knowing he would soon be making the difficult trek to New York during a time when weather would be uncertain. He also knew from experience that he needed to arrive in time to do some business before other members of Congress arrived. His journey may be difficult but travel for other members of Congress was even more time-consuming, and many of them had just learned of their election. Nevertheless, Madison was determined to arrive early, having learned that preliminary preparation and discussions with other early-arriving delegates was always helpful to his cause, the cause of liberty and the Constitution.

Preparing for a New Government

Madison also wanted to stop in Mount Vernon to meet with president-elect George Washington, before traveling on to New York. As it turned out, stopping to see Washington was time well spent. The president had previously sent Madison a copy of his proposed inaugural address. The address had been written by Washington and David Humphreys, Washington's secretary. The proposed address was lengthy—seventy-three pages, including an extensive discussion of Washington's proposed legislative agenda. Madison believed the address was deficient in two major respects: (1) it was simply too long; and (2) it was inappropriate for the president to prescribe the legislative agenda for a co-equal branch of government, Congress. Madison ultimately persuaded Washington on both points and added language to the address that was well crafted to confirm the confidence of the people who had entrusted Washington with the reigns of leadership at a momentous time.

It is often easier to write a lengthy address than to write a short, succinct, and inspiring address. But Washington, Humphrey, and Madison collectively proved equal to the task. Madison's imprint is all over the final product. Washington decided to omit lengthy references to an extensive legislative agenda, but he did include a recommendation regarding amendments to the Constitution. With Madison's assistance, Washington wrote, "Besides the ordinary objects submitted to your care, it will remain with your judgment to decide how far an exercise of the occasional power delegated by the fifth article [the power to amend] the Constitution, is rendered expedient at this present juncture by the nature of objections which have been urged against the system, or by the degree of inquietude which has given birth to them."[18] The President added, "For I assure myself that whilst you carefully avoid every alteration which might endanger the benefits of an United and effective Government, or which ought to await the future lessons of experience; a reverence for the characteristic rights of freeman, and a regard for public harmony, will sufficiently influence your deliberations on the question.[19]" Washington's inaugural address was offered on April 30, not long after the convening of Congress. It also played directly into Madison's legislative agenda: adopt a bill of rights and avoid all other alterations in the structure of government that were being advocated by Anti-Federalists. Madison argued that consideration of the structural changes proposed by the Anti-Federalists should be delayed until actual deficiencies in the government became evident.

Travel to Mount Vernon had been extremely difficult, with roads made almost impassable by snows and mud. Madison left Mount Vernon on February 30, beginning his travels to New York in earnest, finally arriving in New York on March 14. The trip was arduous and physically tiring. Madison arrived after several other members of Congress but before a working quorum was present. Upon arrival in the city, James promptly settled in to familiar accommodations, a room at a boarding house operated by Vandine and Dorothy Ellsworth. Once again, it was a familiar and commodious place to reflect and work.

With a difficult journey behind him, Madison spent more time in preparation and acquainting himself with other members of Congress.

---

18. "Washington's Inaugural Address of 1789, April 30, 1789, National Archives and Records Administration, accessed October 12, 2018, https://www.archives.gov/exhibits /american_originals/inaugtxt.html.
19. Ibid.

His typical day left room for few, generally four or at most five hours, of sleep, a habit that he had formed while a student at the College of New Jersey. He spent the day in meetings, getting a feel for the positions of others. After dinner and discussions with other members of Congress, evening passed into night. Madison toiled day after day for many hours, working late into the night, by the flickering light of a candle, studying and writing. Those late-night hours were consumed with preparation for the next day and with writing lengthy letters to friends, family, and supporters. Already frail, those endless hours of work were taxing on Madison's health. The endless hours of work and the heat of summer, beginning slowly in May and reaching a crescendo in August, took their toll on Madison. The conditions also frayed the tempers of other members of Congress. The ill humor of members was further exacerbated by lengthy speeches, as members wrestled over the substance of the legislative agenda and the future of the nation. They all understood that they were laying the foundation, for good or ill, of the newly formed United States. The weight of this task often made their personal weaknesses painfully evident.

New York was justifiably proud of the extensive and costly renovation and enlargement of its former City Hall. It was part of the city's effort to make a case for New York as the nation's capital. The focal point was the strikingly beautiful Federal Hall, where the First Congress met. The building was elegant, with its lofty ceilings and exquisite marble, but it was hardly ideal for the leading advocate for the Bill of Rights, James Madison, whose softness of speech made it difficult for other members of the House to hear his voice.

Furthermore, the House, unlike the Senate, decided to open its proceedings to the public. Visitors to the House Chambers were seated in distant galleries and expected to hear the proceedings. They were often unable to hear Madison as he spoke. Many visitors and some members were left with a less than favorable impression of Madison as a speaker. To many, he did not live up to his reputation as one of the new nation's ablest advocates. Among many who did not know him, Madison was little more than a small and frail man, dressed in a dark coat, with a voice that was difficult to hear. In a chamber filled with representatives, sweltering in the heat and humidity of a New York summertime, "Little Jemmy Madison" was at a serious disadvantage. It seemed as if the very elements were once again conspiring against Madison. His eloquence had to be found in the substance of words and not the flourish of his oratory. It was a time that demanded just such eloquence.

The elements were aligned against Madison, but they were the least of the threats he faced in securing adoption and ratification of the Bill of Rights. The Federalists remained unpersuaded of the need for a bill of rights and believed debates over that topic impeded the all-important tasks associated with forming a government and providing the revenue necessary to operate the national government. Anti-Federalists, in turn, were persuaded of the need for a bill of rights. Some, however, opposed Madison's efforts for two reasons. First, they wanted a bill or declaration of rights, but they also wanted amendments designed to change the structure of government to ensure the preeminence of state power. Some more devious Anti-Federalists went so far as to want Madison to fail in his effort to secure adoption of any bill of rights. Failure to adopt a bill or declaration of rights would increase public opposition to the Constitution and raise support for efforts to hold a second constitutional convention. Furthermore, even if Madison garnered support for the general cause of amending the Constitution with the adoption of a written bill of rights, the substantive content of those amendments was certain to be divisive.

The obstacles to adoption of a written bill of rights were monumental. Madison believed rights to be inalienable, a gift from God. He would need another series of providential gifts to enshrine those rights into a single written bill of rights. A wise prophet-leader, Isaiah, described the miraculous work of God in such instances in these memorable words, "For precept must be upon precept, precept upon precept, line upon line, line upon line."[20] This would prove to be true with regard to the miracle of adopting the Bill of Rights in New York, just as it was true of the miracle of adopting the Constitution in Philadelphia. One inspired decision would have to follow another

---

20. Isaiah 28:10, *King James Bible Online,* accessed October 12, 2018, https://www.king jamesbibleonline.org/Isaiah-28-10/.

equally inspired decision, each principle building on another, with little room for error. To best understand the miracle of the adoption of the Bill of Rights, it is necessary to describe chronologically each step along the way, which requires returning to Madison's arrival in New York on March 14, 1789.

The Adoption of the Bill of Rights

Congress was scheduled to convene on March 4, ten days before Madison arrived. The first effort to form a quorum for business fell far short. On March 4, only eight out of twenty-two senators had arrived, and only thirteen of fifty-nine representatives were present. Members of both chambers continued to straggle in to New York, often traveling miles along poor roads and through inclement weather. It was not until April 1, 1789, two weeks after Madison's arrival, that the House had sufficient numbers to form a working quorum.

Two early actions on the part of the First Congress are of particular note. They had to determine the appropriate title for the president, and each chamber of Congress, the House and the Senate, had to establish rules. The Senate recommended a more elitist title for the president: "His Elective Highness, the President of the United States of America, and protector of their Liberties."[21] This title confirmed the concern of and commitment to liberty, on the part of most members of Congress, although it is unclear whether they were referring to the liberty of the people or the states.

Despite his unequivocal support for liberty, this title was disturbing to Madison for two reasons. It suggested that the president was the protector of the liberties of the states, representing the united *states* and not we the *people*, thereby implying that liberty was a privilege subject to protection by a beneficent leader or government, raising the specter of a tyrannical majority. It was also too lofty, too elitist, suggesting a king, "His Exalted Highness." Representatives in the House, including Madison, found the title to be unacceptable and recommended that

---

21. See Lorraine, Boissoneault, "Why America Has a 'President' Instead of an 'Exalted Highness," Smithsonian.com, accessed October 12, 2018, https://www.smithsonianmag .com/history/why-america-has-president-instead-exalted-highness-180961841.

the president simply be known as president of the United States. The less-elitist House prevailed.

The other early task involved the providing of rules of order and resolving the issue of whether the proceedings of each chamber should be open to the public. The Senate, the more elitist of the two houses of Congress, voted to work in private. The House, in turn, voted to open their proceedings to the public. The Senate's decision translated into their keeping of poorer records of their proceedings, generally just tallies of votes, than was the case in the House. In five years, the Senate reversed course and joined the House in opening its proceedings to the public. Each chamber also adopted further rules of order, which permitted them to begin the substantive and difficult work of governing.

With general procedures and rules of order in place for each chamber, Congress quickly had to establish a viable government. On April 8, recalling a great deficiency of government under the Articles of Confederation, the failure to provide revenue sufficient for the work of the national government, Madison moved to provide revenue in the form of direct taxation for operating the federal government and as a means of paying the debts of the government, as he promised to do during his campaign for Congress, against the non-tax candidate, James Monroe. Madison was committed to fulfilling promises made to the electorate. After prolonged debates over the nature of and need for revenue for federal operations, Congress voted to support direct taxation.

Congress turned next to the process of providing for the departments of government, including the judiciary and establishment of an executive department or cabinet to serve President Washington and the nation. Madison worked closely with President Washington in the effort to obtain the legislative approval necessary to form a cabinet and executive branch. That work was not completed before Washington offered his first inaugural address to the nation, the very address that Madison helped write, which drew attention to the amendment process. Washington reportedly was visibly embarrassed and trembled as he delivered his first inaugural address in conjunction with his taking the oath to serve as the first president of the United States. He did not relish public speaking and was far more comfortable on the field of battle than he was delivering a major address to a large crowd, including the nation's most respected public servants. His anxiety may have contributed to his appearing stiff. Washington's address was also delivered in a monotone, yet all present acknowledged the president's sincerity and commitment to service. When he sat down, Washington and all present were surely pleased that the address was shortened from its initial seventy-two pages to a mere eight-page, solemn address.

The response to the substance of Washington's address was positive. Nevertheless, both chambers of Congress, as coequal branches of government, believed that they needed to respond to the president's address, even though it did not include a specific legislative agenda, like the one he had included in Washington's first draft. The House directed Madison to chair the committee tasked with formulating a response to Washington's inaugural address. Madison played the primary role in formulating the response to the president's first inaugural address, which he had also largely penned. Washington turned to Madison, once again, and asked him to respond on the president's behalf to the House and Senate responses to Washington's inaugural address. Madison readily agreed and did as bided by the president. Thus, it can fairly be said that Madison was a primary draftsman of Washington's inaugural address, of the House's response to it, and of the president's final words in response to the messages of the House and Senate. Madison and Washington trusted each other. It is little wonder that Madison was often referred to as President Washington's prime minister during those early formative months of the new government under the Constitution.

For Madison, serving President Washington was an honor. He reveled, as the nation did, in the inauguration of our nation's first president. After a day of celebration, however, Congress went back to work. It quickly had to create a viable governmental structure, including providing for the executive and judicial branches of government. Those issues were difficult and divisive. It is not surprising that they proved to be time consuming, as well. Any deviation from those responsibilities was viewed with suspicion and as a distraction by most members of Congress.

It was not until May 4, 1789, therefore, that Madison was able to begin the process of keeping the second and primary promise he had made to the electorate. He stood, taking the floor of the House, quietly announcing his intention to introduce amendments to the Constitution to provide for a written bill of rights. He set the date for introduction of the amendments for some three weeks later, on May 25. Madison did not want to interrupt the flow of congressional business, but he wanted to put his colleagues on notice that he was determined to introduce a bill or declaration of rights. He also reminded other members of the necessity of acting on amendments to avert a crisis, in the form of efforts by some Anti-Federalists and opponents of the Constitution to dismantle the government for want of a written bill of rights.

Evidence of the crisis came quickly. Early in May, Theodorick Bland, an Anti-Federalist and member of the House from Virginia who had opposed ratification of the Constitution, presented Virginia's petition demanding a second convention to consider the defects of the Constitution. Bland was a close ally of Madison's nemesis, Patrick Henry. Bland was joined the next day by John Laurance from New York, who presented his state's demand for a new convention. Thus, before Madison had a chance to offer amendments and thereby allay the concerns of opponents who believed that the Constitution was defective for want of a written bill of rights, he had to deflect the call for another convention.

Madison argued that Congress lacked the power to deliberate on its own with regard to the holding of a convention. In doing so, he used a state's right argument against the pro-state, Anti-Federalist forces. Madison correctly noted that the call for a convention required a vote of two-thirds of the states, not a request from disgruntled representatives for a convention. Madison argued further, with support from Elbridge Gerry of Massachusetts, that the petitions should be tabled until there were a sufficient number of applications. Bland and Madison came to an agreement that forestalled the crisis presented by the Anti-Federalist call for a new convention. They agreed to enter this petition into the journal of the House, without acting directly at that time on the petition.

May 25, the day designated by Madison for presenting the amendments, came and went, due to concerns on the part of his colleagues that there were more pressing matters of business to be considered. Madison was somewhat disappointed and wrote Thomas Jefferson to inform him that the subject of amendments was postponed so that more urgent business would not be delayed.

Part of that press of business included Madison's own proposal on behalf of President Washington, calling for the creation of three executive departments—foreign affairs (the state department), treasury, and war (the defense department). Despite widespread respect for the president, Madison's proposal was questioned by members of the House. Some representatives were troubled by the issue of whether the president had power to remove members of his cabinet, once confirmed. Madison pressed for the president's removal power, but the debate continued. Ultimately Madison and the forces supporting the president's removal power finally prevailed, but it took more precious time.

Madison was becoming anxious. He understood that demands of opponents to the Constitution for inclusion of a bill of rights could not be put off much longer. Nevertheless, he used the time wisely, parsing every word in the introduction of the amendments. He spent hours working and reworking the speech to ensure that each argument was presented persuasively and with clarity. Madison knew that this speech was likely to be one of the most important speeches he would deliver on the floor of the House during the First Congress. It is a speech that has been given sparse attention among scholars, but it is significant in understanding Madison's motivation in introducing the Bill of Rights. His speech also helps clarify the intended nature and scope of the amendments that became the basis for our Bill of Rights.

Introducing the Bill of Rights

Opposition prevailed, however, and the House declined to hear the amendments as a Committee of the Whole. Having failed in his motion to have the amendments considered by the that committee, as opposed to being assigned to a select committee, Madison declared, "I am sorry to be an accessary to the loss of a single moment of time by the house. . . . I will withdraw the motion, and move, sir, that a select committee be appointed to consider and report such amendments as are proper for Congress to propose to the state legislatures of the several States, conformably to the 5th article of the constitution."[22] He added, "If I thought I could fulfill the duty which I owe to myself and my constituents, to let the subject pass over in silence, I most certainly should not trespass upon the indulgence of this house. But I cannot do this; and am therefore compelled to beg a patient hearing to what I have to lay before you."

Madison then launched into his argument supporting the amendments and the substance of the amendments themselves. He began by emphasizing the importance of "proposing to the state legislatures"[23] amendments designed to secure liberty. Madison described the devotion of the American people to "liberty and a republican government" and the need "to extinguish from the bosom of every member of the community any apprehensions, that there are those among his countrymen who wish to deprive them of the liberty for which they so valiantly fought and honorably bled."[24] He noted further that "there is a great number of our constituents who are dissatisfied with [the government under the Constitution]; among whom are many respectable for their talents, their patriotism, and respectable for the jealousy they have for their liberty, which . . . is laudable in its motive."[25] Seeking to invoke the "principles of amity and moderation,"[26] Madison sought to bring parties together under a single banner, "the great rights of mankind secured under this Constitution."[27] Madison was directly confronting the seemingly impossible task of unifying the Federalists and Anti-Federalists, who distrusted each other personally

---

22. "James Madison, House of Representatives, 8 June 1789, The Founders' Constitution (University of Chicago), accessed October 12, 2018, http://press-pubs.uchicago.edu/founders/documents/v1ch14s50.html.

23. Ibid.

24. Ibid.

25. Ibid.

26. Ibid.

27. Ibid.

and ideologically. Many Federalists doubted the need for amendments and were fearful that the scope of those amendments would be enlarged to include disruptive structural changes and not just to provide for individual rights, thereby undercutting the Constitution. On the other hand, Anti-Federalists feared that Federalists were consolidating too much power in the national government, placing liberty in jeopardy. Madison, however, maintained his hope that the parties agreed regarding liberty and natural rights, but differed only as to how best to secure those rights. He also believed that North Carolina and Rhode Island soon would join the union if they were assured that their liberty was secure.

After making a series of prudential arguments favoring a written bill of rights, Madison turned to substantive arguments favoring his recommended amendments. He stressed, "If all power is subject to abuse, then it is possible the abuse of powers of the general government may be guarded against in a more secure manner than is now done, while no one advantage, arising from the exercise of that power, shall be damaged or endangered by it."[28] He added, "It is necessary to proceed with caution,"[29] and thereby avoid opening the door to structural amendments, while at the same time securing individual rights. Madison was moving through a narrow and precarious strait. Madison had to chart a moderate course, taking care at every turn. He also recognized that, to be successful, his efforts had to earn a "concurrence of two-thirds of both houses, and the approbation of three-fourths of the state legislatures,"[30] to be ratified and become part of the Constitution.

Madison acknowledged that the Anti-Federalists objected to the Constitution on structural grounds, believing the various branches of the national government had too much power. Nevertheless, he declared his belief, "that the great mass of people who opposed [the Constitution], disliked it because it did not contain effectual provision against encroachments on particular rights."[31] He also

---

28. Ibid.
29. Ibid.
30. Ibid.
31. Ibid.

believed this objection could best be obviated by providing for written rights, without "endangering any part of the Constitution," as a structural matter.

With that, Madison turned to his amendments. His amendments began with a preamble, declaring, "That all power is originally vested in and consequently derived from the people."[32] Under that declaration, "government is instituted, and ought to be exercised for the benefit of the people; which consists in the enjoyment of life and liberty, with the right of acquiring and using property, and pursuing and obtaining happiness and safety."[33] After that general declaration, Madison added, "[T]he people have an indubitable, unalienable, and indefeasible right to reform or change their government, whenever it be found adverse or inadequate to the purposes of its institution."[34] This latter point was intended to assure the Anti-Federalists that, if at some future point in time the government proved to be too powerful, as a structural matter, or if it failed to preserve rights, it could be changed as a matter of right under the existing Article V amendment process. It was subject to amendment for this very purpose. That argument, in time, came to satisfy most Anti-Federalists, particularly once a written protection of rights was included in the Constitution.

Madison recommended a housekeeping amendment regarding the number of representatives and a second amendment regarding compensation of members of Congress. Those matters were likely placed before substantive amendments protecting rights not because they were more important to Madison—they were not—but because they were matters of a more procedural nature that needed to be dealt with at the outset. Madison then turned to the heart of the matter—the rights that were to be protected.

Madison's first substantive rights provision dealt with the right he considered to be of greatest importance—the right of conscience. That recommended amendment provided, "The civil rights of none shall be abridged on account of religious belief or worship, nor shall any national religion be established, nor shall the full and equal rights

---

32. Ibid.
33. Ibid.
34. Ibid.

of conscience be in any manner, or on any pretext infringed."[35] This amendment was reminiscent, in many respects, of the provision recommended by Madison for inclusion in the Virginia Declaration of Rights in 1776. It provided that no "national religion" was to be established under the Constitution. It declared, as well, that the "*full* and equal rights of conscience" were to remain inviolate or placed beyond the reach or touch of government. The addition of the word "full" made it clear that no part of the right of conscience was subject to government limitation. The words "in any manner, or on any pretext infringed" strengthened this limit on government power to infringe directly or indirectly on religious conscience for any reason. What was clear, in Madison's proposal, was that the right of conscience was the most significant right and must be carefully placed beyond the reach of government. Madison turned next to the rights of speech, press, and assembly, followed by the right "to keep and bear arms." Madison added, "The exceptions here or elsewhere in the constitution, made in favor of particular rights, shall not be construed as to diminish the just importance of other rights retained by the people; or as to enlarge the powers delegated by the constitution."[36] With this addition, he acknowledged that his list of rights included only those that most Americans readily agreed to, while agreeing that other natural rights might exist. Madison was painfully aware that future generations might constrain such rights to further their ends, or public purposes, and thereby depreciate rights. Madison was ever-fearful, to use his own words, that, "There are more instances of the abridgment of the freedom of the people by gradual and silent encroachments of those in power than by violent and sudden usurpations."[37] He understood that the power of the words protecting liberty might be weakened with time, becoming brittle. This is true, given what we now know as the law of intransitivity.

Under the law of intransitivity, applied in the constitutional context, we begin with case A, the words of the original public meaning of the Bill of Rights, case B then interprets case A, case C interprets case

---

35. Ibid.
36. Ibid.
37. Ibid.

B, case D interprets case C, etc. After a series of cases, the latest case, let us say, case E, no longer agrees with the original public or intended meaning of the actual constitutional provision. Madison wisely, and perhaps prophetically, understood that the failure to remain focused on the original public meaning of the words of provisions protecting rights invariably leads to interpretations that change or constrain the meaning of the words, sometimes transforming them into something far different from, and perhaps even antithetical to, the intent of the original words. In the hands of a tyrannical majority, seeking to further some perceived public good, the law of intransitivity is compounded or quickened, because the majority often acts in its interests in ignoring the original intent or meaning. Government (a tyrannical majority) is motivated to alter the meaning of the words securing rights to weaken those rights and strengthen the power of the majority to do what it thinks is right. In implicitly recognizing the law of intransitivity in this governmental context, Madison emphasized, yet again, that recognizing these rights in written form did not imply any power on the part of the government to limit such rights in the future in furtherance of some intended good. Government and its representative's first obligation is always to adhere to a broad original meaning of the rights and the Constitution which gave them life.

Madison's proposed fifth amendment turned from limiting the power of the national government to limiting the power of the state government regarding the vaunted right of conscience. It provided, "No state shall violate the equal rights of conscience, or the freedom of the press, or the trial by jury in criminal cases."[38] This amendment proved to be controversial, but it makes clear that Madison intended a broad scope for the rights that are today contained in the First Amendment, particularly the preeminent right of conscience. It took many years for this amendment to be given life, through incorporation under the auspices of the Fourteenth Amendment and equal protection of the law, but it is further evidence that Madison clearly wanted to provide the fullest protection possible for the rights of conscience, press, and trial by jury. In doing so, he simply believed that he was furthering rather than restricting natural rights.

---

38. Ibid.

In listing each right, Madison addressed where it should be placed within the existing text of the Constitution. Madison initially wanted the provisions incorporated directly into the text of the existing Constitution, because he feared that adding them as appendages, or as a bill of rights, might render them little more than an aspirational afterthought. He wanted each provision to be an actual limitation on governmental or enumerated power, avoiding any possibility that the rights enumerated might be viewed as aspirational or mere suggestions. They were intended to be part of the Constitution's core. Madison failed to prevail on the issue of the interlineation of the amendments, but his hope that they might be recognized has largely been fulfilled.

Having already indulged on the patience of those present, each of whom was straining to hear and understand each word, Madison continued with care. All present knew how carefully Madison had worked on the placement of each word and idea in his speech, and they respected him enough to continue to listen as intently as possible. Yet, the heat, the stuffiness, and acoustics of the room were all taking their toll. Madison's exertions were now causing him to sweat as he strained to speak more loudly. For their part, those present were struggling to remain attentive and engaged. Madison plodded on, intent on persuading those present of the urgent need to support the amendments.

Madison knew that there were those, largely among the Federalists, who believed in the unwritten British constitution based on the Magna Carta. Under the Magna Carta and the unwritten constitution in Britain, however, some rights were not included. Foremost among those rights, Madison argued, were "trial by jury, freedom of the press, or liberty of conscience." He emphasized a point that he would return to later in his life, when he authored the Virginia Resolutions and the Report thereon. He declared, "The freedom of the press and rights of conscience, those choicest privileges of the people, are unguarded in the [unwritten] British constitution."[39] Madison repeatedly referred to the importance of securing these future First Amendment rights. To take one's conscience meant taking that which

---

39. Ibid.

is most dear or important to that individual, the duty to obey God with exactness. Similarly, the right of the press was essential to effectuation of the right of self-governance. No just government held the legitimate power to limit those choicest rights, except under the most limited of circumstances.

Madison reiterated his change of mind in coming to support "parchment barriers," in the form of written amendments securing rights, during his remarks. He also acknowledged the deficiencies of such written limitations, deficiencies that he understood well. Nevertheless, he concluded that written amendments "have a tendency to impress some degree of respect for them, to establish public opinion in their favor, and rouse the attention of the whole community [as means] to control the majority from those acts to which they might otherwise be inclined."[40]

Madison further responded to the Federalist argument that "[I]n the federal government [written amendments] are unnecessary, because the powers are enumerated, and it follows that all that are not granted by the constitution are retained: that the constitution is a bill of powers, the great residuum being the rights of the people; and therefore a bill of rights cannot be so necessary as if the residuum was thrown into the hands of the government."[41] Echoing the conversations he had with Thomas Jefferson during the course of the Virginia ratifying process, Madison reflected, "[E]ven if government keeps within those limits, it has certain discretionary powers with respect to the means, which may admit of abuse to a certain extent, in the same manner as the powers of the state governments under their constitutions may to an indefinite extent."[42] Madison knew that the "necessary and proper" clause might be interpreted expansively and thereby contribute to exercise of discretion that could become a tool in the hands of tyrannical majorities to limit individual rights. Thus, because he had made the same argument, Madison understood well the Federalist argument that in pursuit of some general good, the national government might trample, however indirectly, on rights. He

---

40. Ibid.
41. Ibid.
42. Ibid.

had seen this happen under state declarations of rights. Nevertheless, he believed such declarations were necessary, as a means of limiting or at least warning states before they exercised their power to limit a right. In the same sense, a written bill of rights was salutary at the national level, if for no other reason than that it operated as a caveat to the exercise of broad power that infringed on a right.

Madison also understood another argument made by some Federalists, who asserted that state declarations of rights provided sufficient protection for rights. Those rights had not been expressly disavowed by entry into a compact at the national level. But he stressed "some states have no bills of rights" and others have only "very defective ones."[43] Madison then turned to a related argument that he found to be "very plausible"—the argument that any enumeration of rights would "by implication" give the government the power to limit "rights which were not singled out [in a written bill or declaration of rights]."[44] He responded to this argument by adding the language, in the form of the current Ninth Amendment, providing that rights not enumerated were nevertheless retained by the people and not placed within the domain or reach of government.

The issue of enforcement of a bill of rights remained. Madison responded, "If [those rights] are incorporated into the constitution, independent tribunals of justice will consider themselves in a peculiar manner the guardians of those rights; they will be an impenetrable bulwark against every assumption of power in the legislative or executive; they will be naturally led to resist every encroachment upon rights expressly stipulated for in the constitution by the declaration of rights."[45] This was a resounding affirmation, on Madison's part, of the special role of an independent judiciary in protecting rights against encroachment by a tyrannical legislative or executive action. The courts were the least democratic branch, a branch specifically designed to be above the fray of democratic politics. Furthermore, courts, by their nature, should see themselves as guardians of the rule of law, including laws protecting rights against the tyranny of the majority. As such, the

---

43. Ibid.
44. Ibid.
45. Ibid.

courts were established as an institutional matter, to serve as guardians of the rights of minorities against tyrannical majorities.

In addition to protection by the federal judiciary, Madison made an argument designed to appeal to Anti-Federalists who believed that the states were the repositories of liberty. He declared, "The greatest opponents to a federal government admit the state legislatures to be sure guardians of the people's liberty."[46] But Madison warned that the states themselves could become threats to liberty. To rectify potential excesses on the part of state governments, Madison added a provision providing "that no state shall violate the equal right of conscience, freedom of the press, or trial by jury in criminal cases."[47] James emphasized that it was proper "that every government should be disarmed of powers which trench upon those particular rights."[48] His use of the term "trench" is revealing. As he used the term, it means to prevent or protect against states intruding anywhere near the line protecting those rights.

Anti-Federalists, in turn, were concerned that powers not enumerated might be assumed by the national government. Madison responded with what became the Tenth Amendment, providing that "powers not [enumerated], should be reserved to the several states."[49] He acknowledged that this amendment might be deemed "superfluous" by many but added that there "can be no harm in making such a declaration."[50] Madison believed, at a minimum, that states could invoke this amendment to draw attention to any excessive use of an unenumerated or implied exercise of national power. He also anticipated that the courts would be sensitive to the rights of states, when the national government exceeded their enumerated powers.

After seeking to allay concerns of Anti-Federalists, Madison once again addressed the Federalists. Raising his already feeble voice a decibel or two, he stressed his belief that all gentlemen "will readily admit that nothing is in contemplation . . . that can endanger the beauty of the government in any one important feature, even in the eyes of its

46. Ibid.
47. Ibid.
48. Ibid.
49. Ibid.
50. Ibid.

most sanguine admirers."[51] Madison concluded, "We can make the constitution better in the opinion of those who are opposed to it [Anti-Federalists], without weakening its frame or abridging its usefulness, in the judgement of those who are attached to it [Federalists]."[52] In this argument, Madison reminded supporters of the Constitution that adoption of a written bill of rights would allay the concerns of Anti-Federalists, who in good faith wanted further written assurance that rights would be protected under the Constitution. By allaying the concerns of Anti-Federalists, who genuinely wanted to secure rights, the base of support for the Constitution would be expanded.

Nearing the end of his speech, introducing and defending his proposed written bill of rights, Madison reemphasized his opening remarks regarding his desire to avoid imposing on the time of members of the House. He concluded, "I shall content myself for the present with moving, that a committee be appointed to consider of and report such amendments as ought to be proposed by congress to the legislatures of the states, to become, if ratified by three-fourths thereof, part of the constitution of the United States. By agreeing to this motion, the subject may be going on in committee, while other important business is proceeding to a conclusion in the house."[53] He recognized the need to get on with the formation of the newly founded government, without failing to begin in earnest the effort to secure a written bill of rights that "should . . . fortify the rights of the people against the encroachments of the government."[54]

Madison's speech introducing the Bill of Rights is too often consigned to obscurity. Its enduring importance in the cause of securing liberty makes it worthy of more attention. His speech, together with discussion regarding the motion to refer the amendments to committee, had consumed hours of time. Madison had poured his mind and heart into a speech he knew to be critical to the future of the United States. Fisher Ames was a representative from Massachusetts and considered to be a respected member of the First Congress. He found

51. Ibid.
52. Ibid.
53. Ibid.
54. Ibid.

Madison's form of speech too timid and hard to hear, but he praised Madison for his perspicacity. Madison had used the time he was granted to impress with ideas, not delivery. Feeling weak and tired by his strenuous efforts, Madison sat down and was immediately greeted with a cacophony of disheartening arguments against his motion and the need for written amendments securing rights.

Representative James Jackson, a lawyer from Georgia and a strong opponent of the need for bill of rights, renewed common complaints of his fellow Federalists. His voice, stronger than Madison's, reverberated through the hall as he opposed the dangerous idea of inserting a declaration of rights within the text of the Constitution. Jackson argued that "inserting a declaration of rights in the constitution" was "dangerous and improper" or at a minimum "unnecessary." Jackson renewed the Federalist argument that the federal government simply had no power to regulate the press or other rights included by Madison in his proposed bill of rights. He was apprehensive that failing to get to the more important work of forming a government, would send a message throughout the states and abroad that the government was unstable and an "object of scorn."[55] He added, "This is not the time for bringing forth amendments. . . . The imperfections of the government are now unknown."[56] He also was fearful that the House could be distracted by a protracted discussion regarding the subject of amendments, a topic that he believed to be of limited importance.

Not long after Jackson took his seat, a fellow Federalist, Samuel Livermore from Massachusetts suggested that the House inquire to ascertain the disposition of the Senate regarding the usefulness of the amendments. If the Senate was uninterested or unsupportive, the House would be "wast[ing] its time,"[57] in considering a bill of rights. Like Jackson, Livermore appeared to believe that, at best, the addition of a bill of rights was unnecessary and, therefore, a poor use of valuable time.

---

55. *Annals of Congress*, House of Representatives, 1ˢᵗ Congress, 1ˢᵗ Session, Gales & Seaton's History, June 8, 1789, 461.
56. Ibid.
57. Ibid., 465.

Roger Sherman of Connecticut (one of the architects of the Great Compromise that helped secure adoption and ratification of the Constitution), William Smith of South Carolina, and John Vining of Delaware joined in initially opposing the amendments. They agreed with Jackson; they asserted that it would be improvident for the House to spend time considering amendments. Madison's amendments were, in their opinion, encroaching on time that could be used to far better ends. They believed a strong national government would actually help to secure liberty. With each new voice of opposition, Madison's hopes dimmed.

Elbridge Gerry of Massachusetts rekindled the glimmer of hope, however, when he agreed that the amendments were of lesser importance than the formation of the government but stated his willingness to hear the matter again on July 1, after more important matters could be disposed of. Representative Thomas Sumter of South Carolina joined in offering his supports for the amendments, believing them "to be of such great importance to the Union, that I shall be glad to see it undertaken in any manner."[58] Sumter did not care whether the amendments were considered by the Committee of the Whole or assigned to an appropriate committee—he simply wanted to reemphasize their importance.

By this time Madison "found himself unfortunate in not satisfying [his colleagues] with respect to the mode of introducing the business; he thought, from the dignity and peculiarity of the subject that it ought to be referred to the Committee of the whole."[59] John Page, who also represented Virginia and roomed in the same boarding house as Madison, and who surely discussed the amendments with Madison, spoke next. He argued that it was important to hear the amendments in a timely fashion. The day ended on a positive note for Madison, as the House decided against referring the amendments to a committee, where they might languish. The House agreed to a motion by Representative Lawrence to the Committee of the whole.[60]

---

58. Ibid., 466.
59. Ibid., 468.
60. Ibid.

The amendments were scheduled for debate before the whole House for July 21, thereby ensuring that they would be given a full and fair hearing.

As if on cue, on July 21, Madison reminded his colleagues that they had agree to hear his proposed amendments. Once again, however, rather than debating substance, recalcitrant House members expressed their reluctance to hear the amendments. Jackson continued to be "[S]orry to see the House was to be troubled any further on the subject; he looke upon it was a mere waste of time; but as he always chose the least of two evils, he acquiesced in the motion for referring it to a special committee."[61] Fisher Ames and others pushed anew to have the amendments committed to a select committee, rather than wasting the time of the full House. Ames feared that a public hearing of the amendments would result in endless discussion of a wide variety of substantive and structural amendments. Elbridge Gerry, however, favored hearing the amendments before the full House. He was joined by Thomas Tudor of South Carolina, who wanted to assure the public that the matter of amendments securing rights had been fully heard. In time, members tired of rehashing familiar arguments. By a vote of 34–15, the House declined to hear the amendments in the Committee of the Whole, preferring to refer the Bill of Rights to committee.[62] Ultimately, this was wise. Had the amendments been heard before the full House, without full vetting in committee, it is likely that virtually every amendment offered in state ratifying committees would have been raised and debated. There might have been grandstanding to the public in the House galleries as well. Madison was confident that the amendments would receive a full and fair hearing in committee.

A committee of eleven, including Madison, was formed. Most members of the committee initially appeared inclined to be lukewarm regarding the need for the amendments. Madison, again, had his work cut out for him, if he was to garner necessary support for the amendments. He was heartened when the committee report was issued just a week later. Despite some apparent weakening of the amendment securing the right of conscience, for example, the committee included

61. Ibid., July 21, 1789, at 687.
62. Ibid., 690.

Madison's provision securing the right of conscience against limitation at both the national and state levels. Once again, Madison largely prevailed within the committee, a venue in which he was at his most effective. When given an opportunity to convince others, and the time to do so in a smaller room where he could easily be heard, Madison proved himself to be a very capable and respected advocate. He helped Federalists and Anti-Federalists on the committee better understand the importance of the amendments.

Despite success in the committee, however, Madison still faced a series of significant hurdles. First, it was not enough to report the recommendations out of committee—as a procedural matter, they had to receive a hearing before the full House. Second, if time for such a hearing before the full House was granted, agreement regarding the substance of the amendments would have to be forged within the House of Representative *and* the Senate. Madison was less confident that the amendments would be adopted in the Senate, where many members shared views like those of Patrick Henry, who had vigorously opposed Madison. Undaunted, however, Madison trudged onward in what for him had become a matter of conscience, a mission, not just hearing but in also securing the actual adoption of the bill of rights.

The first challenge was getting a hearing date set. On August 3, when the report of the committee was presented, Madison pushed to have the amendments heard on August 12. The hearing was postponed for another day until Thursday, August 13, 1789. At last, the time had come. Hearings before the full House ensued over the space of eleven days. While opposition to the amendments, as a general matter, was occasionally raised, the focus of members of the House turned to substance.

The Bill of Rights Are Heard before the Committee of the Whole

On the August 13, Representative Richard Lee of Virginia moved that the House "resolve itself into a Committee of the whole"[63] to consider

---

63. Ibid., August 13, 1789, 730.

the amendments. He was followed by his colleague, Representative Page. Page had surely spoken often with Madison and urged consideration of the amendments, recognizing that citizens were concerned regarding the status of their rights under the new government. Page believed the work of the House in considering the amendments would be "expedited by the simplicity and self-evidence which the [amendments] reported possessed, as it was impossible that much debate could take place."[64]

Representative Theodore Sedgwick, a Federalist from Massachusetts, next stood to voice his opposition to consideration of the amendments. Sedgwick, a respected lawyer, had studied theology and law at Yale, and was a charter member of the Academy of Arts and Sciences. Sedgwick was so respected by members of his party that he later served as the fourth Speaker of the United States House of Representatives. He "was sorry that the motion was made, because he looked upon this as a very improper time to enter upon the consideration of a subject which would undoubtedly consume many days."[65] Reflecting past procedural opposition to hearing the amendments, Sedgwick added that there were far more important matters that demanded the attention of the full House.

Madison felt compelled to respond. He reminded his colleagues that the people wanted to be assured that their rights would be respected by the national government and added, "If this is an object worthy of such a numerous part of our constituents, why should we decline taking into our consideration, and thereby promote that spirit of urbanity and unanimity which Government itself stands in need of for its more full support?"[66] With a patience that was wearing thin, he said, "Already has the subject been delayed much longer than could have been wished. If after having fixed a day for taking it into consideration, we should put it off again, a spirit of jealousy may be excited, and not allayed without great inconvenience."[67]

Representative John Vining, a Federalist from Delaware and member of the Committee of Eleven that had considered the

---

64. Ibid., 730–31.
65. Ibid., 731.
66. Ibid.
67. Ibid.

amendments, joined in Madison's anxiety. Vining was a strong supporter of the administration and was respected for his conscientiousness as a legislator. He noted, "In point of time, [the motion to consider the amendments] had priority; in point of importance, every candid mind would acknowledge its preference."[68] Vining added that he "conceived the House was bound to pay attention to it as early as possible; as they had given leave for a bill to be brought in, they ought not to neglect proceeding onwards with it."[69]

Unpersuaded, Sedgwick quickly rose to reiterate his opposition to wasting time considering a bill that was of less importance than many others. He doubted that the people were anxious to have the bill considered. Sedgwick was joined by Representative William Loughton Smith, who believed the judicial bill "was entitled to preference."[70] Smith was a Federalist and a strong supporter of the Washington Administration and a leader in the House. He doubted that the rights amendments were self-evident and believed the debate over them would be lengthy, particularly given that "some members are pledged to support them with all the arguments their fancy or ingenuity can suggest."

Representative Thomas Hartley, a Federalist from Pennsylvania, joined in opposing the motion because consideration of the judicial bill was of greater importance and would do more to secure freedom than the proposed amendments. He leveled an attack against the Anti-Federalists when he added, "As to the artful and designing, who had clamored against [the Constitution], he had not the smallest desire to gratify them: he hoped and trusted their numbers were but a few."[71] Elbridge Gerry who later served as Madison's vice president, agreed with Hartley that the judicial bill was more important and feared that consideration of the amendments would be time consuming. Gerry added that representatives from two states were duty bound to raise amendments of a structural nature that would add to the time consumed by consideration of the amendments. Representative Lawrence agreed that the amendments were untimely, because the people were

---

68. Ibid.
69. Ibid.
70. Ibid., 732.
71. Ibid.

most anxious regarding formation of government. Lawrence added, rather derisively, that "the people in general are more anxious to see the Government in operation, than speculative amendments upon an untried constitution."[72]

It was clear to Madison that it was time to speak again, to calm concerns and draw residual support from those who represented states, like Virginia, where members of the House had agreed to present amendments securing liberty. Drawing on his experience and wisdom, Madison declared, "I should not press the subject at this time, because I am well aware of the importance of the other business enumerated by the gentlemen who are adverse to the present motion, but from an apprehension that, if it is delayed until the other is gone through, gentlemen's patience and application will be so harassed and fatigued, as to oblige them to leave it in an unfinished state until the next session; besides, were the Judicial bill to pass now, it could not take effect until others were enacted, which probably at this time are not drawn up."[73]

Representative Thomas Fitzsimons, one of only two Catholics to sign the Declaration of Independence and a Federalist from Pennsylvania, was tiring of the incessant back-and-forth. He moved that the question be put, to determine whether the amendments should be heard. Representative Page rose just long enough to second Fitzsimmons's motion and remind his colleagues of the need to hear the amendments to satisfy the confidence of constituents who sought assurances that their liberty would be protected under the newly formed national government.

The motion carried in the affirmative and the House resolved itself into the Committee of the Whole. No sooner had the motion passed than Representative Roger Sherman, of Connecticut, stood to oppose "interweaving [the amendments] into the [Constitution]."[74] He offered the following motion, "Resolved by the Senate and House of Representatives of the United States in Congress assembled, That the following articles be proposed as amendments to the constitution, and when ratified by three-fourths of the State Legislatures become valid to

---

72. Ibid., 733.
73. Ibid., 734.
74. Ibid.

all intents and purposes, as part of the same."[75] The concluding words of Sherman's resolution were, in part, an effort to allay Madison's concerns that, if placed in amendment form at the end of the Constitution, the rights therein would be weakened.

Unpersuaded, Madison made a final argument supporting incorporation of the rights into the existing document: "There is a neatness and propriety in incorporating the amendments into the constitution itself; in that case the system will remain uniform and entire; it will certainly be more simple. . . . It will be difficult to ascertain to what parts of the instrument the amendments particularly refer; they will create unfavorable comparisons; whereas, if they are placed upon the footing here proposed, they stand upon as good foundation as the original work."[76] Madison believed that the rights would carry more weight if interlineated. He nevertheless feared becoming bogged down in another debate over largely non-substantive matters. Madison, therefore, concluded, "I am not, however, very solicitous about form, provided the business is but well completed."[77]

A lengthy discussion ensued regarding the placement of the amendments. Representatives droned on, discussing the virtues and vices attending placement of the proposals contained in the Committee of Eleven's report. Elbridge Gerry tired of the statement, and restatement, of various positions. He suggested that the placement of the proposals as amendments, as opposed to incorporating them in the text, would not weaken them in the least. He opined, "For my part, I have no doubt but a ratification of the amendments, in any form, would be as valid as any part of the constitution."[78] Gerry added, "The Legislatures are elected by the people. I know no difference between them and conventions."[79]

Sherman remained adamant, arguing, "The gentlemen who oppose the motion say we contend for matter of form; they think it nothing more. Now we say that we contend for substance, and therefore cannot

---

75. Ibid., 735.
76. Ibid.
77. Ibid.
78. Ibid., 744.
79. Ibid.

agree to the amendments [being incorporated into the existing text]."[80] He warned Madison and others, "If they are so desirous of having the business completed, they had better sacrifice what they consider but a matter of indifference to gentlemen, to go more unanimously along with them in altering the constitution."[81] It was clear Sherman and others were serious, but the time for a vote had come. Sherman's motion failed. It appeared for the moment that Madison's wish, that the amendments would be interlineated in the Constitution rather than being added as an addendum, had been granted.

Near the close of the day, Representative Livermore raised another serious procedural matter when he inquired "to know, whether to carry a motion in a committee that two-thirds should agree."[82] Representative Hartley supported Representative Livermore's suggestion that the House could not hear the reported amendments without a two-thirds vote out of committee. The Committee of Eleven's report had carried by a solid majority, but it was just short of two-thirds. If Livermore and Hartley were right, and a two-third vote was necessary, the report would not be heard. Not surprisingly, given the lateness of the hour and the general acrimony that attended a suggestion that the House was not even permitted to hear the amendments reported by the Committee, the House records state, "Some desultory conversation took place on this subject, when it was decided by the chairman of the committee that a majority of the committee were sufficient to form a report."[83] Consideration of the Bill of Rights had avoided another last-minute bullet in the form of an effort to keep the House from hearing the report, without concurrence of a super-majority in committee.

Consideration of the amendments was the next matter of business, with the proposals being considered as part of the text, as suggested by Madison and the Committee of Eleven. Sherman, however, remained unconvinced and would yet prevail in having the proposals added as amendments. Placement of the amendments became a bargaining chip that Madison and proponents of the Bill of Rights used later to secure

---

80. Ibid.
81. Ibid.
82. Ibid.
83. Ibid.

additional support for the amendments. They would need that chip, at a later juncture, to garner the two-thirds vote of support that was necessary for the House and Senate to adopt the amendments and send them to the states, where a three-fourths vote was required.

Of more concern to Madison than placement of the amendments was Representative Tucker's raising of the issue of whether "the deliberations of the [House] were intended to be confined to the propositions on the table."[84] Tucker wanted to raise structural issues. Madison was unalterably opposed to any amendments that would tamper with the structure of government. These concerns made it easier for him to yield on placement of the proposals, so long as the debate remained focus on rights and not structure.

Madison returned to his room that evening pleased that a series of procedural questions had been resolved without hindering consideration of the substance of the amendments. He, however, had little time to rest. Madison had to prepare for serious business on the Friday, August 14, when the substance of the amendments, the Bill of Rights, were on agenda for the full House. Having labored late into the night, Madison awakened early on the 14th, fully prepared to begin the serious work of securing adoption of the amendments.

The first matter considered on August 14 was the Committee's recommended preamble, which recognized that government was "intended for the benefit of the people and the rightful establishment thereof [was] derived from their authority alone."[85] There was some wrangling over the substance of the preamble. Some believed that the states were the final authority, not the people. Ever attentive to precision in drafting, Madison responded, "The original expression is neat and simple; that loading it with more words may destroy the beauty of the sentence; and others say it is unnecessary . . . Be it so, in their opinion; yet, still it appears important in the estimation of three States, that this solemn truth should be inserted in the Constitution."[86] The reference in the preamble effectively recognized that natural rights belong to the people and are not merely a privilege, a matter of government

---

84. Ibid., 736.
85. Ibid., August 14, 1789, 745.
86. Ibid., 746.

permission or proclamation, by the state or the national government. This was a simple and self-evident truth for Madison and most members of the House. Madison's statement in support of the preamble, with its reference to recommendations of three state ratifying conventions that such language be included, also shows the thoroughness of his research and preparation. The grueling hours of work paid off, as it would throughout the debates. The language in the preamble was initially supported by a vote of 27–23.[87]

The House turned next to consideration of the recommendations regarding the size of the House and compensation for members. Those recommendations, which had little to do with substantive rights, were discussed at length but were later dropped. Consideration of these issues consumed the entire day. Determined to make progress regarding the substantive amendments, the House convened again on Saturday, August 15. The real substance of the Bill of Rights was the next item on the agenda. Madison had been preparing for years to discuss these issues.

Debating Religious Freedom in the House

Discussion began with consideration of the Committee's recommended language for what later became the First Amendment and was the first substantive rights provision in the Committee's proposal. In the very first reference to a right, the Committee recommended the following text: "No religion shall be established by law, nor shall the equal rights of conscience be infringed."[88] The Committee's recommendation was a condensed version of Madison's original proposal which provided, "The civil rights of none shall be abridged on account of religious belief or worship, nor shall any national religion be established, nor shall the full and equal rights of conscience be in any manner, or any pretext infringed."

Representative Peter Sylvester, a lawyer and Federalist from New York, who may be best known for serving as a mentor to President Martin Van Buren, the eighth president of the United States, opened

---

87. Ibid., 747.
88. Ibid.

the deliberations. Sylvester was devout, a leader in his local Episcopal congregation, St. Peters Church in Albany. He worried that the language of the amendment "might be thought to have a tendency to abolish religion altogether."[89] Sylvester remained concerned that the language might harm religion rather than secure the right of religious liberty and respect for religion.

Representative Vining, chairman of the Committee of Eleven, rose immediately to address Sylvester's concern. Vining recommended that the language be transposed, placing the right of conscience before the non-establishment language. Vining wanted to emphasize that the Committee believed the right of conscience to be the heart of the amendment, and that it was designed to promote rather than abolish faith. Non-establishment was simply a part of the right of conscience, which ensured that no national religion was to be established. If the government preferred a particular religion or group of religions, that preference would violate the right of conscience of those who did not agree with the national religion. In short, Vining and the Committee recognized that establishment of a national religion would harm the *equal* right of conscience.

Gerry, somewhat surprisingly, followed Vining. Gerry was considered obstinate by some of his colleagues. He could be strongly partisan, sometimes immoveable, and is best remembered for having sought to "*gerry*mander" districts to favor his party while serving as Governor of Massachusetts. Gerry sought to allay Sylvester's concerns. He suggested that the amendment would read better if it stated, "No religious doctrine shall be established by law."[90] For Gerry, and others present, the amendment was not intended to diminish religion in the public square. It was designed to prevent any sectarian doctrine from being embraced at the federal level, to the exclusion of minority sects.

Representative Sherman, who resisted incorporating the amendments into the text, was in fact strongly opposed to the amendments. He spoke next, noting that he "thought the amendment altogether unnecessary, inasmuch as Congress had no authority whatever delegated to

---

89. Ibid.
90. Ibid., 757.

them by the constitution to make religious establishment."[91] His effort to strike the non-establishment language did not receive any traction, but it further evidenced a sense on the part of most House members that the amendment was not intended to harm religious establishments.

Representative Daniel Carroll of Maryland, a strong Anti-Federalist, rose to offer his support for the amendment. He argued, "As the rights of conscience are, in their nature, of peculiar delicacy, and will bear the gentlest touch of the government's hand; and as many sects have concurred in the opinion that they are not well secured under the constitution." His language "will bear the gentlest touch of the government's hand,"[92] captured a sentiment widely held among members of the House. Carroll also believed the words of the amendment secured the equal rights of conscience and thereby conciliated "the minds of people to the Government [more] than almost any other amendment he had heard proposed."[93] He recognized that people of multiple sects demanded that their duty to God, their right of conscience, be spared even the "gentlest touch of the government's hand."

Eyes turned next to Madison, who rose to speak. He began by responding to Sylvester's concern that the amendment might harm religion. Madison "apprehended the meaning of the [non-establishment] words to be, that Congress should not establish a religion, and enforce the legal observation of it by law, nor compel men to worship God in any manner contrary to conscience."[94] He then responded to the Federalist concern that the amendment was unnecessary, noting that, "Whether the words are necessary or not, he did not mean to say, but they had been required by some of the State Constitutions, who seemed to entertain an opinion that under the clause of the constitution, which gave power to Congress to make all laws necessary and proper to carry into execution to constitution, and the laws made under it, enabled them to make laws of such a nature as might infringe the rights of conscience, and establish a national religion; to prevent these effects he presumed the amendment was intended, and he thought it

---

91. Ibid.
92. Ibid., 757–58.
93. Ibid., 758.
94. Ibid.

as well expressed as the nature of language would admit."[95] Madison had impliedly accepted Vining's suggestion that the right of conscience be placed before the non-establishment concern to clarify that the primary purpose of the amendment was to secure the right of conscience. It was clear from Madison's interpretation of the language that government was precluded from limiting or infringing upon religious conscience even when it did so with the belief that such an infringement was necessary and proper under an enumerated power.

Representative Benjamin Huntington of Connecticut next addressed the proposed amendment. Huntington was a respected lawyer, who received an honorary degree from Yale. As a Federalist, he may have believed that the amendment was unnecessary. Like Sylvester, Huntington "Feared . . . that the words might be taken in such latitude as to be extremely hurtful to the cause of religion."[96] He was concerned that government aid in supporting ministers and building houses of worship at the state level might be limited under the amendment. Sylvester then used the example of Rhode Island, where the lack of a religious establishment and government aid to religion had been harmful. He concluded with his hope that "the amendment would be made in such a way as to secure the rights of conscience, and a *free exercise* of the rights of religion, but not to patronize those who professed no religion at all."[97] This was an early use in the debates of the words "free exercise . . . of religion," the language which ultimately found its way into the First Amendment, as adopted by Congress. It was also a strong statement favoring government solicitude to religious liberty.

At this juncture, Madison interjected his belief that "if the word national was inserted before religion, it would satisfy the minds of honorable gentlemen."[98] He added that "the people feared one sect might obtain a pre-eminence, or two combine together, and establish a religion to which they would compel others to conform."[99] Adding the word "national" helped secure the equal right of conscience—no sect or group of sects would be established or preferred at the national level,

95. Ibid.
96. Ibid.
97. Ibid.
98. Ibid.
99. Ibid

and the right of conscience, therefore, remained equal. Madison clearly liked the language "free exercise," which helped make it clarify that the exercise of conscience was an individual right worthy of full protection. Indeed, years before, Madison had stressed, in his proposed amendment to the Virginia Declaration of Rights that, as a matter of natural law, "all men are entitled to the full and free exercise of conscience."

This was not enough, however, to fully satisfy Representative Samuel Livermore, who had offered the motion to ratify the Constitution in New Hampshire, the critical ninth state that gave the Constitution the full force of law. Livermore had served as Chief Justice of the New Hampshire Superior Court and later served with distinction in the United States Senate, where he was named president pro tempore. Not surprisingly, as a Federalist, he "did not want to dwell long on the subject [of the amendments],"[100] but he believed the amendment should be "made to read . . . that Congress shall make no laws touching religion, or infringing the rights of conscience." He wanted to emphasize the Federalist belief that the national government had no power to pass laws "touching on religion, or infringing the rights of conscience."[101]

Reflecting his continuing unhappiness with Madison's defense of the amendments, Elbridge Gerry said he "did not like the term national."[102] He noted that during the ratifying conventions, "Those who were called antifederalists . . . complained that they had injustice done to them by [use of the title national], because they were in favor of a Federal Government."[103] The term *national* implied an independence of power in the government, and the term *federal* implied a government that was simply a federation of the states.

Madison responded that he did not suggest the term *national* in this context to imply that the federal government was itself national in the sense alleged by Gerry. Nevertheless, Madison withdrew his motion to include the term *national*, which left Livermore's motion to adopt the language "Congress shall make no laws touching religion, or infringing the rights of conscience" on the table. A vote was taken,

---

100. Ibid., 759.
101. Ibid.
102. Ibid.
103. Ibid.

with Livermore's language being adopted by a vote of 31–20,[104] and the Committee of the Whole proceeded to discuss further amendments. The concern over the word *national*, instead of *federal*, when referring to the government evidences that House members were particularly concerned with issues of federalism. They wanted to provide an inalienable right of conscience, but they did not want to intimate that such a right could be used to increase the power of the federal government at the expense of states.

The Livermore amendment was revisited on August 20, 1789, at the insistence of Fisher Ames of Massachusetts. Ames recommended that the religious conscience provision read as follows: "Congress shall make no law establishing religion, or to prevent the exercise thereof, or to infringe the rights of conscience."[105] We know little of the reasons behind the change, because there was no recorded debate. Ames's proposal was simply moved and passed by a majority. Given the quick passage, it is likely that the amendment was simply a reflection of the essence of what had already been debated. As such, it supports the supposition that the right of conscience is best furthered when the state has extremely limited power to infringe on the right to freely exercise one's religious conscience, even if the restriction is passed in furtherance of a perceived public good. By the same token, religious conscience protects against government treating religious institutions in a preferential manner (establishment of a national church or preferring one religion over another), because to prefer one religion over another would violate the equal right of conscience.

On August 20, the Committee of the Whole debated what was then referred to as the Sixth Amendment. That amendment protected the rights of conscientious objectors. It provided, "No person religiously scrupulous shall be compelled to bear arms."[106] Representative Thomas Scott, a Federalist and strong supporter of ratification from Pennsylvania, who had served in the Pennsylvania ratifying convention, rose to express his opposition to the provision. Scott's opposition is significant, in part, because he was from Pennsylvania, a state with

---

104. Ibid.
105. Ibid., August 20, 1789, 796.
106. Ibid.

many Quakers. Quakers believed that taking up arms to kill or harm another in furtherance of a governmental interest violated their solemn duty to God. Taken in that light, to violate the Quaker's solemn duty to God was a heinous act, because it deprived the individual of something greater than life itself—one's own best self, defined by his or her perceived duty to God. To Madison, it was the taking of the most sacred of all property, a taking that must be avoided except in the most extreme cases. Scott clarified his view further by stating that "if this becomes part of the constitution, such persons can neither be called upon for their services, nor can an equivalent be demanded; [and] a militia can never be depended upon."[107] He added, in an obvious reference to the Quakers and others, "There are many sects I know, who are religiously scrupulous in this respect; I do not mean to deprive them of any indulgence the law affords; my design is to guard against those who are of no religion. It has been urged that religion is on the decline; if so, the argument is more strong in my favor, for when the time comes that religion shall be discarded, the generality of persons will have recourse to these pretexts to get excused from bearing arms."[108] Scott only feared that non-religionists might use religion as a pretext for avoiding fighting in a war initiated by their government. As such, he was also concerned that those exempted would fail to provide some alternative means of service or support.

Elias Boudinot

Representative Elias Boudinot, from New Jersey, spoke in support of the amendment. Boudinot was devoutly religious, a Presbyterian, with commitment to the liberty of conscience rooted in the Scottish Enlightenment. Elias graduated from and later served on the Board of Trustees at the College of New Jersey. He largely aligned with the Federalists but never joined a party. Elias wrote a religious response, *The Age of Revelation*, to Thomas Paine's tract, *The Age of Reason*. Boudinot was a strong supporter of the Bill of Rights and believed that they were a gift from God. In that spirit, when the Bill of Rights

---

107. Ibid.
108. Ibid.

was adopted, he believed the work of the Constitution was complete. On September 26, 1789, after the adoption of the Bill of Rights by the House and Senate, in a spirit of profound gratitude to God, Boudinot proposed a joint congressional resolution, requesting that President Washington declare a day of thanksgiving. The Resolution, which was adopted by Congress as a whole, provided as follows: "Resolved, that a joint committee of both Houses

Elias Boudinot

be appointed to wait on the President of the United States, to request that he should recommend to the people of the United States a day of public fasting and prayer, to be observed acknowledging with grateful hearts, the many signal favors of Almighty God, especially be affording them an opportunity peaceably to establish a constitution of government for their safety and happiness."[109] Prior to his service in the First Congress, Boudinot led a respected life of public service, serving as president of the Continental Congress and as a colonel in the revolutionary army with special responsibilities for prisoners of war. Elias was a successful landowner and was known for his generosity. For example, he gave 13,000 acres to Philadelphia to be used as park land. Elias was also widely known for his support for the rights of slaves and Native Americans. He was respected as a man of deep religious conscience, a true Christian in word and deed, one fully committed to the right of conscience.

In expressing his support for the amendment providing for the rights of conscientious objectors, Boudinout argued that the amendment or something like it "was necessary." With a passion bred of deep faith, it was his "hope that in establishing this Government, we may show the world that proper care is taken that the Government may not interfere with the religious sentiments of any person. [B]y striking out the clause, people may be led to believe there was an intention

---

109. Ibid., September 25, 1789, 949.

in the Government to compel all citizens to bear arms."[110] The words "in person" were added and the amendment was passed. It now read, "No person religiously scrupulous shall be compelled to bear arms in person." The "in person" language responded to Representative Scott's concern that states be permitted to ask conscientious objectors to serve in other ways or provide funding for those who did not refuse to serve on the ground of religious conscience.

The House included yet another provision supporting the right of conscience. On August 17, a provision was debated that had been penned about the intent of expressly preventing states from infringing on the right of conscience. That provision provided: "No state shall infringe the equal rights of conscience, nor the freedom of speech, or of the press, nor the right of trial by jury in criminal cases."[111] Madison included this amendment in his draft and was a strong supporter of adding written insurance that the state governments would be prohibited from depriving their citizens of the equal right of conscience, the freedom of speech, and the right of trial by jury—three primary natural rights.

Representative Tucker of South Carolina, a strong proponent of the rights of states, rose and stated the sentiments of many members of the House when he declared, "It will be much better, I apprehend, to leave the State Governments to themselves, and not to interfere with them more than we already do; and that is thought by many to be rather too much."[112] Tucker, and Gerry, both of whom shared the Anti-Federalist opposition to a strong central government, became thorns in the sides of Madison and proponents of the Constitution and Bill of Rights. They valued states' rights more than the human or natural rights, which Madison and others wanted to secure against *any* government action.

Madison was quick to respond to Tucker's assertion that the power of the state governments would somehow be harmed by recognizing the natural right of conscience. With emphasis, he declared his view that this was "the most valuable amendment in the whole list. If there

---

110. *Annals of Congress*, August 20, 1789, 796.
111. Ibid., 783.
112. Ibid., 783–84.

was any reason to restrain the Government of the United States from infringing upon these essential rights, it was equally necessary that they should be secured against the State Governments."[113] He added that protecting those "essential rights" against the national and state governments was "necessary to [protect the state and national governments against each other], and [he] was satisfied that it would be equally grateful to the people."[114] Madison understood that states were subject to being captured by a given religious sect or group of religions, in exclusion to the others. Once captured, those groups or sects could use the state's power to limit conscience of non-preferred seats. Madison could well have gone a step further, arguing that every state is benefited by having citizens of conscience. People of conscience, he might have argued, are often more patriotic, viewing such patriotism as an expression of gratitude to their government for recognizing their duty to God. They are more willing to protect and secure the rights and property of others, because their own most sacred property, conscience, was protected.

Representative Livermore largely agreed but suggested that the provision could be made more affirmative if it was worded as follows, "the equal rights of conscience, the freedom of speech or of the press, and the right of trial by jury in criminal cases, shall not be infringed by any State."[115] Livermore's strengthening of the language, by placing the rights first and the limited power of the states last, was quickly agreed to, and Representative Tucker's motion to eliminate the provision protecting the right of conscience against the States was rejected by the House.[116] The House's strong support for the right of conscience was particularly gratifying to Madison and evidenced a strong commitment to the equal rights of conscience, even as applied to the states.

The debate over what is today regarded as the remainder of the First Amendment went almost as smoothly. The Committee of the Whole considered the following provision, on August 15, "The freedom of

---

113. Ibid., 784.
114. Ibid.
115. Ibid.
116. Ibid.

speech and of the press, and the right of people peaceably to assemble and consult for their common good, and to apply to the Government for redress of grievances, shall not be infringed."[117] Members disagreed regarding the language and whether some of the rights (e.g., assembly) were simply derivative of other rights expressed in the same amendment. Representative Sedgwick, for example, believed that some rights were implied by other rights. He argued, "If the people freely converse together, they must assemble for that purpose; it is a self-evident, unalienable right; it is certainly a thing that never would be called in question."[118] On this ground, he moved to delete the language "and the right of the people peaceably to assemble and consult for their common good, and to apply to the Government for redress of grievances,"[119] as being implied and redundant. Sedgwick's motion failed by a large margin.[120] In a sense, however, Sedgwick made a good point in arguing that many of these rights are in some measure derivative of one another. That observation adds weight to the argument that such rights are in some ways interdependent. As was the case with the right of conscience, and with little equivocation, members of the house overwhelmingly agreed that the rights of free speech, a free press, and assembly, were expressly or implicitly inalienable.

The Threat of Additional Amendments

Not surprisingly, members offered substantive changes to some of the proposed amendments and sought to add other amendments. As members began to offer major changes, Madison was particularly concerned that it would not be possible to get the necessary votes to adopt and ratify the bill of rights. Madison urged his colleagues to join with him in confining "ourselves to an enumeration of simple, acknowledged principles, [so that] ratification will meet with little difficulty. Amendments doubtful in nature will have the tendency to prejudice the whole system."[121] This statement is significant, because it makes it clear

---

117. *Annals of Congress*, August 15, 1789, 759.
118. Ibid.
119. Ibid.
120. Ibid., 761.
121. Ibid., 766.

that Madison and members of the House and ultimately the Senate understood that the rights included in the Bill of Rights were widely accepted as being among the foremost natural rights. The words, and intentions of the framers of those amendments, therefore, were simply reflective of a larger public view regarding these natural rights. The debates, in this regard, therefore, make it clear that the Representatives believed that the broader public (the people) intended to include those rights, including the right of conscience, in the Constitution.

Gerry supported a motion offered by Representative Tucker designed to provide a means by which the people could "instruct" their government regarding issues of concern. In supporting Tucker and the need to perfect the Constitution by obtaining instruction from constituents, Gerry could not resist a personal attack on the amendments' author. Referring specifically to Madison and his warning against consuming time and becoming bogged down in the detail of new amendments, Gerry asserted that Madison was unduly "fond" of his own work and was seeking to keep it from being "disfigured by other hands."[122] Gerry droned on, "That honorable gentleman brought forward a string of propositions; among them was the clause now proposed to be amended; he is no doubt ready for the question, and determined not to admit what we think an improvement."[123]

Having tired of the lengthy debate on an issue he believed to be of little significance, Representative Vining, and not Madison, called the question. In doing so and with some exasperation,,he referred directly to Gerry when he said, "The gentleman last up has insinuated a reflection upon the committee for not reporting all the amendments proposed by some State conventions."[124] He then explained why the Committee of Eleven declined to report out all the amendments: "The committee conceived some of them superfluous or dangerous, and feared many of them so contradictory that it was impossible to make anything of them; and this is a circumstance [Gerry, who served on the Committee] cannot pretend ignorance of."[125] Vining then amplified

122. Ibid., 768.
123. Ibid.
124. Ibid., 770.
125. Ibid.

his attack, "Is it not inconsistent in that honorable member [Gerry] to complain of hurry, when he comes day after day reiterating the same train of arguments, and demanding the attention of this body by rising six or seven times on a question? I wish, sir, this subject discussed coolly and dispassionately, but hope we shall have no more reiterations or tedious discussions."[126]

The push for more amendments had worn on many members of the House, but the debate raged on, with increasing vindictiveness. Despite tiring of the incessant wrangling, Madison was again moved to speak. Madison opened by stating that he "was unwilling to take up any more time of the committee; but, on the other hand, [was] not willing to be silent after the charges had been brought against the Committee."[127] He declined, however, to engage in any further personal attack, preferring to push the substance of his argument and to emphasize that the rights being considered were widely accepted by those attending the state ratifying conventions. He stated, "I appeal to the gentlemen who have heard the voice of their country, to those who have attended the debates of the State conventions, whether the amendments now proposed are not those most strenuously required by opponents to the constitution?"[128] He continued, "While I approve of the [Committee's amendments], I . . . oppose the consideration at this time of such [amendments] as are likely to change the principles of the Government, or that are of doubtful nature; because I apprehend there is little prospect of obtaining the consent of two-thirds of both Houses of Congress, and three-fourths of State Legislatures, to ratify propositions of this kind; therefore, as a friend to what is attainable, I would limit it to the plain, simple, and important security that has been required."[129] In short, Madison recognized that some members of the House were being dilatory or, worse yet, were using subterfuge to derail consideration of the amendments and undermine the Constitution.

---

126. Ibid.
127. Ibid., 775.
128. Ibid.
129. Ibid.

The question was called on the Tucker amendment, and it failed by a resounding margin of 41–10.[130] The first amendment, including the freedom of speech, the press, and assembly, as proposed by the Committee, was then adopted. Debate over other amendments followed, with many efforts by Representative Tucker and others to derail the process. It was evident, however, that Madison already secured much of what he hoped for in the House, as evidence of support for the amendments and the rights they were designed to protect from the hand of government.

Madison found the work to be "difficult and fatiguing" due to what he believed to be "dilatory artifices" on the part of Anti-Federalists. Elbridge Gerry and Thomas Tucker had made the work tedious and sometimes acrimonious. Madison was personally attacked but resisted the urge to respond in kind. As was his custom, he endeavored to avoid personal invective and sought conciliation and compromise in his effort to obtain House support for amendments securing essential rights.

The Bill of Rights and the Senate

On August 24, 1789, the House finally forwarded the amendments to the Senate for their consideration. Still fatigued by the difficulties faced in the House, Madison remained less confident about what might happen to the amendments in the Senate. The Senate was more elitist and less sensitive to the need for strong protection of individual rights at the national level. As it turned out, the Senate joined the House in supporting the amendments, with some important changes. The Senate's deliberations and actions regarding the amendment securing the right of conscience provide examples of how members of the Senate treated the amendments. Unfortunately, the Senate's proceedings were private, and arguments were not included in the record, nor were voting results. The records, as such, were sparse. There is, however, a record of proposals presented together with a notation of whether they were adopted.

---

130. Ibid., 776.

On August 25, 1789, the House amendments were read on the floor of the Senate. Senator Ralph Izard, who represented South Carolina and was a known opponent of the Bill of Rights, was the first to speak. Izard was a strong defender of slavery and became the president pro tempore of the Senate, before retiring to manage his estate. His commitment to the new nation was widely acknowledged by his colleagues, who were aware that Izard had pledged his estate as collateral to support the revolutionary cause. His credentials as a patriot were unquestioned, even though his colleagues often disagreed with his substantive positions.

As an outspoken opponent of the Bill of Rights, Senator Izard moved to postpone consideration of the amendments until the next session. If supported, his motion would have dealt a serious blow to the Bill of Rights and the Constitution. Senators Robert Morris of Pennsylvania and Langdon of New Hampshire joined Izard in expressing their ardent opposition to the amendments. Morris went so far as to say, "Poor Madison got so Cursedly frightened in Virginia, that I believe he has dreamed of amendments ever since."[131] Morris had somewhat reluctantly signed the Declaration of Independence, yet he eventually signed and strongly supported the Constitution. Morris and Roger Sherman of Connecticut were the only two men to sign the Declaration of Independence, the Articles of Confederation, and the Constitution. It is regrettable that he failed to support the Bill of Rights.

As a strong Federalist, Morris believed the amendments constituting the Bill of Rights were unnecessary and perhaps even harmful. Senator Morris doubted that the amendments would pass. Morris was confident that the amendments would never be able to overcome the many obstacles that stood in the way of their adoption and ratification. Morris was so devoted to passage of the Judiciary Act and helping to place the new government on sound footing, that he strongly believed any time spent on the amendments was time wasted. He feared that failure to establish a sound and effective federal government and fiscal policy would play into the hands of those who opposed the Constitution itself.

---

131. See Richard Labunski, *James Madison and the Struggle for the Bill of Rights* (Oxford: Oxford University Press 2006.

Despite opposition from powerful Senators, the discussion of the amendments began and continued until September 14, when the Senate passed their version of the amendments, which included *twenty-six* significant changes. Senator Richard Henry Lee, an Anti-Federalist from Virginia who had opposed ratification of the Constitution, was, nevertheless, a supporter of adding a written bill of rights. Lee was not, however, happy with the Senate's effort to protect rights, which he believed to be little more than a "mutilated and enfeebled" version of rights.

The nature of the consideration in the Senate of various drafts regarding the right of conscience, clarifies the broad public meaning attributed to that right. The first proposal in the Senate dealing with the right of conscience read, "Congress shall make no law establishing one religious sect or society in preference to others, or to infringe the rights of conscience."[132] The Senate initially adopted this version, but later rejected it, all without any record of what was said.

After rejecting that provision, the Senate considered the following language: "Congress shall not make any law infringing the rights of conscience, or establishing any sect or society."[133] This version transposed the right of conscience, placing it first, and included the non-establishment language suggested by Livermore in the House. The debate continued and yet another version, a mix of the first two, was proposed: "Congress shall make no law establishing any particular denomination of religion in preference to another, or prohibiting the free exercise thereof, nor shall the rights of conscience be infringed."[134]

This version was an improvement, making it clear that the debate was moving in the direction of defining non-establishment in non-preferential terms, providing that no "particular denomination of religion" should be preferred. This language is also quite significant because it includes the "prohibiting the free exercise [of religion]" language. It embodied much of Madison's view regarding the right of conscience—a right of full and free exercise coupled with equality or non-preference among religious sects or denominations.

---

132. Ibid., September 8, 1789, 70.
133. Ibid., 75.
134. Ibid., 77–78.

On September 9, the Senate finally settled on language and adopted a version that stated, "Congress shall make no law establishing articles of faith or a mode of worship or prohibiting the free exercise of religion." Clearly, many Senators shared concerns expressed in the House that the amendment not be viewed as denigrating religion. They also did not want the national government to establish any religious or theological doctrine as its own. This version, which was forwarded to the House, also included the very important language securing the free exercise of religion. Senators used the term religion rather than conscience, but the terms were largely interchangeable among members of the founding generation.

In an act that troubled Madison, the Senate inexplicably refused to adopt the amendment securing the right of conscience against state action. Professor Labunski notes that, "Madison was irritated by the Senate's rejection of that amendment, telling Edmund Pendleton that the 'difficulty of uniting the minds of men accustomed to think and act differently can only be conceived by those who have witnessed it.' A short time later, Madison told Pendleton that it was going to be difficult for the House and Senate to reconcile their differences over several key amendments.'"[135] Madison was actually somewhat pleased that the process was moving forward, even though he was not entirely satisfied by the Senate's actions regarding the amendments. Madison understood that opposition in the Senate to limiting state power regarding the right of conscience was based on a fear of encroachment of the national government on the power of the state governments and not due to a lack of support for the concept of the right of conscience.

The Conference Committee

Given opposition in the House, from Madison and others, to the Senate's somewhat weaker version of a bill of rights, it is not surprising that the House requested a conference between leaders in the House and Senate, to iron out their differences. The Conference Committee was made up of influential members of the Senate and House, including

---

135. Richard Labunski, *James Madison and the Struggle for the Bill of Rights* (Oxford: Oxford University Press, 2006), 237.

Madison, Sherman, and Vining from the House and Senators Ellsworth, Carroll and Paterson from the Senate. This able group convened on September 21. Members of the Committee had worked together in the past and were committed to working out their differences.

John Vining Jr. of Delaware was known as a colorful speaker and inclined on occasion to flourish. He was also known as a capable lawyer and draftsman. His talents and wealth enabled him to serve in variety of significant positions at the state and federal levels. He assumed a prominent role in debates over the Bill of Rights.

Conference members had their differences, but they were also jointly committed to adopting a bill of rights worthy of adoption and ratification. Vining was recognized as collegial and often encouraged efficiency and compromise in any deliberation. With those attributes, which he generally shared with Madison, he became an important member of the conference committee. Vining was personable and had an open disdain for personal attacks, often reminding his fellow representatives of the need for collegiality. His colleagues all generally joined in his commitment to civility of the kind that welcomes candor and often leads to compromise.

Their candor as to differences was evident from long before they were named to the Committee and was no doubt a reason for selecting them to confer on this challenging subject matter. They, nevertheless, represented the divisions that existed in the House and Senate, respectively. On the issue of the right of conscience, for example, Representative Sherman had argued that Congress had no authority to act in the area; Representative Vining had chaired the Committee of Eleven and had recommended transposing the right of conscience and the non-establishment provisions to make it clear that religion was not being disfavored; and Madison was the strongest advocate for a vibrant right of conscience. Differences needed to be bridged, but all delegates shared a commitment to the right of conscience in some form.

We know less regarding the views and differences of Committee members from the Senate because the Senate debates were not recorded. Senator Ellsworth was educated at the College of New Jersey, like Madison, and was influenced by the Scottish Enlightenment, with its commitment to the right of conscience. Carroll, in turn, was a faithful

Catholic. Not surprisingly, he had a track record of being fully committed to securing the rights of religious minorities (fittingly, a residence hall at the University of Notre Dame is named after him). Paterson also graduated from the College of New Jersey and, like all graduates from that august institution, had been influenced by teachers steeped in the Scottish Enlightenment and a commitment to natural rights. Three of the six members of this Conference Committee, one of the most significant committees in the founding era, therefore, were graduates of the College of New Jersey. Those graduates and other members of the Committee worked conscientiously to secure the right of conscience, as the preeminent natural right, which Witherspoon and other faculty members had consistently emphasized at the College of New Jersey.

The Committee worked well together, melding differences between the Senate and House drafts into a single set of coherent and widely accepted amendments. The right of conscience was secured in an amendment that has the hand of Madison written all over it: "Congress shall make no law respecting an establishment of religion, or prohibiting the free exercise thereof." The national government—Congress—was prevented from passing any law *respecting* an establishment of religion," furthering Madison's strong belief that no religious sect or group of sects should be preferred over minority sects. Government was also left without the power to make laws, direct or indirect, that had the effect of "prohibiting the free exercise [of religion]." The free exercise of conscience, the most sacred of all rights to Madison, therefore, found its way into the Bill of Rights, in what would become the First Amendment.

We have no record as to why the Conference Committee declined to include the language prohibiting states from infringing on conscience. It may be that members of the committee were fearful that states would view such an act as an infringement of state sovereignty and power. It appears evident, however, that members of the conference committee, including Madison, believed that the right of conscience was already secure, as a natural right. Madison would, nevertheless, have preferred that this truth be clarified in the Bill of Rights, as further insurance that a widely accepted right was beyond the reach of any legitimate or just government. Madison sadly recognized, however, that the right was sometimes wrongly relegated to a mere aspiration and was, therefore, often violated. He was comforted, however, by the fact that the right of conscience was widely recognized as a natural right given of God and, as such, was included in most state declarations of rights, including Virginia's.

Ever the optimist and caught up in the spirt of the broad call for liberty that was a part of the revolutionary cause, it is likely that Madison believed the right of conscience would also be recognized as an "immunity" under the privileges and immunities clause in the Constitution. Madison and others of the founding generation were widely aware of the influential work of William Blackstone. In his *Commentaries on the Law of England*, which were published and widely disseminated by Clarendon Press at Oxford University in 1765–1769, Blackstone used the terms "privileges" and "immunities" to refer to the natural rights of life, liberty, and property. Madison believed the most sacred of those rights was the right of conscience. For Madison, it is likely that the "privileges and immunities clause" (Article IV, Section 2, Clause 1) largely secured the natural right of conscience against state action. Madison, no doubt, believed that the right of conscience was secured against state action by the Ninth Amendment, which provided, "The enumeration in the Constitution, of certain rights, shall not be construed to deny or disparage others retained by the people."

Madison remained confident that the right of conscience would be recognized in every state. He may have been guilty of misplaced optimism, but it is evident that Madison and others believed that they had set in motion the cause of liberty, including the full recognition of the liberty of conscience, in a manner that would result in securing each natural right against government action. To this very day, however, the right of conscience continues to be contested, especially by those who believe that the federal and state governments have the power to act to further a majoritarian agenda even when it opposes the most sacred of all property, the right of religious conscience. Had Madison recognized that this would prove to be the case, he would have insisted on including the protection against state intrusion on the right of conscience.

It is likely that, at the time of the adoption of the Bill of Rights, the Conference Committee joined in Madison's optimism and intention to secure the inviolable right of conscience. Members of the House and Senate repeatedly supported a broad right of conscience and used language carefully crafted to secure that precious liberty and to ensure that religion could not be harmed by government. Similar efforts were made to secure other self-evident rights. Those efforts and that language was legitimized through the ratification process, which followed adoption of the Bill of Rights in the First Congress.

Later in life, after having much time to reflect on the Constitution as a matter of theory and practice, Madison had the opportunity to emphasize the importance and public meaning of the actual language used in the Constitution and Bill of Rights. He did so in a letter to Henry Lee. Madison wrote, "I entirely concur in the propriety of resorting to the sense in which the Constitution was accepted and ratified by the nation. In that sense alone it is the legitimate Constitution."[136] Madison added that, if the intent or public understanding of the generation that framed and ratified the Constitution and Bill of Rights is "not the guide in expounding it, there can be no security for a consistent and stable, more than for a faithful exercise of its powers. If the meaning of the text be sought in the changeable meaning of the words composing it, it is evident that the shape and attributes of the Government must partake of the changes to which the words and phrases of all living languages are constantly subject."[137] He continued, "What a metamorphosis would be produced in the code of law if all its ancient phraseology were to be taken in its modern sense!"[138] Writing this letter in 1822, less than a generation after the framing and ratifying of the Constitution, Madison had already observed the propensity of a new generation to change the public meaning of the Constitution and Bill of Rights, as ratified, not through the amendment process but through interpretation to fit their desires, through the guise of an enlightened modernization of its meaning, thereby permitting the will of the majority to regularly trample upon the people's rights. The likelihood of such modernization, without utilizing the amendment process, was a matter of grave concern to Madison, just as it should

---

136. Letter From James Madison to Henry Lee, 25 June 1824, Founders Online (National Archives), accessed October 12, 2018, https://founders.archives.gov/documents/Madison/04-03-02-0333.

137. Ibid.

138. Ibid.

be to every generation. If the meaning of the language or text of the Constitution can be altered through interpretation designed to modernize its language, rather than through the constitutionally required amendment process, the Constitution, and the system of government and rights it secures, is in serious jeopardy.

The Bill of Rights Is Adopted

The language of the Bill of Rights, as agreed to in the Conference Committee, was forwarded to the House and Senate. Just three days later, on September 24, the House considered the amendments. Madison knew that they needed thirty-four votes to obtain the required two-thirds vote for adoption. There was little room for error, given that some members of the House had voiced their strong disapproval of the amendments. Much to Madison's relief, the House voted overwhelmingly, 37–14, to support the amendments. Representatives Gerry and Tucker, who had consistently opposed the amendments, remained among the few who were adamant in their opposition to the Bill of Rights. Surprisingly, Representative Page of Virginia voted against the amendments, as well, despite efforts from Madison and others to persuade him to support them. Roger Sherman, who served ably on the Conference Committee had been nudged to accept the amendments, believing them to be "harmless [to opponents]" and "satisfactory [to supporters]." One day later, on the September 25, two-thirds of the Senate voted in favor of the amendments. Even the mild final opposition to the Bill of Rights should not necessarily be read as actual opposition to the rights themselves. Some voted no because they favored addition of other rights—a stronger set of rights. Others continued their opposition to a bill of rights claiming the Constitution itself intruded on the sovereign rights of the states and provided for too strong of government at the national level. The fear that the Bill of Rights might be read to limit the rights of individuals and the prerogative of the states to protect such rights led many members of Congress to oppose it. What is clear is that the founders overwhelmingly supported the idea of limiting the power of government at all levels to trample upon rights.

The President Signs the Bill of Rights and Offers a Prayer Resolution

Upon adoption in Congress, the Bill of Rights were then forwarded to the president. It was clear to all that President Washington was strongly supportive of the Bill of Rights. He previously evidenced his support in his inaugural address, in words that might have been penned by Madison. Washington also provided Madison with a letter of support of a Bill of Rights to protect the liberty he had fought so hard to secure. Washington encouraged Madison to use that letter with Federalists who doubted the need for such amendments. Historians concede that the victory in the House and Senate was, in significant measure, a testament to Madison's careful draftsmanship and able advocacy and was attributable to Washington's support. A week after receiving the amendments, Washington forwarded them to the states, with Boudinot's resolution recommending a public day of fasting and thanksgiving for the "signal favors of the Almighty God, especially by affording them an opportunity to peaceably establish a constitution of government for their safety and happiness."[139]

Representative Aedanus Burke, of South Carolina, opposed adoption of the prayer resolution, arguing that he "did not like this mimicking of European customs, where they made a mere mockery of thanksgivings."[140] Interestingly, Representative Tucker, Burke's fellow South Carolinian, also opposed Boudinot's resolution. Tucker argued that adoption of the resolution was "a business with which Congress have nothing to do; it is a religious matter, and, as such, is proscribed to us."[141]

John Adams, the second president, followed Washington's example and issued a resolution of fasting and prayer, like the one Boudinot fashioned in the First Congress. Jefferson, the third president, declined to issue a prayer resolution believing that the government of the United States is constitutionally precluded from "intermeddling with religious institutions, their doctrines, disciplines, or exercises."[142] Madison, the

---

139. *Annals of Congress*, September 25, 1789, 949.
140. Ibid.
141. Ibid., 950.
142. See, A. Stokes & L. Pfeffer, *Church and State in the United States* (New York: Harper & Row, 1964), 88.

fourth president, charted a moderate course, during the War of 1812, when he issued a resolution calling on "religious societies, so disposed, to offer at one and the same time, their common vows and adorations to Almighty God, on the solemn occasion produced by war."[143] President Madison appreciated the prayers of the faithful, but he did not want to imply that government had the power to require them. Later, Madison went a step further by suggesting that even greater care should be taken in offering such resolutions. In 1820, in his *Detached Memoranda*, Madison indicated that he was worried that prior prayer resolutions were subject to being drafted narrowly to fit "the standard of the predominant sect."[144] As always, Madison was cautious in binding the religious conscience of minority religionist or of the government establishing any doctrine as its own. Nevertheless, such prayer resolutions have continued to our present day. On May 4, 2016, for example, President Barack Obama issued the following proclamation calling for a day of prayer: "I, Barack Obama, President of the United States of America, by virtue of the authority vested in me by the Constitution and the laws of the United States, do hereby proclaim May 5, 2016, as National Day of Prayer. I invite the citizens of our Nation to give thanks, in accordance with their own faiths and consciences, for our many freedoms and blessings, and I join all people of faith in asking for God's continued guidance, mercy, and protection as we seek a more just world."[145]

On September 2, 2017, President Trump tweeted, "Remember, Sunday is National Prayer Day (by Presidential Proclamation)!"[146] His formal proclamation provided,

> I, Donald J. Trump, President of the United States of America, do hereby proclaim September 3, 2017, as a National Day of Prayer for the Victims of Hurricane Harvey and for our National Response

---

143. Ibid., 99.

144. Madison's Detached Memorandum, 31 January 1820, Founders Online (National Archives), accessed October 12, 2018, https://founders.archives.gov/documents/Madison/04-01-02-0548.

145. "Presidential Proclamation—National Day of Prayer, 2016," by the President Barack Obama, May 4, 2016, The White House, Office of the Press Secretary, accessed October 12, 2018, https://obamawhitehouse.archives.gov/the-press-office/2016/05/04/presidential-proclamation-national-day-prayer-2016.

146. "Remember, Sunday is National Prayer Day (by Presidential Proclamation)!", accessed October 13, 2018, http://trumpingtweets.com/remember-sunday-is-national-prayer-day-by-presidential-proclamation/.

and Recovery Efforts. We give thanks for the generosity and goodness of all those who have responded to the needs of their fellow Americans. I urge Americans of all faiths and religious traditions and backgrounds to offer prayers today for all those harmed by Hurricane Harvey, including people who have lost family members or been injured, those who have lost homes or other property, and our first responders, law enforcement officers, military personnel, and medical professionals leading the response and recovery efforts. Each of us, in our own way, may call upon our God for strength and comfort during this difficult time. I call on all Americans and houses of worship throughout the Nation to join in one voice of prayer, as we seek to uplift one another and assist those suffering from the consequences of this terrible storm.[147]

When he initially arrived at Congress early in May 1790, Madison understood that adoption of the Bill of Rights in the House and Senate was hardly assured. He faced an uphill battle and had to navigate between the Federalist belief that amendments were unnecessary and perhaps even harmful, in that they could be used to limit the natural rights of the people, and the Anti-Federalist desire to undercut the Constitution itself by sowing seeds of discontent against the national government. Ratification would prove to be even more difficult, but as usual, Madison was steeling himself for another battle, unable to take much time relishing a victory that would be meaningless without state ratification.

---

147. "President Donald J. Trump Proclaims September 3, 2017, as a National Day of Prayer for the Victims of Hurricane Harvey and for our National Response and Recovery Efforts," September 1, 2017, accessed October 13, 2018, https://www.whitehouse.gov/presidential-actions/president-donald-j-trump-proclaims-september-3-2017-national-day-prayer-victims-hurricane-harvey-national-response-recovery-efforts/.

Chapter Seven

Ratification of the Bill of Rights: Completing the Miracle

"Without liberty, law loses its nature and its name, and becomes oppression. Without law, liberty also loses its nature and its name, and becomes licentiousness."[1]

James Wilson

"In Europe, charters of liberty have been granted by power. America has set the example . . . of charters of power granted by liberty. This revolution in the practice of the world, may, with an honest praise, be pronounced the most triumphant epoch of its history, and the most consoling presage of its happiness."[2]

James Madison

Proponents of the Bill of Rights, as adopted by Congress, including Madison, returned home to face a new set of challenges. Ratification of the Bill of Rights by three-fourths of the states, in turn, was hardly a given. The framers were aware of significant opposition forming in some of the states, including Virginia. Patrick Henry, Madison's old nemesis, was already opposing the Bill of Rights, believing that they harmed the cause of liberty.

---

1. James Wilson, *Of the Study of the Law in the United States* (1790), Founders' Library, accessed October 13, 2018, http://founding.com/founders-library/american-political-figures/james-wilson/of-the-study-of-law-in-the-united-states.
2. *National Gazette,* 18 January 1792, Founders Online (National Archives), accessed October 13, 2018, https://founders.archives.gov/documents/Madison/01-14-02-0172.

Henry desperately wanted structural amendments. He believed the federal government was too powerful and sought to limit its power, even, if necessary, against the inclusion of the Bill of Rights. He was also prepared to raise the major issue that separated Madison and the Anti-Federalist candidate, James Monroe, in their run for a seat in the United States House of Representatives—the power of the national government to engage in direct taxation. The stage was being set in Virginia and elsewhere for a battle over ratification of the Bill of Rights.

Despite being exhausted from the extended ordeal associated with his work in the First Congress, Madison's efforts to secure a written bill of rights remained far from finished. As was so often the case, after working on a project of great importance for many days, Madison was suffering ill health. He struggled to gain enough strength to do the most mundane tasks, such as keeping up with customary correspondence. He certainly was not healthy enough to return home to Virginia, where his presence was needed to help secure ratification of the Bill of Rights. Madison was also waiting for his friend, Thomas Jefferson, to arrive in New York. In Madison's absence from Virginia, opposition forces were rapidly gathering and forming a seemingly ironclad strategy to defeat ratification.

Realizing that he was needed at home and could wait no more, Madison finally departed New York, arriving at Montpelier early in 1791. When he arrived, he was greeted with encouraging news that New Jersey, the home of William Paterson, who had served on the Conference Committee, had voted to ratify most of the amendments. However, it declined to pass what was then the second amendment, an amendment regarding compensation for members of Congress. The first two amendments dealt with matters other than rights and neither one was ultimately ratified by the requisite number of states. Many states soon adopted all the amendments intended to secure rights. Madison was particularly heartened to learn that even South Carolina, the home of Representative Tucker and Senator Izard, two of the strongest opponents of the amendments in Congress, ratified all the amendments.

Madison rejoiced in learning that Massachusetts also voted to ratify. Governor John Hancock, whose dramatic signature was the first to be affixed to the Declaration of Independence in 1776, was a tireless proponent of the amendments in Massachusetts. Hancock was a man of deep faith who believed the amendments were "of great consequence" and would complete the Constitution. It was the same John Hancock who, as a founder of the Sons of Liberty, had rallied support for the revolutionary cause with his words, "Resistance to tyranny becomes the Christian and social duty of each individual. . . . Continue steadfast and, with a proper sense of your dependence on God, nobly defend those rights which heaven gave, and no man ought to take from us."[3] In February, with continual prodding by Governor Hancock, Massachusetts approved the ratified every amendment containing a substantive right.

Madison was deeply dismayed, however, to learn that his native Virginia was mounting a vigorous opposition to the Bill of Rights. Patrick Henry continued to seek to derail the new government under the Constitution, to achieve his goal of holding a second convention. Senators Richard Henry Lee and William Grayson, who had been elected to the Senate with Henry's support, at the time that Madison was refused a seat in the Senate, joined Henry in opposing the amendments. Patrick Henry continued to exert great control in the Virginia State Senate and was a power to be reckoned with. Henry's hold on the popularly elected House of Delegates, however, was waning. Senators Lee and Grayson, together with other like-minded Anti-Federalists, believed that the amendments provided weak security against what they considered to be a powerful national government, which threatened the rights of states and their citizens.

The Battle in Virginia

Unfortunately, in this fight Madison was relegated to battling on the sidelines—he was neither a member of the Virginia Senate nor the House of Delegates. He did, however, have many friends serving in the Virginia legislature, and his influence continued to be felt from a

---

3. Steve Straud, "John Hancock, "Provincial Congress, Resolution to Massachusetts Bar, October 1774," The Federalist Papers, September 8, 2018, accessed October 13, 2018, https://thefederalistpapers.org/founders/john-hancock/john-hancock-provincial-congress -resolution-to-massachusetts-bay-october-1774.

distance. Madison knew that Virginia, as one of the largest and most powerful states in the union, was critical to the ratification process and the securing of the Bill of Rights. He feared that the Virginia Senate was likely to demand additional amendments of a structural nature. The likely result in the House of Delegates, on the other hand, was less apparent. Obtaining support for the Bill of Rights, without additions and without postponement, therefore, was a formidable undertaking.

Ever an astute politician and advocate, Patrick Henry understood that most Anti-Federalist concerns regarding the Constitution were placated by the addition of a Bill of Rights. Politically, most Anti-Federalists also understood that the people were generally satisfied with the amendments, and they personally feared that they might not be re-elected if they directly opposed amendments securing rights. Another opposition strategy unfolded, therefore, at the direction of Patrick Henry and Senators Lee and Grayson. They called for a post-ponement of a vote until after the next commonwealth elections. In adopting this tactic, opponents argued that the people had not been able to vote on the amendments. They believed that the people should be directly permitted to deliberate and voice their opinion at the ballot box before elected representatives in Virginia decided whether to ratify the amendments. This dilatory strategy was a clear threat to the timely ratification of the Bill of Rights.

Their ploy was generally an effective one, somewhat reminiscent of Madison's efforts to derail the Assessment Bill providing for direct aid to Christian religions, by letting the people express their sentiments prior to passage of that bill in the Assembly. Patrick Henry's strategy, in this regard, helped unify those who disfavored the amendments, including those who believed the amendments were too weak and others who were concerned about preserving state power. Initially, the House of Delegates rejected Henry's motion for postponement with a significant majority voting against it. An unlikely ally joined the opponents' cause. Former Governor Edmund Randolph was known as a strong supporter of the Constitution, but he was concerned about possible interpretations of the Eleventh and Twelfth Amendments, which are currently the Ninth and Tenth Amendments. Those amend-ments were designed to ensure that "enumeration in the Constitution, of certain rights, shall not be construed to deny or disparage others retained by the people" (9th Amendment) and "powers not delegated to the United States by the Constitution, nor prohibited by it to the states, are reserved to the states respectively, or to the people" (10th Amendment). Randolph specifically feared that those amendments did too little to secure rights of the people and the states from the power of the national government. He wanted to limit the powers of the national government.

Madison was unpersuaded and wrote friends, including George Washington, to clarify his understanding that the amendments were designed to limit and not expand, directly or by implication, the power of the federal government. He wrote Washington and acknowledged that "the rights declared in the first ten of the proposed amendments [the 1st through 8th amendments today] were not all that a free people would require the exercise of, and that as there was no criterion by which it could be determined whether any other particular right was retained or not."[4] He, however, worried that the drafting of such rights was a daunting task since such rights were not easily put into language with "definitive certainty." Madison was raising an argument that he long believed—reducing rights into written form, particularly those which were less self-evident, might threaten rather than secure such rights. Madison added in his letter to Washington, that Randolph's raising of this argument was "really unlucky [and to be] regretted as it springs from a friend to the Constitution."[5]

Unlucky or not, Randolph's concerns gave new hope to the opposition forces. Fortunately for Madison and other proponents of the Bill of Rights, however, Henry departed for home to be with his family before the final decision was made regarding ratification of the amendments. Some historians speculate that he believed the cause was lost. Henry's early departure proved to be providential and contributed to securing passage of the amendments. The House of Delegates first deadlocked, at 62–62, with Speaker Thomas Matthews, a former general in the

---

4. Letter to George Washington from James Madison, 5 December 1789, Founders Online (National Archives), accessed October 13, 2018, https://founders.archives.gov/documents /Washington/05-04-02-0261.
5. Ibid.

Revolutionary War and a leading Free Mason, breaking the deadlock, giving proponents of the Bill of Rights a razor-thin victory.

The battle raged on, however, fueled by Randolph's influence and opposition. The next vote dealt directly with Randolph's concerns. The vote in favor of removing the Eleventh and Twelfth amendments (Ninth and Tenth today) was 64–58, a heartening result for opponents, particularly given that it occurred in House of Delegates. Just days later, however, the House reversed its vote and supported the whole of the Bill of Rights by a thirteen-vote margin.

Deliberations in the Senate continued, with the result remaining uncertain. Members of the Senate who opposed the Bill of Rights argued that many of the amendments, including the Third, which protected the right of conscience, did not go far enough. The Senate voted to postpone consideration of the Bill of Rights because of perceived deficiencies in the amendments. The House of Delegates rejected the Senate's proposed changes and the Virginia legislative body was bogged down in what really were petty differences. As so often can tragically be the case, partisan differences resulted in indecision and postponement of action.

It was not until October 1791, that the Virginia House of Delegates formally reconsidered the amendments and began, in earnest, the process of building momentum toward ratification. On December 5, the House adopted all the amendments—unanimously! Just ten days later, the Senate followed suit and passed the amendments by a slim margin. Two weeks later, President Washington reported to Congress that Virginia finally voted to ratify the amendments. Virginia had provided the crucial vote, as the tenth of fourteen states that had voted to ratify all the amendments designed to secure rights. The proposed first and second amendments, which dealt with issues other than rights, were not ratified and did not become part of the Constitution.

It was not until March 1, 1792, however, that Washington's Secretary of State, Thomas Jefferson, sent notification to the governors that the Bill of Rights had been ratified. The very first provision in the First Amendment protected the right of religious conscience. That right was followed by the freedom of the press, freedom of speech, the freedom to assemble, and the right to petition the government. Some contemporary opponents of those preeminent rights like to say they were not the first amendments included in the original Bill of Rights as proposed to the states. That is true. It also true, however, that the third amendment, in fact, included the first substantive rights included in the Bill of Rights. Among all of the rights included in the ten substantive amendments, the right of conscience was intentionally placed first, with inclusion of the language "Congress shall make no law respecting an establishment of religion, or prohibiting the free exercise thereof." That language was placed first in the litany of our primary rights because the right of conscience was the deemed by Madison and the other architects of the Bill of Rights to be the preeminent, or most sacred, of all rights. Other significant *first* amendment rights followed the right of conscience with the language, "Congress shall make no law . . . abridging the freedom of speech, or of the press; or the right of the people peaceably to assemble, and to petition the government for a redress of grievances."

Insights to Understanding the Meaning of the First Amendment

As Madison taught, constitutional analysis appropriately begins with the public meaning of a given constitutional text. The First Amendment was carefully crafted, in a manner that reflects Madison's adept use of language and his education, including his understanding of antithesis gleaned from his study of Hebrew. Eimi Priddis argues that "respecting" and "prohibiting" are used in a parallel structure, making it clear that both terms are verbs. She explains, "If both phrases of the First Amendment are understood to be participial phrases, the First Amendment is also revealed to be a beautiful instance of antithesis. The grammatical structure of the two phrases is identical, and the phrases even have the same number of syllables."[6] Priddis continues, "The rhetorical appeal of the parallel structure is enhanced by the fact that both participial phrases are equal in importance, but opposite in meaning, each working together to prohibit a separate but equal type

---

6. Eimi Priddis Yildrim, "A Rhetorical Revolution: The Antithesis of the First Amendment," manuscript in author's possession, 23.

of infringement of religious liberty. In other words, the antithetical means of infringing religious freedom—granting particular favors to a religion and imposing particular disabilities on a religion—would be beautifully juxtaposed in identical grammatical structures."[7] She concludes, "It would be difficult to believe that such beautiful rhetorical antithesis in the First Amendment was accidental, especially given the time period during which the text was written. It is much more likely that the Founders intended respecting to be a present participial verb all along."[8]

Read as verbs, "respecting" and "prohibiting" turn the first part of the First Amendment into a single balanced provision, designed to protect a single complementary right—the right of conscience. The right of conscience, according to Madison, protects the full and free exercise of religion and, therefore, necessarily protects against any establishment of religion. The establishment of *a* single sect or even a group of religions would violate the equal liberty of conscience of minority sects and individuals who were not part of that established religion or group of religions.

The establishment language of the First Amendment, according to Madison, was designed to prevent Congress (the government) from granting favors (emoluments) or preference (unequal treatment) to religious sects or establishments. Madison had a clear understanding of the Latin roots for words used in the amendment. Respecting comes from the Latin verb *respicere*, which means to "look back at, regard." Interestingly, when used as a verb, respecting also means to "act to harm or interfere with" or to "care or provide for." The addition of the phrase *"an* establishment of" makes it clear that the Conference Committee drew on Madison's thinking and drafting skill. Clearly, Congress (the national government) was prohibited from making direct payments to religious establishments or sects. Congress was securing the right of conscience without harming or showing special regard for an establishment of religion, as Madison emphasized in his response to those in Congress who believed his initial language might be read to harm religion generally.

---

7. Ibid.
8. Ibid.

The national government was also precluded from treating religious establishments unequally by showing preference to any single denomination or group of denominations. The language clearly protected the right of conscience, the right that secured protection for all religions and religionists, by demanding that they be treated equally by the federal government. That text also protects against special benefits being conferred on any particular religion or group of religions, mirroring Madison's objections to the Assessment Bill in Virginia.

The right to the "full and freely exercise" one's religion was also directly secured or protected by the language "Congress shall make no law . . . prohibiting the free exercise [of religion]." Prohibiting comes from the Latin words *prohibeo* or *interdico*, each of which means to disallow or officially proscribe. Proscribe, in turn, means to legally prohibit, limit, or prevent something from being done, whether directly or indirectly. Repeatedly, with the urging of Madison, members of the House and Senate used language that made it clear that they did not believe that the right of religious exercise was to be full and free from government infringement in any form, from even the slightest touch of the government hand (power). "Free," according to the Oxford Dictionary, means "able to act [or to do] as one wishes, not under the control of another." It also means to not be "subject . . . to despotic government." The prohibiting language incorporated Madison's long-held view that government may not interfere with the free exercise of religion except to protect the exercise of an equal right of religious conscience or to prevent religious exercise from "manifestly endangering" the state. Madison understood that if the state was manifestly endangered, all liberty would be threatened, including the right to exercise one's religion freely and fully.

Some theorists argue that the establishment clause was intentionally placed first, to make it clear that those who adopted and ratified the First Amendment believed that restricting religious establishments was more important than protection of the right of free exercise. One could just as easily argue that the free exercise clause was placed second as a sort of crescendo. In truth, however, the clear intent was to protect a single, complementary right—the right of religious conscience.

Read in this light, the freedom of conscience provision, the *first* right recognized in the *First* Amendment, protects against government making payments to or preferring one religious sect or establishment over another, thereby preserving the equal right of conscience. It also prohibits the government from interfering directly or indirectly with the full and free exercise of religion of individuals and sects, or groups of individuals, except when such exercise manifestly endangers the existence of the state or interferes with the exercise of the equal right of religious conscience by another. The establishment and free exercise limitations on governmental power are, therefore, complementary and fulsome.

In March 1792, the same month that Thomas Jefferson, President Washington's Secretary of State, sent notification to the governors that the Bill of Rights had been ratified, James Madison wrote a significant and often disregarded essay published in the *National Gazette*. Indeed, that essay, which was dated March 29, 1792, may be the best explanation of the original meaning of the First Amendment, as understood by Madison. The essay helps clarify Madison's understanding that the right of conscience, like other major rights, is both a right and a form of property. Madison's essay on property also helps explain the meaning of other First Amendment rights—the freedom of speech, the freedom of the press, the right to peaceably assemble, and the right to petition the government. It is tragic that this essay, which explains with clarity the intended meaning of the First Amendment, is rarely examined in contemporary efforts to better understand the public meaning of the right of conscience and the First Amendment at the time it was ratified.

Madison begins the essay by defining property as "that dominion which one man claims and exercises over the external things of the world, in exclusion of every other individual. In its larger and juster meaning, it embraces every thing to which a man may attach a value and have a right; and which leaves to every one else the like advantage."[9] Madison elaborated on his fulsome view of property and

---

9. James Madison, "Property," 29 March 1792, The Founders' Constitution (University of Chicago), accessed October 13, 2018, http://press-pubs.uchicago.edu/founders/documents/v1ch16s23.html.

rights by beginning with the most obvious case, the right of property in the form of lands and money. He then moved to the right of opinions and expressions, noting that "a man has a property in his opinions and the free communication of them."[10] Madison then emphasized that man "has a property of peculiar value in his religious opinion, and in the profession and practice dictated by them."[11] Madison added that a man has "property very dear to him in the safety and liberty of his person" and "an equal property in the free use of his faculties and free choice of the objects upon which he employs them."[12] He then wisely summarized this point by stating, "In a word, a man is said to have a right to his property, he may be equally be said to have a property in his rights."[13] He concludes this thought by explaining, "The end of government, that alone is a just government, [is to] impartially secur[e] to every man, whatever is his own."[14] Thinking of rights as the most personal and sacred of all forms of property helps explain why rights are so precious and need to be guarded in every generation. Indeed, if people better understood that the deprivation of First Amendment rights is like taking a part of another's very person or identity, and in the case of conscience his or her soul, it is likely that rights would be better understood and, therefore, carefully protected.

In a further discussion that illuminates his hierarchy of rights, Madison points out that praise should be sparingly allowed to a government which "does not protect [its citizens] in the enjoyment and communication of their opinions, in which they have an equal, and in the estimation of some a more valuable property."[15] He then emphasized that praise should be even more sparing "where a man's religious rights are violated by penalties, or fettered by tests, or taxed by hierarchy. Conscience is the most sacred of all property; other property depending in part on positive law, the exercise of [conscience], being a natural and inalienable right."[16] To reiterate his emphasis on the right

---

10. Ibid.
11. Ibid.
12. Ibid.
13. Ibid.
14. Ibid.
15. Ibid.
16. Ibid.

of conscience, with an example, Madison continues, "To guard a man's house as his castle, to pay public and enforce public debts and enforce private debts with the most exact faith, can give no title to invade a man's conscience which is more sacred than his castle, or to withhold from it that debt of protection, for which the public faith is pledged, by the very nature and original conditions of the social act."[17]Madison conceived of religious conscience as a natural right of a peculiar nature, a right more sacred than other rights which were, in some measure, a matter of positive law and dependent on government for their existence.

Madison discussed some examples and then made the following important point near the end of his explanatory essay: "If there be a government then which prides itself in maintaining the inviolability of property; which provides that none shall be taken directly even for public use without indemnification to the owner, and yet directly violates the property which individuals have in their opinions, their religion, and their persons, and their faculties; nay more, which indirectly violates the property which individuals have in their property . . . [is not a government that is] a pattern for the United States."[18] He concludes this revealing essay by admonishing, "If the United States mean to obtain or deserve the full praise due to wise and just governments, they will equally respect the rights of property, and the property in rights: they will rival the government that most sacredly guards the former; and by repelling its example in violating the latter, will make themselves a pattern to that and all other governments."[19]

For Madison, government's primary responsibility is to secure rights—rights in tangible property, expressive rights, and the right of conscience. Rights in real property, under the Fifth Amendment, shall not "be taken for public use, without just compensation." Any real property, therefore, may only be taken by government when "just [not merely fair] compensation" is awarded. By their nature the right to one's opinions or expression, in turn, may not be taken with just compensation, because no such monetary or tangible compensation is possible. Property is tangible and may be the subject of just compensation.

17. Ibid.
18. Ibid.
19. Ibid.

Expression, on the other hand, is personal and generally not tangible. There is no way for government to compensate for the taking of a right that is so personal. Rather, if justice is to be done, such rights must be treated equally and broadly protected. Only the most compelling reasons warrant an invasion of the rights of expression and assembly. Additionally, the government must treat all such rights equally—taking one right of expression without taking other related rights is unjust. The most sacred right, the right of conscience, in turn, is clearly property that is, by its nature, beyond the reach of government. There is absolutely no way to compensate, with even a modicum of justice, the taking of such property. To take one's conscience is to take that which is most sacred, personal, and unique from the believer. It is to deprive persons of a part of their soul, a solemn duty owed God. In natural rights terms, that sacred duty is prior to the existence of the social compact and, therefore, beyond the reach of government. No just government may intrude on such a sacred right—personal property at its most intimate—according to Madison, except in two limited circumstances: when an equal right of conscience would be taken without government intervention (equivalent rights of religious conscience must be treated equally); or when the government and all liberty would be lost unless the right of conscience in that case is limited or taken by government. In other words, unless the government would be manifestly endangered if the right is not taken or limited.

John Locke and William Penn also referred to rights as property in the context of conscience, but it was Madison who added much light to the topic, particularly as it relates to the hierarchy of rights included in the First Amendment and the importance of those rights, particularly the foundational or preeminent right of conscience. The right of conscience was preeminent for Madison, because so many other rights were means to the end of expressing and exercising one's conscience, one's most deeply held beliefs. For example, speech is a means, in many respects, to expressing one's conscience. Madison understood that many in his generation, and hopefully in ours, want to speak primarily to express that which is most important or meaningful in their lives. Many also desire to share their religious conscience as missionaries to bring others the joy of their faith. Speaking about matters considered to be expressions of our own most deeply held views is a means of building community with other fellow believers, which is essentially the right of assembly or association. The rights protected in the First Amendment, therefore, are interrelated and are serve as means or instruments to the end of expressing and exercising one's deeply held beliefs or conscience.

Contemporary Examples of the Importance of Religious Liberty

Understanding the right of conscience, in Madisonian terms, as the most sacred of property is, indeed, illuminating. Every citizen enjoys an equal right of conscience. The way individuals exercise their respective rights of religious conscience may differ, but everyone individual's chosen form of exercise is protected. That is what equality means in this context. To take the right to exercise one's conscience, in any instance, is to rip the heart and soul out of a person who feels bound by her or his conscience to obey God. Only a tyrant of the worst sort would deprive another of what is most precious and sacred to that individual, his or her very soul. Each American share, whether they acknowledge it or not, equally in the right of conscience this most sacred of all property, regardless of gender, ethnicity, sexual orientation, or religion. Furthermore, to deprecate this most sacred of all property (right) weakens all other rights, particularly the rights contained in the First Amendment.

Madison also understood that citizens who willingly accept duties greater than themselves are essential to the perpetuation of any just government. Madison certainly agreed with and, in fact, may have written the following words that were included in President George Washington's famous Farewell Address: "Of all the dispositions and habits which lead to political prosperity, religion and morality are indispensable supports. In vain would that man claim the tribute of patriotism, who should labor to subvert these great pillars of human happiness, these firmest props of the duties of men and citizens."[20]

---

20. "Washington's Farewell Address, 1799," The Avalon Project (Yale Law School), accessed October 13, 2018, http://avalon.law.yale.edu/18th_century/washing.asp.

Washington concludes, "Let us with caution indulge the supposition that morality can be maintained without religion. Whatever may be conceded to the influence of refined education on minds of peculiar structure, reason and experience both forbid us to expect that national morality can prevail in exclusion of religious principle."[21] George Washington and James Madison jointly understood that a sense of duty, particularly religious duty, provides the foundation of true patriotism and morality.

A few short contemporary examples may help clarify Madison's insights regarding the rights contained in the First Amendment. The first is from the life of Anjeze Gonxhe Bojaxhiu, who is best known as Mother Teresa. As a matter of religious conscience, Mother Teresa was inspired or called to serve among the poorest of the poor in Calcutta, those who were often forgotten and viewed as untouchables. Initially, she faced strong opposition from local Hindu leaders, who were unwilling to grant a Roman Catholic the right to serve their poor, particularly the untouchables.

If those leaders continued to flex their muscle or power as the dominant religious group in Calcutta, they could have put an end the work of Mother Teresa. The cost would have been high. Those whose lives were blessed by Mother Teresa's service would have failed to feel the touch of her loving hands, if she were prohibited from exercising her religious conscience. Mother Teresa and members of her order viewed themselves as agents of their God and attributed their acts to the touch of their Master's hands. They were being obedient servants to the Lord their God. Mother Teresa and those who were called to serve with her would have suffered a serious blow to their conscience and souls, if the government of Calcutta had sided with a local religious majority. Their very reason for being, their souls, would have been taken from them. The people served would have suffered needlessly as well.

Under the right of conscience, when viewed as a sacred property, if the government prevents individuals from following their conscience, it constitutes an illegal taking, a taking of that which is precious above all else. Their service and souls would also be protected under the "no law respecting an establishment of religion" language. To ban Mother

---

21. Ibid.

Teresa from serving would constitute an act of preferring the majority religion. Such an act would have violated two requirements of the non-establishment limitation on government action: (1) it would have shown preference to a religion supported by the majority; and (2) it would have harmed a minority religion. In using the example of Mother Teresa, it is important to note that the First Amendment does not apply directly, as a matter of law, to India or other nations. It is, nevertheless, an apt example of the value of the right of conscience and the operations of a just government.

Another example can be drawn from the life of Dr. Martin Luther King Jr. King firmly believed that he was "called" to serve as a voice for civil rights and racial equity, when he undertook his leadership role regarding the bus boycott in Montgomery, Alabama. Late one night, early in the boycott, a rock with a note cascaded through his window. It fell at Dr. King's feet. He picked it up and carefully read the angry words written on the note. Those words were a clear threat to his life and the lives of his family members. In an era when death threats were real, Martin was shaken and went upstairs to comfort his baby daughter. He swept her up in his arms, believing he was about to comfort his infant daughter by assuring her that he would do all that was within his power to keep her safe. As a young minister and father, he was initially determined to assure his daughter's safety by stressing that he had decided to focus on building his church and keeping his family safe rather than serving as a spokesperson for a highly controversial and dangerous boycott. According to Dr. King, in that instant, as he held his infant daughter, he knew God was calling him to serve as a spokesperson for righteousness and racial equity. Indeed, he was being called for the sake of his daughter and all children. Martin knew that the "call" (commandment) was from God and could not be disregarded without doing irreparable damage to his soul.

Despite imprisonment and efforts to stop him from speaking, Martin remained faithful to that "call" until the threat contained in the note became a reality, years later, when he was mercilessly murdered by a cowardly assassin. A voice of conscience was momentarily quieted by a ruthless, racist murderer. As was true of Mother Teresa, depriving Dr. King from the right to freely exercise his religious conscience from entering the public discourse and leading the civil rights movement, would have taken a part of his soul and the blessings felt by many because of his inspired work. He exercised his most sacred property, his conscience, to fulfill a personal duty to God. In doing so, he strengthened his soul as he blessed many by his heeding the clarion call he had been given to support the cause of liberty and racial equity. Like John Witherspoon, another prophetic preacher-teacher before him, Dr. Martin Luther King Jr. used his religious voice to impact those he served as a minister *and* contribute to the public discourse.

Today, sadly, there are some who want to prevent religious leaders from speaking and engaging in the world of politics and policy, arguing that religious speech and advocacy somehow violates the establishment limitation of the First Amendment. Those opponents of religious exercise and speech may believe that they are performing some public good, but the lives of Mother Theresa and Dr. King, together with so many others who have served well in heeding a call to conscience, stand as evidence that Madison and Washington were right—"reason and experience both forbid us to expect that national morality can prevail in exclusion of religious principle."

Not all examples of the exercise of conscience are so dramatic. Some are simply quiet, personal efforts to be true to one's duty to God or to something they consider greater than themselves, something worth living and dying for. For example, some belittle the right of conscience of a baker to refuse to bake a cake for reasons that he sincerely believes violate his conscience, his sense that he is to use his talents, which he believes to be God-given or magnified, in ways acceptable to the God he worships.[22] The taking of such a right does, in fact, implicate his duty to God, as he sees it, and his soul. In a related sense, a LGBTQ couple may legitimately believe their identity is harmed when that same baker refuses to bake a cake for their wedding – they feel the very real sting of discrimination.

The most difficult cases arise when rights conflict. Generally, such rights and identity, or self-definition, can be balanced, particularly if both parties respect the right and identity of the other. Indeed, if we viewed the other as a friend, or a loved one we disagree with, we would

---

22. See *Masterpiece Cakeshop, Ltd. v. Colorado Civil Rights Commission*, 584 U.S. (2018).

surely endeavor to find ways of demonstrating respect for their right of conscience or identity, knowing that the denigration of that right or identity was the taking of a right of great importance. If, for example, the LGBTQ couple can obtain the cake elsewhere, the baker's right of conscience can be protected, without irreparably harming the LGBTQ couple. The couple in that instance, if they respected the right of the baker, would buy the cake elsewhere. Certainly, the couple and those who feel the sting of discrimination with them are free to view the baker as a bigot and boycott his bakery. In turn, a cost of exercising one's conscience may be disparagement in the marketplace and society generally. There are legitimate costs, therefore, to exercising one's rights of conscience, but the right must, as Madison understood, remain inviolate The truly difficult case comes when the couple are unable to obtain a cake elsewhere—a case in which the rights of the baker or the identity of the couple would be irretrievably harmed and a balance is not possible. Fortunately, those cases of irretrievable conflict are exceedingly rare—they are more the product of lawyerly hypotheticals than reality in the contemporary world. Certainly, they would be rare in a world of friends, where the rights of the other were important.

A recent Pew Research Center Study found, "Three-quarters of U.S. adults say religion is at least 'somewhat' important in their lives, with more than half (53%) saying it is 'very' important. Approximately one-in-five say religion is 'not too' (11%) or 'not at all' important in their lives (11%)."[23] Pew also reports that over 50 percent of the following religious groups or sects view their religion as *very* important—"Jehovah's Witness (90%), Historically Black Protestant (85%), Members of the Church of Jesus Christ of Latter-day Saints (84%), Evangelical Protestant (79%), Muslim (64%), Catholic (58%), Mainline Protestant (53%), and Orthodox Christian (52%)."[24] Thus, for a majority of Americans, their religion or religious conscience is very important. Madison understood that religious stalwarts consider their religious duty to be their most sacred property, the very essence of who they are. He saw this, as a boy, in the case of Baptist ministers

---

23. Pew Research Center, "Chapter 1: Importance of Religion and Religious Beliefs," November 3, 2015, accessed October 13, 2018, http://www.pewforum.org/2015/11/03/chapter-1-importance-of-religion-and-religious-beliefs/.

24. Ibid.

who were jailed for failing to obtain (pay for) a license to preach. For Madison, every person of conscience should be protected against governmental tyranny.

A similar experience in my childhood made this truth real to me. As a third grader, I was deeply moved as I observed a courageous act on the part of a classmate, Patricia. Each day, we stood in unison as a class to pledge allegiance to the American flag and our nation. Patricia, however, declined to do so, choosing to be true to her faith as a Jehovah's Witness. All other members of the class stood as she sat quietly at her desk. The result was to be expected—many of her classmates ridiculed her, making her feel lonely, an outcast. Our teacher, Mrs. Stokes, who was patriotic and was a member of the World War II generation, saw what was happening and intervened to teach us that we were reciting the Pledge of Allegiance and singing the National Anthem as a testament to those who gave their lives protecting liberty, including Patricia's right of conscience, which required that she remain seated. Mrs. Stokes' explanation made sense to the class. From that day forward, many of us felt a small measure of Patricia's pain, courage, and faith. Strangely, it increased our allegiance to the country we were pledging allegiance to, because we felt we were pledging our allegiance to protect our classmate, Patricia's, right of conscience. Mrs. Stokes' teaching found its way into our childlike hearts. A classroom of third graders had come to understand that Patricia's sitting in allegiance to her conscience is exactly the kind of liberty we are pledging our allegiance to protect. We saw it as a courageous, patriotic act, not as an act running counter to the public good and patriotism. My only regret is that I never took the time nor had the courage to tell Patricia how much I respected her for her allegiance to her religious conscience despite occasional sneers and rejection from some of her peers.

In *Minersville School District v. Gobitis*,[25] decided in 1940, the United States Supreme Court held that public schools were permitted to require students, like Patricia, to pledge allegiance and salute the flag, even if standing, saluting and pledging violated their most sacred property, their religious conscience. That decision reflected the strong sentiment of the majority in the United States at that time,

---

25. 310 U.S. 586 (1940).

who believed that respect for the flag and our nation justified forcing individuals to stand and recite the Pledge of Allegiance, even though it inflicted harm on the conscience of some individuals who were a member of a minority religious sect.

In a remarkable, some would say miraculous, turn of events, just three years later, the Court reversed itself, proving that a change of mind can be a sign of strength. During the throes of World War II, the Court decided *West Virginia State Board of Education v. Barnette.*[26] In *Barnette*, the Court held that the First Amendment prevents schools and school officials from forcing students to pledge allegiance and salute the flag. The Court treated the student's right as a right of expression, however, and not as a right of conscience. Nevertheless, conscience was really what was at stake in Patricia's case and in the *Barnette* case. The Jehovah's Witness students were not simply trying to express themselves or persuade others; they were seeking to exercise their freedom of religious conscience, their willingness to obey the Lord their God, just as the Baptist ministers did during Madison's youth.

Churches and institutions directly affiliated with religious sects also perform the function, in part, of exercising the collective rights of their members, rights protected under the right of conscience. Members of a religious sect or institution have voluntarily agreed to be a part of or to associate with the sect, because it reinforces their conscience, their duty to God. Some even feel "called" to serve God by joining a given church or religious body. As a student and faculty member, I was involved directly with three institutions, each of which was religiously affiliated and embraced the beliefs of differing minority sects or faiths. In each instance, it was easy to see the joy and sense of affirmation religious minorities—students, faculty, and staff—felt because they were able to affiliate with others who shared their faith. Attendance at the institution furthered their right of conscience. As minorities they felt a bit less alone when they were able to join with fellow believers. Churches and religiously affiliated institutions are rightly protected under the non-establishment and free exercise and association values, as understood by Madison and members of the founding generation. The government may not harm religious establishments, even when members of the

---

26. 319 U.S. 624 (1943).

governmental majority may be seeking to further a perceived public purpose. To do so is a direct or indirect preference for one sect or group of sects (those that agree with the majority) over the religiously held beliefs (conscience) of a minority sect. To limit the minority individual, sect, or institution is, as Madison well understood, an act of tyranny on the part of the majority.

It is worthwhile to point out that there is a natural and constitutionally permissible cost borne by all religious institutions and individuals protected by the right of conscience. They may not establish their theological doctrine as the doctrine of the state. Under Constantine, most Christian sects set forth a creed, which Rome adopted as its own. That creed preferred one religion or group of religions over others. Minority Christian sects and adherents of non-Christian faiths, who did not adhere to the Creed, suffered in Constantine's effort to unify his people under a single statement of belief.

Minority religionists and religions suffered theologically, as well, when the government put its stamp of approval on or awarded special benefits (emoluments) to a sect with differing doctrinal views. The Christian majority wielded this power in a manner that led to the imprisonment of disbelievers, Christians and non-Christians who did not follow the majority's doctrines. When empowered in this way, religious majorities almost always use government power, directly and indirectly, as they did in Rome, to persecute or harm minority religions and believers. Under the non-establishment value, religions are not permitted to gain control of the power of government of the United States to help protect believers in all sects.

There is another side to the non-establishment limitation on government action, as Madison and the founding generation conceived of it. The non-establishment value embodied in the First Amendment also limits possible majority religious groups in ways that non-religious groups are not limited. For example, many environmentalists or non-environmentalists (e.g. the Green Party) may use government to pursue their ends to the exclusion of others. They may even elect their leader as president to further their religious views. A political majority of environmentalists, who believe in a version of global warming, for example, are permitted to enact treaties and impose their policy choices on others. Those who believe otherwise, including a significant albeit shrinking minority of environmentalists and others who may question the science of the majority, must accept the decision or doctrine of the majority. Environmental majorities, unlike religious majorities, may enforce their policy choices and commandeer the government to their ends, establishing their belief or theories as the policy of the nation. Given the non-establishment value embodied in the First Amendment, religionists may not, however, commandeer the government. Part of the price religious believers pay for their right to freely exercise their religion and obey the Lord their God is being subject to the establishment limitation that demands equality or non-preference.

An inviolable right of religious conscience provides protection against the slightest touch of the government's (majority's) hand; but it does so at a cost to religious believers. A religious sect or group of sects may not impose their beliefs (doctrine) on other minority religious sects and the non-religious. Throughout history, majority religious sects often have sought to impose their religious beliefs on others through governmental action. For example, in many countries where it holds a majority, Islam seeks to impose Shariah law, declaring the nation to be an Islamic republic, despite the objections of members of minority religions residing in that nation. In exchange for giving up the power to impose their theology on others, churches, religious institutions, and individuals exercising their religious conscience are exempt from government interference with their right to fully and freely exercise their religion. In property terms, the government (a tyrannical majority) may not take that which is most sacred in a person, their right of religious conscience, from individuals or congregations of believers (sects). In turn, religious sects may not commandeer the state to their religious ends.

Relatedly, religious leaders like Martin Luther King Jr., John Witherspoon, as well as contemporary religious leaders, may freely exercise their conscience or moral voice in the public square, but they may not impose their sectarian theology or doctrine on others through governmental action. Additionally, religious institutions and leaders may not seek special benefits or emoluments for their sect for government. In short, they may not be treated preferentially. The sacred right of conscience, therefore, is a wonderfully symmetrical right. All share in it, regardless of race, religion, social orientation, gender, and so on. Every individual has or retains an inalienable right of religious conscience, whether they choose to exercise it or not. As Madison saw so clearly, it is a natural right, a gift from God that is inalienable and largely beyond the reach of any just governmental action, a gift that protects one's soul. The words of the First Amendment are clearly reflective of Madison's views and drafting skills and provide for a rich and wonderfully complementary right of conscience: "Congress (government) shall make no law respecting [preferring or harming] an establishment of religion, or prohibiting [directly or indirectly touching upon] the [full] and free exercise thereof."

Madison's Greatest Vexation Becomes a Matter of Hope

As a young man, Madison was vexed by government takings of the right of conscience, as he observed Baptist ministers incarcerated for their religious beliefs. With the ratification of the Constitution and Bill of Rights, he put into place what many appropriately consider to be a providential and miraculous work, the preservation of the right of conscience. That sacred right was secured in the *first* provision of the *First* Amendment of the Bill of Rights, amending the Constitution with the express intent of securing rights. The right of conscience was pre-eminent in Madison's enumeration of rights and in the eyes of those who adopted and ratified the Bill of Rights. Madison took solace in his having accomplished a measure of his reason for being on this earth, a significant part of what he believed he was called to do as a matter of conscience—to use his time and talent, his public service, to secure the adoption and ratification of the Bill of Rights. He also understood and was painfully aware that every generation must take its turn protecting the rights secured in the bill. If a subsequent generation ceased to adhere to the rights as enumerated and ratified, Madison knew the enumeration of those rights in the Constitution could quickly become little less than a parchment barrier, mere words on an aging piece of paper. The Revolution and the adoption and ratification of the Constitution and Bill of Rights had demanded the best efforts of Madison and so many others. A question remained, that every subsequent generation must also answer: Can our fragile form of constitutional government and rights be maintained?

Having led the effort to secure rights, including the right of religious conscience, Madison continued to serve in Congress and thereafter filled other major public offices, including service as Secretary of State in the Jefferson administration and as the fourth President of the United States. From the time he first entered public service, Madison's life was a whirlwind of determined activity. While it may fairly be said that Madison's greatest and most lasting contributions to the new nation were his work on the Constitution and Bill of Rights, there was more for Madison to accomplish, in a professional and personal sense. The Constitution and Bill of Rights were in place, but the future success or failure, the very existence, of the government under those documents remained uncertain. Madison played a continuing role in securing the rights protected in those inspired documents during the fragile first generation of the United States, a generation that would help determine whether a nation conceived in liberty could, in fact, be protected by the constitutional rule of law. Two questions that every subsequent generation must also answer remained: Can our fragile form of constitutional government and rights be maintained? Will Madison's legacy and the sacred right of conscience long endure, or will it become little more than a string that has become brittle from disuse and disregard that tenuously links his generation to our generation?

Chapter Eight

Service as Party Leader
in Tumultuous Times

"If men were angels, no government would be necessary. If angels were to govern men, neither external nor internal controls on government would be necessary. In framing a government which is to be administered by men over men, the great difficulty lies in this: you must first enable the government to control the governed; and in the next place oblige it to control itself."[1]

James Madison

"There are seasons in every country when noise and impudence pass current for worth; and in popular commotions especially, the clamors of interested and factious men are often mistaken for patriotism."[2]

Alexander Hamilton

Madison's battles with his nemesis, Patrick Henry, were at an end. Madison always understood that Henry was motivated by good intentions. Madison admired Henry as a great orator and patriot and never expressed any ill-will or animosity toward him. Two of the great figures of American history had stood toe-to-toe, for more than a decade, over issues related to whether the Constitution and Bill of Rights, as drafted, should become the law

---

1. *The Federalist Papers* (Mineola: 2014), No. 53, 254,
2. Publius Letter, II, [26 October 1778], Founders Online (National Archives), accessed October 13, 2018, https://founders.archives.gov/documents/Hamilton/01-01-02-0622.

of the land. Madison prevailed. The Constitution and Bill of Rights were adopted and ratified. Given the series of close calls or grand coincidences required to adopt and ratify first the Constitution and later the Bill of Rights, the constitutional foundation of the United States of America was clearly miraculous, an act of Providence, in the eyes of Madison and others in the founding generation.

Having won and lost great conflicts, Patrick Henry returned home, tired and in need of the succor of family. He remained deeply concerned over the fate of the nation under the Constitution and Bill of Rights. The battering endured in one political battle after another had taken its toll. Patrick was now determined to direct his full attention to caring for his family and property. He had served his nation well, even when he opposed the Constitution. In doing so, he had effectively helped ensure that it would include a Bill of Rights. Tired and fully prepared to reorder his priorities, Patrick wrote his daughter, Betsey, "It is time to me to retire. I shall never more appear in a public character."[3] He added that his fondest wish was "to pass the rest of my days as may be unobserved by the critics of the world, who show but little sympathy for the deficiencies to which old age is so liable."[4] Patrick closed that letter with these endearing words, "May God bless you, my dear Betsey, and your children."[5]

Patrick had acquired a massive estate, but he was concerned about his indebtedness. He directly owned over 100,000 acres and held an indirect ownership of millions of additional acres. Patrick Henry, George Washington, and the Lee family were the largest land owners in the Commonwealth of Virginia. Patrick Henry was a wealthy man, in terms of property, but managing those lands in a profitable manner was no easy task. In addition to his managerial responsibilities, Henry also found joy in the simple things of life. He delighted in playing the violin—we might call it the fiddle—and being with his wife, children, and grandchildren, after a life of public service that had so often removed him from his family. President Washington tried to

---

3. See Harlow Giles Unger, *Lion of Liberty: Patrick Henry and the Call to a New Nation* (Cambridge: Da Capo Press 2010), 264.
4. Ibid.
5. Ibid.

lure him out of retirement, first to serve as Secretary of State and later as Chief Justice of the Supreme Court. The nature of these significant offices reflected Washington's abiding respect for Patrick Henry, even though Henry had so often opposed the policies that Washington held dear. Political differences never diminished the respect and fondness President Washington and Patrick Henry had for one another.

After some soul-searching, Patrick declined President Washington's offers to serve as Secretary of State and Chief Justice of the Supreme Court. In reluctantly declining those opportunities to serve, he reflected, "To disobey the call of my country into service when her venerable chief makes the demand of it must be a crime unless the most substantial reasons justify declining it."[6] Ever the lawyer, Henry then carefully outlined his reasons: "My domestic situation pleads strongly against a removal to Philadelphia, having no less than eight children by my present marriage, and Mrs. Henry's situation [Dolly was pregnant] now forbidding her approach to the small pox, which neither herself nor any of our family have ever had. To this may be added other considerations arising from loss of crops and consequent derangement of my finances [caused in part by his lengthy public service]—and what is of decisive weight with me, my own health and strength I believe are unequal to the duties of the station you are pleased to offer me."[7] Patrick died not long thereafter, in 1799, and his remains rest to this day next to his dear wife, Dorothea or Dolly, on the family estate, Red Hill. Patrick had purchased Red Hill, a plantation located adjacent to the Staunton River, to serve as a beautiful residence for Dolly during their final years together. Patrick aptly referred to Red Hill as "the garden spot of the world."[8]

Madison, on the other hand, having prevailed over an able adversary to secure adoption and ratification of the Constitution and the Bill of Rights, had years of public service in front of him. If he had the luxury of time to pause to think about such matters, however, Madison might well have envied Patrick's family life, surrounded as he was by

---

6. Ibid., 266.

7. Ibid.

8. See "The Magic of Redhill," Patrick Henry Foundation Red Hill, accessed October 13, 2018, https://www.redhill.org/about/redhill.

a loving wife, children, and grandchildren. Madison surely wondered whether, and if so when, he would ever be blessed to enjoy the companionship of a faithful spouse, like Patrick Henry's beloved Dolly.

For the present, Madison had little time to rest and spent his time focused on his work in Congress. He was about to face a set of new trials and yet another force to be reckoned with, in the form of his former ally in writing *The Federalist Papers*, Alexander Hamilton. Those new political battles, in turn, would soon drive a wedge between Madison and President Washington. Madison always referred to Washington as General Washington or Mr. Washington. He also referred to Thomas Jefferson as Mr. Jefferson or President Jefferson. Madison reserved the high respect for his own father. Madison closed a 1770 letter to his father with the following words: "With my love to the Family, I am, Hon. Sir, Your affectionate son, James Madison."[9] Throughout his lifetime, Madison consistently referred to his father as Honorable Sir or Mr. Madison. The use of Honorable Sir reflected the great respect, and deep affection, James had for his father. The use of the respectful title of "Mr.," in turn, was reserved for few men in Madison's life: his father, Jefferson, and Washington.

Times were changing. Patrick Henry the former political leader in Virginia was safely ensconced at home, and Madison was about to be assume new leadership responsibilities. He soon became leader of the newly formed Democratic-Republican Party. Madison had served as the most prominent leader in the First Congress and was about to bear what was for him a burden, leadership of a new party, as the United States began to suffer under a condition of fierce partisanship. As party leader, Madison was destined to differ with President Washington and particularly his Secretary of the Treasury, Alexander Hamilton, while often agreeing with Jefferson, Washington's Secretary of State.

Hamilton soon became the voice of many of the policies of the Washington Administration, particularly those designed to create a strong economic foundation for the nation and, what was for Hamilton

---

9. Letter from James Madison to James Madison, Sr., 23 July 1770, Founders Online (National Archives), accessed October 13, 2018, https://founders.archives.gov/documents /Madison/01-01-02-0008.

a related issue, a strong executive branch of government, designed to effectuate those powers. Furthermore, Hamilton strongly believed that the government under the Articles of Confederation had unduly favored the power of the state governments, creating an imbalance of power that made it difficult for the national government to strengthen the economy and defend against threats from foreign powers. For Hamilton, a strong executive translated into a growing economy and a strong national government able to act effectively against any foreign threat. Hamilton was, therefore, determined to solidify the role of the national government in the balance of power between the state and national governments. The national government, under Hamilton's view, had to be more powerful than the state government. Increasingly, Washington accepted Hamilton's vision of a much stronger national government and the need for a powerful executive to lead that government.

Jefferson, Washington's Secretary of State, in turn, served as a strong counterpoint to Hamilton's positions in Washington's Cabinet. Jefferson favored stronger state government and feared the development of a powerful, and what he believed to be elitist, executive branch of government. Jefferson, however, found himself increasingly relegated to a distant second position in the Administration, even in advising the president regarding foreign affairs. Any allegiance Madison had to Hamilton was also quickly dissipating. As Jefferson's voice became less powerful within the Washington Administration, Madison became the leader of opposition in Congress to the Hamiltonian view of government. Madison had previously agreed with Hamilton that the imbalance between the state and national governments needed to be addressed in the new federal government. He, nevertheless, believed that there should generally be equilibrium or equality of power so that the national and state governments could each act as a check and a balance against the power of the other. Such a balance of power, for Madison, could best secure liberty. Similarly, Madison feared increases in the power of the executive branch, at the national and international levels. Increases in executive power, at the expense of the power of the other branches of government, also created a disequilibrium or imbalance that Madison firmly believed to be a threat to liberty.

Hamilton proved to be a highly capable adversary, often partisan and ever-willing to engage in invective directed to those who opposed his policies. Consistent with his character, Madison generally endeavored to avoid personal attacks on his opponents. As a party leader, however, it was impossible for Madison to avoid partisanship. Nevertheless, he largely remained focused on liberty and the importance of limited government and balanced power. The playing out of the battles between the Hamiltonian and Madisonian views of government made for powerful political theater at the time they occurred and continue to play themselves out in today's politics. Hamilton gave content to a strong view of the strong national government and executive branch. It was Washington who gave the breath of life to that view of government by providing Hamilton and his allies with the power to effectuate those views. Jefferson, on the other hand, was clearly a strong and often obstinate force in the formulation of what came to be known as Republican or Democratic-Republican ideas. Madison certainly shared in giving life to those Republican ideas and values, ultimately providing the counter-balance to Washington in terms of political power, by becoming the leader, first of the legislative branch of government, and later the Democratic-Republican Party.

Hamilton and Madison had served the nation well as significant collaborators in helping to secure ratification of the Constitution, through coauthorship of the *Federalist Papers*. That collaboration had drawn to an end and a new era was opening, a time of increasing opposition between two former allies. Hamilton became a strong nationalist, with a belief that the needs of the nation demanded a strong national government. Without a strong national government, Hamilton feared that the United States would disintegrate into many bickering states and risk being overcome by other unified world powers. He also believed that issues related to debt threatened the union.

Madison, on the other hand, remained a small "f" federalist. He believed in a federal system, with a balance of power between the states and federal government. Madison also shared Jefferson's fear that Hamilton espoused an oligarchy, a government of the elite and rich, particularly those who became rich through stocks and investments in mercantile or related business interests. Like Jefferson, Madison believed the future of the new nation could best be secured by alle-giance to Republican ideals that were founded in respect for common people, particularly farmers, planters, and others representing agrar-ian as opposed to mercantile interests. Most of all, however, Madison believed liberty had its roots in limited government. In the end, just as the collaboration of Hamilton and Madison had helped secure a great good, in the form of ratification of the Constitution, their opposition would provide to create the kind of dynamic tension that helped form a more perfect union. The unfolding of that dynamic, under the watch-ful and deliberative eye of President Washington, proved fundamental to the creation of a viable but not all-powerful national government.

Hamilton was a strong Anglophile—a supporter of all things English. Hamilton was known to emphasize that the people of the United States "think in English," as a way of stressing the natu-ral connection between the United States and Britain. Madison, on the other hand, followed his friend and intellectual partner, Thomas Jefferson's, lead in international matters. Madison shared Jefferson's fear that Britain posed the gravest threat to the welfare of the new nation. Madison also understood that other nations in Europe con-stituted a real, albeit secondary, threat to America. Madison felt a natural allegiance to France, given their support for the revolutionary cause against the British during the Revolutionary War. Madison also understood the importance of counter-balancing the power of Britain by maintaining a strong relationship with France. He was apprehen-sive of all foreign powers and was particularly determined to minimize their influence in lands to the west. Britain had built forts and alliances with Native tribes, in the north and west, which Madison viewed as a threat to the westward movement of the new nation. Madison was also personally supportive of the French people and efforts to obtain freedom from their monarch. Additionally, Marquis de Lafayette was a dear friend and a great general in the eyes of Jefferson and Madison. These factors contributed to Madison's belief that strong ties with France were crucial to the survival of the still fragile United States. The close personal and political ties between Madison and Jefferson, and differences with Hamilton, intensified a growing rift between Madison and Jefferson and Hamilton, and secondarily President Washington.

Hamilton and Madison each acknowledged the great strengths of the other. Shortly before his death, Madison told Charles Ingersoll that Hamilton was a great man and that he bore him no ill will.[10] Hamilton, in turn, referred to Madison, "as a clever man,"[11] who was "Uncorrupted and Incorruptible."[12] Hamilton, in less flattering terms, added that Madison was a bit provincial, "[un]acquainted with the world."[13] Interestingly, Hamilton wisely added that he and Madison had the "same End in view,"[14] but differed significantly as to the "mode of attaining it." Two great men, who once miraculously united their talents to build the nation, now were divided as to the best means for securing its future. In retrospect, without their joint efforts, it is doubtful the Constitution would have become the foundation, the supreme law, of the land. Hamilton and Madison worked closely and tirelessly to lay the constitutional foundation for the national government. It is unfortunate that this great partnership did not last, and once great allies became fierce adversaries.

The Rise of Partisanship

In January 1790, a schism was quickly developing between Hamilton and Madison. Hamilton, a committed nationalist, believed in concentrating power, particularly economic power, at the *national* level. Madison, in turn, believed the power of the *federal* government should be limited or checked by the power of the states as a means of protecting liberty. Madison feared the consolidation of power at any level, in any governing body, or in any individual. That fear was tied to his love of liberty. The protection of liberty was a matter of conscience for Madison. His priority was limiting government to only those powers necessary to effectuate the basic needs of government, at the national and state levels, without infringing on the rights of the people. Such limited natural power was necessary to achieve the basic ends of the

---

10. See Ralph Ketcham, *James Madison* (Charlottesville: University of Virginia Press 1990), 305.
11. Ibid.
12. Ibid.
13. Ibid.
14. Ibid.

government and was also critical to maintaining liberty. Hamilton, on the other hand, was tireless in his effort to achieve his priority of building a strong national government to place the new nation on a sound economic footing.

Hamilton represented the mercantile or business interests of the northern colonies, and Madison was more supportive of agrarian interests of the southern colonies. These two men held diametrically opposed views on nearly every political front, which contributed to the growing rift between these former allies and ultimately led to a major sectional divide in the nation that has persisted throughout the history of the United States. Those differences manifested themselves in highly partisan ways. Such partisanship played an important role in the creation of two political parties at the national level: The Federalists (the party largely espousing Hamilton's views), and the Democratic-Republicans (the party led by Madison and espousing more Jeffersonian views). The partisan rift between these two formidable statesmen also had a surprising affect upon Madison's relationship with his great friend, President Washington. Washington retained a disdain for the fierce partisanship that developed during his administration and sought with limited success to moderate the differences between Hamilton and Jefferson, and with Madison in Congress.

In January 1790, Hamilton prepared two significant reports: a "First Report on the Public Credit" and a "Report on a National Bank." A year later, he added two additional important reports: one dealing with the "Establishment of a Mint" and another constituting a "Report on Manufactures." These reports provided the intellectual basis for a stronger national economic policy and government. They also were designed to reduce the national debt. Hamilton's efforts were critically important in placing the national government on sound economic footing, thereby securing the perpetuation of the United States. While necessary in many ways, Madison found Hamilton's efforts to be troubling for numerous reasons, which soon became evident.

An early example of the differences between Madison and Hamilton dealt with their respective views regarding payment of national debts. Hamilton proposed to pay the nation's debts in full both nationally and internationally. By doing so, Hamilton was confident that the new nation's status among creditors would be secure. Madison, ever moderate, but increasingly the partisan, disagreed in part. Madison was generally supportive of Hamilton's efforts to pay debts owed other nations, although he believed Hamilton was too generous with the British. Madison also believed that Hamilton's plan for assuming national debts was inequitable. Madison knew that many soldiers in the Revolutionary War had been paid with certificates that were initially worthless. With pressing personal obligations, those revolutionary heroes were essentially forced to sell those certificates at much less than their face value, sometimes for as little as ten cents on the dollar. Hamilton proposed to pay those debts—the certificates held by current creditors—at face value. As a result, creditors, part of the mercantile class, were going to earn a windfall, largely at the expense of citizen soldiers and their original lenders, who had sold the certificates for much less than face value. Additionally, Madison, ever the fiscal conservative, feared that full payment of such debts might threaten to bankrupt the national government. At a minimum, in Madison's view, full assumption of the debts would result in a need to increase direct taxation significantly to pay the value of those certificates. This was classic Madison, seeking to find a balance between interests and values. He wanted to pay the debts, but not in full, thereby putting the nation on a sound fiscal footing without creating a windfall for speculators who had purchased those certificates for pennies on the dollar.

Finally, Madison believed that Hamilton's plan impacted the states in an unequal manner. States, like Virginia, had already endeavored to pay its debts in full. If states that had failed to pay their debts were fortunate enough to have their non-paid debts assumed by the national government, states that were fiscally responsible would be placed at a disadvantage. For Madison, Hamilton's plan incentivized speculation and rewarded nonpayment of debts by some states, all at significant cost to taxpayers and debtors. If the national government assumed such broad economic power, it also created an imbalance of power with the states.

It is not surprising, therefore, that Madison played a significant role in structuring a compromise on the debt assumption issue. Jefferson arranged for a dinner at the White House, which included only two guests, Hamilton and Madison. Jefferson used Madison, as he often did, then and during his presidency, to help achieve compromise, whenever a compromise was possible. He also knew that Madison and Hamilton had a strong, prior working relationship. Madison was willing to yield on his argument that states that had worked to honor their debts, like Virginia, were being treated unequally, if Hamilton would agree on another issue of importance to Madison's constituents—placement of the nation's capital in Virginia. Thus, Virginia would benefit for having honored its debts.

Originally, the capital was to be placed on the Susquehanna River in Pennsylvania. Philadelphia and New York City were also vying for placement of the capital. Hamilton was willing to deal. In exchange for Madison agreeing to support aspects of Hamilton's debt assumption proposal, Hamilton agreed to secure the critical vote of Robert Morris, a Representative from Pennsylvania, to support placement of the future capital on the Potomac River.

Some historians have criticized Madison for being more political than principled in his willingness to negotiate on the debt issue to ensure that the capital was placed on the Potomac. Madison understood the need for compromise between conflicting principles: the payment of debts and the balance of power. He was, however, seeking to ensure that his state, which had been fiscally responsible, should not be penalized for acting with integrity. Building a new capital and city in the area helped soften the inequity of Hamilton's plan to Virginia. Overarching all of this was a further principle—representatives should support the interests of their constituents so long as the interests of their constituents do not offend matters of conscience or harm the government in ways that threatens rights. Madison understood that he was acting in the interests of those who had elected him, which may be considered a foundational principle of Republicanism and representative government. Such constituent support is also a matter of liberty—the democratic right of the people to elect representatives to further their interests. Madison understood that principles often come into conflict, requiring compromise and balancing. So long as the government remained representative and in balance, compromise was the best means of securing effective government.

Another issue that evidenced the differences between Jefferson and Madison and their adversary, Hamilton, the leading policy voice of the Washington Administration, dealt with Hamilton's proposed national bank. He was determined to create a national bank and a common currency, in the form of paper money. Relying on a national bank and the printing of paper currency was appealing to Hamilton, because it provided for efficient fiscal operations at the national level. It also helped consolidate national power. As a constitutional matter, Hamilton believed the bank constituted a necessary and proper exercise of enumerated power, as a means of achieving the legitimate needs of the national government. For Hamilton, without the bank and other related fiscal programs, the national government would be unable to operate effectively. He believed the survival of the nation dictated that such policies were necessary and proper, even if they were not clearly included among the enumerated powers granted to Congress. Hamilton believed that securing survival of the national government was a necessary, albeit implied, power.

Jefferson and Madison firmly disagreed. Jefferson, who was then serving as President Washington's Secretary of State, argued that the creation of a national bank was neither necessary nor proper under any enumerated power granted Congress or the executive ranch of the federal government. Jefferson added that the concept of implied powers largely expanded the power of the national government and constituted a threat to liberty. Madison was also a strong advocate of acting within the bounds of clearly enumerated powers under the Constitution. Enumerated powers were essential to the constitutional model of government Madison believed to be mandated by the Constitution. Such a model secured liberty by limiting the power of government, and the national government had no express power to create a bank. Madison naturally sided with Jefferson. But it was Madison who had to lead the effort in Congress, because Jefferson was increasingly powerless in an administration dominated by Hamilton's ideas. Jefferson's increasing powerlessness was attributed, in part, to his unwillingness to bend on principle to find a common ground. He failed to understand that often principles come into conflict and must be balanced. In this instance, to survive, and thereby ensure the perpetuation of liberty, the federal government needed to be placed on firm economic footing. Jefferson, however, was unwilling to read the Constitution with sufficient breadth to make this possible.

Madison had strong views regarding the issue of implied powers as well, but he was more inclined to understand the need to balance principles. He expressed the reasons for his opposition to the National Bank in the House of Representatives. Madison argued, "The doctrine of implication is always a tender one. The danger of it has been felt in other Governments."[15] He further noted that the implied powers argument offered by Hamilton, to justify creation of a National Bank, was a strained and inappropriate construction of the necessary and proper clause. Madison believed that the creation of a National Bank also constituted an unconstitutional monopoly and, thereby, violated his belief that economic liberty was furthered through a free market. In making this argument, he added, "If implications, thus remote and thus multiplied, can be linked together, a chain may be formed that will reach every object of legislation, every object within the whole compass of political economy."[16] As a guardian of individual and economic rights, Madison believed that such an expansive reading of the power of the national government was, by its very nature, a serious limitation on the liberty secured under the Constitution. He also feared that, if unchecked, Hamilton's National Bank proposal placed the new nation and Constitution on a slippery slope, a slope that could lead to ever-increasing national power at the expense of the states and the people.

Madison's arguments were vigorously opposed by Hamilton's allies in Congress. Representative Sedgwick joined other Federalists in claiming that Madison, who had coauthored the *Federalist Papers* with Hamilton, was an "apostate" for abandoning "his formal principles." Madison was unmoved, knowing that he had not abandoned his commitment to the principles of limited government and federalism. He supported the existence of a viable national government. His beliefs in the principles of federalism and limited government, however, were based on checks and balances, including the requirement of acting

15. Ibid., 320.
16. Ibid.

within the ambit of the expressly enumerated powers granted to the national government and any branch therein. He resisted the urge to respond in kind to Sedgwick, by asserting that it was Hamilton and the federalists, Sedgwick included, who were apostates to the Constitution, given their desire to expand greatly on the limited powers expressly enumerated in Article I of the Constitution. They were, in Madison's mind, refusing to follow the principles of limited government set forth in the Constitution. Hamilton and his allies were also engaging in a form of broad constitutional interpretation that could, with time, change the very meaning or intent of the Constitution in dramatic ways. Characteristically, however, Madison declined to get drawn into personal attacks and remained focused on dealing with actual issues.

The Controversy over a National Bank and Other Issues

The nation's needs were great, but differences on fiscal issues including creation of a national bank were real. Madison strongly believed that a decision, like this one, could have a profound impact on the nature of the Republic. Economic interests were, however, aligned against him. Many in Congress believed the bank would increase prosperity and help secure the nation against foreign foes. Madison used all his capacity for argument, his brand of eloquence through persuasion, but he lost by a margin of nearly two-to-one. It was a difficult loss to swallow, but Madison and Jefferson held fast to one remaining hope. They believed President Washington could be persuaded to decline to sign the bill creating the National Bank on constitutional grounds. They knew Washington agreed with the policy behind the bank, but they also believed that he would take his constitutional oath seriously and veto the bank bill because it exceeded the power granted the executive branch under the Constitution.

Washington sought counsel from Jefferson and other members of his Cabinet. He also solicited Madison's counsel on the different occasions. Attorney General Edmund Randolph sided with Madison and Jefferson. Madison, Jefferson, and Randolph strongly reiterated their constitutional arguments, supporting a government constitutionally constrained by enumerated powers. They also argued that the Republic and the liberty fought for in the Revolutionary War was threatened more by a broad reading of the Constitution than by some future ill-defined threat. If and when such a threat arose, it could be dealt with, but not until the threat was actually manifest. For Madison, taking of rights could only be justified by real, not perceived, threats.

Hamilton knew Washington agreed with of the economic policy behind the bank, but he rightfully worried that the president might succumb to the arguments raised by Jefferson, Randolph, and particularly Madison. He responded with his powerful pen. Hamilton quickly wrote a memorandum supporting the policy and the constitutionality of the bank to garner public support for his effort. On the constitutional side, Hamilton asserted, "Nothing is more common than for the laws to express and effect more or less than was intended."[17] The bank passed constitutional muster, for Hamilton, if a "fair" reading of the constitutional text supported the creation of a bank. He focused on the text and not the public meaning or intent behind the language of the Constitution when ratified. Hamilton was a textualist, committed to a broad reading of the power granted under broad terms of the Constitution. The need for a bank, together with other solid economic policies formulated at the national level, was critical to the welfare of the new nation.

Washington kept putting off the signing of the bill providing for a national bank. He was deeply conflicted, and days passed by without any action on his part, adding to the suspense on the part of the Hamiltonian and Madisonian sides of the argument. During this deliberative process, Washington counseled formally and informally with Madison. All sides to the argument had a full and fair hearing with the president. On the final day for signing, Washington finally affixed his signature to the bill. He had heard and deliberated over every argument in a painstaking manner, seeking to do what was right. In the end, he supported the bank and Hamilton. Washington remembered what it was like to suffer with his troops at Valley Forge

---

17. "Hamilton's Opinion as to the Constitutionality of the Bank of the United States: 1791," The Avalon Project (Yale Law School), accessed October 13, 2018, http://avalon.law.yale .edu/18th_century/bank-ah.asp.

due to an ineffective, weak, and inadequately funded national government. As president, he continued to harbor the fear that the existence of the nation was gravely threatened, absent implementation of sound national fiscal policy. For Washington, the existence of the nation and the liberty fought for in the Revolutionary War hung in the balance. Necessary governmental strength at the national level demanded a sound fiscal footing and the bank helped secure that footing. The president believed that threats from abroad and internally were real and could do more to undercut liberty and the Constitution than would failure to implement Hamilton's fiscal strategy. Such policies were necessary and proper, under the Constitution, in President Washington's view.

Hamilton won on the substance, the bank was lawful. He was also the winner in President Washington's Cabinet. His broad reading of governmental power, and executive authority, had prevailed. Jefferson, as Secretary of State, who was unbending and sometimes difficult to deal with on a personal level, found himself increasingly isolated in President Washington's administration. As the power of Jefferson's voice decreased, dependence on Madison, as the opposition leader or counterpoint in Congress, increased. Madison was on the losing side of the deliberations over the bank, but he remained a powerfully eloquent voice in Congress. His integrity and willingness to seek common ground also earned sometimes grudging respect from Hamilton and members of the Federalist Party. Naturally, however, his standing as a counselor to the president suffered. Madison found himself increasingly opposing policies advocated by the president and Hamilton. The need for a strong opposition, which could check increasing national power, particularly within the executive branch, was necessary, as a constitutional and policy matter.

Within weeks after passage of the bill authorizing a National Bank, Madison expressed his fear that the new bank law would lead to excessive. speculation and fraud within the nation. Madison continued to favor a free market, but he feared that speculators necessarily enriched themselves through inside information and manipulation of the political process. For Madison, every act of speculation was performed at the expense of a victim. Speculation meant winners and losers and was, by its nature, divisive. He also shared Jefferson's disdain for what he saw as a rising oligarchy, with all the trappings of elitism. Madison hammered away at Hamiltonian economics, arguing that they promoted speculation which, in turn, gave rise to "monarchy and aristocracy." He argued that Hamilton's economic policies were not founded on sound constitutional principles. Rather, Hamiltonian economics expanded the power of the national government well beyond the rightful powers enumerated in the Constitution.

The second session of the First Congress drew quietly to a close on March 3, 1791. Much had been accomplished. A strong national foundation was laid—the Constitution had proven to be effective and a Bill of Rights was adopted, which helped secure the rights of the people against the tyranny of the majority. The adoption and ratification of the Bill of Rights also allayed concerns on the part of many. How the Constitution should be interpreted, in turn, foreshadowed future battles regarding how best to construe the Constitution—broadly, to further desired policies (the Hamiltonian broad textualist interpretation), or in a fashion limited by public meaning, the intent of the framers and those who ratified the Constitution (the Madisonian originalist interpretation). Hamilton helped place the nation on a sound fiscal footing, and Madison played a significant role in demanding that the Constitution be adhered to.

Sadly, however, unity at the national level was declining precipitously. Disputes over economic and international policy were beginning to divide the nation in significant ways. Two clearly delineated parties were developing. Strident partisanship was displacing unity and civility, which disappointed President Washington and Madison. Nevertheless, the articulation of partisan principles was necessary to ensure that the government was effective and remained within its constitutionally delineated bounds. Partisanship—the articulation of conflicting principles and values—is, in many ways, necessary to good government under the Constitution, but it is always difficult to maintain civility, another necessity of good government, in such an environment.

Early in 1791, during a time of relative peace, only weeks after the Bill of Rights was officially ratified and sent to the states, Madison penned a series of significant essays. Two of the essays, one regarding "Money," in which he argued for caution in fiscal matters, and the other, "Property," in which he argued that rights are the most treasured form of property, are significant statements of his understanding. The essays appeared in the *National Gazette*, which was edited and published by Madison's old roommate at the College of New Jersey, Philip Freneau. Madison and Jefferson had encouraged Freneau to start what would today be referred to as an opposition press, a vehicle for disseminating the views of the fast-developing Democratic-Republican Party. The *National Gazette* was, from its inception, highly partisan. Battle lines were being established, with each party having its own newspapers to fuel their subscribers with partisan information and arguments. The Federalists, particularly Hamilton, often turned to the *Gazette of the United States*, which was edited by John Fenno, as a vehicle for sharing Federalist positions. Madison was a strong believer in freedom of the press and believed that dissemination of partisan views could inform the public by challenging the government in power and by exposing the public to the opinions of strong proponents of differing views, which were ever-vying to win public support for their positions. He also believed that a large republic, together with a free press, which could widely disseminate differing views, was preferable to a smaller government which could be commandeered by a single powerful group.

Madison's belief that a large republic and a free press could secure greater liberty than a small one, given the diversity of interests and sects at the national level, effectively turned the conventional wisdom of that age on its head. Prior to ratification of the Constitution, many Americans believed that liberty could best be secured in a small government. This, however, was an area in which Madison had a great impact—he persuaded many Americans, including his fellow Virginian Edmund Randolph, that a larger national government could, if properly limited by strict enforcement of enumerated powers, do much to protect liberty, as a structural matter. Ironically, Hamilton and Madison had both supported increased prominence for the national government, but they did it for different reasons. Madison did so to ensure liberty, and Hamilton did so to provide power and vitality to the national government, including the power to act in fiscal matters. At the time of the framing and ratification of the Constitution, Madison and Hamilton joined forces as the leading intellectual advocates for the Constitution, which provided for a stronger national government. Many historians wonder why Madison and Hamilton parted ways in the First Congress, but the reason is clear. For Madison, a stronger and more unified, but carefully limited, national government was necessary to ensure liberty. Hamilton, on the other hand, was more concerned with power, particularly economic and military power—power to be used to place the new nation on sound fiscal footing and to protect against international threats.

The differences between Madison and Hamilton were destined to be exacerbated, as new issues were about to arise in the Second Congress. One of the reasons Madison could spend so much time providing essays to the *National Gazette* was because he was so popular within his district that he ran unopposed in seeking a second term in the House. He was pleased to avoid the physical and emotional rigors of campaigning. He delighted in the prospect of returning home to Montpelier and using his time writing and preparing for the Second Congress, laying the foundation for his theoretical support of the Democratic-Republican Party in a series of essays. Even though differences were developing, and Madison was fast becoming the leader of the opposition party, he remained on cordial terms with President Washington.

Washington's Fourth State of the Union Address

Madison was invited, once again, to work with Alexander Hamilton in drafting the president's Fourth State of the Union address. The address largely focused on three issues. The first was "Indian hostilities which have for some time past distressed our Northwestern frontier,"[18] an issue that greatly concerned Madison and the growing

---

18. "Fourth Annual Message of George Washington," November 6, 1792, The Avalon Project (Yale Law School), accessed October 13, 2018, http://avalon.law.yale.edu/18th_century /washs04.asp.

western population. The second dealt with the state of the judiciary. In the first Congress, Hamilton, representing the executive branch, and Madison, from the perspective of the legislative branch, disagreed over the way the Constitution should be interpreted. Madison and Hamilton both believed that the judicial branch of government was uniquely suited to interpret the Constitution to secure rights and provide for limited government. The third issue involved national finances. Using language that appears to have been supplied by Hamilton, Washington addressed fiscal matters when he declared, "I entertain a strong hope that the state of national finances is now sufficiently matured to enable you [Congress] to enter upon a systematic and effectual arrangement for the regular redemption and discharge of the public debt, according to the right which has been reserved to the Government. No measure can be more desirable, whether viewed with an eye to its intrinsic importance or to the general sentiment and wish of the nation."[19]

In words that are likely to have been suggested by Madison, the president also took time to express his gratitude for all that had been accomplished in the First Congress. He was particularly grateful for efforts to secure the rule of law through the Constitution and Bill of Rights. Washington stated, "The results of your common deliberations hitherto will, I trust, be productive of solid and durable advantages to our constituents [by] strengthen[ing] and confirm[ing] their attachment to that Constitution of Government upon which, under Divine Providence, materially depend their union, their safety, and their happiness."[20] The president then concluded his remarks with words that sadly, yet prophetically, warned against increasing partisanship and lack of civility in public affairs. Washington, the "father" of the new nation, pleaded, "Still further to promote and secure these inestimable ends there is nothing which can have a more powerful tendency than the careful cultivation of harmony, combined with a due regard to stability, in the public councils."[21] Madison agreed, but he harbored declining hope that unity and civility would prevail. For his part,

---

19. Ibid.
20. Ibid.
21. Ibid.

Washington was tiring of the growing bickering within the nation and his cabinet and desired to return permanently to Mount Vernon.

With the growing rift between Jefferson and Hamilton in Washington's administration, the president's plea for civility and harmony in public councils proved to be wishful thinking. The nation was becoming divided in a fiercely partisan way. That rift found its way into Congress and public affairs generally. Despite generally trying to maintain civility, as he had in his campaign against James Monroe, Madison felt an increasing need to state vigorously positions supporting Jefferson and the policy choices he supported. Like Jefferson, Madison was fearful that agrarian, egalitarian, and limited government views of government were being displaced with Hamiltonian views favoring a strong national government, mercantile interests, and alliances with the British.

Discontent and the Lack of Civility

Hamilton was correct in his observation that Madison seemed unhappy in his role as a party leader. Madison was naturally discontented in his new role as leader or primary voice of the Democratic-Republicans. That discontent had much to do with Madison's aversion to the acrimony and vindictiveness that often occurred during debates over highly charged partisan differences. Madison did not like the rough and tumble of partisan politicking. He favored thoughtful discussions and deliberation in preference to highly partisan bickering and debates, bickering that often manifested itself in brutal name-calling and personal attacks. He knew from experience that civil discourse, accompanied by counseling together, often led to compromise and optimal results. Some partisans on both sides, however, could not resist the urge to engage in personal attacks and rigid defenses of their prospective partisan differences.

Madison was discontent, even vexed, a word he often used to describe his feelings when facing deeply troublesome issues, by comments from his detractors who confused his leadership of the opposition to Federalist measures with a desire for personal power and a willingness to consistently promote the interests of Virginia, even when those interest were clearly contrary to needs at the national level. Fisher Ames was a moving speaker who mixed personal attacks with legitimate differences over substance. He declared, "Virginia moves in a solid column, and the discipline of the party is as severe as the Prussian. Deserters are not spared."[22] He added, "Madison is become a desperate party leader."[23] Madison found it increasingly difficult to remain focused on substance, as the ferocity of personal attacks on all sides reached a crescendo.

Differences simmered as financial speculation reached what Madison considered to be a frenzy. Hamilton further fueled the fire with his Report on Manufacturing, which proposed more close interaction between government and business. It provided for direct government aid, in the form of what Hamilton referred to as "bounties," paid out of higher tariffs, to certain businesses. One of the early recipients of such government aid was the fishing industry. Cod fishermen were awarded bounties or government payments to strengthen the industry and provide for growth in the economy. Madison was appalled by the developing tie between government and business. He went so far as to declare that the national government was engaging in such an expansive reading of the Constitution, to further the end of growing the economy, that threatened to interpret the Constitution so broadly that it would become wholly ineffectual in limiting the power of the national government.

Washington shared Madison's distaste for incivility. President Washington was so dismayed, and tired of serving, that he seriously considered submitting his resignation in conjunction with the election of 1792. The victims of such incivility are often the leaders America needs most, men and women with a devotion like that of Washington and Madison. Incivility also leads to bad policy, because the various sides in any significant policy dispute represent differing but meritorious values, which are conflicting. Civil expression of partisan positions, therefore, creates a respectful dialogue that often leads to meaningful compromise, in the form of a balancing of values of merit. Facilitating, even crafting, such compromises were part of Madison's genius. During

---

22. See Ralph Ketcham, *James Madison* (Charlottesville: University of Virginia Press 1990), 332.
23. Ibid.

the growing partisanship during his presidency, Washington went so far as to ask Madison to write a letter describing why he was unwilling to continue serving as president. Despite often disagreeing with the president as to matters of policy, Madison argued that Washington should stay the course, because the nation desperately needed his service. Madison understood that Washington provided a critical stabilizing influence, and a deliberative approach to governance that was necessary in maintaining a viable government under the Constitution, especially in an increasingly divisive world. Washington responded that he questioned his own competence to manage the government, reiterating his desire to return to the peace of Mount Vernon where he would be free from the incessant partisan bickering. The president was physically and emotionally tired. Madison and others, however, ultimately persuaded Washington that his continuing leadership was critical to the future of the fledgling nation, which he and so many dear to him had fought for with such devotion. Washington steeled himself to finish his term. His race, as , had turned into a marathon, the final few miles or years of which he knew would be brutal.

At the close of that marathon, the end of his difficult second term in office, Washington openly shared his sentiments. In his "Farewell Address," Washington referenced the resignation letter he had been persuaded not to make public and the sacrifice that attended his service when he declared, "The acceptance of, and continuance hitherto in, the office to which your suffrages have twice called me have been a uniform sacrifice of inclination to the opinion of duty and to a deference for what appeared to be your desire. I constantly hoped that it would have been much earlier in my power, consistently with motives which I was not at liberty to disregard, to return to that retirement from which I had been reluctantly drawn." He added, "The strength of my inclination to do this, previous to the last election, had even led to the preparation of an address to declare it to you; but mature reflection on then perplexed and critical posture of our affairs with foreign nations, and the unanimous advice of persons entitled to my confidence, impelled me to abandon the idea."[24]

---

24. "Washington's Farewell Address 1796," The Avalon Project (Yale Law School), accessed October 13, 2018, http://avalon.law.yale.edu/18th_century/washing.asp.

In that oft-cited Farewell Address, Washington further referenced growing partisanship in words that also reflected Madison's sentiments. Washington did so in the following heartfelt words:

> Let it always be remembered to your praise, and as an instructive example in our annals, that under circumstances in which the passions, agitated in every direction, were liable to mislead, amidst appearances sometimes dubious, vicissitudes of fortune often discouraging, in situations in which not unfrequently want of success has countenanced the spirit of criticism, the constancy of your support was the essential prop of the efforts, and a guarantee of the plans by which they were effected. Profoundly penetrated with this idea, I shall carry it with me to my grave, as a strong incitement to unceasing vows that heaven may continue to you the choicest tokens of its beneficence; that your union and brotherly affection may be perpetual; that the free Constitution, which is the work of your hands, may be sacredly maintained; that its administration in every department may be stamped with wisdom and virtue; that, in fine, the happiness of the people of these States, under the auspices of liberty, may be made complete by so careful a preservation and so prudent a use of this blessing as will acquire to them the glory of recommending it to the applause, the affection, and adoption of every nation which is yet a stranger to it.[25]

Washington's hope that the spirit of liberty would spread throughout the world was tempered by increasing partisan criticism at home. Some of that criticism was directed personally at him, as the policies of his Administration enjoyed varying degrees of success. Madison refrained from attacking his respected friend in public. Even he, however, was unable to bridle his growing uneasiness with the president's willingness to expand executive power beyond its rightful constitutional limits. Madison feared the expansion of executive power, understanding that others would follow Washington and might use such increased executive power to limit the liberty of the people. Washington, in Madison's view, was setting a precedent for a perilous expansive reading of implied powers under the Constitution. Aggrandizement of power in the executive, or any other branch of government, was a threat to liberty. Ever vigilant regarding matters implicating liberty, Madison had openly

---

25. Ibid.

expressed his opposition to aspects of the creation of a National Bank and the assumption of debts in a manner designed to benefit creditors and mercantile interests through the exercise of executive power. To Madison, it was clear that broad use of the necessary and proper clause to create implied rather than express powers in constitutional governance was inconsistent with the public understanding of enumerated powers, even if the desired end of government action was a good one. Madison became even more concerned as the president began to use the threat of war as a means of expanding executive power to deal with actual or perceived international crises. Madison saw such aggressive executive action in foreign affairs as an expansion of the power of the presidency and a diminution of the power of Congress, particularly in declaring and funding war. Later, during his own presidency, Madison would come to better understand why Washington had acted as he had.

Madison was principled in his interpretation of the Constitution, an interpretation that he believed to be fully consistent with the public meaning of those who ratified the Constitution. He asserted that the foremost concern of the people was to maintain liberty and implement a Constitution that secured such liberty through checks and balances (balanced power among the branches of government), enumerated powers (express limitations on the lawmaking powers of the national government), and the Bill of Rights (securing natural and other rights recognized by those who ratified the amendments). He knew that power can corrupt, even among the best of men and women, when it remains unchecked. Madison acknowledged that one's conscience provides a check in some individuals, which helps to ensure that they do not use their power to limit the liberty of others; but conscience alone was insufficient, because men "are not angels" and access to unbridled power is hard for even the most conscientious to resist.

In a related sense, he also personally opposed elitism, which he and other Democratic-Republicans often referred to as monarchism. He also favored an independent judiciary as a further check regarding constitutional rights and governance. Justices and judges, as a profession, were taught to abide by the law and were shielded from the pressures of having to seek reelection. As a group, lawyers and judges were also trained in the importance of abiding by the law, and in the importance of rights, even when such allegiance ran counter to their own personal policy choices. Judges were also free from the pressures of satisfying the present needs or demands of constituents. Lawyers and particularly judges, therefore, would take seriously their oath to abide by the express terms of the Constitution.

Madison also believed that the oath to abide by the Constitution taken by members of Congress and the executive branch should provide a check on individuals working in those branches of government. Madison, however, did not believe the oath to abide by a Constitution would do much good in the hands of a despotic leader or of leaders who place their own personal interests or the interests of their constituents above the Constitution and the rights of individuals, who might be harmed by some executive or legislative act. The oath, while a helpful reminder, might not be of much value as a limitation on tyrannical action even in the hands of a conscientious leader seeking to do good. Even Washington, a man of conscience, refused to yield to what Madison saw as the express limits on executive power, when the president signed laws that were beyond the constitutionally limited powers to achieve a common good, fiscal responsibility. Senator J. William Fulbright, who spent much of his time as Chairman of the Senate Foreign Relations Committee, during the twentieth century, captured these sentiments well when he reflected, "When we violate the law ourselves, whatever the short-term advantage may be gained, we are obviously encouraging others to violate the law; we thus encourage disorder and instability and thereby do incalculable damage to our own long-term interests."[26]

Madison was increasingly fearful and distressed by the way the executive branch was using a variety of what he considered to be constitutionally inappropriate means to augment its power to make and unilaterally change treaties. Madison's concerns with Hamilton's expanded use of federal powers in creating a bank and exercising expanded executive power in economic matters were amplified by his alarm at efforts to increase the power of the executive in foreign affairs,

---

26. See Jim Lobe, "The Arrogance of Power," September 1, 2002, accessed October 13, 2018, https://fpif.org/the_arrogance_of_power/.

as well, and to do so without any check from Congress. Madison firmly believed that the Constitution dictated that the branches counsel together in such matters.

The Rift Expands to International Relations

In the realm of international relations, Madison believed that the French Revolution evidenced a laudatory, if sometimes excessive, rise in republicanism and the embrace of the principles of liberty by the French people. He was also a proponent of a balance of power between France and Britain as a means of protecting the safety of the United States. The Washington administration, on the other hand, feared the French Revolution, believing it to be volatile and destabilizing. The beheading of Louis XIV early in 1793 appalled Washington and supported his foreboding regarding relations with France. These differences as to relations with France had the effect of increasing Hamilton's role within the Cabinet.

The Washington Administration responded to unrest in France and increased tension between Britain and France by declaring its version of a policy of "neutrality." Madison believed that Washington's proposed "neutrality" favored Britain, because trade with Britain far exceeded trade with France, and Britain often used its trading power and dominance of the seas to influence policy in the United States. He was deeply apprehensive that the Administration's conception of neutrality was creating an imbalance in power between two powerful nations—Britain and France—both of which must be kept at bay. More significantly, from a constitutional point of view, Madison believed that the Administration, under the sway of Hamilton's able direction, was using international instability as a means of increasing the power of the executive branch at the expense of Congress. A war of words between Hamilton and Madison ensued.

Hamilton, writing as *Pacificus*, articulated the pro-neutrality view. Madison, responding as *Helvidius*, argued for a balance of power, internationally and constitutionally between the executive and legislative branches of government and world powers. Madison's use of the pseudonym *Helvidius* is interesting. Helvidius Priscus was a stoic

philosopher, who fearlessly advocated the cause of republicanism in
Rome, despite opposition from a series of Roman rulers. Hamilton
wrote, "The general doctrine of our Constitution is that the Executive
Power of the Nation is vested in the President; subject only to the
exceptions and *qu[a]lifications which* are expressed in the instrument."[27]
He continued, "It is the province and duty of the Executive to preserve to the Nation the blessings of peace. The Legislature alone can
interrupt those blessings, by placing the Nation in a state of War."[28]
Hamilton clearly believed the Administration had the power to implement a policy of neutrality, even though it violated the letter and spirit
of an existing treaty supporting France.

Madison responded, "The power of treaties is vested jointly in the
President and in the Senate, which is a branch of the legislature."[29]
He added, "From this arrangement merely, there can be no inference
that would necessarily exclude the power from the executive class:
since the senate is joined with the President in another power, that
of appointing to offices, which as far as relate to executive offices at
least, is considered as of an executive nature. Yet on the other hand,
there are sufficient indications that the power of treaties is regarded
by the constitution as materially different from mere executive power,
and as having more affinity to the legislative than to the executive
character."[30] According to Madison's understanding, the Constitution
mandated that the treaty power was to be shared with the Senate. Even
more significantly, he wrote, "In no part of the Constitution is more
wisdom to be found than in the clause which confides the question of
war or peace to the legislature, and not to the executive department."[31]
To Madison, it was clear that the increasing concentration of power
in the executive branch of government, in the international relations or foreign affairs area, created a constitutionally impermissible
imbalance of power between the executive and legislative branches

---

27. Hamilton, "Pacificus No. 1, [29 June 1793]," Founders Online (National Archives), accessed
October 13, 2018, https://founders.archives.gov/documents/Hamilton/01-15-02-0038.
28. Ibid.
29. Madison, "Helvidius, No. 1, [24 August] 1793," Founders Online (National Archives),
accessed October 13, 2018, https://founders.archives.gov/documents/Madison/01-15-02-0056.
30. Ibid.
31. Ibid.

of government. It also reflected British "royal prerogatives" and not American values. Madison declared, "The power of making treaties and the power of declaring war, are royal prerogatives in the British government, and are accordingly treated as Executive prerogatives by British commentators."[32] Once again, Madison believed that Hamilton was leading the Washington administration along a precarious path that favored the British model of government, not the Constitution of the United States. As a constitutional matter, therefore, Madison asserted that the treaty and war-making powers are shared, and therefore anticipate collaboration and counsel between the branches. To ignore that check on executive power was a threat to liberty and the structure of government intended under the Constitution.

It must be acknowledged that Washington acted with foresight when he expressed concerns regarding the excesses in the French Revolution. The French were volatile and hardly a paragon of virtue or consistency when it came to the cause of liberty. Nevertheless, Madison also exercised foresight. His fear that the executive branch's increased power to dictate the nation's foreign policy, often with little consultation or cooperation with Congress, would carry precedential weight and threatened to lay the foundation for an imperial presidency. Madison warned that increased and unchecked executive power, at the expense of its counterpart, Congress, would yet lead to executive excesses, including creation and control of a standing army by the executive branch. Madison was right. Today, the executive branch is the most powerful branch in international relations, effectively dictating and executing on foreign policy, leaving Congress with little more than the power to declare war, an ominous act that is seldom exercised, and the power to refuse to fund executive deployment of forces and resources, which is so fraught with risk that it is rarely used. Refusing to fund deployments already taken under executive power might jeopardize troops in the field or weaken trust with other nations, making it problematic for Congress to exercise this power. For Madison, the Constitution provided for a means of counsel and compromise among the branches. Such deliberation, in turn, is more likely to result in wise

---

32. Ibid.

policy and provides a necessary check and balance by Congress on excessive use of the power of the presidency.

In a letter to Jefferson, Madison made it clear that he feared the executive branch had a propensity to use, and occasionally foment, foreign policy threats as a means of increasing the imbalance of power between the executive and legislative branches of government. He wrote, "You will understand the game behind the curtain too well not to perceive the old trick of turning every contingency into a resource for accumulating force in the government."[33] Elsewhere, Madison put it this way, "In war honors and emoluments of office are to be multiplied; and it is the executive patronage under which they are to be enjoyed. It is in war, finally, that laurels are to be gathered, and it is the executive brow they are to encircle."[34]Interestingly, during his service as president, Madison found it necessary to use some of the very powers he expressed such grave concern over during the Washington administration.

Despite the force of Madison's arguments, with each new revelation regarding rising terror and excesses in France, following the bloody French Revolution, the American public grew more supportive of President Washington. The public believed that, once again, Washington was leading with vision and wisdom. After all, he had predicted the darkness that would attend the French Revolution. The increasingly outrageous behavior of the French minister or ambassador to the United States, Edmond-Charles Genet, also alienated the American people, bringing them back to the fold that supported the Administration's vision of a British-leaning form of "neutrality." Public support for the Administration's pro-British policies grew, with little regard to constitutional arguments made by Madison.

Genet supported bringing British ships, which had been captured and pillaged by the French, into American ports. He also commissioned Americans in the west to fight against Spain, raising tensions on yet another unwelcome front. Each new act of incompetence on

---

33. Letter from James Madison to Thomas Jefferson, 14 March 1794, Founders Online (National Archives) , accessed October 13, 2018, https://founders.archives.gov/documents /Madison/01-15-02-0179.

34. Madison, "Helvidius No. 4, [14 September] 1793," Founders Online (National Archives), accessed October 13, 2018, https://founders.archives.gov/documents/Madison/01-15-02-0070.

the part of the French Minister, Genet, threatened to bring the United States into an unwelcome war against European nations. Washington was livid. Despite maintaining support of the French Revolution on a theoretical level, Jefferson and Madison eventually had to concur in Washington's assessment of Genet. Jefferson wrote Madison that Genet was "hotheaded" and "disrespectful." Madison went even further, declaring Genet to be a "madman." As Secretary of State, Jefferson joined other members of the Cabinet in unanimously calling for the recall of Minister Genet. Public support of the Hamilton and Washington "neutrality" position was nearly unanimous in the northeast, where trade with Britain was the basis for a strong economy. Even southerners were increasingly drawn to support the vision of "neutrality" embraced by Washington and Hamilton by troublesome acts on the part of the French government. Once again, the Hamiltonian view of a strong national government, led by a powerful executive branch, won the day, and partisan differences deepened.

Yellow Fever

All these concerns regarding international affairs were soon eclipsed as matters of public concern by the specter of "yellow fever" in the nation's capital, Philadelphia. The fever was carried by mosquitoes, which thrived in Philadelphia during the late summer and early fall. In 1793, heat, humidity, and heavy rains contributed to the accumulation of pools of water, which provided a breeding ground for the disease-carrying mosquitoes. Grave epidemics or plagues are often aptly referred to as black, because they bring darkness in their wake. "Yellow fever" is rightfully named, in turn, because its victims suffer jaundice, which brings a yellowish hue to their skin. Philadelphia became increasingly enveloped in an epidemic that was deadly, sparing few households. Children were particularly susceptible to the disease, but no generation was spared.

By September 9, the date of a scheduled Cabinet meeting, the fever was spreading quickly throughout Philadelphia. Hamilton was unable to attend the meeting, having reported that he and his wife, Eliza, were stricken by the fever. Hamilton and Eliza took some solace in the fact that their children were in New York and were spared the risk and ravages of a dreaded disease. On the 9th, Washington wrote his Secretary of War, Henry Knox, a note that referenced the outbreak: "I think it would not be prudent either for you or the Clerks in your Office, or the Office itself to be too much exposed to the malignant fever, which by well authenticated report, is spreading through the City; The means to avoid it your own judgment under existing circumstances must dictate."[35] Washington left the next day to attend to responsibilities related to the location of the future capital on the Potomac and to needs at Mount Vernon. Hamilton and his wife survived, but many did not.

The fever came on quickly with a chill. Chills that wracked the body were followed by fits of nausea, muscle pain, and fatigue. Toward the end, victims were wracked with vomiting episodes, in which they would heave up material with a blackened hue. As symptoms intensified, victims became exceedingly lethargic. Their will to live also weakened, as death drew closer and claimed many victims. Many parents watched as their children suffered death in their arms, only to shortly thereafter feel themselves in the death grip of yellow fever. Generally, within a week, the victim was dead. Some, like Alexander and Eliza Hamilton survived; but many did not. Dolley Madison, James's future wife, for example, suffered greatly losing her first husband, John Todd Jr., and an infant son on the same day to the dreaded disease. Some living in the city, including Jefferson, were spared entirely from the fever, but their hearts were filled with sorrow at the horror of death that surrounded them. By the time the weather cooled, and the deadly mosquitoes died, one out of every ten residents of Philadelphia had fallen victim to the disease. Congress had completed its work prior to the outbreak, so Madison was home at Montpelier. He felt the pain of the outbreak, however. He lost many loved ones, including his younger brother, Ambrose, to yellow fever. Madison's wife-to-be, Dolley Payne Todd, suffered profound loss from the epidemic, losing a newborn son and a husband.

---

35. See, "George Washington and Yellow Fever," Yellow Fever Casebook, accessed October 13, 2018, http://fevercasebook.blogspot.com/2012/01/george-washington-and-yellow-fever.html.

The impact of the yellow fever epidemic had a sobering effect, quieting the incessant bickering among partisans in Philadelphia for a time. But, with the cold weather, the end of the epidemic, the resignation of Thomas Jefferson as Secretary of State, and the gathering of the Third Congress, significant new disputes arose. Madison arrived back in Philadelphia in November 1793, at a time when the threat of yellow fever was past. He returned in time to hear Washington's fifth annual state of the union address, which was given on December 3. In that address, Washington renewed his strong support for his neutrality proclamation. He also invoked the need for readiness should the United States be drawn into war. Standing erect, and reminding all present of his service in war, Washington stressed, "If we desire to secure peace, one of the most powerful instruments of our rising prosperity, it must be known that we are at all times ready for war."[36] In assuming his role as the leader of Congress, which mandated that he respond to the president, Madison had little desire to engage in a vigorous attack over principle with the president. There would be time for that, when actual executive actions and policies were at issue. For the present, Madison simply chose to reiterate the respect of all for President Washington, as a wise, virtuous, and deliberate man. Madison also joined in some of the president's sentiments regarding Genet, the French minister.

Genet was recalled but concerns regarding France continued. A radical new government, the Jacobins, had come to power in France. The Jacobins were ruthless, having initiated a reign of terror orchestrated to take the lives of their opponents. The new government demanded that Genet return to France, where he certainly would be executed. Genet stayed in the United States, however, simply moving northward, to New York. Despite his excesses, Genet was dashing and soon married Governor George Clinton's daughter, Cornelia. Ironically, in 1808, Genet published an article, "Madison as a 'French Citizen,'" to promote his father-in-law's campaign for the Presidency against Madison. In the process of attacking Madison, Genet also took aim at Jefferson's embrace of the agrarian life, arguing that Madison

---

36. Draft for George Washington's Fifth Annual Address to Congress, Founders Online (National Archives), accessed October 13, 2018, https://founders.archives.gov/documents /Hamilton/01-15-02-0358.

and Jefferson intended to turn New Englanders, who relied heavily on mercantile interests, into farmers. Ironically, Genet himself lived the life of a Gentleman Farmer on a beautiful farm, aptly named Prospect Hill, overlooking the Hudson River.

As his final act as Secretary of State, Jefferson delivered a "Report on the Privileges and Restrictions on the Commerce of the United States in Foreign Countries." That report went into detail regarding trade and was an attack on so-called neutrality with Britain. Jefferson saved his strongest language for the preferred treatment Britain was receiving under existing trade policy. He noted, "Great Britain received our pot and pearl ashes free, whilst those of other nations pay a duty of two shillings and three pence the quintal."[37] Jefferson went on to discuss a series of areas in which Britain was receiving preferential treatment, including tobacco, tar, fish, etc. He saved his strongest criticism for trade limitations imposed by the British, declaring, "Our ships, though purchased and navigated by their own subjects, are not permitted to be used, even in their trade with us."[38] Jefferson emphasized further that, "While the vessels of other nations are secured by standing laws, which cannot be altered but by the concurrent will of the three branches of the British legislature, in carrying thither any produce or manufacture of the country to which they belong, which may be lawfully carried in any vessels, ours, with the same prohibition of what is foreign, are further prohibited by [British law] from carrying thither all and any of our own domestic productions and manufactures."[39] He called for equivalent prohibitions on British goods, until they relented and agreed to fair trade. In language clearly aimed at British trade prohibitions, Jefferson fumed, "Should any nation, contrary to our wishes, suppose it may better find its advantage by continuing the system of prohibitions, duties and regulations, it behooves us to protect our citizens, their commerce and navigation, by counter prohibitions, duties and regulations, also. Free commerce and navigation are not to

---

37. Jefferson, "Report on the Privileges and Restrictions on the Commerce of the United States in Foreign Commerce," December 16, 1793, accessed October 13, 2018, http://avalon.law.yale.edu/18th_century/jeffrep2.asp.
38. Ibid.
39. Ibid.

be given in exchange for restrictions and vexations; nor are they likely to produce a relaxation of them."[40]

Jefferson's final words, as Secretary of State, resonated with Madison, who believed true neutrality demanded free trade and equality of treatment of all parties. Jefferson and Madison believed that liberty was being undercut, under the guise of so-called neutrality, which effectively permitted the British to limit free trade. With Jefferson's resignation, Washington had to find a new Secretary of State. Somewhat surprisingly, but as a vote of confidence, the president offered the position to Madison. Madison wisely declined, realizing that his differences with the Administration and particularly Hamilton were too great.

Jefferson departed for Monticello, leaving Madison to serve as the leader of the developing Democratic-Republican Party in Congress and within the broader government. Only days after Jefferson's delivery of his report regarding commerce, Madison introduced seven resolves designed to create fair and balanced trade in Congress. Those resolves called for the imposition of reciprocal duties on goods traded by nations that placed prohibitions on goods traded by the United States. Essentially, he was calling for retaliation against British imposition of prohibitions on trade from merchants in the United States. Support for Madison's effort to balance trade with Britain was strengthened by the issuance of "Orders in Council," by the British government. Those Orders authorized the British Navy to seize ships of neutral nations, including the United States, seeking to trade with France. The Orders were, in fact, followed by seizure of vessels from the United States seeking to deliver goods to France.

Despite the soundness of his arguments calling for fair and balanced trade, and his opposition to Britain's execution on the "Orders of Council," Madison was faced with an uphill battle in Congress. Much of American trade was with Britain, and imposition of limitations would surely result in further prohibitions of trade with Britain. Madison responded to such concerns on the floor of the House. He argued that Britain would capitulate if it felt the pain of reciprocal prohibitions. One can almost hear the cadence behind Madison's words as he sought to assure his colleagues: "[Britain's] merchants would feel

---

40. Ibid.

[the weight of reciprocal prohibitions]. Her navigation would feel it. Her manufacturers would feel it. Her West Indies would be ruined by it. Her revenue would deeply feel it. And her government would feel it through every nerve of its operations."[41]

Those in attendance were captivated by Madison's remarks, which stretched on for over two hours. Madison almost persuaded those present that imposition of reciprocal prohibitions on Britain would work, even though he acknowledged that some short-term sacrifice would be required by all Americans. President Washington, however, who knew much of sacrifice, opposed such prohibitions. Washington's opposition, together with concerns by merchants regarding short-term losses in income and rising alarm regarding atrocities being committed in France under the Jacobin "Reign of Terror," doomed Madison's efforts to establish free and equal trade with all nations. Madison's efforts were also overshadowed by incessant Federalist efforts to stir up the American people with the possible threat of war. President Washington chose a less risky and moderate course by appointing a delegation, led by John Jay, to negotiate a treaty with Great Britain that would cover trade and related issues.

Madison worried that any such treaty with Britain would merely ratify existing trade inequities with Britain. He also feared that any such treaty might alarm the French, who feared British influence over its former colonies. To allay such concerns, Washington decided to send a delegation to France as well to assure the government that relationships with France would not suffer under any agreement with France. Madison declined Washington's invitation to lead the delegation to France. He believed the delegation was doomed from its inception and he was reluctant to travel. Indeed, Madison longed to return to Montpelier.

Even the idlest visitor to Philadelphia could see that the national government had grown in power since the ratification of the Constitution. There was a vibrancy and a growing tension that best described the growth of the national government in a mere six years, a legacy to

---

41. Madison, "Commercial Discrimination," [14 January] 1794, Founders Online (National Archives), accessed October 13, 2018, https://founders.archives.gov/documents /Madison/01-15-02-0120.

the new nation left by Hamilton and Washington. Perhaps, most surprising to Madison, however, was the growing power of the executive branch. He and other delegates to the Constitutional Convention had feared excesses in legislative power more than growth in the executive branch during the convention. After only a few years, however, it was now evident to Madison that growth in the executive branch posed the greater threat to the balance of power in government and liberty.

Whisky Rebellion

The growth in the national government and the executive branch came with costs. To help fund the growing expenses of government, Hamilton and others devised an excise tax that covered many products, including whisky. Understandably, this tax hit a nerve with some of the independent, rough-and-tumble, whisky-drinking citizens in the west. Opposition to the tax was particularly strong in the western part of Pennsylvania. A small group of incensed opponents vented by taking the law into their own hands. They set the house of a tax collector on fire and took perverse pleasure in watching it burn to the ground. The anti-tax furor was reaching a fevered pitch, as approximately six thousand angry men gathered near Pittsburg to protest the tax. The protest was nonviolent, but President Washington was becoming increasingly alarmed.

The potential for violence had to be quelled. Washington gathered an impressive militia of ten thousand men to march west and deal with what became known as the Whisky Rebellion. The president was determined to serve as a true commander-in-chief and personally led the armies into a possible battle to secure peace and order in the nation. Washington certainly did not want such outbreaks to occur, but he did delight in riding at the head of an army. The fact that he was willing to lead the army, with a clear show of power, contributed to an utter lack of resistance on the part of the anti-tax rebels. The Whisky Rebellion was easily quelled, without the firing of a single rifle, but the underlying issues remained unresolved.

Madison believed the burning of the tax collector's house was a lawless act that warranted punishment. He viewed leaders of mobs, engaged in violence, as little more than petty despots. Just as he had worried about the implications of Shays' Rebellion, he was concerned by the gathering of the anti-tax forces in protesting their government through violent means. Madison, nevertheless, strongly supported the right of tax protesters to gather and petition the government, but not in a violent manner. Not surprisingly, Madison was concerned by the government's response and the president's role in that response. The gathering of a militia, ten thousand strong, by the national government, led by the president, worried Madison. He believed the government's response was excessive, and feared that, had there been resistance, the government would use the threat of internal rebellion as an excuse to create and fund a standing army. Hamilton's enthusiasm for the effort to deal with the rebels by a strong show of national force was also troubling. Madison's fears may have been overstated, but he was genuinely apprehensive that Hamilton was using the incident to stoke the fire of support for strengthening the power of the national government and the executive branch within that government. Madison's fear that the national government, and particularly the executive branch, would use so-called crises to augment their power to engage in battles in the future. Once the executive branch had such power, it would not willingly relinquish it. The formation of a national standing army would be a serious step in that direction, giving the executive branch the opportunity to deploy forces without Congressional approval. The use of purported crises to deploy troops or exercise power would surely result in an imbalance of power among the branches of government, making it difficult to recalibrate the appropriate balance.

At generally the same time that the Whisky Rebellion rose with a clamor and fell with a whimper, grassroots groups were forming to support the Democratic-Republican cause. Individuals were drawn to such groups out of a desire to promote liberty. They were exercising their rights to assemble and express themselves. Those groups shared the fears of Madison and Jefferson that the national government was becoming too powerful. They perceived that growth in government threatened their rights. Furthermore, they actively celebrated the libertarian roots of the French Revolution and maintained a strong distrust of the British, their former colonial masters.

The Administration's response to the formation of these grass-roots societies was, again, excessive. Fearing threats from within and without and tiring from the weight of the mantle of the presidency, Washington did something out of character for him—he directly attacked the growth of these political groups. He, once again, played the fear of rebellion card. In his opening address to Congress, in words that may have been crafted by Hamilton, the president warned that such groups or societies were extra-legal creations that were helping to instigate rebellion. They were a serious threat from within. Fisher Ames went a step further and claimed that such groups were akin to the Jacobin clubs in France, that helped foment and execute the Reign of Terror. Raising the Reign of Terror, with visions of beheadings, was clearly inflammatory.

Madison was again asked by fellow members of the House to respond to the president's state of the union remarks. He believed the president had committed one of the gravest errors of his political life when he attacked societies that were forming to further political ends, particularly the cause of liberty. To equate those societies with rebellious forces, was a clearly partisan, Federalist act that weakened Washington and the Presidency. Madison warned in his response that the executive branch was using the "tendency of insurrection to increase the momentum of power." The use of the development of grassroots political groups to challenge the government was far less of a threat, in Madison's mind, than the president's use of such societies as an excuse to further increase national power and to encourage deprivation of the right to petition one's government.

As 1794 closed, with increased bitterness among partisans and the cold and snow of winter, Madison proposed naturalization legislation that furthered his vision of liberty. He did so under clear constitutional authority. Article I, Section 8, Clause 4 of the Constitution empowers Congress, and not the executive branch, to "establish a uniform rule of naturalization." The bill, as passed, provided for liberal naturalization, included only four limitations: (1) five years of (lawful) residence within the United States; (2) a "good moral character, attached to the principles of the Constitution of the United States, and well-disposed to the good order and happiness of the United States"; (3) the taking of a formal oath to support the Constitution and to renounce any foreign allegiance; and (4) the renunciation of any hereditary titles. In a later letter, written in 1813 to express his opposition as president to efforts to use public land to induce immigration, Madison stated, "It is not either the provision of our laws or the practice of the Government to give any encouragement to imigrants, unless it be in cases where they may bring with them some special addition to our stock of arts or articles of culture."[42] He was not opposed to immigration, but he was opposed to the unconstitutional use of executive power to incentivize immigration. In immigration and naturalization, he believed he was furthering liberty, the rights of those legally present in the United States with a liberal naturalization system and liberty through limiting the power of the national government to act outside its expressed powers. Congress, in Madison's view, had the power to pass legislation regarding immigration and naturalization, and the president had power to agree to or disagree with such legislation.

The Federalists opposed Madison's naturalization bill, largely claiming it was too liberal. Some argued for a longer period of residency. Other Federalists, led by Representative Samuel Dexter of Massachusetts, an ordained minister, sought to use religious bigotry to stir up the electorate and legislators to oppose Madison's legislation. Dexter, and those who agreed with him, argued that Roman Catholics posed a threat to peace and vilified them as "Papists." Papists was a derogatory term used by some to disparage Catholics by arguing that their first allegiance is to the Pope and not the Constitution. They should, therefore, be limited in their right to become naturalized. Madison responded to Dexter's arguments with characteristic concern over any effort to persecute or belittle religious conscience or liberty. Madison argued that he "did not approve the ridicule thrown on the Roman Catholics. In their religion was nothing inconsistent with the purest republicanism."[43] He reminded other members of Congress, as well, that Catholics had "proved to be good citizens during the

---

42. Letter from James Madison to Morris Birkbeck, [ca. 9 November] 1817, Founders Online (National Archives), accessed October 13, 2018, https://founders.archives.gov/documents/Madison/04-01-02-0140.

43. Madison, "Naturalization," [1 January] 1795, Founders Online (National Archives), accessed October 13, 2018, https://founders.archives.gov/documents/Madison/01-15-02-0337.

Revolution." Madison's naturalization bill was adopted and signed into law as the Naturalization Act of 1795.

Jay Treaty

Matters largely remained quiet, in the early months of 1795, as Congress and the Executive went about their daily responsibilities without much fanfare and with few partisan flare-ups. Concerns mounted, however, as rumors regarding the efforts of John Jay, and those working with him, to agree to a treaty unduly favorable to Britain. In March 1795, President Washington saw the treaty, which came to be referred to as the Jay Treaty, for the first time. Shortly thereafter, in accordance with their powers under the Constitution, the Senate adopted the Treaty, and Washington, albeit with some reluctance, signed it into law. For this part, Madison had grave concerns regarding the Jay Treaty.

The negotiation of the Jay Treaty, designed to avoid war with Britain, intensified the differences between Madison (the Democratic-Republicans) and Hamilton (the Federalists), who had used his influence to get a somewhat reluctant Washington to sign the Treaty. Madison initially helped frame the issues, but he happily turned the leadership role in opposing the treaty to a rising star within the Democratic-Republican Party, Albert Gallatin. Gallatin became a dear friend and ally of Madison and proved to be a powerful leader and gifted speaker. He also offered a counterpoint to Hamilton's nationalistic financial theories. He would soon relieve Madison of one of the greatest burdens he had to carry during his lifetime of public service—the role of party leader in an increasingly partisan political world.

Abraham Gallatin

A native of Switzerland, Gallatin emigrated to the United States at the age of nineteen after the death of his parents. Gallatin was elected to serve as a delegate to the Pennsylvania constitutional convention in 1789. After distinguishing himself as a delegate, Albert was elected to serve in the state legislature. At the age of thirty-one, Albert was then elected to the United States Senate. As a Democratic-Republican,

Gallatin was opposed by the Federalists, who mustered the necessary votes to remove him from office on a straight party-line vote. The Federalists argued that he had not lived long enough in the United States to meet the citizenship requirement for service in the Senate. The Constitution required that he be a citizen for nine years. Some questionable evidence was mustered to support the efforts of the Federalists to prevent Gallatin from serving in the Senate. Gallatin's French accent helped fuel the opposition on the part of the Federalists, as well, given their disdain for the excesses of the French Revolution. Throughout his lifetime, many Federalists, with anti-French and pro-British leanings, derisively referred to Gallatin as a foreigner. The Federalists prevailed in their effort to deny Gallatin a seat in the Senate. Defeated, he returned home to Pennsylvania, more committed to being engaged in politics.

After returning to Pennsylvania, Gallatin earned further respect through his efforts to help resolve the differences between the parties to the Whisky Rebellion. He was thereafter elected to the United States House of Representatives in 1795, where he came into direct contact with Madison. Gallatin's commitment to liberty and his command of the issues, particularly financial policy, quickly made him a leader in his party. His understanding of economics and financial issues, together with his allegiance to the principles of the Democratic-Republican Party, made Gallatin a natural and able opponent to the Federalists and Alexander Hamilton.

As Gallatin assumed more leadership responsibility, Madison was more than pleased to spend more time enjoying his life with his bride, Dolley. Madison was gladly willing to yield leadership of the party to Gallatin, a persuasive and articulate leader. He, like Madison, was a strong defender of the Bill of Rights and of the need for limited government, to secure those rights. Gallatin once stated his position in the following words, "The whole of the Bill of Rights is a declaration of the right of the people at large or considered as individuals [and it] establishes some rights of the individual as unalienable and which consequently no majority has a right to deprive them of."[44]

---

44. Albert Gallatin, New York Historical Society, October 7, 1789, see, "Constitutional Limitations on Government," accessed October 13, 2018, http://econfaculty.gmu.edu/wew /quotes/govt.html.

With his command of economics and interest in fiscal issues, Gallatin helped create the Committee on Finance in the House of Representatives, as a means of counterbalancing Hamilton's power in the executive branch. Gallatin strongly influenced financial and related issues as a leading member of the Finance Committee. He later served as Secretary of the Treasury in both the Jefferson and Madison administrations. Gallatin also later played a major role in negotiating the Treaty of Ghent, which was signed on December 24, 1814, bringing an end to one of our nation's most contentious wars, the War of 1812. He even assisted in planning the Lewis and Clark expedition. After a sometimes-tempestuous life of public service, which included serving as Ambassador to both France and England, Gallatin returned to New York City, where he continued to put his talents to work in service. His continuing interest in education contributed to his efforts to help found New York University. With a mind and heart that knew few borders, Gallatin also became interested in what today is known as Native American Studies and earned the title of "the father of American ethnology." After leaving public service, Gallatin used his understanding of economic theory in his service as president of the New York City Branch of the National Bank, which became known as the Gallatin bank. He thereafter assisted in the effort to charter a Second Bank of the United States. He was devoted to liberty, but like Madison, he was also pragmatic and resilient, open to the ideas of others. Those qualities helped make him an able political leader.

Upon arriving for his service in the House of Representatives, Gallatin found himself quickly thrust into party leadership. He was soon matched against Hamilton, Ames, and other leaders of the Federalists. They proved to be able adversaries, the kind of adversaries who help negotiate the compromises that make for wise governance. Gallatin soon discovered that his skills were honed, in part, because he had to respond to arguments from some of the great minds of the early republic. Gallatin proved to be an effective leader of the opposition to Federalist policies, and a friend to Jefferson, Madison, and the Democratic-Republican cause.

Gallatin and the Jay Treaty

Early during his time in the House, Gallatin joined forces with Madison in opposing the Jay Treaty, which they both believed to be unduly favorable toward Britain. Madison and Gallatin agreed that the British withdrawal of their military forts in the western territory of the United States was of value. They were aware, however, that the British had already essentially agreed to withdraw from the territories east of the Mississippi River that had been ceded to the United States in the peace treaty ending the Revolutionary War, so that positive in the treaty was essentially a given. British traders were also given free access to the Northwest Territories and, of more significance to Madison and Gallatin, they were given full access to the Mississippi River. The treaty indicated that Britain would examine issues related to the seizure of American ships. But that promise was little more than a possible agreement to agree at some time in the future. Sadly, that agreement was only achieved after the War of 1812.

The treaty did not deal with issues of extreme importance to the Democratic-Republicans. It failed to respond to concerns regarding British capture of slaves and the impressment of American sailors. Of greatest concern, the treaty failed to address the issue of free trade with France. In short, it perpetuated favored status to Britain at a time that they were at war with France. That favorable status for Britain, essentially indicated the Administration's preference for or siding with the British in the war. Madison declared it to be a "ruinous bargain." It raised fears of possible war with France because the French were likely to view the treaty as a statement favoring, or taking sides with, Britain in violation of an existing treaty between the United States and France. Madison found the Jay Treaty to violate the freedom of commerce, in a manner that decidedly favored the British. In short, for Madison and for Gallatin, the Jay Treaty was a bad substantive deal for the United States, as a matter of foreign policy and further violated principles of free trade and economic liberty.

Hamilton helped persuade an ever-deliberative and, in this case, somewhat reluctant President Washington to sign the Jay Treaty. Understanding that the public questioned the fairness of the Jay Treaty,

Hamilton proceeded to write over twenty newspaper articles support-ing the treaty. Despite efforts by Jefferson to get Madison to respond, he declined. Madison had easily won re-election to the House. The new Congress included an increasing number of Democratic-Republicans. Madison believed it would be better to wait until the seating of the new and more favorable Congress before taking the issue up again. He was also tiring of incessant partisan wrangling with Hamilton, who seemed to relish such battles. Finally, Madison's heart had been cap-tivated by the widow, Dolley Payne Todd, who had become his wife. He sought a respite from the cacophony of Congress and was attuned to events at Montpelier and to his joyous, even mirthful, relationship with his wife, Dolley. Madison was distracted and was simply unwill-ing to take up his pen again.

Hamilton's articles, which went largely unanswered, helped assuage some concerns on the part of the public. Hamilton was also aided by changing economic conditions. The Jay Treaty had reopened trade with Britain. Since far more trade took place between Britain and the United States than with France or any other nation, the nation's economy began to grow. With exports up as much as 50 percent, and with declining import costs related to trade with Britain, Americans were enjoying very good economic times. There are few things more likely to capture the hearts and minds of an electorate, and their rep-resentatives, than the prosperity that attends economic growth. The prosperous economy strongly influenced the American people to accept the Jay Treaty, despite its infirmities.

Nevertheless, with Congress back in session, Madison's attention had refocused on matters of government. He launched a strong attack on the Jay Treaty, with assistance from Gallatin. The Senate had rati-fied the Jay Treaty. Madison argued that the House had the power to decline to fund matters associated with implementation of the Treaty. He argued further that the House had the right to examine the diplo-matic papers related to the Jay Treaty. Madison's arguments had some merit. Madison fashioned his demand by declaring that, if in exercis-ing its treaty power, "the president and Senate can regulate trade, they can also declare war, they can raise armies to carry on war, and they can procure money to support armies."[45] Treaties could lead to war, as was clearly true in this instance. France had already made it clear that the ratification of the treaty was akin to a declaration of a lack of neutrality, an implied act of war. If treaties could lead to war, Madison argued that the House of Representatives had the power under the Constitution to refuse to implement the treaty.

Madison's argument was strained and was likely wrong on constitutional grounds. The framers and the Constitution understood that the treaty power was shared between the Senate and the president. No direct treaty power had been given to the House. In the end, as a constitutional matter, the House's sole power was to use its rightful power to fund or refuse to fund, as a check on aspects of a treaty, after the fact. Madison hoped that his policy arguments favoring consultation with the House would be substantively strengthened by release of diplomatic papers related to negotiation of the treaty. The president, however, refused to release the papers, arguing that the secrecy necessary in such negotiations would be compromised by releasing the papers to the democratically elected House of Representatives. Chief Justice Ellsworth supported refusing to grant the House's desire to receive documentation related to a treaty. Madison saw this as bad policy. He also believed it constituted an elitist slight to the democratically elected House of Representatives. Madison's arguments were of little avail.

Madison's reputation suffered in some quarters, because of his strong opposition to the Jay Treaty. The Treaty was widely supported by the prevailing view regarding the president's treaty-making power *and* by the general economic prosperity that it brought in its wake. Madison's standing was also harmed somewhat by his refusal to respond to questions regarding his understanding of the intent of the delegates to the Constitutional Convention regarding the treaty power. He refused, claiming his belief as to the intent was not as important as the public intent of those ratifying the Constitution. He was, however, cast as being somewhat duplicitous for failing to offer his own opinion regarding the intent of the framers with respect to the treaty power in the Constitution. Madison's arguments proved futile and served to

45. Madison, Jay's Treaty, [10 March] 1796, Founders Online (National Archives), accessed October 13, 2018, https://founders.archives.gov/documents/Madison/01-16-02-0174.

tarnish his reputation somewhat among a number of his Congressional colleagues. William Cobbett, writing as Peter Porcupine, jubilantly declared, "Citizen Madison was formerly reckoned as a sort of chief, but he has so sunk out of sight this campaign that we can look upon him, at least, no more than an aide-de-camp . . . without any hope of repairing his reputation. As a politician he is no more; he is absolutely deceased, cold, stiff and buried in oblivion for ever and ever."[46]

Madison's arguments had also worn on his colleagues and had worn on Madison himself. Gallatin responded by picking up the baton and making eloquent arguments supporting the Democratic-Republican viewpoint. Fisher Ames, who had been ill, responded with a fiery attack on Gallatin and the Democratic-Republicans. Ames's attack, which was at times characteristically personal, lasted for more than two hours. Ames engaged in some fear-mongering, using the prospect of increased strife with the Native tribes in the west, which would surely be followed by bloody attacks against settlers, attended by the cries of mothers as they watch their children shudder in fear at the sounds of "warhoop[s]."[47] He concluded his highly charged address with words that reverberated throughout the hall, "I can fancy that I listen to the yells of savage vengeance, and the shrieks of torture; already them seem to sign in the western wind; already they mingle with every echo from the mountains."[48] At this point in his emotional remarks, Ames managed to evoke tears on the part of many present. More importantly, he had persuaded more members to support his arguments favoring the Jay Treaty.

Madison was profoundly vexed by Ames's remarks. Madison viewed Ames's address as pure demagoguery, and he found himself tiring from incessant and vitriolic partisanship, coupled with declining deliberation and compromise. Madison was tiring of public service in such a rancorous political climate and was pleased that the Democratic-Republican cause in such times was now in the able hands of Gallatin, whose talents better suited him to battle against such

---

46. See Ralph Ketcham, *James Madison* (Charlottesville: University of Virginia Press 1990), 365.

47. Ibid., 363.

48. Ibid.

rhetorical flourish and fierce partisanship. Gallatin was now clearly the voice of the Democratic-Republicans.

Longing for Home

Madison was tired and pined for the quiet of Montpelier. He longed for more time with Dolley and, with some joy, announced that he would not seek re-election. It was clear he would have won, but he simply lacked interest in continuing to serve. He, nevertheless, revived his interest and enthusiasm one last time before returning home. Madison joined in Washington's effort to create a national university, an idea initially proposed by Benjamin Rush during the Constitutional Convention and long supported by Madison. Madison was supportive of the idea from its inception. President Washington offered the reasons why he supported the concept of a national university: "[O]ur Country, much to its honor, contains many Seminaries of learning highly respectable and useful; but the funds upon which they rest, are too narrow, to command the ablest Professors, in the different departments of liberal knowledge, for the Institution contemplated, though they would be excellent auxiliaries. Amongst the motives to such an Institution, the assimilation of the principles, opinions, and manners of our Country men, but the common education of a portion of our Youth from every quarter, well deserves attention."[49] Washington then concluded, "The more homogenous our Citizens can be made in these particulars, the greater will be our prospect of permanent Union; and a primary object of such a National Institution should be the education of our Youth in the science of Government."[50] As was the case with the Rush's national university proposal in the Convention, Washington's university would respect the right of conscience and would create a university that was non-preferential as to matters of religion.

All four of the first presidents supported the creation a national university, as a means of increasing civic and professional education and promoting unity in a diverse nation. None did so with greater

---

49. George Washington, Eighth Annual Message to Congress, December 7, 1796, Miller Center (University of Virginia), accessed October 13, 2018, https://millercenter.org/the -presidency/presidential-speeches/december-7-1796-eighth-annual-message-congress.
50. Ibid.

commitment to the concept than did Madison, who believed that a national university would help enshrine liberty and civility, by bringing diverse groups of students together at the national level. He believed that such a university would open the doors to students from all part of the nation and, in doing so, would help the nation avoid the rising partisanship and sectionalism, between the south and north and promote understanding and liberty. In each instance, the proposal failed. With Madison and Washington both supporting the concept, however, it came the closest to passing in the House of Representatives during the closing days of Washington's Presidency.

Washington and Madison were both delighted to be going home to Virginia and family. Many of the early parts of Washington's famous Farewell Address were written by Madison. It was, in many senses, a valedictory address for Washington and Madison. The constant bickering had taken their toll on two great leaders who had a disdain for bitter partisanship and a desire for deliberative and collaborative government. Their greater collective fear, however, was that party was becoming more important than country. Washington declared, "The unity of government which constitutes you one people is also now dear to you. It is justly so, for it is a main pillar in the edifice of your real independence, the support of your tranquility at home, your peace abroad; of your safety; of your prosperity; of that very liberty which you so highly prize."[51] These two great Virginians understood that liberty without unity was likely to be short-lived. Washington went on to reflect that, it "is easy to foresee that, from different causes and from different quarters, much pains will be taken, many artifices employed to weaken in your minds the conviction of this truth."[52] Madison had come to empathize with the president as reflected in words that Madison, again, likely drafted and Washington spoke with conviction, "The impressions with which I first undertook the arduous trust were explained on the proper occasion. In the discharge of this trust, I will only say that I have, with good intentions, contributed towards the organization and administration of the government the best exertions

51. Washington's Farewell Address to the People of the United States, September 19, 1796, U.S. Senate, accessed October 13, 2018, https://www.senate.gov/artandhistory/history/resources/pdf/Washingtons_Farewell_Address.pdf.
52. Ibid.

of which a very fallible judgment was capable. Not unconscious in the outset of the inferiority of my qualifications, experience in my own eyes, perhaps still more in the eyes of others, has strengthened the motives to diffidence of myself; and every day the increasing weight of years admonishes me more and more that the shade of retirement is as necessary to me as it will be welcome."[53] Two giants were ready to retire, to return home.

Madison was sincere about retiring. Many talked of him as a candidate for the presidency, but the idea held little present attraction for Madison. He was tired and wanted to take refuge in Montpelier and make up for years of having lacked the companionship of a soulmate. James and Dolley loaded their belongings and began a relatively slow and leisurely trek home to Montpelier. They were joined by other family members, including Dolley's young son, Payne. They stopped along the way to visit family. It was a time of joy for Madison, as he felt the mantle of years of public service being lifted from off his shoulders and the warmth of his wife's hand in his own. Madison was returning home to enjoy a respite of sorts. John Adams, however, better understood Madison, in such matters, then he understood himself. John Adams wisely reflected, "Mr. Madison is to retire. It seems the mode of becoming great is to retire." Adams added, "Madison I suppose after a retirement of a few years is to be president or V.P." Adams understood that "political plants grow in the shade."[54]

The summer months would arrive soon, bringing sweltering heat, which even shade did little to cure. But those would be good times, because Madison would have time to reflect and think, freed from the daily demands of office. He rejoiced in following President Washington into retirement. His opponents had won a victory of sorts by creating a toxic political environment that was deeply offensive to leaders like Madison and Washington. He would return, but he welcomed an interlude from his all-consuming life of public service. Over a period of two decades of tireless public service, Madison had been a party to a series of providential events that led to the adoption and ratification of

---

53. Ibid., 2.
54. Letter from John Adams to Abigail Adams, 14 January 1797, Massachusetts Historical Society, accessed October 13, 2018, http://www.masshist.org/digitaladams/archive/doc?id=L 17970114ja.

the Constitution and Bill of Rights, causes his sense of duty drove him to support, with a relentlessness bred of a conscience, and a deep faith in America. In heeding his call to public service, Madison had changed America and the world in profound ways, securing liberty through the constitutional rule of law. As a man who was himself called and driven by conscience, who had so willingly acknowledged the aid of Divine Providence at every step in the formation of the United States of America, it is not surprising that he did so much to secure the most sacred of all property.

Despite his having done more than any other single individual to secure adoption and ratification of the Constitution and Bill of Rights, Madison was giving little thought to such a monumental view of his public service, something he believed to be best left to historians. This frail man, who spoke with a whisper and had clearly earned the title of Father of the Constitution and the Bill of Rights, was simply glad to be going home to Montpelier. In time, Madison would again feel the call to serve, together with Dolley, to join his family and enjoy a well-deserved respite from a glorious time of public service. In time, however, conscience would call both James, the father of religious liberty, and Dolley, who would soon become America's first First Lady, into service at a time of great national need.

Acknowledgments

I owe so much to so many, each of whom have helped make this book possible. One group, however, is particularly noteworthy. Without the support of my family, beginning with my wife, Danielle, and including my eight children and twenty-six grandchildren, this book would never have been completed. Many days that should have been spent with them were used to research, write and rewrite this book. They never complained about time lost and were a source of encouragement and inspiration. Indeed, this book was written because I want others, particularly my children and their children, to know more about the formative role James Madison played in the founding of the United States of America, as the "father" of the Constitution, the Bill of Rights, and the right of religious conscience. One of my sons deserves special thanks. At a time when I was struggling mightily due to my inability to write a book worthy of being read by a broad audience, my son simply reminded me to "try to see Madison as God sees him." While I know that I failed to begin to capture Madison in that lofty light, I did find my son's counsel to be liberating.

Judge Arlin M. Adams, Dean Rex E. Lee, President Dallin H. Oaks, and my father, Willis J. Smith, the four lawyer-servants to whom this book is dedicated, also deserve special acknowledgment. Judge Adams and Dean Lee helped lay the groundwork for this book and my life in the law. Dean Lee, who later served in historic fashion as Solicitor General of the United States, taught me during the first week of my first year of law school. Rex left me always wanting to learn more about constitutional law, the supreme law of the land. Judge Adams taught me about the historic and legal roots of religious liberty for two consecutive semesters at the University of Pennsylvania Law School, while serving as a judge on the Third Circuit of Appeals. Dallin H.

Oaks, who now serves as First Counselor in the First Presidency of The Church of Jesus Christ of Latter-day Saints, has helped shape my thinking about religious liberty and life in ways that I can never repay. In one letter, after kindly reviewing an article I had written about the right of conscience, then Elder Oaks suggested that he was "almost persuaded"—he believed I had failed to distinguish the right of religious conscience from a more generalized right of conscience. He was right and, in the process, helped me see the right of conscience more clearly through the eyes of James Madison. Finally, Willis J. Smith is my father—the greatest lawyer I have ever known. Dad taught me a deep respect for the rule of law and for its capacity to bless lives. Dad joined with my mother, Georgi Ana, in also helping me to believe in myself, despite my many evident weaknesses which they knew so well.

Three other teachers deserve special acknowledgment: Beverly Bedwell, Bob Campbell, and Glenn Barkan. Mrs. Bedwell, my eighth-grade teacher, taught me that life is about learning, and learning is about joy. Mr. Campbell, who taught my senior civics class and led by example by later serving as mayor in our small town. Bob taught me that public service is a great call, ever reminding me that it was a call. I was blessed to have Glenn Barkan as a professor during his first year of full-time teaching. He taught about the founding era in a way that captivated my interest in enduring ways.

Other professional colleagues and friends deserve special note. Cole Durham, who taught me during my last year of law school, has become a colleague and friend and has shown me much of the world through the lens of religious liberty. Marcia O'Kelly, a colleague at North Dakota, who also taught constitutional law, helped me make the transition to teaching, by kindly challenging my thinking day after day. Robert Justin Lipkin or Bobby, as he was known among his friends, taught with me at Widener University and has since passed away. Bobby always drove me to think with more clarity and openness to new ideas. Oh, how I miss our times together. Fred Gedicks, another friend in the professoriate, has always challenged my thinking in the First Amendment area. He has also become a dear friend, who makes my life fuller, even in trying times. Finally, Tim Lytton, who I hired as a new faculty member at the University of Arkansas right after he graduated from Yale Law School, taught me what it really means to be a scholar-servant.

My colleagues at the Center for Constitutional Studies, Scott Paul, Andy Bibby, and Carl Scott, have also been very supportive, often assuming some of my administrative responsibilities so that I could continue to work on "Madison." As part of my work at the Center for Constitutional Studies, I have been blessed to work closely with Dr. Nicholas Cole, a Senior Research Fellow and Director of the Quill Project at Pembroke College (Oxford). As an accomplished historian of the founding era and a dear friend, Nicholas teaches and tutors me whenever we are together.

Executive Vice President of Academics Jeffery E. Olson and President Matthew S. Holland of Utah Valley University have encouraged me to finish this project and devote my professional life to the task of increasing constitutional literacy. Space will not allow to acknowledge so many others, but you know who you are.

As is true of any teacher, my students have had a wonderful influence on me. They have inspired me and have made teaching and sharing the life of James Madison a joy. The Wood Assistants at the Center of Constitutional Studies have also been particularly helpful. Kristee Hone, our office assistant, has helped with all the little things and has done so promptly, with her characteristic desire to serve.

The team at Cedar Fort have also been exceedingly helpful and have kept the book moving along at a breath-taking pace. Thanks to Kathryn Watkins, Carolyn Nelson, Vikki Butler, Melissa Caldwell, and Kaitlin Barwick, who have been on the front lines throughout the process.

About the Author

R odney K. Smith directs the Center for Constitutional Studies at Utah Valley University. Dr. Smith came to Utah Valley University from the Sandra Day O'Connor College of Law at Arizona State, where he served as the Distinguished Professor of Practice and founding director of the sports law and business program. Dr. Smith received his J.D. from the J. Reuben Clark Law School at BYU and holds an LL.M. and SJD from the University of Pennsylvania. He previously served as the president of Southern Virginia University and as a law school dean at Capital University, the University of Montana, and the University of Arkansas at Little Rock. He held the Herff Chair of Excellence in Law at the University of Memphis, where he emphasized constitutional law, sports law, and ethics. His work, particularly in the First Amendment and sports law areas, has been widely cited by scholars and courts at all levels, including the United States Supreme Court. He has testified before state and congressional committees, including testimony in the Clarence Thomas confirmation proceedings, and has written for USA Today, the Christian Science Monitor, and other national newspapers. He frequently writes for the Deseret News and Meridian Magazine. Dr. Smith regularly appears on radio and television news programs.

Scan to visit

www.rodneykeithsmith.com